"If any American does not already own a good, comprehensive work on World War II, this is the book he or she should buy."
—*St. Petersburg Times*

"Convincing . . . fascinating. . . . Astor's deep knowledge and the amazing experiences of his subjects come through clearly."
—*Publishers Weekly*

"Oral history at its very best."
—*BookPage*

"A sweeping, imaginative oral history . . . succeeds by the thoughtful coupling of a narrative that touches on most of the war's most important engagements with the reminiscences of hundreds of participants. . . . Astor offers the most salient facts in what otherwise could have been an overwhelming mass of detail. He also turns up some surprises. Invaluable to historians, with much to interest general readers as well."
—*Kirkus Reviews* (starred review)

"Will make you feel as though you were there in the midst of the fighting. A moving account . . . remarkable."
—*West Orange Times*

more . . .

"Strong, effective, absorbing . . . a genuine tour de force . . . brilliant text and breathless pace . . . stimulating and down-to-earth. . . . My compliments and congratulations go, with great admiration, to Gerald Astor."

—Martin Blumenson, author of *The Battle of the Generals*, from his review in *Parameters* magazine

"Astor succeeds admirably, creating the finest . . . oral history available of the American soldier in World War II . . . Well-chosen entries . . . fast-paced, smoothly flowing narrative. . . . Astor has written the first oral history to include all of the services and theaters of the war. Highly recommended."

—*Library Journal* (starred review)

"A remarkable job of weaving together an extraordinary amount of oral evidence with more traditional narrative, turning out a quite readable seamless treatment of the war . . . a valuable addition to the literature of the war."

—*New York Military Affairs Symposium (NYMAS) Newsletter*

"If you want to buy your grandchildren a gift they will remember, spend the money for this living reference book."

—*Veterans Voice of Austin*

THE GREATEST WAR

VOLUME I

FROM PEARL HARBOR TO THE KASSERINE PASS

GERALD ASTOR

WARNER BOOKS

A Time Warner Company

WARNER BOOKS EDITION

Copyright © 1999 by Gerald Astor

This Warner books edition is published by arrangement with Presidio Press.

Cover design by Jerry Pfeifer
Flag photo by Philip James Corwin
Inset photo by Bettman/Corbis

Warner Books, Inc.
1271 Avenue of the Americas
New York, NY 10020

Visit our Web site at
www.twbookmark.com.

For information on Time Warner Trade Publishing's online publishing program, visit www.ipublish.com.

 A Time Warner Company

Printed in the United States of America

First Warner Books Printing: September 2001

10 9 8 7 6 5 4 3 2 1

For the late Donald I. Fine

Contents

Preface   ix

Acknowledgments   xi

1. "This Is Not a Drill!"   1

2. Preattack Maneuvers   28

3. The Philippine Defenses   43

4. Still Asleep   71

5. Early Engagements   102

6. Retreat   125

7. The East Indies   156

8. The Fall of Bataan   189

9. The Death March and Morale Missions   227

10. Final Defeat in the Philippines   262

11. At Sea and in the Air   282

12. American Airpower Concepts   319

13. Opening Offensives   337

14. Paratroopers, Raiders, Rangers,
    Marauders, Alamo Scouts   369

15. Torch   390

16. Grim Glimmers   422

17. Defeat   450

18.	Tunisia	487
	Roll Call	509
	Bibliography	534
	Index	545

Preface

When I told Gen. George Ruhlen that I intended to write a book covering the battles fought by Americans during World War II, he wrote to me, "How many pages are you projecting, 5,000 or squeeze it into 3,000?" His comment was well taken, for an encyclopedic account of what happened to Americans in World War II would require many volumes and in fact the historian Samuel Eliot Morison produced something on the nature of twenty books covering just the engagements of the Navy and the Marines.

However, my intention was not to cover the war from objective to objective nor was it to describe the details of strategy and tactics. I freely confess that, even in an oversize manuscript, I have omitted many hard-fought battles, units, and individuals who underwent the same hardships, terror, and sorrow, and who, in spite of their ordeals, overcame. Instead I hope to present a sense of what the American fighting man (women in World War II were restricted to clerical and service positions although as the book indicates, some nurses underwent much of what the men did) experienced in terms of what he thought, felt, saw, heard, and tried to do. Words on a page cannot match those moments under fire but by their own voices the soldiers, sailors, and airmen reveal the nature of that war well beyond anything shown in films or TV, except perhaps for *Saving Private Ryan*. (Even here one might quibble about the premise upon which the story unfolds.)

Having written six books on World War II, I am well aware that eyewitness accounts or oral histories have their weaknesses due to faulty memories, skewed perspectives, and the common human resort to self-service. On the other hand, these same deficiencies also afflict official reports. In his letter to me, George Ruhlen remarked that a friend of his named Brewster commanded a task force whose mission was to regain possession of a crossroads during the Battle of the Bulge. "Some 20 accounts were written by 'historians' who were never there, most inaccurate, but only one writer ever contacted Colonel Brewster for his recollection of that action."

I expect there will be some who will dispute an individual's version of some events in this book, but I believe that by relying on as many sources and veterans as I have the essential truth of the experiences is correct. Although many of the sensations and the reactions of those on the scenes seem similar—the most replicated comment was "Suddenly, all hell broke loose"—there were significant differences from year to year, from campaign to campaign, from area to area.

It was the biggest of all wars and those who fought the battles deserve to be heard.

Acknowledgments

So many people have shared their memories and experiences with me that I cannot cite them individually. Their words are credited to them in the text and to some extent through Roll Call.

I received special help from Paul Stillwell of the United States Naval Institute in Annapolis; Joseph Caver of the United States Air Force Historical Research Center at Maxwell Field, Alabama; Dr. David Keough at the United States Army History Library at Carlisle Barracks, Pennsylvania; the United States Naval Historical Center; Debbie Pogue at the United States Military Academy Library; Jim Altieri; William Cain; Tracy Derks; Len Lomell; Benjamin Mabry; Jason Poston.

Small portions of this book appeared in some of my previous writings on World War II.

1

"This Is Not a Drill!"

MARTIN LOW, A TWENTY-TWO-YEAR-OLD FIGHTER PILOT ASsigned to the U.S. Army Air Corps' 78th Pursuit Squadron at Wheeler Field on Oahu, recalled, "That night, I had too many as usual, woke up about 7:30, and then retrieved the newspaper that had been delivered to my room. I heard the unique sound of a dive bomber. The Navy would often make passes at Wheeler as part of their practice runs but when I looked up and saw the wheels were down I thought, 'that guy is really in a hurry.' Then I saw a 100-pound bomb leave the belly; they used spotting charges to mark their drops—and it landed right in the middle of a hangar. I thought, 'Oh my God, is that guy in trouble.' There was a tremendous explosion and at that moment I saw the rising sun insignia on the airplane."

John Alicki, a sergeant with the 53d Antiaircraft Brigade, his enlistment time up and ready to sail to the mainland for civilian life, remembered, "On that Sunday morning, they got me up a little early and held me to my promise to go to church. We were entering the church just before 8:00 A.M. when we heard in the distance something like firecrackers. As we went into the church the sound became more audible. When I stepped outside, I saw the red disk emblem on the sides of the planes."

Arthur Price, an aviation metalsmith with the Navy's Patrol Wing 2, had spent Saturday night with friends in an enlisted-housing area at Kaneohe, a newly constructed naval air station on the eastern shore of Oahu. A few days before, his unit had concluded an exercise that involved the Army Air Corps, with blue the designation for the Navy and red for their opposite numbers.

"I was awakened by enemy airplanes buzzing the housing area. There was an observation tower nearby, and to the Japanese it must have looked like an aircraft-control tower, because the first thing they did was strafe the tower. That woke us up.

"My first reaction was, 'I thought those maneuvers were over on Friday. What are they doing today? It must be the damned red army again.' The planes flew by, and then, all of a sudden, one of us said, 'That's not a star. That's a red ball. The only thing that's got that is Japanese. What the hell is he doing here?' At that point we didn't see any bullets flying around or anything, even though the planes were pretty low. Then we heard the rat-a-tat-tat of strafing on the beach and knew this was for real. We got into a car and drove to the squadron hangar arriving just about the time everybody else was showing up from the barracks nearby."

Seaman Adolph Leonard Seton, who had enlisted in 1939, was on deck. "That morning, when I saw a dark olive-drab plane with a 'meatball' insignia passing close aboard, astern of the St. Louis (a light cruiser) in the navy yard near Battleship Row, my first reaction was: 'That stupid bastard!

He'll be court-martialed for this!' I thought it was a lone, berserk Japanese pilot, who somehow had gotten to Pearl and now would be in trouble with his navy and ours."

Ensign Ted Hechler Jr., a 1940 graduate of the United States Naval Academy, rolled over in his bunk aboard the cruiser USS *Phoenix* at 7:55 A.M., awakened by a loudspeaker that sounded an alert condition for a duty section. "I was not planning to respond. Instead, I grumbled something to my roommate. I complained about yet another damned drill and in Pearl Harbor on a Sunday morning, no less. In probably no more than ten or twenty seconds, this was all changed. I heard the sound of feet running on the deck overhead. Then came the sounds of the Klaxon horn and the announcement, 'All hands, general quarters.' This meant us, and we started to move out of our bunks. The voice on the loudspeaker now became shrill as the message changed to 'All hands, general quarters! Man the antiaircraft batteries. This is *not* a drill! The words 'This is not a drill' were repeated over and over, almost pleadingly." Indeed, earwitnesses cite that five-word declaration as having echoed and reechoed throughout the day.

Officially, the alarm went out between 0757 and 0758. At the Ford Island command center, as a color guard prepared to hoist the flag at 0755, Lt. Cmdr. Logan Ramsey of Patrol Wing 2 with responsibility for aerial reconnaissance of the ocean observed a plane diving over the station. He called upon a subordinate to get the aircraft number for disciplinary action. The latter reported a red band on the offender and moments later a black object dropped, followed by an explosion. Ramsey understood immediately. He charged into the radio room and ordered all operators at the sets to send in English the message, "Air Raid, Pearl Harbor, This is not a drill!"

Aboard the battleship *Oklahoma*, Ens. Paul H. Backus, USNA 1939, heard a slightly different version. "When the attack started, I was in my cabin, in my bunk, half-awake. The general alarm jerked me out of my dozing state. Its clamor was paralleled by an announcement over the general announcing system. 'This is a real Jap air attack and no shit.' I recognized the voice. It was Herb Rommel, a senior reserve ensign, who had grabbed the microphone on his way to his battle station in turret four. Only under the most unusual circumstances would an officer personally make an announcement in those days of formal battleship routine. And the use of obscene language by anyone over the announcing system was just unheard of. So this had to be real; moreover, right after the last word of the announcement, the whole ship shuddered. It was the first torpedo hitting our port side."

At the Marine barracks in the Pearl Harbor installation, the flag-raising ritual, replete with bandsmen and leathernecks was about to begin. Captain Samuel R. Shaw, USNA 1934, commanded A Company. "The old and the new guard marched on and were standing at ease, waiting to begin the ceremony of morning colors. The men were equipped with M1 rifles and each man had three clips of ball ammunition. The men looked idly around as a column of planes apparently guiding on the road from Honolulu passed over the main gate area, flying at a surprisingly low altitude, headed toward the ships moored along the length of Ford Island.

"The sergeant of the old guard, a man who had a lot of time in Shanghai and seen much of the Japanese forces there, did a double take, a long and careful second look. He turned to the officer of the day and said, 'Sir, those are Japanese war planes.'

"The officer in turn took a hard look and said, 'By God,

you're right! Music, sound call "Call to arms!" ' As the first notes from the bugle sounded, the harbor shook with the explosion of a torpedo in the side of one of our battleships. Without another command, the Marines in guard formation loaded their rifles, took aim and began firing."

Marine lieutenant Cornelius C. Smith Jr. had been drinking coffee in a mess hall when the first blast rocked the building and bounced his oversize coffee cup onto the deck. From the lanai he watched a dry dock erupt in flames and smoke hundreds of feet into the air: ". . . the bombs are falling. They whistle to earth with ear-shattering explosions. You can see the morning sunlight glisten on the bombs as they fall—silvery flashes like trout or mackerel jumping out of the water.

"Who said the Japs were cross-eyed, second-rate pilots who couldn't hit the broad side of a barn door? Maybe so, but I'm standing on our Navy Yard parade ground looking up at them, while they're making a sandpile out of the yard. They're kicking the hell out of Pearl Harbor, and it's enough to turn your stomach.

"Friends back home used to ask about the Japs. 'Hell, we could blow them out of the water in three weeks!' But here we are with our pants down and the striking force of our Pacific fleet is settling on the bottom of East Loch, Pearl Harbor. Who wouldn't be ashamed?"

Captain Brooke Allen, commander of a B-17 squadron based at Hickam Field, Hawaii, burst from his quarters, clad only in a bathrobe that flapped open as he waved his arms at an overhead raider while shouting, "I knew the little sons of bitches would do it on a Sunday! I knew it!" He quickly regained his composure, paused long enough to hastily don clothing, and rushed to the flight line to see if he could get planes airborne.

Immediately after he realized that those overhead were enemy planes, Martin Low said, "I got my best friend from across the hall and told him we're under attack. I started to drive in my car to the hangar and when I was about fifty feet from it, I heard a 'rat-a-tat-tat' against the side of the car. We jumped out, and hid under the theater. We watched in utter consternation. Because they were worried about sabotage, the planes had all been lined up in neat rows where they could be easily guarded. One burst of fire could hit all the ships in a line."

Gordon Austin, the CO for the 47th Pursuit Squadron temporarily housed at Haleiwa Field, a sandy strip ordinarily used for training exercises, had flipped a coin with his operations officer on whether the squadron would fly on 7 December. "It came down 'give the boys a day off.' " Austin and some friends flew to Molokai that Saturday evening and early Sunday went deer hunting. "Somebody rushed up to us and said, 'The Japanese have attacked Pearl Harbor.' We flew back in a B-18 [an obsolete precursor to the B-17] and as we crossed the channel from Molokai to Oahu, they were saying, 'Boy, they sure are making this realistic'—we'd had so many exercises like this. Navy planes used to come in on Sunday morning from off the carriers. They would come over Wheeler Field and when they got there they would run the prop pitch up and make an awful racket and wake everybody up about 7:30 in the morning. But over the radio we could hear, 'This is not a drill.' Still dubious, we decided to stay airborne and when we saw the smoke off Pearl Harbor, again the word was 'realistic.' We were over Diamond Head and suddenly we were in a sea of flak. The U.S. Navy was firing on us. My heart jumped up in my mouth. I never got scared like that the rest of the war. We landed at Wheeler

Field. The P-40s' tails were gone. They were sitting nose up; all of them burning."

A flight of eighteen Navy aircraft, from the USS *Enterprise* steaming a course 200 miles due west, encountered similar trouble. Several were shot down by Japanese fighter cover before the Americans even discovered their home base was under attack. Others who had been instructed to land at Ford Island reeled under hails of shrapnel and bullets from friendly forces aiming at anything in the skies.

The same hostile reaction beset a flock of eleven B-17Es, the latest model four-engine Flying Fortresses that had taken off from a California airfield for the 2,400-mile trip to Hickam Field, first stop enroute to bolster the air arm in the Philippines. Their bombsights and machine guns were neatly packed in crates stowed in the fuselages. American sailors on ships and soldiers on the ground cut loose at the big bombers lumping them in as part of the attack.

Even as Brooke Allen struggled to take aloft one of the still airworthy B-17s from his squadron, a few minutes after eight o'clock, the Fortresses from the States approached Oahu. Major Truman H. Landon, the officer in command of the bombers, observed oncoming aircraft and assumed it was the Air Force out to welcome them. But when the "hosts" suddenly fired upon them, Landon realized they were Japanese. To conserve fuel for the 2,400-mile trip, the American planes carried a skeleton crew, not enough men to man their machine guns even if they had been installed. With no ability to defend themselves, the B-17s scattered, ducking into the clouds or opting for a quick touchdown at any open field, including an emergency landing on a golf course.

Richard Carmichael, one of almost a quarter of the 1936 graduates of West Point who elected an Air Corps career, commanded a B-17 bound for Hickam Field. "I had been stationed at Wheeler Field, flying P-12s and P-26s [early-model fighter planes], so as it broke dawn coming in to the Hawaiian Islands, I was pointing out all the various sights. We came around with Diamond Head on our right, Waikiki Beach, the Hawaina Hotel, the Royal Hawaiian, and the harbor. Somebody tapped me on the shoulder and said, 'Look at all those white puffs up there in the air ahead.' I looked up and said, 'Well, the Navy must be practicing.' We had heard maybe they were having a maneuver of some sort on Sunday morning. We didn't get very excited about it until we had to get up really close.

"We got close enough to hear the control tower was under fire. By this time we could see airplanes. We alerted and I called in and asked for landing instructions. The answer came back, 'Land from west to east, but use caution, the field is under attack.' We had to fly around the ships and as we started into this pattern on the downwind leg, the navy started shooting at us. At the same time, somebody said, 'We have a pursuit airplane, a Japanese plane on our tail.' Things had gone to hell in a handbasket. Everything was happening. All the battleships, all that smoke there—they had already been hit and were on fire.

"I said, 'to hell with this. I am going up to Wheeler and see if I can get into my old home base.' To get away from the fighter on our tail, I remembered there were always clouds over the Koolau Mountain Range on the eastern side of Oahu. I got up in the base of the clouds before this guy shot us down, or maybe he wasn't even shooting at us.

"We could see the whole hangar line of Wheeler was on fire. I thought about fuel and another place to land. I checked with Sergeant Carter and he said, 'We have about forty-five minutes of fuel left.' That would give me enough time to fly around the north end of the Koolau Mountains and take a look at Waimanalo, our old gunnery camp. In the meantime, someone spotted another field and said, 'There are U.S. fighters down there, P-40s at our old officers' swimming beach, Haleiwa,' but I continued on down to Waimanalo. When I got there, there was an airplane on fire on the runway, one of Ted Landon's. There were PT boats in the harbor and some were on fire. The place was under attack and I decided to go back to the fighter squadron at Haleiwa and landed there.

"The field at Haleiwa was now under attack and we taxied over to the trees to get close enough to [hide] our B-17s out of the way. We got out and the sergeants started unloading the guns and mounting them. Jim Twaddell and I looked up and saw a fighter coming right down the runway, firing at us. We decided to take cover in a hell of a hurry. This was right close to the beach and we ran there, saw a big rock with an open space under it.

"I said, 'Come on, Jim, we'll get under the rock.' We didn't know it but the waves were out at that particular time. Just as we got under, here came the waves. They almost drowned us. It ruined our watches and everything. There we were, the brave squadron commander and the weather officer, hiding under the rocks, and all the sergeants were out trying to shoot down the enemy."

Lieutenant General Walter C. Short, commissioned after graduation from the University of Illinois in 1902 and a veteran of the American Expeditionary Force in France during World War I, commanded the Army's Hawaiian Department whose primary responsibility was to protect the bases there and the fleet. Like his opposite number, Adm. Husband E. Kimmel, Short arrived on station in February 1941.

On the evening of 6 December Short and his wife had attended a party at the Schofield Barracks Officers' Club, leaving the festivities an hour or so before midnight. The route home took them by Pearl Harbor, crammed with ships ablaze with lights. Short remarked to an associate, "What a target that would make!" But it was a casual aside rather than a foreboding.

Lieutenant Colonel James A. Mollison, chief of staff for the local Air Corps, who like so many others at first thought the explosions came from Navy or Marine pilots who inadvertently dropped ordnance, had rushed to his headquarters at Hickam Field. From there he telephoned Short's chief of staff, Col. Walter Phillips, still trying to decide the source of the noise. When Mollison informed him the islands and bases were under attack, the incredulous Phillips snorted, "You're out of your mind, Jimmy. What's the matter, are you drunk? Wake up, wake up!"

Exasperated, Mollison held the receiver out to enable Phillips to hear the sounds of bombs and machine guns. Even then Phillips vacillated, until a second staff officer called with the news. The chief of staff scurried next door to Short's quarters.

"I heard the first bombs," said Short, "and my first idea was that the Navy was having some battle practice, either that they hadn't told me about or that I'd forgotten that they had told me about it. When some more dropped I went out on the back porch to take a look at what was going on, and about that time the chief of staff came running over to my quarters around three minutes after eight and said he had just gotten a message . . . that it was the real thing."

Short hurried to his headquarters at Fort Shafter where wounded men already lay on stretchers beside the base hospital and soldiers frantically dug trenches. While the general now knew Pearl Harbor itself was under attack he had no knowledge of events there since the anchorage was not visible from Shafter. A colonel whose home overlooked the harbor arrived to breathlessly inform Short, "I just saw two battleships sunk."

"That's ridiculous!" insisted Short.

When the attack began, Adm. Husband E. Kimmel, a 1904 graduate of the Naval Academy and commander in chief of the United States fleet (CinCUS), also was in his residence dressing as he awaited confirmation of a report that one of his destroyers, the USS *Ward*, had sunk a submarine trespassing near the islands. He was on the telephone with the duty officer at naval headquarters when a yeoman burst into the latter's office shouting, "There's a message from the signal tower saying the Japanese are attacking Pearl Harbor and this is no drill." The officer relayed the shocking news. Kimmel slammed down the receiver and as he buttoned his white uniform jacket ran outside. From the lawn of the residence of Mrs. John B. Earle, wife of a navy captain next door, Kimmel could clearly see Battleship Row being hammered, bombers circling the hapless vessels, dumping tons of devastating explosives.

Mrs. Earle recalled, "[they] could plainly see the rising suns on the wings and would have seen the pilots' faces had they leaned out." She described the admiral as watching "in utter disbelief and completely stunned," his face "as white as the uniform he wore."

Kimmel would say, "I knew right away that something terrible was going on, that this was not a casual raid by just a few stray planes. The sky was full of the enemy." Horrified, he saw "*Arizona* lift out of the water, then sink back down—way down."

It is unlikely that the appalled admiral actually realized the devastation of what he witnessed. A bomb had struck the

Arizona close to its No. 2 turret and detonated the forward
magazine. The blast wiped out nearly 1,000 men including
the skipper Capt. Franklyn Van Valkenburg and RAdm.
Isaac Kidd, commander of the First Battleship Division. The
explosion showered the adjoining repair vessel USS *Vestal*
with debris—pieces of the battlewagon, whole human bodies, some alive, legs, arms, and heads. The force of the erup-
tion hurled some 100 men from the *Vestal* overboard,
including her skipper, Comdr. Cassin B. Young. Dripping oil
and seawater he clambered back aboard to cancel an "abandon ship" order. For the hapless *Arizona* the torment continued with more bombs and torpedoes until it settled in the
harbor, with fewer than 200 survivors from a complement of
1,400.

Paul Backus, aroused on the *Oklahoma* by the profanity
uttered by a fellow ensign over the loudspeaker, had to
shake awake his cabinmate, Ens. Lewis Bailey Pride Jr., who
slept through both the general alarm and the announcement.
"We threw on some clothes. While doing so, we asked each
other how in hell the Japs managed to get in without being
detected by the PBYs [from Patrol Wing 2]. These were the
big seaplanes based at Ford Island. Every morning, these
flying boats used to roar down the channel and stagger into
the air for their daily surveillance patrol. When the battleships were in port, this very early takeoff was damned an-
noying. As the large planes applied full power down past
Battleship Row, they awakened all the junior officers. (The
senior officers didn't mind because they lived ashore.)"

Actually, three PBYs from Arthur Price's squadron had
flown the customary search mission. One of them spotted
the submarine outside the harbor and dropped a smoke
bomb as part of the attack upon the invader by the destroyer
Ward. However, the PBYs, on patrol since four or five in

the morning, did not range to the north, the direction from which the Japanese convoy approached the islands.

Backus made his way topside. Unknown to him, he had been the last to see his friend Bailey Pride. He saw a Marine acquaintance endeavoring to close a hatch. No one who survived the attack would ever again see that man alive either. Hurrying by the gun deck where the 5-inch/25 antiaircraft mounts were located he noticed the sailors were not manning the weapons. "I asked why. It turned out that the boxes containing the ready ammunition were padlocked and there was no compressed air for the rammers. The padlocks were broken and the ammunition hand-rammed into the breeches. Then the gun crews discovered there were no firing locks on the breech blocks. They had been removed and were down in the armory being cleaned for a scheduled admiral's inspection. As a result, not a shot was fired from these guns before the ship rolled over.

"The gunnery officer, Lt. Comdr. Harry H. Henderson, wanted to keep a portion of the antiaircraft battery manned and ready while we were in port. He is reported to have been overruled by the captain. Apparently, Captain Bode believed the threat of an attack was insignificant, and it was more important to get ready for the inspection that was scheduled for Monday. As part of our preparation for the inspection, some of our blisters were open when the attack took place. The manhole covers had been removed in some instances so that the blisters could be aired out for a later cleaning. Obviously our resistance to flooding was minimal when the torpedoes hit. When the blisters dipped under, flooding had to be massive.

"The *Arizona* blew up at about this time. A huge spout of flame and gray-black smoke shot skyward way above her foretop. The explosion sounded like many depth charges going off simultaneously. I found out later that the only *Arizona* officer forward of her stack to survive was Ens. Douglas Hein. A classmate of mine, Doug told me that he was with the admiral and captain on the flag bridge when the explosion occurred. When he regained consciousness, he was in the water, not knowing how he got there. He was badly burned on his back, head, and hands, but otherwise intact. Doug recovered fully, but the tragedy is that he was lost later in an aircraft accident.

"About the same time, the lines securing the *Oklahoma* to the *Maryland* had started to pop as the list on the ship increased rapidly. The executive officer [Comdr. J. W. Kenworthy] watching all of this from his station, gave the word to abandon ship. This word was picked up and passed along topside by shouts. I think by this time power had been lost and the general announcing system was out. In retrospect, fewer lives might have been lost if those of us topside had made more effort to get the word to those below decks to abandon ship.

"I can recollect distinctly only that first torpedo explosion that helped roust me out of my bunk, although there had been at least four or five hits by this time. Ensign Norm Hoffman counted five torpedo hits during the time he was running from the wardroom to his turret via its lower handling room and the climb up the center column to the turret booth. There were two more hits while he was in the booth testing telephones before William F. Greenaway, the leading boatswain's mate in the second division, put his head up the hatch in the overhang and relayed Commander Kenworthy's order to abandon ship." The severe list of the *Oklahoma* indicated the mortally wounded battleship was about to capsize.

"Before going over the side," said Backus, "I remember

seeing some of the *Maryland*'s guns firing with *Oklahoma* sailors helping to man them. Avoiding the torpedoes and the possibility of a quick rollover, I went over the high side, which was the starboard side. I can't remember climbing over a bulwark or going through the lifelines, but I do remember sliding down the side of the ship behind some members of the Marine detachment and ending up on the antitorpedo blister. Once on the blister, I ran forward a few frames before going into the water between the ships. I remember thinking that I probably could not make the climb from the water to the *Maryland*'s blister, that there might be a boat tied up under the *Maryland*'s bow into which I could climb and, if not, Ford Island's shore wasn't that far away."

Survivor Backus said, "The water between the ships was covered with fuel oil, but it was not burning as it was in other parts of the harbor. The swim up to and around the bow of the *Maryland* was uneventful. There was a *Maryland* motor whaleboat tied directly under her huge starboard anchor. Two *Oklahoma* sailors, one a boatswain's mate, second class, were already in the boat. Another joined us soon after I climbed in. I had a look at the engine and found it was a new diesel with which I was unfamiliar. I could not find the starter. All three sailors indicated that they, too, were strangers to the engine, so the four of us sat in the boat until there was a lull. I remember looking up at the gigantic anchor right over our heads and thinking that if a bomb hit the *Maryland*'s forecastle we would have had it. (I was told afterward that a bomb had hit her forecastle but obviously it did not damage the chain stopper.) [During] the lull the boatswain's mate remembered where the starter switch was. I told him to take over as coxswain, I'd be engineer, and the other two would help survivors out of the water.

"We made at least two, possibly three or four, trips be-

tween the waters around the *Oklahoma* and the Ford Island
fuel dock. A few bigger boats were in the area. There were
quite a few people in the water. They were covered with fuel
oil. Many were choking and spitting. The *Oklahoma*'s senior medical officer, Comdr. Fred M. Rohow, an older man,
was in trouble. Dr. Rohow either had been wounded or had
been hurt getting off the ship. We got him and some others
aboard for one boatload. At one point while we were re-
trieving survivors, I realized the guns were roaring again. I
looked up and could see what looked like bombers at high
altitude. Even more nerve-wracking was the shrapnel from
our own guns which was splashing all around us. All of this
was associated with the second wave of the Japanese attack."

Backus and his comrades pulled a "Filipino or Chamoro"
steward from the water. "He had just come out of the porthole of a second-deck compartment on the starboard side.
The porthole was by this time several feet under water, the
ship having rolled all the way over to port. He was almost in
a state of shock. He had had to fight his way out against the
surging flood of water entering through the porthole. There
were many others in the compartment for whom he did not
have much hope. No others surfaced in the immediate vicinity during the next few minutes.

"On our last run by the overturned hull of the *Oklahoma*,
I noticed an officer in dress whites, with spy glass and white
gloves, standing on the overturned hull near the stern. There
were a couple of sailors with him in undress whites. As we
swung in close aboard, I realized the officer was Ens. John
'Dapper Dan' Davenport, a good friend and classmate. He
was the junior officer of the deck and was manning the quar-
terdeck. As the ship rolled over, he and the sailors on watch
with him just rotated their station to keep up with the roll. At

that point there was plenty of room in the boat for the three of them but 'Dapper Dan' refused to ride with us. The boat was filthy with oil and he would have nothing to do with us. He and his watch were taken off a short time later by, presumably, a much cleaner boat.

"There were no more *Oklahoma* survivors evident in the water. We delivered our last load to the fuel dock, my crew left me when I indicated I wanted to go back out to help around the *California*. There seemed to be fires in the water alongside her and some swimmers in the water in the vicinity. Other boats were headed for them and, I believe, pulled them out. We beached the *Maryland* whaleboat by the fuel dock and went ashore." Hundreds of bedraggled men, blackened with oil, burned, wounded, exhausted, staggered ashore, paddling there on their own or else rescued by a small flotilla of boats crisscrossing the harbor to pluck sailors from the water.

Equally beset by the marauding enemy aircraft, the battleship *West Virginia* absorbed a torpedo during the second pass at Battleship Row. Then another pair struck home and the ship listed to port just as flames broke out in a turret, followed by another massive explosion. The *West Virginia*'s skipper, Capt. Mervyn Bennion, and her navigator, Lt. Comdr. T. T. Beattie, met on the bridge to determine what action to take. As the pair discussed their options, a half-dozen torpedoes wracked the hull and a pair of bombs exploded topside. A large chunk of shrapnel ripped open Bennion's stomach. As he lay dying, another officer summoned help. A chief pharmacist's mate applied first aid and mess attendant Dorie Miller arrived to help remove the stricken officer from further danger. Bennion died within a few minutes. Miller, an African American and like all blacks restricted to steward ranks, with no training, then helped man a machine gun.

Credited with knocking down a pair of enemy aircraft, Miller won a Navy Cross for heroism, but only after pressure from outside the Navy.

As an assistant control officer for antiaircraft aboard the cruiser *Phoenix*, Ted Hechle, while responding to "general quarters," moved into high gear at the sound of the ship's .50-caliber machine guns yammering overhead. He raced up three decks above the main one to his station in "sky forward," an aerie above the bridge to control the four 5-inch/25 guns of the starboard battery. "I was propelled on my journey by the sight of a torpedo plane that flew past the *Phoenix* at deck level. It carried a big red ball on the side. As I reached my station, our battery was already training out. The awnings which were still up from the admiral's inspection had to be taken down so the guns could train out. Locks were chopped off the ammunition boxes.

"Because of the lack of high-level horizontal bombers—the kind of planes I was capable of directing fire at—during the initial stages of the attack, I found myself an unwilling occupant of a front-row seat from which to witness the proceedings. The sky seemed filled with diving planes and the black bursts of exploding antiaircraft shells. Our batteries were among those firing shells in 'local control,' which meant the fire originated from the guns themselves. The Japanese planes were too close for us to take advantage of the more sophisticated automatic control which was normally provided by my station. In essence, the guns were laying out a pattern of steel in the hope that the Japanese planes would fly through it and be damaged in the process. I have often described the experience as akin to trying to swat an angry swarm of bees in the confines of a telephone booth. To make matters worse, our shells were set with a minimum peacetime fuse setting which would not permit them to explode until they had reached a safe distance from the ship. In addition, some of the fuses were defective with the result that the exploded projectiles were coming down ashore. Our best weapons under these conditions were the machine guns, which accounted for a number of enemy aircraft.

"By shortly after 8:00 A.M. the harbor was a riot of explosions and gunfire. I looked at the battle line from which huge plumes of black smoke were rising. As I watched, I saw the *Arizona* wracked by a tremendous explosion. Her foremast came crashing down into the inferno. Since I was in the corresponding station in my own ship, I naturally thought about what my own fate might be in the next few minutes.

"Bombs were exploding on the Naval air station at Ford Island and the Army air base at Hickam Field. A Japanese torpedo plane came down our port side. It couldn't have been more than 150 feet above the water and looked as if the pilot had throttled down, having just launched his torpedo at the battle line. He banked to the left as he got opposite us, as if to turn away. I could see .50-caliber tracer slugs going right out to the plane and passing through the fuselage at the wing joint. Suddenly, flames shot out from underneath, and he continued his turn and bank to the left until he had rolled over onto his back. A great cheer went up from our crew, because his demise was apparent. Unfortunately, he crashed onto the deck of the seaplane tender *Curtiss*, inflicting a number of casualties.

"Another plane came in, low over the water, toward our starboard quarter. This time I saw a cross fire of tracers from the *Phoenix* and other ships. There was an explosion on the plane and in the next instant there was nothing left but its debris descending to the water. Moments later, I heard the 'zing' of a bullet whistling by. Later, we discovered a hole in the shield of a range finder below us. The air was so full of flying bullets and shrapnel by that time it was impossible to tell the source, but that bullet constituted the total damage inflicted on the *Phoenix* that day."

At Kaneohe, aviation metalsmith Arthur Price Jr. came upon a scene of ruins. "The first wave of planes had strafed all the PBYs we had sitting out on the beaching ramp, and they were all burned. Our fire trucks were there, but they couldn't do much with burning aluminum. Even the planes out on the water were on fire. One of our boys who had been on watch in a plane out in the bay was strafed, but he had sense enough to crawl onto the ramp. I went over and picked him up, but he was already dead. I put him in the back of the squadron truck and wrapped him in a cloth. There was nothing else I could do for him, so I just left him there.

"Meanwhile, our men were setting up machine guns outside the VP-14 hangar. I went over to try to help out, and then somebody shouted, 'Here comes a group of bombers.' Our skipper said, 'Let's get the hell out of here.' So he and I and another man jumped into the truck and we started heading over toward another hangar. When we got there, we looked up, and there came a formation of eight to twelve bombers, flying in a beautiful Vee formation at about 1,200 feet. As soon as we saw them approaching the hangar, we got out of the truck and dove under some construction material. The planes got right above us and let their bombs go. That was the end of our new hangar.

"About that time, a Zero fighter came down. We thought he was going to strafe us, because his guns were going, but evidently the pilot had been shot already. He just flew straight into the ground right ahead of our truck, shooting the whole way. He hit the ground maybe 500 feet from us, and was thrown out of the plane. He was dead, of course, and all chopped up, so we threw him in the back of the truck. So here we were carrying the dead American from the seaplane ramp and the dead Japanese from the Zero.

"We drove back to our hangar, and there encountered Chief Aviation Ordnanceman John Finn, a man who was later awarded the Medal of Honor for his heroism that day." Finn had mounted a machine gun atop a construction scaffolding to shoot at the enemy planes. Blazing gasoline surrounded him but he kept firing until hit by strafers. "He [Finn] was all shot up—looked as if he'd been peppered with small stuff, .30-caliber machine guns. So it was back into the truck once more to take the chief to sick bay. He and the skipper and I were in the front, and the two corpses were in back.

"When we got to our destination, wounded men were flaked out all through the passageways because there were so many of them that there was no place to put them. I thought the medical people would keep Chief Finn there, he was in such bad shape. But he said, 'No, I just want to get patched up.' He wouldn't stay. Twenty minutes later he was right down at the skeleton of the hangar getting the ordnance things organized.

"By nine o'clock, when things had died down [at Kaneohe but not immediately around Pearl Harbor] our three PBYs came back from patrol and they didn't have a scratch on them. Those were the only planes we had left, because we lost thirty-three of our thirty-six that morning."

Returning from the hunting expedition, Gordon Austin met Lt. George S. Welch, the assistant operations officer of the 47th Pursuit Squadron. "Where have you been?" asked Austin.

"I've been shooting down Japs," Austin quoted Welch. "There's one off the road there." Inspection of the wreckage revealed the bodies of three crewmen from a torpedo bomber. Welch and a fellow pilot, Lt. Kenneth Taylor, had spent the evening carousing, and in an all-night poker game that did not break up until shortly before 8:00 A.M. When Japanese gunners strafed the officers' club, the pilots jumped into their car and sped off to Haleiwa.

The Japanese apparently were unaware of the field for it went untouched. As elsewhere the American aircraft were, in Taylor's words, "lined up in perfect line right down one side of the field. At Haleiwa we had no revetments, and we just parked them there just to look nice and also keep them bunched so we could guard them easier." However, word of the assault had reached the base and by the time Welch and Taylor came to the flight line, crews were already loading the fighters.

The two roared off in their P-40s and headed for Wheeler Field to arm their guns with .50-caliber ammunition. Landing between attacks by the Japanese they stocked their weapons and went in search of the foe. In a scrap with half a dozen or so enemy planes, Welch said, "We took off directly into them and shot down some. I shot down one right on Lieutenant Taylor's tail." Subsequently, the pair landed, rearmed, and headed for the Marines' Ewa Field. "At that time there was a whole string of planes looking like a traffic pattern," said Taylor. "We went down and got in the traffic pattern and shot down several planes there. I know for certain I had shot down two planes or perhaps more."

Adolph Seton, passing out sound-powered phones for antiaircraft stations on the *St. Louis*, was struck by the response of his shipmates. "Our crew acted as though this was another drill except for outbursts of cheering every time a plane was hit within our limited firing bearings. Seton's skipper, Capt. George A Rood, recalled that no one issued an order to commence firing. "Our battery people knew what was up, knew what to do and [they] took the initiative and opened fire with everything that would bear." Subsequently, the *St. Louis* claimed six enemy planes shot down but officially received credit for three.

While the gunners blazed away, Rood conned his ship toward the open sea with as much speed as his reduced boiler power could generate. "I knew that if any Jap submarines were present, they would be lying off the entrance ready to torpedo outgoing vessels and so we buckled on speed." As the cruiser headed for the open sea a steel cable from a dredge blocked the way. Captain Rood called for full speed ahead and he says his ship "hit that cable a smashing blow and snapped it like a violin string."

Churning through the water at twenty-two knots in an eight-knot zone, the *St. Louis* cleaved through the narrow channel at the harbor entrance. At flank speed, the cruiser nevertheless made an easy prey since the narrow lane rendered torpedo evasion tactics impossible—Kimmel's predecessor had described the harbor as "a goddamn mousetrap."

Indeed, an enemy midget submarine lurking at the entrance launched a perfectly lined-up pair of torpedoes at the oncoming cruiser. The lead missile set to hit on the starboard side apparently ran too deep, for it struck a spit of coral and exploded, soaking crewmen with seawater. The second one, possibly knocked off course by that detonation, veered into coral and also blew up. Had either missile found its mark and the *St. Louis* foundered, the hulk would have bottled up the harbor.

Lightened by the release of its tin fish, the midget sub popped to the surface. Gun crews from the cruiser instantly opened fire and claimed a hit on the conning tower of the raider, which disappeared. As the *St. Louis* set its course for the open sea, the 7 December, 1941, raid passed into history with a finale of strafing sorties on airfields. Some two hours after the first Japanese planes roared over the anchorage, the last of them vanished to rendezvous with the carriers. They left behind 8 battleships, 3 light cruisers, 3 destroyers, and 4 auxiliary craft that either sank, capsized, were heavily damaged, or less so. The naval air arm reported 13 fighters, 21 scout bombers, 46 patrol bombers, and a handful of other planes lost. The Hawaiian Air Force wrote off 4 B-17s, 12 B-18s, a pair of A-20s [two-engine bombers], 32 P-40s, 20 P-36s, plus a considerable number of other aircraft including 88 pursuit or fighters and 34 bombers damaged. In addition, installations catering to both Navy and Air Corps needs had been ravaged. Worst of all was the cost in lives, more than 2,400, with 2,000 from the Navy. Another 1,178 required treatment for injuries, horrible burns, and grievous injury to limbs and organs. The raiders escaped with only 29 planes down, 1 full-size submarine, and 5 midget subs destroyed.

Within two hours after the raid began, the Pearl Harbor anchorage was choked with sunken or smashed ships that for days oozed oil whose fires would burn for weeks. Ashore, the Navy docks and maintenance shops lay in ruins. At Wheeler and Hickam Fields, along with lesser airfields, heaps of often barely recognizable scorched metal sat smoldering. Hangars, operations buildings, and barracks showed gaping holes if not reduced to piles of debris. Amid frantic efforts to rescue those trapped on sunken or blazing ships and buildings could be heard the sirens of ambulances, the occasional drone of aircraft, and the sporadic discharge of weapons in the hands of trigger-sensitive defenders who now believed a full-scale invasion might be imminent.

Brooke Allen, the B-17 pilot who first tried to get off the

ground with an empty Fort, admitted that in his haste he flooded an engine and rather than try to make it on only three abandoned the effort. On a second attempt, with a bomb load, he went in search of the Japanese carriers. "I found an American one to the south. With a personal feeling that the Japanese had come from the north, I made a maximum range search. The weather was bad and I'd have to get down on the deck at times and up to altitude also to take maximum advantage of visibility. With only one airplane it would have been unusually fortunate if I had stumbled across the task force. I returned with a minimum of fuel and a heart full of disgust that I had been unable to locate them."

Martin Low recalled getting airborne in a P-40 shortly after 10:00 A.M. and scouring the skies for signs of the enemy. "When I got near Pearl Harbor, they opened up on me and I realized they were a little tender. The Japanese were long gone. The rest of the day, we just sat around. We had an alcoholic colonel in command and every five minutes he claimed there were Japanese fighters over the waterworks, the electrical plant, or whatever. We kept busy filling every container with water, moving the remaining planes into revetments, setting up tents.

"At 8:00 P.M. our squadron went to a naval air station on the other side of the island to take over planes that had been at the gunnery camp [Haleiwa]. We traveled in a staff car in a total blackout. We had our .45s pointed out of the windows. Every wave that hit the beach we saw as another landing barge."

Enroute to Pearl Harbor on 7 December was a trio of U.S. submarines. Aboard the *Pompano* sailed a former Naval Academy football star, Slade Cutter, a native of Chicago. "On the morning of the seventh, about five minutes of 8:00 A.M.," remembered Cutter, "the radioman came up through the conning tower, reached up, and handed the officer of the deck a dispatch, which read, 'Air raid on Pearl Harbor. This is no drill.' " On the *Pompano*, said Cutter, were several officers traveling to take command of other submarines and they along with his own skipper, Lewis Parks, had served in China. "They got to talking about the Japs: 'That's just like those yellow bastards. They'd do something like that.' And they believed it right away."

Because of engine trouble, the *Pompano* had been delayed for repairs. Had the sub arrived on schedule, 6:00 A.M. at Pearl Harbor, *Pompano* would have become another target of opportunity in the anchorage. The vessel, however, still came under fire. "We were about 135 miles northeast of Pearl Harbor on the great circle route from San Francisco to Pearl, when we were attacked by Japanese aircraft." The *Pompano* and its companions, in an attempt to make up for lost time, hastened toward the islands, traveling on the surface. "We had pumped out all of our variable water, to lighten us, to make more speed through the water. As soon as this message came in, Parks said, 'Rig ship for dive and compensate. Get the water back in so we can dive.'

"We weren't done when we got attacked by the first wave coming back [from Pearl Harbor]. And we were strafed. The other submarines went under. We weren't damaged."

By the time the three submarines reached Hawaii, it was night and they were instructed to submerge until the following evening. Escorted by a destroyer they headed into the harbor. "We didn't know anything that had gone on," said Cutter. "We had no idea of the damage. The first thing we saw on the reef was a Navy fighter. It had been crash-landed but it didn't look like it had been damaged very much. A little farther, Hickam Field was just burning. Ford Island, that was burning. Right ahead of us was the *Nevada*, which was beached. Then we turned the corner and saw the battleships, this way and that—the masts—all of them didn't sink on an even keel. We passed the floating dry dock where the *Shaw* had been blown up. When we came closer, there was the *Oklahoma*, upside down. The *Utah*, upside down and the *Arizona* was still burning and it looked like there were six inches of oil on the water. It was a very depressing sight. We got into port to tie up. There were a bunch of people on dock but we couldn't get people to handle our lines. It was like they were all in a daze."

A day after the attack, Gordon Austin and the commander of the 14th Pursuit Air Wing, Brig. Gen. Howard Davidson, toured Pearl Harbor in the company of an admiral. Austin remembered Davidson telling the admiral, "Except for the human misery, the human disaster, the human losses in the attack, it is the best thing that ever happened to the U.S. Navy."

"As a young captain I was just gasping for air hearing that comment to a black shoe [seagoing rather than aviator] sailor. Davidson said, 'If the war had started and you people had gone to sea with all your battleships, the Japs would have sunk them all at sea and you would have lost all hands.' " Davidson had a point in that a few weeks later, the British dreadnoughts *Prince of Wales* and *Repulse* were both sunk in the South China Sea by enemy aircraft with heavy loss of life. The enemy was long gone, having successfully achieved its first strategy, neutralization of the U.S. fleet.

2

Preattack Maneuvers

BY THE MID-1930S, THE MORE AGGRESSIVE ELEMENTS OF THE Japanese industrial complex, responding both to an Imperial tradition and the ravages of a worldwide depression, dominated political policy in the country. In 1931, a bogus incident in the Chinese province of Manchuria provoked a full-scale attack. Japan conquered the unorganized defenders and created a puppet, "independent" state called Manchukuo.

Over the next few years, a series of attempted coups and assassinations shook Japan. Ultimately, the proponents of a greater Japan crushed the opposition. Expansion became the goal. Achievement mandated a substantially larger army and navy. The Nipponese government circumvented the limitations of the naval treaties, secretly building a pair of huge battleships, the *Yamato* and the *Musashi*. These were much bigger than anything launched by the United States. If the United States had matched these dreadnoughts it could not have moved them through the Panama Canal.

To Western diplomats and military strategists the Sino-Japanese War of 1937 and the bellicose pronouncements from Japan ordained a collision course between East and West. Americans sympathized with the Chinese as newsreels showed the ravages of war inflicted upon civilians by the Japanese invaders. In 1937, when Japanese bombers sank the U.S. Navy gunboat *Panay* on the Yangtze River, Americans turned angry and hostility remained even after an apology and indemnity payment. Diplomats, missionaries, business representatives, and service personnel in China perceived a growing arrogance that bordered on contempt from Japanese military whom they encountered.

Satisfaction of Japanese aims could not be accomplished with indigenous resources and the only way to sustain the Empire lay in a southern advance. That route meant bumping heads with the British, Dutch, French, and American interests rather than the Soviet Union, a northern military threat but less of a reservoir of scarce raw materials. The new power in the Far East threatened to slam doors opened to Western trade by gunboats in the nineteenth century. A newspaper reputed to speak for the foreign office in 1940 bluntly asserted, "Japan must remove all elements in East Asia which will interfere with its plans. Britain, the United States, France, and the Netherlands must be forced out of the Far East. Asia is the territory of the Asiatics."

Along with more bites of Chinese territory, a further series of actions by the Japanese affronted the Western democracies. On the heels of Germany's smashing defeat of the French in June 1940, Japanese soldiers moved into northern French Indochina [what would become Vietnam, Laos, and Cambodia] and few doubted that the troops would soon march southward. In retaliation for the invasion of Indochina, President Franklin D. Roosevelt declared an embargo on further shipments of scrap iron and steel. By the end of the year, the sanctions would begin to pinch the Japanese economy and its war-making potential.

On 27 September 1940, Japan signed the Tripartite Pact, a treaty that pledged Germany, Italy, and Japan to "assist one another with all political, economic, and military means when one of the three Contracting Parties is attacked by a power at present not involved in the European War or in the Sino-Japanese conflict." Clearly, the only country that qualified as a target was the United States since the Soviet Union still held a nonaggression pact with Hitler. Germany had lost the Battle of Britain in the skies during the summer of 1940 and as the Nazi legions prepared to chew up the Soviet Union the Third Reich thus tried to enlist Japan in an active role, urging an attack upon Singapore and British possessions in the Far East. To sweeten the proposal, the Hitler government even pledged ". . . if Japan got into a conflict with the United States, Germany on her part would take the necessary steps at once. It made no difference with whom the United States first came into conflict, whether it was with Germany or with Japan."

Harsh rhetoric from both sides generated intense discussions at the top levels of government in Tokyo and Washington. A new ambassador, Adm. Kichisaburo Nomura, presented his credentials in Washington. Nomura seems to have negotiated in good faith but he had little influence at home. Although Washington offered to accommodate the Japanese hunger for Indochina's rice and minerals, the Imperial Army overran the colony toward the end of July 1941. Roosevelt promptly froze the assets of both Japan and China (with the agreement of the Chinese Chiang Kai-shek) and a week later leveled an embargo on high-octane gasoline and crude oil, vital to the military forces.

As the tension with Japan had increased, Army and Navy brass had taken a number of steps to improve their readiness for war. In the Far East, the Asiatic Fleet under Adm. Thomas Hart had grown in size, although hardly enough to match what the Japanese could muster. The Army Air Force beefed up its Philippine arsenal, adding fighter planes and a new group of B-17 Flying Fortress bombers, with more like those destined for the Far East that arrived during the attack on Pearl Harbor.

In July 1941, Douglas MacArthur, formerly the military advisor for the Commonwealth of the Philippines, had been recalled to active duty as commander in chief, United States Army Forces in the Far East. He continued to develop an ambitious plan to defend the Philippines with a bulked-up nexus of U.S. soldiers plus the redoubtable Philippine Scouts and an army of indigenous conscripts. Meanwhile, as December approached, Admiral Hart prudently sent many of his vessels to sea rather than pen them up in the vulnerable Manila Bay.

Throughout this period, Washington through the State Department, the secretaries of the army and the navy, and the uniformed heads of the armed forces continually advised their commanders in such major bastions as the Philippines and Hawaii of the tension with Nippon. There was no shortage of messages counseling the likes of MacArthur, Hart, Short, and Kimmel of the need to ready themselves for a possible outbreak of war.

On the other hand, there was at least one serious error in the distribution of intelligence. Enemy agents, directed by the Japanese consulate in Honolulu, fed information on military matters to Tokyo. On 24 September the consulate was asked for precise information about the location of warships in the anchorage. Having broken the Japanese diplomatic code, American intelligence deciphered the dispatches that later would become known as the "bomb plot message." Unfortunately, the authorities in Washington failed to advise either Kimmel or Short of the specific request for details about the deployment of the fleet in Pearl Harbor that implied plans for an attack. In their defense the authorities insisted the Japanese, like all nations, routinely sought such material. Whether Kimmel and Short would have acted differently if privy to the "bomb plot" is unknown.

When Short assumed his command he operated under the policies of the Army's chief of staff, George C. Marshall, who stressed, "The risk of sabotage and the risk involved in a surprise raid by Air and by submarine constitutes [sic] the real perils of the situation. Frankly, I do not see any landing threat in the Hawaiian Islands [Short commanded 25,000 ground troops to repel an invasion] so long as we have air superiority." Marshall specifically instructed his subordinate, "Please keep clearly in mind in all of your negotiations [with military and civilian authorities in the islands] that our mission is to protect the base and the Naval concentrations."

Short, upon inspection of his fief, perceived obvious weaknesses in his air force, and attempted to disperse and shield his fighters and bombers. He advised the adjutant general in Washington, "The concentration of these airplanes at Wheeler Field and at Hickam Field presents a very serious problem in the protection against hostile aviation." Short asked for $1.5 million worth of bunkers in which to stash 142 single-engine fighters, 121 double-engine pursuit ships, 25 two-engine bombers, and 70 four-engine bombers. It was a fairly modest sum even in 1941 dollars but Washington never acted on his plea.

Half-hearted efforts to open up more air fields to spread out assets had created a few strips like Haleiwa but these were more in the nature of training or emergency sites rather than functioning bases. As an infantry officer, Short may well have been unaware of the quality of his Hawaiian Air Force. By December 1941, the war planners, convinced that the Japanese would hit the outermost Pacific bases including the Philippines, Wake, and Guam, shipped available aircraft toward these points, stripping Hawaii of some of its planes in the process. Short may not have known, indeed many of those more directly concerned with the Air Corps did not realize, just how weak was the U.S. in the skies. The pursuit or fighter-plane force included obviously obsolescent P-36s and P-37s as well as early and inadequate P-40 models. The B-18 bomber, a woefully underpowered ship, at best could barely muster 170 to 180 miles per hour. Only a handful of the new B-17 or two-engine A-20s were available.

The head of the Hawaiian Air Force, Maj. Gen. Frederick L. Martin, and RAdm. Patrick N. L. Bellinger, both aviators, in an example of armed-services cooperation, at the instigation of their bosses, Kimmel and Short, produced a plan for a joint action in the event of an attack upon Hawaii and the fleet. On 31 March 1941, the authors noted, "A successful, sudden raid against our ships and Naval installations on Oahu might prevent effective offensive action by our forces in the Western Pacific for a long period. . . ." They cautioned a raiding force could come without any advance information from intelligence and it might consist of carriers that steamed within 300 miles.

The Martin-Bellinger Report stated, "The aircraft at present available in Hawaii are inadequate to maintain for any extended period from bases on Oahu, a patrol extensive enough to insure that an air attack from an Orange [the designation of an enemy] carrier cannot arrive over Oahu as a complete surprise."

Daily patrols that covered an arc through 360 degrees seaward were the most effective means to discover intruders,
but Martin-Bellinger admitted the Hawaiian command
lacked the personnel and planes to carry out such missions.
Under an agreement reached between the Army and Navy,
long-range reconnaissance was the responsibility of the
Navy and its PBYs. The Army would scout only twenty
miles offshore, of value perhaps for locating submarines but
useless against a surprise air attack.

Another study by an Air Corps officer in the summer of
1941 raised again the specter of carrierborne raids. The in-
vestigator noted the routes the enemy must take—either
north or south in a westerly direction—to avoid shipping
lanes, pinpointed the probable time of an attack—early
morning—and what it would require to combat a force composed of half a dozen flattops. The report recommended an
allotment to Hawaii of 180 B-17s or similar four-engine
bombers and 36 torpedo-bearing medium bombers. The in-
fusion of aircraft would have eased the Navy's patrol-search
burden and theoretically deployed a puissant attack force
upon the enemy fleet. But at the time, the entire Air Corps
owned only 109 B-17s, with many of them committed to
MacArthur, mainland defense, or Great Britain.

Short was perceptive enough to focus on the need for a
system to provide an early warning of air attacks. Early in
his tenure he asked his superiors to obtain permission from
the secretary of the interior for permission to construct a
radar-detection apparatus atop Haleakala, a mountain on
Maui and one of the highest elevations in the islands. The
National Park Service as a subset of the Department of the
Interior governed Haleakala. And while agreeing to allow
temporary use of the promontory, the service demanded approval of all plans and structures, giving advance notice that

nothing that altered the natural appearance of the reservation or interfered with sightseeing would be permitted. The view from the mountaintop held priority over national defense. That officials of the National Park Service could reject the War Department's petition indicates the degree of confusion and lack of leadership in official Washington.

Frustrated in that direction, Short counted on radars placed elsewhere in the islands, but at best the detectors could pick up approaching aircraft at a distance of seventy-five miles, minimal time to scramble interceptors and man antiaircraft batteries. How seriously Short took his aircraft control and warning (ACW) net is problematical. At the inquiry after the disaster of 7 December, he remarked, "At the time we had just gotten in the machines and set up. I thought this was fine training for them. I was trying to get training and doing it for training more than any idea that it would be real."

About an hour before the first Japanese planes commenced the attack, Pvt. George E. Elliott, a trainee working the oscilloscope at the Opana Mobile Radar Station on the northern tip of Oahu, picked up an odd array of blips. His companion, an experienced technician, Pvt. Joseph L. Lockard, decided, "It must be a flight of some sort." The radar indicated some 50 planes coming from the north at a distance of 136 miles. After discussion on whether to report what was probably a Navy operation, Elliott phoned the Fort Shafter Information Center.

Lieutenant Kermit Tyler, a pilot in the 78th Pursuit Squadron, only vaguely familiar with the capabilities of radar and on duty in the information center, answered. He knew of scattered reports of aircraft from other radar stations but this was the largest flight sighted. Aware that B-17s were expected from the mainland, Tyler either assumed the incoming traffic was that bunch or else it was some Navy operation. He advised Lockhard, "Well, don't worry about it." The Opana station tracked the images until they were forty-five miles out, and then shut down. Had the radar warning been heeded, the American forces would have had as much as fifty minutes of advance notice of the attack. Possibly Short's dismissal of the ACW's usefulness was transmitted to the lower echelons.

Along with the radar advisory, the destroyer *Ward*'s encounter with a submarine some fifteen minutes or so earlier in the morning was another signal missed by the defenders. The sub, on the surface in restricted waters, first was noticed by a supply ship that notified the *Ward*, and then a PBY on morning patrol also spotted it. Having dropped depth charges, both the destroyer and the PBY notified superiors. Admiral Kimmel was still trying to interpret the meaning when he heard the bombs.

The strike on Pearl Harbor was enhanced by an American obsession with the potential for sabotage. Occidentals, both in the States and those in residence in Hawaii, focused on a population that included 160,000 of Japanese background, 37,500 of whom were foreign born. Publicity about the successes of "fifth columns" organized by the Germans to ease their conquests skewed decisions on Hawaii. In the final week of November 1941, Short discounted the possibilities of a Japanese attack. His conversations with the Navy indicated the Japanese fleet was either in home ports or else headed south. (Observers had reported a convoy moving in that direction and it eventually moved at other targets in the Pacific.) He zeroed in upon sabotage as the primary threat. As a consequence, aircraft, instead of being dispersed with guns loaded, were stripped of their ammunition that was safely under lock and key, lined up in neat, easily guarded formation fit for mass destruction.

On 7 November, at a cabinet meeting Secretary of State Cordell Hull spoke candidly of the international situation. He emphasized, "relations were extremely critical" and that "we should be on the lookout for a military attack anywhere by Japan at any time." On that same date, Saburo Kurusu as a special envoy embarked on the *China Clipper*, ostensibly for another try at resolving differences. After Kurusu reached Washington, representatives of the two countries conferred in search of a rapprochement. Neither side budged from its positions. Japan demanded a free hand in China, the end of all embargoes, refused to commit itself to evacuation of French Indochina, and did not deign to even mention its support of Hitler. The American position, submitted on 26 November, was based on principles of respect for the territorial integrity and sovereignty of nations, noninterference in those countries' internal affairs, equal commercial opportunity, and maintenance of the status quo in the Pacific except through alteration by peaceful means. Acceptance by Japan would roll back all of its expansion and limit the future of the empire.

While Hull, Roosevelt, Nomura, and Kurusu negotiated, Japanese ships were already at sea, with one group headed for the British-governed Malaysia, another aimed at a Philippine invasion, and the third bound for the waters off Hawaii.

In Hawaii there was a sense of war in the near future with Japan, but while some considered shooting imminent, few believed they were directly in the line of fire. Admiral Kimmel spoke in terms of war at sea. He arranged for all of the capital ships when in the narrow channel to face out to sea rather than have egress blocked by the need for a bat-

tlewagon to steam in a circle in order to head for the ocean.
But he, as had his predecessor, refused to have antitorpedo
nets installed on the grounds they reduced room to maneuver and because the shallow water protected against a submarine attack. The idea of torpedoes delivered from the air
seems not to have occurred to Kimmel and his staff. He directed a perfunctory surveillance of the seas, using his carriers *Enterprise* and *Lexington* for reconnaissance in the
outlying areas, while a handful of patrol planes based in
Hawaii reconnoitered limited sections of the nearer approaches. Left untouched were the northern reaches, where
wind directions most favored a carrier-based assault on the
American base.

General Short, too, saw no reason to fear a blow at Pearl.
He was unaware that the Navy patrols covered only a small
portion of the ocean. However, he had specific instructions
from the War Department that he use his assets, B-17s and
B-18s, to assist the Navy in this responsibility.

While their commanders wrestled with their obligations
based on their understanding of the geomilitary situation,
the lower echelons saw only modest modifications in their
lives. Ted Hechler of the *Phoenix* remembered "the customary prewar ways lasted right up to the time war started." He
noted that on the morning of 6 December, the commander of
Cruiser Division 9 carried out the traditional inspection.
"The men were in their whites, lined up in rows for personnel inspection. When it came to the inspection of the ship
herself, RAdm. H. Fairfax Leary had on his white gloves so
he could check for dust."

Paul Backus noted, "There was a great feeling of cocki-
ness among those with whom I worked and played. I don't
recall anyone ever expressing any concern about potential
combat, naval or otherwise, with the Japanese."

In Washington, however, there were grave doubts about the future. The code breakers on 29 November cracked a pair of messages that became known as the "winds" dispatches. In these the foreign ministry advised Ambassador Nomura that in the event of an emergency—severance of diplomatic relations and the cutoff of international communications—the daily short-wave radio news from Tokyo would use Japanese words for "East wind rain" to signify a danger point with the U.S. Other climactic turns covered relations with Great Britain and the Soviet Union. The precaution convinced all but the most optimistic American foreign policy people of an approaching crisis. Military authorities were duly informed of the gravity portended by the "winds" system.

On 6 December, Foreign Minister Shigenori Togo notified Nomura that the ministry would transmit a fourteen-part response to the American proposals. The procedures employed for sending the lengthy message, in retrospect, suggest the foreign ministry was in no hurry to see the contents delivered. At the same time, the Japanese held up an appeal from President Roosevelt to Emperor Hirohito for more than ten hours. Meanwhile, American Navy technicians utilizing decrypting machines labored to unscramble the text. By late evening all but the last part had been handed by the decoders to top Navy and Army brass, the State Department, and the White House. According to Lt. Lester Shulz, who physically brought the document to the president, Roosevelt read through the fifteen pages, a flat-out rejection of all American ideas, and handed them to Harry Hopkins, his close advisor. When Hopkins had gone through the papers, Roosevelt said, "This means war."

The chief executive, however, did not immediately sound a loud alert. He waited until Admiral Stark returned from an evening at the theater before calling him. Stark later claimed nothing Roosevelt said indicated hostilities were any closer, although there was already consensus that Japan was likely to attack at any time. Nor was the Army greatly aroused by the latest news. Brigadier General Sherman, the head of that branch's intelligence, decided the Japanese statement carried "little military significance." As a consequence, Miles saw no reason to disturb Gen. George C. Marshall, the chief of staff.

On 7 December, while the intelligence sections finally delivered a last element of the message at about 8:30 A.M. Washington, D.C., time [2:30 A.M. at Pearl Harbor], which offered no wiggle room, a brief note from Togo to Nomura stunned Col. Rufus S. Bratton, the Army's intelligence expert in the Far Eastern Section. Togo ordered Nomura not to deliver the fourteen-part statement to the American authorities until 1:00 P.M., Washington time. Ordinarily the diplomatic corps took Sundays off. But more significantly, no previous directive from Tokyo ever specified a precise hour. In fact, at that moment, the first of the Japanese planes would be a few minutes from Pearl Harbor to begin unloading their bombs and torpedoes.

Bratton was convinced that the Japanese expected to attack an American installation in the Pacific. However, he later agreed, "Nobody in ONI [Office of Naval Intelligence], nobody in G-2 [Army Intelligence] knew that any major element of the fleet was in Pearl Harbor on Sunday morning the 7th of December. We all thought they had gone to sea . . . because that was part of the war plan, and they had been given a war warning."

The cabinet officials and military leaders in Washington tried to guess what area would be most vulnerable at that appointed hour. Based on their limited knowledge of Japanese naval movement the most likely target appeared to be Kota Baharu, on the coast of Malaysia. It was agreed by Admiral Stark and General Marshall that all outlying possessions should be advised of the imminent threat.

The notices promptly went off to the first addressees, the Caribbean Defense Command, MacArthur in the Philippines, and the Presidio on the California coast. But atmospheric conditions blocked the radio channel for Hawaii. Instead of going to the Navy, which maintained better communications with the islands, the officer from the War Department Signal Center chose to use teletype through Western Union with a relay from San Francisco, via RCA, to Hawaii. Unfortunately, transmission of messages under this system did not instantly put the word out. The message would first need to be put in code, then deciphered by the receiving station for delivery to the likes of Short and Kimmel.

Honolulu recorded Marshall's warning at 7:33 A.M., as the first wave of airplanes droned on, a mere thirty-five miles from Oahu. The message carried no priority stamp and was placed with a batch of other cables scheduled for delivery by a motorcycle-borne delivery boy. The first bomb exploded about 7:55. The caution from Marshall never reached Short or Kimmel.

Somewhere between 1:30 and 2:00 P.M. a naval commander handed a dispatch from Hawaii to John H. Dillon, an assistant to Secretary of the Navy Frank Knox conferring with top aides. Dillon recalled the message, "We are being attacked. This is no drill." Knox gasped, "My God, this can't be true. This must mean the Philippines." Admiral Stark quickly checked and said, "No, sir, this is Pearl."

At 4:00 P.M. eastern standard time, Japanese Imperial Headquarters announced that a state of war existed between

Japan and the United States and the British Empire. On the following day, Roosevelt spoke to the American people by radio about "a date which will live in infamy" as he called on Congress for a declaration of war.

3

The Philippine Defenses

THE SMASHING SUCCESS OF THE ATTACK ON PEARL HARBOR resulted from perfectly plotted strategy backed by excellent logistical support. The raid benefitted hugely from American complacency, underestimation of Japanese military power and prowess. The U.S. commanders demonstrated a lack of imagination as they stressed a potential fifth column while blind to the possibility of a much more devastating type of assault. The continuation of a spit-and-polish Navy rather than a combat-prepared one meant that shipboard guns could not operate with requisite swiftness. Luck all fell to the attackers. American planes and ships in their limited reconnaissance did not blunder upon the fleet. At the appointed hour the harbor happened to be crammed with targets; only the two aircraft carriers were out of reach. The weather was perfect. The failure to sound an alarm at the radar sighting in large part resulted from the coincidence of the B-17s enroute. Atmospheric conditions blocked a potentially last-minute warning to the base. Even an hour of grace might have greatly reduced the losses, but from the Japanese standpoint everything that could go right did. From the American side it was a total disaster. Luck would have no role in the next major achievement by the Japanese.

For the United States, the Philippines, which blocked access to the Dutch East Indies, the British South Pacific possessions including Australia, and American outposts at Guam and Wake, were an obvious target for any military moves. The northernmost reaches lie less than 350 miles from mainland Asia. Flight distance from Formosa [Taiwan], the big island wrested away from China by Japan, is perhaps 700 miles to the Philippines' largest city, Manila.

After the U.S. had decisively defeated the Spanish fleet in the Battle of Manila Bay in 1898 and routed the occupying army, Spain ceded the territory to the U.S. By the 1930s, America had lost its appetite for territory so far from the mainland and for rule so inimical to the tradition of freedom. That these colonial holdings no longer seemed profitable also weighed upon the minds of government officials, particularly as the Great Depression blighted the economy. Responding to needs at home and the agitation within the islands, an agreement between the U.S. and local leaders specified that the Commonwealth of the Philippines, established in 1935, would receive complete independence in 1946. Until that time, the U.S. would control only matters of foreign affairs and defense, with participation in these activities by the local government. The citizens elected Manuel Luis Quezon as the first president of the Commonwealth.

Eager as the islands were to escape from American rule, the political powers recognized the threat from Japan. In this, the desires of both the Philippine authorities and the U.S. were the same. Aware of the potential for a conflict with Japan, in 1935, Quezon recruited his old friend Gen.

Douglas MacArthur, then outgoing chief of staff for the U.S. Army. The new military adviser to the Philippines was on familiar turf. His father, Gen. Arthur MacArthur, a Civil War veteran, had participated in the campaign to oust the Spanish and then subdue a rebellion against American rule while Douglas studied at West Point.

Immediately after graduation from the U.S. Military Academy as top man in the class of 1903, Douglas MacArthur worked as an engineer to help map the territory. "The Philippines charmed me. The delightful hospitality, the respect and affection expressed for my father, the amazingly attractive result of a mixture of Spanish culture and American industry, the languorous laze that seemed to glamorize even the most routine chores of life, the fun-loving men, the moonbeam delicacy of its lovely women, fastened me with a grip that has never relaxed." It was not all lush, tropical romance, for on one occasion, MacArthur shot it out with a pair of "desperadoes," killing both with his pistol.

By World War I, MacArthur, who had been recommended for but did not receive a Medal of Honor during the altercation with Mexico's bandit-patriot Pancho Villa, had advanced to the rank of colonel, serving as chief of staff for the U.S. 42d Division, part of the American Expeditionary Force that fought in France. MacArthur continually led his men out of the trenches and his personal bravery plus his adept strategy and tactics as a brigade commander added four more Silver Stars and a pair of Distinguished Service Crosses. A brigadier general by the time of the armistice and commander of the 42d, MacArthur achieved a reputation for personal courage under fire and irregular military dress.

Always dapper, younger than most senior officers, MacArthur developed a rapport with the doughboys of that era. His successes and his style also generated a hearty dis-

dain in some colleagues and superiors. During the late
1920s, MacArthur returned to the Philippines for a three-
year stint and became friendly with the former rebel and
now political leader, Manuel Quezon. Earlier, he did a tour
as superintendent at West Point and finally ascended to the
post of Army chief of staff in 1930. For a time he adroitly
managed to avoid political bear traps during a time of turmoil, ranging from the court-martial of Gen. Billy Mitchell,
the early exponent of air power, to the pressure of disarma-
ment forces, and the ever thinner budgets for the military.

He studied the past and thought of the future. He foresaw maneuver and movement as decisive, recognizing that
planes, tanks, and mechanization meant the end of World
War I–style trench combat with massive, immobile armies
confronting one another. He argued in favor of stockpiling
the strategic materials that would become so critical for
World War II and he reestablished the Order of the Purple
Heart, a medal issued to those wounded or killed due to
enemy action.

But in 1932, he stumbled. Some 25,000 World War I veterans, accompanied often by their families, had encamped
in Washington, D.C., while they sought an appropriation of
a federal payment for their service during the war. They
dubbed themselves the Bonus Expeditionary Force (BEF)
and MacArthur, always hostile to any group that seemed to
lack respect for the forces of law and order, imbued with the
habits of a lifetime in a military environment, scoffed at
what he perceived as a rabble of malcontents: "In the end,"
said MacArthur, "their frustration combined with careful
needling by the Communists, turned them into a sullen, ri-
otous mob."

According to *American Caesar*, William Manchester's biography of MacArthur, he considered 90 percent of the bonus

marchers fakes although a Veterans Administration survey found 94 percent had army or navy service records, with more than two-thirds having served overseas. MacArthur mobilized troops to deal with the squatters. After members of the BEF scuffled with soldiers near the Capitol, the general defied orders from President Herbert Hoover and directed his forces to evict the main body of supplicants from a campground across the Anacostia River. In the ensuing melee, tents, shacks, and makeshift shelters were put to the torch, tear gas and bayonets routed the civilians leaving two babies dead and a child lacerated by a bayonet. (In his book, *Reminiscences*, MacArthur insisted no one was killed.)

President Franklin D. Roosevelt, inaugurated little more than six months later, bent on curing the Depression, and suspicious of MacArthur's ambitions, kept him and his army on a short leash and starved for funds. Tarred by a personal scandal involving a mistress, described as a "Eurasian beauty," buffeted by cliques in the military establishment whose animosity dated back to World War I, and resented by veterans for his treatment of the BEF, MacArthur, after Roosevelt refused to extend his tour as chief of staff for more than a matter of months, expected to retire.

Franklin Roosevelt arranged for Congress to fund a U.S. military mission in the Philippines. Commonwealth president Manuel Quezon found MacArthur delighted to accept the post of military advisor, with $33,000 a year added to his salary as a U.S. major general, a considerable stipend for the 1930s. To serve as MacArthur's chief of staff, the War Department assigned Maj. Dwight David Eisenhower, who had been an aide while the general served as the chief of staff for the U.S. Army. (The experience led Eisenhower to respond later to a question of whether he knew MacArthur, "I studied dramatics under him for four years in Washington and five in the Philippines.")

The general had taken up residence in a six-room penthouse atop the Manila Hotel and immersed himself in building the Philippines into a defensive stronghold, "a Pacific Switzerland." Under the strategy created by his predecessors in the War and Navy Departments, MacArthur was expected to operate in accord with War Plan Orange (WPO), modified slightly over the years and coded as WPO-1, WPO-2, and finally WPO-3. The War Plan Orange scenario envisioned meeting a thrust by the Japanese at the Philippines with a retreat of the defenders into the narrow, jungle-like peninsula of Bataan that lay along the western edge of Manila Bay and was backed up by several fortified islands including the redoubt at Corregidor whose big guns could deny any enemy the use of the Manila anchorage. The resistance would be expected to contain the Japanese until the military might of the U.S., convoyed by the Navy, would cross the Pacific and blast the invaders from the archipelago and any other sites temporarily in their hands.

WPO in any shape hardly fitted MacArthur's vision for waging war. While not openly disavowing WPO, he determined to design an organization that need not retreat to Bataan. Instead of a small, elite military capable of holding off a much larger opposition by dint of carefully prepared, well-stocked positions that employed terrain and vegetation for its own advantage, MacArthur sought to develop enough ground, air, and sea strength to make any strike at the Philippines too costly for the Japanese, even after independence in 1946. He planned an army whose active duty and reserve elements added up to forty Filipino divisions, 400,000 soldiers, trained, equipped, and led by a cadre of officers schooled at a local replica of West Point. His navy would be fifty speedy, torpedo-armed boats that would ply the surrounding waters with such swiftness and stealth that they could disrupt the approach of any large ships. For control of the sky he considered 250 aircraft necessary. To go from blueprints to reality, MacArthur estimated a period of ten years and an expenditure of a quarter-billion dollars by the Commonwealth along with subsidies from the U.S. to meet its responsibilities.

For all of the years he had spent in the Philippines previously and his experiences as chief of staff during the first years of the Great Depression, MacArthur's schemes lacked a sense of reality. The belief that American officers and noncoms along with those Filipino graduates of West Point could transform the conscripts into fully qualified soldiers with five and a half months of training was a fantasy. The men, however willing, were not reared in the kind of industrial society that marked the West. They had neither the experience nor the education to adapt quickly to the demands upon modern troops. When they started to arrive at the training camps in 1937, those charged with transforming the draftees into soldiers discovered their recruits spoke eight distinct languages and eighty-seven different dialects. More than one-fifth, including some designated as first sergeants or company clerks, were illiterate in any tongue. The sharp schisms and deficiencies in language skills and customs seriously hampered instruction and communication.

Equally defeating, the Commonwealth was no more prepared to provide the kinds of appropriations necessary to field the requisite number of men and equipment each year than was the United States with its own armed forces. The original local budget of $25 million annually was almost instantly pared to less than one-third and in the year preceding Pearl Harbor, appropriations came to a measly $1 million.

MacArthur, however, continued to argue that he could and would make the islands impregnable. Both his case and his achievements were hampered by alienation with Washington, D.C. Pacifist elements regarded MacArthur as a warmonger. Few in Congress cared to expend great sums on fortifications or armaments for a place that would soon be free of U.S. control. MacArthur's influence in the States waned further as he was forced to retire from active duty as an American officer when he refused to relinquish his appointment as the Philippine commander with the rank of field marshal.

MacArthur's inability to procure military hardware and money for the defenses of the Commonwealth stirred doubts in Quezon. The Japanese conquests in China persuaded Quezon that a declaration of neutrality might be the one way to avoid turning his country into a battleground. He even contemplated dismissal of MacArthur and shocked his field marshal with a public statement, "It's good to hear men say that the Philippines can repel an invasion, but it's not true and the people should know it isn't." Newspapers in the islands published the conflicting views of the president and his military advisor, causing considerable anxiety among the reading public. Again, MacArthur's memoirs do not indicate any difference of opinion with Quezon.

The bombs and bullets that shattered the peace of Europe in September 1939 emphatically announced that neither negotiations nor appeasement could prevent war. The blitzkrieg juggernaut of Nazi Germany that rolled over Poland, Denmark, Norway, Holland, Belgium, and finally France, the bare escape of British troops from Dunkirk, and the siege of London by Adolf Hitler's *Luftwaffe* cast doubt over the ability of Great Britain to defend its Far East empire.

After the Japanese seized the opportunity to take over French Indochina and pressured Dutch and French colonies to accept Tokyo's concept of a "Greater East Asia Co-Prosperity Sphere," there was little doubt who would be the senior partner and the chief beneficiary. No slouch at exploiting an opportunity either, MacArthur wrote to the current Army chief of staff, Gen. George C. Marshall, and noted that since the Philippine Army soon would be absorbed into that of the U.S.—a leap of the general's imagination, since the War Department had not yet come to that decision—he expected to shut down his office as military advisor. He suggested to Marshall the establishment of a Far East command covering all U.S. Army activities and nominated himself to be in charge.

After dithering over the idea for several months, worsening conditions convinced the policy makers to eventually adopt MacArthur's idea. Along with extra appropriations designed to strengthen the indigenous forces, a cable from Marshall on 27 July 1941 announced creation of the United States Army Forces in the Far East (USAFFE) and, recalling him to active duty, designated MacArthur as the commanding general. In his memoirs, MacArthur remarked, "I was given the rank of lieutenant general, although my retired rank was that of a full general."

MacArthur now had the role he coveted and a platform from which to importune ears no longer deaf to the sounds of Japan's marching feet. But America was close to 10,000 miles away, its defense factories slowly gearing up and their prime customers already in a shooting war with the Axis Powers of Germany and Italy; Great Britain and the Soviet Union also demanded the tools to fight.

Short on money, equipment, and trained fighting men in 1941, MacArthur's USAFFE, however, boasted some war assets, and with the conviction of President Roosevelt that confrontation with Japan appeared inevitable, there was the promise of a substantial enhancement of resources. On hand, the general could count upon a cadre of 297 graduates of West Point. The most senior were MacArthur and a former football all-America, coast artilleryman Col. Paul Bunker, representing the Class of '03. The most junior included several from the Class of '41, infantry lieutenants, like Alexander "Sandy" Nininger and Hector Polla, who arrived only ten days before the attack on Pearl Harbor. Mixed in were officers from almost every class in between—former cavalryman Gen. Jonathan Wainwright '06, infantry specialist Gen. Clifford Bluemel '09, engineer Col. Hugh J. Casey '18, the military law expert Albert Svihra '22, Italian-born infantry leader Floyd Forte '34, and bomber pilot Colin P. Kelly '37. The practice of admitting a few men from the islands to the U.S. institution included nineteen well-schooled Filipino officers like Vincente Lim '14 and Fidel V. Segundo '17, both of whom commanded Philippine Army divisions.

In the delicate minuet to prevent treading on the sensitive toes of the host people, forty-five of the American West Pointers along with a number of non-Academy, regular army officers and noncoms were attached to the existing, largely on paper in some instances, twelve Philippine Army divisions. Although they technically served as advisors to the Filipino officers, in practice, the latter almost always deferred to the Americans.

To achieve his goals, MacArthur, on 1 September 1941, began to mobilize the Philippine Army. Elements of the ten reserve divisions, who theoretically had already undergone some training, were to be called up gradually until the total of 75,000 would be on active duty by 15 December. MacArthur, who received his fourth star as a full general shortly after he assumed his new post, simultaneously hectored Washington to satisfy his dire needs and voiced optimism for the future. In October 1941, MacArthur became privy to a plan known as Rainbow Five, the overall Allied strategy for war with Japan and with the other Axis powers—the British, the Dutch in their colonies, and the Free French were already at war with Germany and Italy—which conceded the loss of the U.S. possessions of Wake, Guam, and the Philippines. The scenario assumed that in a two-ocean, worldwide conflict the Philippines could not be held. In that respect, Rainbow went beyond Orange.

MacArthur, while not opposing Rainbow Five, had argued that it was a mistake to write off the Philippines. Instead, he persuaded Marshall and Adm. Thomas Hart, commander of the Asiatic Fleet, that he could stop the Japanese at the water's edge. He believed the enemy would not make his move before April 1942 and by then MacArthur insisted he would field more than 100,000 well-trained and equipped troops backed up by a strong Air Corps while Hart's fleet would deal with the Japanese Navy.

The decision to scrap first the defensive bastion philosophy of WPO and then revise Rainbow Five to include preservation of the Philippine Islands dictated significant changes in operations by the Philippine military commander. Guarding the potential landing sites among the roughly 250 miles of Luzon beaches demanded a considerably larger army than would have been required to retain only Bataan and the fortified positions at the mouth of Manila Bay. MacArthur thus opted not to augment the highly professional Philippine Scouts with a limited number of well-equipped soldiers and pursued quantity rather than quality. The choice of arena also meant a major shift in logistics, deployment of food, ammunition, fuel, and other supplies where these items could be retrieved by the defenders of Luzon's approaches rather than on Bataan. MacArthur's choice of strategy and its fulfillment would have a critical effect on the struggle to defend the Philippines.

As the portents of war gathered in ever-darker clouds, the highest American civilian official on the scene was Francis Sayre, the U.S. high commissioner. In his State Department capacity, after being warned of the crisis with Japan, he met with Hart and MacArthur on 27 November. Both Sayre and Hart feared an imminent thrust by the Japanese. However, recalled Sayre, "Back and forth paced General MacArthur, smoking a black cigar and assuring Admiral Hart and myself in reassuring terms that the existing alignment and movement of Japanese troops convinced him that there would be no Japanese attack before spring."

Although the public perception, aided and abetted by the strength of his personality and oratory, regarded MacArthur as the man in charge of the Far East, in reality he commanded only the U.S. Army. His opposite number for the Navy, RAdm. Thomas Hart, three years older and an 1897 graduate of the Naval Academy, was stiff-necked, peevish, the epitome of the martinet. He zealously guarded his prerogatives and it was inevitable that frost would govern relations between the two military leaders.

Like MacArthur, Hart had received little in the way of reinforcements as 1941 ebbed. The major additions amounted to a dozen submarines and six PT boats as well as the understrength 4th Marine Regiment transferred from duty in China. The U.S. Asiatic Fleet consisted of Hart's flagship, the heavy cruiser *Houston*; a single light cruiser; thirteen World War I, four-stack destroyers; the subs; and the PT boats plus a handful of miscellaneous craft including tenders, gunboats, minesweepers, and tankers. Conspicuous by their absence were any battleships or aircraft carriers. Two dozen PBYs, the slow-moving amphibious patrol planes, made up the fleet air arm.

As a young destroyer officer, William Mack said that when he came to the Asiatic Fleet in 1939, there was an underlying feeling of trouble ahead. "It was totally a peacetime system. But I think we all knew, in our hearts, that war was just around the corner—the corner being one or two years. About six months later, the ship was given sonar which meant the ships in the Asiatic Fleet were considered the front line. We suddenly realized that they were being serious back in the States—they were giving us something we were going to have to have. Before that time, we had depth charges in the destroyers and that was it. The doctrine for finding a submarine [before sonar] was simply to sight its periscope, take a bearing on it, estimate the range, and run down toward him to drop some depth charges."

The installation of sonar aboard the destroyers was a tangible sign of the approach of war. In November 1940, said Mack, all dependents began to be evacuated. "The fleet tempo changed considerably. We no longer went to China— we stayed around the Philippines. For the last year before the war started we were roughly on a war footing; we still had awnings [for shade against midday sun] and movie machines but we were expecting something to happen." At the same time Mack continued to wear his formal whites and carry a sword when going ashore until just about a month before the start of the war.

Army nurse Madeline Ullom, who reached the archipelago almost a year before war broke out, noticed in May 1941 a change in ambience as "social activities greatly decreased. Curfews were routine. Alerts were frequent. Field exercises were longer and more intensive. The Army-Navy

Game, the event of the year, when reservations at the club were made months in advance, was all but canceled." Still, she remembered, "An American flag moved gently in the breeze above the central entrance to Sternberg [Hospital]. A feeling of security filled the atmosphere. The military corpsmen and Filipino aides were skilled and efficient. A high quality of duty performance was required and obtained. Supervision was meager. Professional dedication at all times was paramount. Inspection days brought no apprehension."

Major Philip Fry, who already had one tour in the Philippines on his record, had returned to the islands in November. Almost immediately upon his arrival, he had noticed a project at the Fort McKinley officers' club. "I started over there with Ted Lilly [an officer acquaintance from a previous tour]. Just outside of the front of the club I saw the entrance to an immense dugout, the shaft down was within twenty feet of the steps of the club. It led down from fifty or more feet. This dugout was beneath the area of the officers' club, the tennis courts, and the commanding general's quarters. It had a series of corridors and compartments and was designed as a divisional command post but it was never completed." The swift passage of events would prevent further work or use.

Another recent immigrant, Sam Grashio, wore the gold bars of a second lieutenant and the wings of silver as a P-40 pilot assigned to the 21st Pursuit Squadron. Two years at Gonzaga University had provided Grashio with enough academic credits to enlist in the Washington Air National Guard and then undergo training in the Air Corps. "I thought of flying only in the narrow sense; taking to the air in the best World War I movie tradition, embellished with goggles and helmet, scarf waving in the breeze. I thought little about *why* I was training and flying so much. Of course I knew that war had been going on in Europe ever since September 1939, but in flying school I thought of it mostly when a fellow cadet of Greek lineage would needle me about what his countrymen were doing to the Italian troops Benito Mussolini had so injudiciously sent to invade Greece.

"My mistaken perception of the world deepened soon after the 21st Pursuit Squadron sailed from San Francisco on 1 November 1941. Our ship was the *President Coolidge*, a former luxury liner then being used as a troop transport. Life was lovely; there were no duties, the food was magnificent, and we did not even know where we were going." Not until the vessel reached Hawaii did Grashio and his colleagues figure out they were bound for Manila.

"Nothing happened that might have suggested, even remotely, that a real war was not far off," said Grashio. "On board the *Coolidge*, there were a number of senior officers who had just graduated from the National War College. Having little to do, I listened to them extensively. To a man they were convinced that there would be no war with Japan because the Japanese would not be so stupid as to start a war they would be certain to lose within a few weeks."

A cold dose of reality should have struck Grashio on 6 December when he heard a speech from Col. Harold George, a senior airman. George warned that war was imminent, that the Japanese had 3,000 planes in Formosa only 600 miles away, and already they had been seen doing aerial reconnaissance over the Philippines. George concluded with remarks indicating he believed Grashio and his fellow fliers were members of a "suicide squadron." Grashio, unconvinced, offered to bet the squadron commander Lt. Ed Dyess five pesos there would be no war with Japan. "Ed took the bet at once and laid another five it would begin within a week."

On that timetable, the members of the 21st had painfully little time to prepare. Their machines were as fresh as the pilots; only eighteen of the twenty-four allotted had been removed from their shipping crates and assembled by 8 December. Four had never even been flown and the others had not yet been adjusted for maximum performance.

At the Navy Department in Washington the experts doubted MacArthur's forces could hold off an onslaught on the beaches and not be forced to retreat along the lines of War Plan Orange. Although Hart wanted to fight it out with the Imperial Navy in Philippine waters, he was instructed to safeguard his vessels by deploying them southward. Furthermore, since his fleet was considered to be part of the overall Rainbow strategy, he had to be prepared to sail to the Dutch East Indies and join with the Allied ships there.

As a young naval officer, Robert Lee Dennison received an assignment from Hart to be a contact with the commander of the USAFFE. "MacArthur had a very elementary understanding of the use of a navy. He, like a good many Army officers of his time, looked on a navy as a seaward extension of the army's flank and that's all. There was no personal contact between Hart's staff, MacArthur's staff, or MacArthur or Hart. MacArthur didn't know what we were up to in terms of ship movements or what our war plans were, nor did we know what his plans were. That was the purpose of my being in this particular capacity."

Those expected to implement MacArthur's strategy on the ground discovered some painful weaknesses. Glen Townsend, as a U.S. Army colonel, assumed command of the 11th Regiment, a component of the Philippine Army's 11th Infantry Division, in September 1941. "I found that the regiment was composed of Ilocanos and Igorots in about equal numbers. I found that they spoke eleven different dialects and that Christian and Pagan had little liking for each other. All of the enlisted personnel had taken the prescribed five-and-one-half-months' training. They were proficient only in close-order drill and saluting. The officers, being mainly political appointees, had less training than the men they were supposed to lead." To "advise" the regiment, the American aides to Townsend added up to ten other officers and seven enlisted men.

The paucity of personal gear possessed by his men and the unit's equipment appalled Townsend. His Filipino soldiers had no blankets, raincoats, mosquito bars, entrenching tools, or steel helmets. They wore rubber-soled shoes and pith helmets. The standard uniform was one pair of khaki shorts and one shirt. They also owned one set of blue-denim fatigues. The antitank company supposed to field 37mm guns had none. The entire regiment depended upon four trucks and eight field telephones. There were 81mm mortars, but no ammunition other than that designed for target practice would be available until three months after the Japanese invaded.

For the basic infantryman's weapon, the U.S. Army had sold the Commonwealth its surplus Lee-Enfield rifles. Unfortunately, the stock of these pieces was too long for the short-statured Filipinos and could not be aimed with the butt in the crotch of the shoulder where the recoil could be comfortably absorbed. Instead, soldiers were forced to brace their Lee-Enfields against their upper arms ahead of the shoulder and incurred nasty bruises while lowering their ability to effectively fire the rifles. On the plus side, Townsend says the would-be soldiers struck him as physically fit, eager to learn, and presented no disciplinary problems.

It seems obvious that MacArthur miscalculated what it

would take to create an effective local army. Clifford Bluemel, who as a young lieutenant in 1914 had served a tour in the islands, was among those who had returned to the Philippines as the war clouds darkened. "I got there in June 1940 to command the 45th Infantry, Philippine Scouts. It was a good regiment, about sixty men to a company. [In August 1941] I was told that three colonels, Brougher, Jones, and Bluemel, would run a school for the training of ten Philippine Army divisions' staff officers. They were all Filipinos, some of them graduates of West Point.

"I ran the school from 8:00 in the morning until 11:30 and from 1:00 to 4:30 in the afternoon. Then we all went out and walked for fifty minutes—everybody. I also ran the school from 7:00 to 9:00 at night. They thought that was terrible, and that I was a rough S.O.B. But I had only six weeks to train them. I even ran it all day Saturday sometimes, and they didn't like that. Sunday they had off. When I threatened to run it on Sunday, I almost had a riot one time."

Around the first of November, MacArthur and his chief of staff Sutherland visited Bluemel at his school. "We had drinks and talked about different things. MacArthur talked about the Tojo Cabinet which had been formed in Japan. He said, 'The Tojo Cabinet is not the war cabinet. The Tojo Cabinet will fall, and there will be another cabinet which will be the war cabinet.' "

MacArthur's conviction that the political process in Japan had not yet reached the war-kindling point indicates his confidence that he still had time to prepare. Bluemel had no intelligence that could contradict his chief but other remarks by MacArthur took him aback. "Before I went to the Philippines, an officer who had been the military attaché in Germany gave a talk on the handling of the three-regiment divisions by the German Army. It was to me an ideal system.

We had that four-regiment division, and it took six hours [for an order] to get the division moving. The former attaché said a German general could get a three-regiment division moving in no time with an oral order. He just gave an infantry colonel his mission and boundaries, attached a battalion of light artillery to him, and so on.

"I asked MacArthur what he thought about it. He talked for half an hour. The man, I think, had never read and found that the Germans had a three-regiment division. It began to shake my confidence in him a little. I thought, 'That man doesn't even know anything about handling a three-regiment division. Yet the Philippine Army has three-regiment divisions.' "

With the school course completed by mid-November, Bluemel was assigned to command the 31st Division of the Philippine Army, organized and mobilized in Zambales Province. Recalled Bluemel, "I went to see this great Philippine Army that MacArthur had trained. The enlisted men of my command were all Filipinos. Most of them spoke Tagalog and some English. Several spoke other dialects. They [the 31st Division] were supposed to have had five months' training prior to induction in the service. The basic training given them during that five-month period was poor. Most of them had fired five rounds or less with the World War I Enfield. Very few fired the .30- or .50-caliber machine gun. Apparently the artillerymen had never fired the 75mm gun and in some cases had never seen one fired.

"There was a Colonel Irwin, who had the 31st Infantry Regiment [part of the 31st Division]. Irwin had been a major in the 45th, and I had utmost respect for him. He was a fine officer—a man who would do things. He had the regiment organized." To Bluemel's shock, Irwin informed him the regiment had never been on the target range. Bluemel instructed Irwin, "The principal thing the infantry must know is how to shoot and how to march. That's basic infantry training, because they've got to be able to march and when they get to their destination, they've got to be able to get fire superiority quickly and beat the enemy." He arranged for the troops to use the target range at the Olongapo Naval Base at Subic Bay. One battalion from the 31st Infantry Regiment managed to expend some fifty rounds per man and a second battalion fired half that amount. The arrival of the 4th Marine Regiment from China at Olongapo closed the range to the army and a third battalion from the 31st never got to squeeze off a single bullet. The troops would not have a further opportunity to use their weapons before they met the enemy in actual combat.

According to Bluemel, toward the end of November, "The Army-Navy Game was to be played. I got a table reserved at the Army-Navy Club. Some people were going to sit there with me, and we were going to have some drinks and listen to the game." (Ordinarily the broadcast of the football game was an excuse for a gala, with the two services enthusiastically partying. However, in deference to the Far East crisis, the celebration had been canceled.)

Still Bluemel figured he could at least quietly enjoy the game at the club and he dropped by MacArthur's headquarters to obtain a pass for the day. To his astonishment, the G-3 plans and operations officer told him no passes were to be granted for the weekend. And he was advised to see Sutherland and ask to see a secret report. "I went in and told him the G-3 sent me and that there's a document I should see. It went something like this: 'The conference with the Nomura delegation [special envoys from Japan to Washington] has been terminated and will not be renewed.' I said, 'My God! That's war! When the Japanese are ready to attack, they don't declare war; they attack, and then declare war.' " As commander of the 31st Division, Bluemel quickly reported to Jonathan Wainwright, in charge of the northern Luzon defenses. Wainwright knew of the radiogram about the breakdown in negotiations. In fact, he had been looking for Bluemel and now directed him to start organizing beach defenses.

The strongest defensive unit was the Philippine Division. It included the U.S.-manned 31st Infantry Regiment that with only 1,800 GIs added up to little more than half of the normal contingent. However, the remainder of the outfit came from the Philippine Scouts, the one local fighting force that from an effectiveness standpoint matched the best from the States. Although the Philippine Army was almost literally a paper tiger, the Scouts, formed into the 45th and 57th Infantry Regiments, were men who had opted for a lifetime military career. The inception of the Scouts dated back to 1901 when the U.S. Congress authorized recruitment of a force of Filipinos for service in the American Army, and whose appropriations would come directly from its military parent rather than from monies designated for the territory. Equipped and armed on a par with the 31st Infantry Regiment, the Scouts brought pride and élan to their job. While certain tribal customs such as a fealty to kinsmen and elders occasionally annoyed their American compatriots, the Scouts also displayed a sense of discipline that earned admiration even from U.S. officers who ordinarily considered Filipinos inferior. Most of the officers in the Philippines, as the war approached, continued to be drawn from the U.S. Army, West Pointers, regulars, and reservists called to the colors. Some Filipino graduates of West Point also occupied command positions. Many of the Scouts achieved the status of noncommissioned officers.

As an elite organization, the Scouts could be selective about admission, and in the quality of personnel the outfit matched the soldiers from the States. The Scouts also equalled the GIs in equipment; the infantrymen carried the latest weapon, the M1 Garand rifle. Some of the Scouts at first disdained the M1 that featured faster firepower rather than the accuracy of the Springfield with which a soldier carefully squeezed off each shot.

Although MacArthur bombarded Washington with requisitions for the new Garand M1 rifles, the other troops labored with either Springfield '03s or the highly unreliable Lee-Enfield. Neither weapon could unleash the number of bullets in a given time as an M1. Ancient machine guns, dud mortar shells, a lack of adequate or big enough artillery, a shortage of vehicles—whatever a modern army needed the USAFFE could only order and hope it would arrive in time. Indeed, early in December MacArthur received word of a covey of cargo and troop ships steaming toward the Philippines under the guidance of the cruiser *Pensacola*. The holds and decks of the vessels carried the mortar and artillery shells so desperately needed and bore the crated aircraft of the 27th Light Bombardment Group whose pilots had already resided in the islands.

The defenders had already welcomed the American-crewed 192d and 194th Tank Battalions, with 108 light tanks as well as some additional coast artillery. In his original prescription for a successful defense of his turf, MacArthur spoke of a fleet of fifty or sixty torpedo boats. Attached to the Asiatic Fleet at the time of Pearl Harbor were only the six seventy-seven-foot craft of Motor Torpedo Boat Squadron 3. Lieutenant John Bulkeley and his fellow torpedo boat crewmen spent their time investigating the waters around the archipelago and prudently located caches of fuel and supplies for future emergencies. "I was damned if I knew what I would be expected to do in the Philippines. I figured my missions would be determined by the theater commander."

The addition of the six torpedo boats hardly added up to the seagoing power that MacArthur envisioned as necessary. The third leg of his planned buildup, however, more closely approached his blueprint. With 8,100 Air Corps personnel—flight crews, mechanics, and other ground-service experts—stationed in the Philippines by 7 December 1941, these troops constituted the single largest complement of Americans. What is remarkable about the Army Air Corps presence in December 1941 is how much had been accomplished in a short period. The first true effort to build an island-based air wing began in May 1941, a bare six months before the first bombs dropped. The War Department dispatched a conservative, old-school officer plagued by poor health, Gen. Henry Clagett, to survey the needs. Fortunately, Clagett's chief of staff, a dedicated aviator who flew during World War I, Col. Harold George, compensated for his superior's lack of imagination with vision and energy. His success or failure, however, rested upon forces beyond the scope of either his wisdom or his industry.

The tasks ahead seemed insurmountable. The men from Washington learned that only four airfields with military capacity existed on Luzon, whose major city of Manila lay just 700 miles from bomber bases on Formosa. Furthermore, only Clark Field could be considered a first-class base. Both Nielson Field, the fighter strip near Manila, and Iba, the base along the western coast, lacked facilities for service of planes. Ground access to Nichols, the principal field for fighter planes, six miles south of Manila, depended upon a single narrow road that crossed a river bridge. One well-placed bomb could isolate Nichols from any entry or exit. Furthermore, although it had hard-surfaced runways, improper drainage rendered one section useless during the rainy season.

Under prodding from George, a handful of aviation engineers had started the slow process of carving out additional strips throughout the islands, but the pace was so slow none were ever completely finished before the enemy struck. With George sounding the Klaxon, and with the backing of MacArthur, authorities hoped that genuine airpower might be enough to halt a Japanese advance at least long enough for a Philippine rescue operation. The best and latest that America could provide began to arrive in the islands. Some of the first pilots shipped to the Philippines in 1940 had been taken aback to discover that in combat they were expected to fly the same outmoded P-26 in which they had trained. But as the sense of urgency heightened, first came P-35s, and then the latest, the P-40 Warhawk.

To bolster the thin ranks of the Air Corps, the 34th Pursuit Squadron, equipped with P-40s, was hastily dispatched overseas. It reached Manila on 20 November 1941, poorly prepared for action. A quartermaster refused to include barrels of antifreeze on the grounds it was not needed in the tropics. The 34th's water-cooled P-40s thus landed in the Philippines lacking a basic fluid for proper operation. The outfit's chief clerk, Sgt. Thomas Gage Jr., a 1940 enlistee from Tulsa, was among those aboard the SS *Coolidge* when it docked after the twenty-day voyage from Hawaii. "When we arrived at Nichols and after we got our P-40s put together," says Gage, "we were ordered to exchange our P-40s for the worn-out P-35s the 24th Group had been flying. The P-35s' engines were completely worn out when we got them. They had [ten months earlier] been on a ship bound for some Swedish colony and when the ship was in Manila they had been commandeered. The instruments were in Swedish." The details of diversion of these Seversky-manufactured aircraft from their original destination to the U.S. Air Corps differ slightly in official accounts but the condition of the planes was as Gage described.

Construction at the Del Carmen airfield had hardly started before the 34th moved in. They were supposed to be only the first of several units to be stationed at what was expected to be a field capable of handling B-17s. Even as the 34th moved in, ordnance people scattered 500- and 1,000-pound bombs in the brush for eventual use by the oversize tenants. There was no running water, no latrine, and only a small river available for the basic amenities. The nearest town lay three miles off but the biggest problem was the strip itself. Dust as much as six inches deep layered the bared ground. Airfield engineers had used molasses to cover the surface as they graded the runways, hoping that would produce a grass resistant to the production of dust, but to little avail. Sometimes, after one pilot took off, the next man in line could see nothing for three to five minutes. The grit fouled the tired engines of the P-35s beyond the aid of primitive maintenance.

"We were issued," says Gage, "twelve Springfield rifles and six drum Lewis machine guns for aerodrome defense. The Lewis guns had no sights and the drums were loaded with no tracers. We dug six pits, six feet deep, and about four in diameter. In the center was placed a steel pole on which a Lewis was mounted. Each pit had a drum, reserve drums were in a central supply, and a runner was to fetch when needed." Antiaircraft defenses at Del Carmen obviously were pitiful.

By the first week of December 1941, the 24th Pursuit

Group listed seventy-two P-40s and eighteen P-35s available for combat. However, some planes had just been assembled and delivered, their machinery untested and requiring tuneups. Additional P-40s were still in crates, awaiting assembly. None of the pursuit ships were outfitted with adequate oxygen equipment. The fliers could not handle enemy aircraft at the higher altitudes. The slower P-35s, lightly armored, with worn-out engines and .30-caliber machine guns, were hardly suitable for 1941 aerial warfare.

Fighter aircraft had never been the first priority of George and MacArthur. Both of them considered the prime requisite for a defense lay in the bomber and particularly the newest version, the B-17 Flying Fortress. An impressive start in dispatch of the four-engine bombers had landed a total of thirty-five in the Philippines—almost triple the number stationed in Hawaii. Backing up the Fortresses, the Philippine command could call on some aging and obsolescent B-18s and B-10s, useful at best for reconnaissance and ferrying supplies. Aware of the danger of keeping all thirty-five Fortresses in one target basket and expecting reinforcements, the Air Force had begun to construct a field on a former pineapple plantation on Mindanao, well out of range of the Formosa threat. On the eve of the Japanese attack, sixteen of the B-17s had been flown to Del Monte Field, Mindanao. The remainder were to follow and make that their base until suitably protected places could be created on Luzon.

The presence of the B-17s appeared to provide a devastating potential against any invasion fleet. But even these bombers, among the earlier models of the Fort, lacked essential features that later became standard equipment. The first B-17s entered battle without the power turrets, heavy armor, and tail guns that would carry the fight deep into Germany and blast Pacific sites late in the war. On paper, the Philippine Air Force bolstered the Americans. But its sixty aircraft was made up of forty-two P-13s, primarily trainers. The planes listed for combat were a dozen P-26s, biplanes successful in knocking King Kong off the Empire State Building but long abandoned as useful for war by the U.S., and three B-10s, equally obsolescent.

Perhaps the worst aspect of the defenses of airfields and other installations was the absence of a functioning early-warning system. The latest radar systems, ones that could detect both heading and altitude of aircraft, key to the summer of 1940 Royal Air Force success against the might of German bombers in the Battle of Britain, were almost totally absent from the islands. To supplement the inadequate electronic systems, inexperienced watchers, still being schooled in aircraft recognition, equipped with binoculars, were expected to spot incoming traffic—through clouds or at extreme altitudes—and then relay the information over an antiquated telephone network. The system as developed in China earlier worked reasonably well, but there the attackers traveled long distances over land where they would be observed while still far from their targets. Against the Philippines, the raiders flew over the water from Formosa or launched from aircraft carriers, invisible to observers on land. The destruction of the U.S. air arm would render the Americans unable to fly effective reconnaissance over the seagoing approaches. Because the shortages of weaponry included proper antiaircraft batteries, the defenders could not mount any opposition to the aerial thrusts.

The pace of preparedness had picked up dramatically in the last month or two before December. But the military might on hand was a long way from the ability to stop a better-organized and better-armed Japan. Whether the forces under MacArthur and Hart would have been ready by April, the general's date for an attack, is conjecture. The Japanese, well supplied with intelligence from countrymen living in the Philippines and aided by dissident Filipinos hostile to the existing government and the American presence, were aware of the effort to prevent any capture of the islands. The move to war reflected the desire of the expansionist elements not to gamble on MacArthur's chances of achieving his goal by springtime.

MacArthur, like others in his command, would express astonishment over the attack on Pearl Harbor, believing the Philippines would always be the first objective. But the Japanese may well have been aware of War Plan Orange, predicated upon the ability of the U.S. Navy to bring relief to the Americans and Philippines holding out on Bataan. The war that began at Pearl Harbor now menaced the Philippines, the closest U.S. stronghold to Japan and an obvious prize if Imperial Japan expected to seize control of the Western Pacific and Southeast Asia.

4

Still Asleep

ON SUNDAY NIGHT, 7 DECEMBER, IN THE PHILIPPINE ISLANDS—
because of the international date line, it was Saturday, 6
December, in Hawaii and Washington, D.C., 5,000 miles
away—the 27th Bombardment Group tossed a bash at the
Manila Hotel in honor of their Army Air Force commander,
Gen. Lewis Brereton. Amid a raunchy affair that featured
the "best entertainment this side of Minsky's" (a reference
to a chain of burlesque houses in the States), General Brereton chatted with RAdm. William R. Purnell, chief of staff
for the top Navy officer in the Far East. Others in the group
were Adm. Thomas C. Hart and Brig. Gen. Richard K.
Sutherland, chief of staff for the supreme commander of
all the American and Philippine military, Gen. Douglas
MacArthur. Admiral Purnell remarked that it was only a
question of days or perhaps hours until the shooting started.
Sutherland agreed, adding that the War and Navy Departments in Washington expected hostilities might erupt at any
moment. Brereton immediately instructed his chief of staff

to place all air units on "combat alert," as of Monday morning, 8 December. The party at the Manila Hotel wound down sometime after midnight. The airmen straggled back to their quarters in the darkest hours of the morning.

Ten minutes after the first explosives rained down upon the hapless Pearl Harbor anchorage, at 2:30 A.M. his time, a startled radio operator at Asiatic Fleet headquarters in Manila intercepted a stunning, unencrypted Morse code message, issued under the aegis of Adm. Husband E. Kimmel, the Honolulu-based Pacific Fleet commander: "Air Raid on Pearl Harbor. This is no drill." Almost simultaneously, a typhoon of torpedoes, bombs, bullets, and shells struck other Japanese targets in Malaya, Thailand, Singapore, and Shanghai.

Because he knew the unique technical style of the Hawaii sender, the Manila radioman realized the communiqué was genuine and alerted his duty officer, Lt. Col. William T. Clement, a Marine, who in turn contacted Admiral Hart. As a youthful naval officer then, Charles Adair remembered, "He [Clement] then called the various staff officers. I was in the apartment house where I was living when I got a call about 3:15, maybe a little earlier. All he said was, 'Charlie, come on down to the office.' I didn't even ask him what had happened because I knew what had happened. I was sure of it. I didn't keep him on the phone. I got dressed as quickly as I could and walked rapidly or ran part of the way through the park and over to where the headquarters was located [in the Marsman Building, at Pier 7 in Manila]. Once I got into the office, the communicators handed me a tape about six feet long or so, and I started pulling it through my fingers. 'This ship sunk. That ship sunk, et cetera,' with the details of some of the things that had gone on."

Commander S. S. Murray, the recently arrived boss of a submarine division operating out of Manila, after a familiarization cruise in the local waters celebrated with a round of golf on Saturday. He retired for the night on a submarine tender. "A few minutes before 2:00 A.M., I was awakened by Cmdr. James Fife, chief staff officer, commander of submarines, Asiatic, saying that Pearl Harbor had been attacked. After Fife awakened me and we had talked to the squadron commander, in the meantime sending for all the submarine skippers, and the message being sent for all submarines to alert them and to tell them to make immediate preparations to be sent on patrol, we started getting them ready."

As a junior officer on the sub *Seadragon*, Norvell Ward shared an apartment with three colleagues in Manila, and missed any official alarm. "We were having breakfast at the Army-Navy Club in Manila, picked up the *Manila Herald*— JAPANESE ATTACK PEARL HARBOR! We caught the ferry over [to the Cavite Naval Yard] and there we were at war."

Destroyer skipper Edward Parker, after a voyage to the Philippines to collect mail flown in from the States, rejoined his division at Tarakan, a port in Borneo. "Early Monday morning, about 3:15, the voice over the tube said, 'Captain, important message coming in from the *Marblehead* [flagship for the destroyer division].' I put on my bathrobe and ran up. 'The Japanese had attacked Pearl Harbor, or something like that. Govern yourself accordingly.' [I thought] What the hell does 'govern yourself accordingly' mean?"

Not until perhaps an hour after the first report received at Manila Navy headquarters did General Sutherland learn of the blow at Pearl Harbor, and then only from a commercial newscast. An enlisted army signalman happened to have tuned in to a California radio station. He immediately reported to his duty officer and the word passed up to Sutherland who telephoned the MacArthur penthouse atop the Manila Hotel.

"Pearl Harbor!" the astounded MacArthur supposedly exclaimed. "It should be our strongest point." Within ten minutes, at 3:40 A.M., a call from Washington, D.C., to MacArthur confirmed the news bulletin. According to MacArthur, he asked his wife Jean to fetch his Bible and he read before rushing off to confer with his staff. (Richard Sutherland once claimed, "His dispatches were replete with references to the deity but he has no more religion than a goat.")

Ten years later, Hart explained the failure to inform the Army of Kimmel's urgent message. He insisted Clement had tried to get through to someone at headquarters for the U.S. Army Forces, Far East, but could not get a response. He allegedly passed the word to a staff officer at his home. While the news slowly percolated into other military services, it reached naval circles much faster. Lieutenant John D. Bulkeley, head of Motor Torpedo Boat Squadron 3, said, "The night of 8 December we were all asleep in the officers' quarters at Cavite when my telephone rang about three in the morning and I first learned the Japs had struck at Pearl Harbor. I was told, 'We are at war' and that Rear Admiral [Francis] Rockwell wanted to see me immediately."

Mary Rose Harrington, a Navy nurse at the hospital compound beside the Cavite navy base remembered, "I was on night duty. It was a beautiful moonlit night and after I'd made rounds of the sick officers' building I thought I'd walk outdoors. But the assistant master of arms came dashing in to say that Honolulu had been bombed. Then I saw a captain and the war plan officer, talking loudly, and we started to wake people up in the middle of the night."

Nor did the Navy advise the Air Force's Brereton of the war's opening salvo. At the main Philippine airbase, Clark

Field, sixty miles north of Manila, someone heard a radio news flash about the Japanese bombardment of Pearl Harbor. In the absence of verification from any official sources, however, during a period in which rumor rampaged through military circles, the only action taken was to notify the base commander.

Sam Grashio, P-40 pilot stationed at Nichols Field, recalled, "About 2:30 A.M. on 8 December, Lt. L. A. Coleman, the officer of the day, banged on the door of the officers' living quarters and yelled to us to report at once to the operations tent. We dressed in a rush, jumped into a waiting vehicle, and sped away. [Lieutenant Ed] Dyess announced enigmatically that there was an emergency, but ten minutes later he told us to go back to our quarters. It seemed to me I had just fallen asleep when Coleman began banging on doors again. This time he shouted at us to get dressed, that Pearl Harbor had been attacked! It was about 4:45 A.M. We dashed back to Nichols. Dyess confirmed that Pearl Harbor had indeed been bombed by the Japanese. He ordered us into our new P-40E pursuit planes and directed us to start our engines and stand by on the radio."

Other U.S. airfields also sounded alerts and then a series of official and unofficial statements brought word of the attack upon the installations in Hawaii. Meanwhile, MacArthur's staff contacted Brereton and told him what they knew—which was limited. There had been no official declaration of war by the Japanese and the information on what had happened at Honolulu remained sketchy. At 5:00 A.M. the Air Force chief checked in at headquarters.

For most of the military personnel in the Philippines the news reached them haphazardly. Some units received word fairly quickly to mobilize and report to their assignments before dawn. Others became aware almost by pure happenstance. West Pointer Harold K. Johnson, a captain serving as operations officer for the 57th Infantry, a Philippine Scouts regiment, said, "We had heard rumors all over Manila on Sunday, 7 December, that an attack had been made on Hawaii but the rumors were not given very much credence because it appeared to be such an illogical action to those of us in the Philippines. We figured we were the prime target and we had mixed viewpoints.

"There was an element of complacency . . . because we listened to and believed the Navy and the boasts that they would drive the Japanese fleet from the sea within a matter of a week or ten days. At the same time we knew we were a long way from the West Coast [of the U.S.] and if the Navy didn't drive the Japanese fleet from the sea, why, we were in trouble.

"It was Monday morning on the 8th before our regiment finally got the word. I was having breakfast in my robe about 6:30 when I got a call from a friend of mine. He said Colonel Clarke wants you to alert the regiment to move out of the barracks. [My friend] was a company commander from a sister regiment, serving in Bataan at the time, doing some survey work and cleaning up trails." Johnson quickly asked for a confirmation of the order from Clarke and with that instantly set to his tasks.

Colonel Clifford Bluemel, USMA '09, commander of the 31st Philippine Division, also swallowed the preliminary facts at breakfast. "On the morning of 8 December I ate with Col. [John] Irwin, Captain Bauer and one other officer. Bauer came into the mess and said, 'Did you hear the radio?'

"I said, 'I don't have any radio. What is it?'

"He said, 'Pearl Harbor, Wheeler Field, and Hickam Field

were all bombed! The planes were destroyed on the ground, and a lot of the fleet was damaged!'

"I said, 'Oh my God! Who did it?'

"He said, 'The Japs did it.'

"I said, 'Well, we are at war now.' "

Lieutenant Colonel Irvin Alexander, of the quartermaster corps, a mustang who matriculated at West Point via the University of Indiana and a stint as a machine gun corporal with a federalized national guard during World War I, was at Fort Stotsenburg, some fifty miles north of Manila. "At breakfast on the morning, our radio told us that Pearl Harbor had been attacked with considerable naval damage. The announcement brought our breakfast to a mournful end, for we knew war was inevitable, and that we were on the hottest of war's seats."

Philip Fry, an infantry officer who had arrived in the islands less than three weeks before, recalled being at Fort William McKinley in the 45th Infantry Regiment's barracks hard by the first golf green and close to the officers' club and the tennis courts. "On the morning of December 8th, just around dawn I was awakened by some officer rushing in and announcing that we were at war. He told of the attack on Pearl Harbor as, dressed in our pajamas, we eagerly crowded around him for the news. I dressed quickly and walked to the club, found the place in an uproar, everyone seeking news. I managed to get a cup of coffee. Left the club and started walking to division headquarters. On the way I saw the 57th and 45th Infantry forming in full field equipment preparatory to taking the field. Decided then to cast my lot with one of these fine old regiments. I had no desire to enter a first-class shooting war with untrained troops. I asked for immediate assignment to the 57th Infantry and got it just like that."

Unlike Mary Rose Harrington, Army nurse Madeline Ullom, stationed at Sternberg General Hospital in Manila a few miles from Cavite, greeted the morning of 8 December blissfully unaware of what had happened. "A generous slice of luscious papaya with a squeeze of tangy lime was ever a good way to begin breakfast. The lithe Filipino lad with the big armful of newspapers wended his barefoot way among the tables. His big brown eyes were solemn. His wide cheery grin was absent. His soft murmur was barely audible as he handed each, 'Your paper, mom.' Big black headlines across the front page blared the attack on Pearl Harbor."

There was a brief lull for the major Air Corps units while the Japanese opened the assault on the Philippines: First on the radio station at Aparri on the northernmost tip of Luzon; then fighter planes operating from a carrier destroyed two Navy PBYs in Davao Gulf near Mindanao, but missed their tender. Shortly after, the enemy hit at the airfield located near Baguio. Missing from these efforts was any sort of offensive blow by the Americans. Behind the failure to initiate any action lies a murky tale, confusions of command and decision. When General Brereton, air commander for the USAFFE, learned of the raid on Pearl Harbor, he had immediately hurried to MacArthur's headquarters, instructing his subordinates to ready the B-17s for a raid, with Formosa the obvious target. But instead of being able to confer with MacArthur, Brereton could not get beyond Chief of Staff Sutherland, an imperious, zealous officer whose arrogant manner made him the most unpopular man on MacArthur's staff.

Sutherland brusquely informed Brereton that his boss was too busy with Admiral Hart to discuss the immediate role for the Air Corps. That MacArthur and Brereton did not confer is the one undisputable fact about what occurred in the early hours of 8 December, Manila time. According to Sutherland's recollections, the airman announced that he would attack Formosa with his B-17s. The chief of staff claimed that after Brereton declared his intentions, Sutherland inquired, "What is the target? Where are the fields?" He did not know. He had no target data. There were twenty fields on Formosa. General Brereton had no notion of what he would attack and he would almost certainly lose his planes. Brereton later insisted he had proposed hitting the Japanese troopships crowded into Takao Harbor on Formosa.

Accounts from various sources indicate that at the hour Brereton attempted to see his commander in chief and obtain permission for the bombing raid on Formosa, MacArthur was unwilling to make any move against the Japanese. Absent a declaration of war from any party, he spoke of warnings from Washington that he not take any action the Japanese might seize upon as provocative. He later explained to an historian, Louis Morton, "My orders were explicit not to initiate hostilities against the Japanese."

Eugene Eubank, who had joined the Army in 1917, commanded the 19th Bomb Group. He remembered, "General Brereton called me early on Monday morning and his exact words were, 'A hostile act has been committed at Pearl Harbor.' I flew down to Nichols Field and while I was there I heard him, two or three times, on the phone, presumably talking to General Sutherland, urging him to give us authority to mount a mission against the Japanese. The question was whether we would go up to Formosa and bomb the airfields or whether we would go against Japanese ships. That required a different type of bomb. You can't load for a mission until you know the target. We could have moved the planes but we were waiting for a mission, for orders to bomb the Japanese in Formosa or in the sea."

In his memoirs, MacArthur remarked that upon word of a

force of enemy bombers over the Lingayen Gulf on course for Manila at 9:30 A.M., he was still "under the impression that the Japanese had suffered a setback at Pearl Harbor, and their failure to close in on me supported that belief. I therefore contemplated an air reconnaissance to the north, using bombers with fighter protection, to ascertain a true estimate of the situation and to exploit any possible weaknesses that might develop on the enemy's front." Subsequently, he said, having learned that the Japanese had succeeded in their Hawaiian venture, he changed his mind. Although the events at Pearl Harbor signaled about as clearly an act of war as conceivable regardless of what was achieved and had been confirmed by Washington, MacArthur, thus in an altogether uncharacteristic fashion, dithered for five hours. Finally, at 10:10 in the morning, through Sutherland, he agreed to photoreconnaissance flights, the first steps necessary for an attack by the B-17s.

The commander of the USAFFE, in the course of denying that he ever consulted with Brereton or knew of any interview the airman had with Sutherland, added, "As a matter of fact, an attack on Formosa, with its heavy air concentrations by our small bomber force without fighter cover, which because of the great distance involved and the limited range of the fighters was impossible, would have been suicidal. In contrast, the enemy's bombers from Formosa had fighter protection from their air carriers, an entirely different condition from our own."

MacArthur was probably correct in his estimate of the outcome of a B-17 raid on Formosa but his reasoning smacks of hindsight. The American bombers with their thin, unarmored fuselages; the cumbersome, manually operated turrets; and absence of tail guns would have made them easy prey. The range of the P-40s fell well short of the requirements to escort the bombers to Formosa and return. And the lack of oxygen equipment for high altitude flight meant the fighters could not stay with their flock.

Few if any U.S. strategists possessed accurate intelligence on the quality of the Japanese air force and MacArthur was dead wrong when he referred to bombers coming from Formosa as being convoyed by carrier-based fighters. In fact, the Japanese Zero had been modified and its pilots trained in ways that added hundreds of miles to its range. The sorties against Luzon that struck the vital American installations early in the war employed land-based Zeros.

As an intelligence officer for the Air Corps in the Philippines, Capt. Allison Ind enthusiastically supported an immediate retaliation on Formosa by the B-17s. "We had no illusions," said Ind. "These folders [descriptions of objectives on Formosa] were not comparable with the exact and elaborate sheets of the RAF and the *Luftwaffe*, prepared as they had been over a dozen, a score and more of years. We had none of their beautifully calibrated bomb-target maps, indicating best approaches and even bomb-release lines for given speeds and altitudes. But we had something complete enough to make this bombing mission a very far cry from the blind stab it would have had to be otherwise. Maybe we could deliver a real hurt, if not a staggering blow, to the enemy, at his very point of departure for an invasion action against the Philippines." Others thought quite differently and the Air Corps settled for a three-bomber photoreconnaissance to take off around noon or a bit later. The mission was delayed while technicians located the proper cameras and arranged for them to be flown to Clark Field from Del Monte.

Whatever the discussions at USAFFE headquarters during the morning of 8 December, the airmen throughout the area responded to a pair of warnings. Brereton's Washington boss, Gen. Henry (Hap) Arnold, telephoned the Philippines to caution against a repeat of the Hawaiian experience. Even without the advice from half a world away, when radar at Iba had indicated incoming hostile traffic, the duty officer at Clark Field had ordered the B-17s to get out of harm's way. The bombers had placidly cruised the skies in great circles for two hours, staying in radio contact with the nearby communications tower. The first series of strikes from the sky ignited a host of defensive missions. The P-40s started patrols to cover Clark Field. Pilots at airbases not involved in these operations remained by their ships, ready on signal to meet the invaders.

At the northern tip of Luzon, the closest point to the Imperial Japanese forces stationed on Formosa, the Philippine Army's 11th Division guarded the beach approaches around the town of Aparri. Like all Philippine military units, Americans either commanded or "advised" the indigenous soldiers. Information about a state of war reached some units there almost eight hours after the news reached Manila. Colonel Glen R. Townsend served as the commanding officer of the 11th Regiment. "About ten o'clock on the morning of December 8th," recalled Townsend, "one of the Filipino officers came to tell me he had heard over his car radio that Japanese planes had bombed Hawaii. I thought of Orson Welles and the men from Mars." [The radio drama in 1939 panicked thousands who believed outer-space beings had invaded the U.S.]

"But Captain Pilar insisted, so I walked with him to his car nearby. When he turned the radio on, the announcer was just telling about the bombing of Baguio [the summer capital of the Philippines and site of some military installations and a resort area]. That convinced me there was a war on, but if more was needed it came an hour or so later. Eighty-four Japanese bombers passed directly over the camp. We later learned that these struck Clark Field."

Word of the Pearl Harbor attack and reports of incoming aircraft had reached operational elements of the 34th Pursuit Squadron at Del Carmen and pilots took off because of the alerts. Tom Gage, working in the squadron offices of the Del Carmen Airfield currently under construction, away from the flight line, remained ignorant that the country was at war. "A little before noon, one of the cooks, Shorty Batson, came running down to tell me they had heard on the Manila radio that Pearl Harbor had been bombed. Shortly after I heard what sounded like distant reports of firecrackers exploding. I stepped out and took a look around the sky and over toward the direction of Clark Field [14 miles to the north] the sky was covered by black dots. My first thought was, 'My God! Look at the enemy planes—there's thousands of them.' It took a few minutes for me to sort out the antiaircraft bursts and barely visible were two lines of very small black dots, flying in formation, above and beyond the shell smoke. I immediately hotfooted across the area and found Lt. Jack Jennings, the squadron adjutant, in his tent, reading a book! I told him Clark Field was being bombed. His reply was, 'Is that official, Sergeant?' I replied, 'Hell, Lieutenant, look out the back of your tent! Clark Field is going up in smoke!' "

At Clark, an hour before noon, with no imminent attack by Japanese planes in the area, most of the aircraft, including P-40s and B-17s, were back on the ground. While ground crews hastily refueled the ships and stocked the prescribed ordnance for the bombers, air crews snatched a few moments of rest or a quick snack. About 11:30, Iba airfield alerted all Air Corps bases of a large formation of planes

coming in from the China Sea, apparently vectored on
Manila, but the heading also meant the enemy would approach Clark Field.

The warning of approaching planes over the China Sea
scrambled flights of fighters from other bases. The 3d
Squadron at Iba saw nothing in the vicinity of their home
field, nor could they spot anything amiss at either Manila or
Clark Field. Running low on gas, the P-40s returned to Iba.
Just as planes formed up for an orderly landing, Iba literally
went up in flash and smoke. Enemy bombers, cruising at
28,000 feet, out of sight and well out of range of the P-40s,
had unloaded devastating strings of explosives across the
base. The place was completely destroyed, the radar station
and its operators wiped out, every building reduced to rub-
ble, anyone not in a foxhole died. Five P-40s were lost and
the surviving flights scattered to emergency sites, with several crashing from lack of fuel or damage from dogfights.

At Nichols Field, P-40 pilot Grashio said, "After the initial alert, we cut our engines, got out of the cockpits, and sat
under the wings, and waited as seemingly endless hours
dragged by. Suddenly about 11:30 A.M. we received an urgent call to prepare for action, though just what action was
unspecified. Soon, Ed Dyess divided our eighteen P-40s into
three groups and led two of them, A and B, into the air. I was
to lead the remaining six, Flight C, and follow him, but a
couple of our planes developed minor engine difficulties
that delayed us just long enough that we lost contact with A
and B Flights. Only at about 11:50 did my flight actually get
into the air. We flew to Laguna de Bay, a huge lake just
south of Nichols Field, and for the first time tested our .50-
caliber machine guns by firing short bursts into the water.
More of the fruits of unreadiness appeared only minutes
later. Two pilots in my flight reported that their engines were

throwing so much oil on the windshields that they couldn't see. They could only go back to Nichols.

"By now Flights A and B were not only out of sight but, for reasons unknown, out of radio contact as well. Since I had received no orders other than to get into the air and follow the other flights, our isolation was complete. Since I had to do something, I radioed [the others] that we should fly toward Clark Field, sixty miles north. It seemed a logical target for Japanese planes flying in from the north." The fighter squadrons, alerted by Iba, prowled the skies, searching sectors over the China Sea, Bataan, and Corregidor. Clark Field, during the period when its own ships from the 20th Pursuit Squadron required refueling, lay naked.

The bombs that smashed the radar installation at Iba eliminated the most definitive source of intelligence on enemy raids. The native observers, trained to report flights approaching the islands, relayed their information over the lines of the notoriously unreliable Philippine telephone system to air headquarters at Nielson Field. In turn, the word passed over the teletype or by radio to the different squadrons. But by midday of 8 December, the wires that normally carried the messages were dead, victims either of sabotage or the frequent technical problems.

"We arrived over Clark Field about 12:20 P.M.," said Grashio. "It was a gorgeous day. The sky was blue and the air smooth as glass. Observing the idyllic look of the area I still could not feel that I might become personally involved in a shooting war at any moment. It may seem incredible that anyone could have been in such an abstracted condition eight hours after Pearl Harbor but I accepted the fact of war only when it hit me in the face, and there were many like me.

"Observing nothing unusual at Clark, C Flight flew westward toward the China Sea. Suddenly I spotted planes at about our altitude (10,000 feet) moving south. We closed in, pulses racing. No sweat! They were only some other P-40s. Before we could get close enough to tell which squadron they belonged to, however, our earphones were suddenly filled with hysterical shouts from the tower operator far below, 'All P-40s return to Clark Field. Enemy bombers overhead.' These ominous words were almost immediately intermixed with the terrifying whoomp of bombs exploding. To my utter astonishment, the formation of P-40s continued serenely on a southerly course, climbing gradually. Obviously they had not heard the frantic order to return to Clark. What happened to their radios? It was the second snafu on a day filled with them."

At 12:30 P.M., about the moment that Grashio recognized a friendly group of P-40s, the 19th Bombardment Group staff continued to plot the assault upon Formosa. The P-40s of the 20th Pursuit Squadron at Clark Field taxied to the runway, ready for the signal to take off. Already, bombs had been loaded into several B-17s, and the aircraft scheduled to collect photo intelligence on Formosan bases rumbled into position for the start of their mission.

Lieutenant Fred T. Crimmins Jr., commander of one plane, started to walk across the field toting a machine gun that required a minor fix. His crew, grabbing lunch, was astonished to hear an unconfirmed radio report that at that very moment Japanese bombers were over Clark Field. Crimmins reached a hangar and passed the weapon to a sergeant for repair when the base Klaxon sounded its urgent alarm. The pilot and the mechanic rushed outside and peered into the sky. In the clear blue above, from over the mountains to the northwest, they saw two precision Vees, one behind the other, serenely droning toward them at 18,000 feet.

The pair heard the engines even as the first of the P-40s roared down the runway, now frantic to get off before the hammer fell.

There had been no warning at all, according to those on the scene, and it was a matter of seconds or perhaps a minute between the sight of the Japanese flights and the fall of the bombs. And when these plummeted to the target the devastation was horrendous. The pattern of the two bomber waves spewed explosives across the field, shattering the officers' quarters, the parked P-40s, the headquarters building, the maintenance shops, and hangar areas. Almost every structure took a hit and many blazed flames without restraint; the apparatus to control fires had been destroyed. No means to summon help existed; the blasts obliterated the communications center. The 200th Coast Artillery, responsible for anti-aircraft defense, coped with ammunition manufactured a minimum of nine years earlier. Most fuses were badly corroded and an expert guess reported that only one of every six of the three-inch rounds actually fired. Tracers and flaming debris ignited nearby trees and the long grass. A giant pall of dust and a thick black cloud from a burning oil dump rose so high in the air that a pilot near Iba saw the sinister cloud. At ground zero, the fumes reduced visibility well below 100 feet.

Flight C from the 21st Pursuit Squadron, with Sam Grashio in command, started to respond to the control tower appeal for help. "Right at this critical juncture," said Grashio, "Joe Cole radioed his engine was throwing oil so badly that he could not see out of his windshield. Like the two others with the same trouble, he had to return to Nichols Field. This left McGown, Williams, and myself. We turned back toward Clark. In the distance I got my first glimpse of the spectacular destructiveness of war. It was astounding!

Where the airfield should have been the whole area was boiling with smoke, dust and flames. In the middle was a huge column of greasy black smoke from the top of which ugly red flames billowed intermittently. Momentarily, I thought how utterly, abysmally wrong the senior officers on the *Coolidge* had been, a reflection almost immediately replaced by pity for those on the ground who must be going through hell. I said a quick prayer, asking God to help them and thanking Him for sparing me, at least for the moment, from being on the receiving end of Japanese bombs.

"About 12:50 P.M., directly over the field, I noticed several enemy dive bombers perhaps 800 feet below us and 2,000 feet above the ground bombing and strafing. All our flight training had been directed toward moments and opportunities like this. I signaled my wingmen to attack. Just then, an enemy dive bomber shot out of the smoke maybe 500 feet below. I looked at once for McGown. He was nowhere in sight. Gus Williams had disappeared, too.

"Instead, about 100 yards behind and above me were two Zeros, closing in. They opened fire. I veered sharply to the left. My plane shuddered as a cannon burst hit the left wing and blew a hole big enough to throw a hat through. For the first time that day I had the hell scared out of me. Momentarily, I was sure I was going to die on the first day of the war. Instinctively, I began to pray again, this time with greater fervor than before. I also remembered what Ed [Dyess] had told me many times; never try to outmaneuver a Zero; go into a steep dive and try to outrace it. I pushed the throttle wide open and roared for the ground. The wind shrieked past me and the earth flashed upward at horrifying speed. Technical manuals specifically warned against a power dive in an untested plane, and I was in a P-40 that had been in the air a grand total of two hours. But with two

Zeros on your tail, the admonitions in technical manuals are not the first things you think about. My luck held. When I tried to pull out of the dive at treetop level just west of Clark the plane responded magnificently. Glancing back, I was overjoyed to see the two Zeros falling steadily behind. The superior diving capability of the P-40 had saved my hindquarters."

Grashio said he saw enemy tracers pass increasingly wide of the mark and eventually the pair of Zeros turned away. "I breathed a prayer of thanks only to break out anew in a cold sweat. Would I be able to land with the gaping hole in the wing? I radioed Nichols tower for advice. I was told to climb to 8,000 feet above an uninhabited area and simulate a landing. Wheels and flaps down. I did so. The hole in the wing presented no problems. Nevertheless, many curious and doubtless apprehensive people stood along the runway when I came down about 1:30, the first pilot to make it back to Nichols from combat."

On the ground at Clark Field, however, rather than celebrating the return of a pilot, the airmen and ground crews not killed or badly wounded struggled to recover, dispensing what medical aid they could to the injured and seeking to arrange transport for them to the Fort Stotsenburg Hospital. But the respite from the onslaught was pitilessly short as dozens of Japanese fighters roared through the smoke. Machine guns and 20mm cannons hammered away at the parked Fortresses, totally exposed to the strafing runs. Only a few had been ruined by the high-altitude attack of a few minutes earlier, but the fighter runs, at a few feet off the ground, completely wrecked all but two or three and even those absorbed some damage. The three ships scheduled to survey Formosa, having never left the earth, lay in smoldering ruins. Four of the P-40s at Clark managed to get airborne before the bombs rendered the field useless. Five others in the process of taking off and five more lined up to await their turn were turned into junk. The quartet that escaped registered three downed Zeros and a handful of other interceptors that rushed to the scene claimed several other kills. But the costs to the enemy were negligible.

The only Fort to survive was that of John W. Carpenter, a 1939 graduate of West Point who had transferred from the field artillery to become a B-17 pilot with the 19th Bomb Group. "The airplane I inherited was a dog, and all the way across the Pacific this thing had been blowing generators. Every time you would turn around, you would blow another generator. My squadron had been ordered to disperse down to Del Monte around the fifth of December but as usual my airplane was out for a generator so I stayed on Clark with the ground echelon.

"Word came around to report to group headquarters. They said the Hawaiian Islands had been attacked and Hickam was gone. At that time we didn't have any orders and couldn't do anything. Our commander then, Col. E. L. Eubank, then tried to get permission to load up and go bomb the Japs—no way. They said, all right, we are not going to get these airplanes caught on the ground here; everybody get out and go. They assigned reconnaissance sectors for the different airplanes. We all took to the air, all except my aircraft, which was out for generators. There wasn't another airplane on the ground. Everybody got to work and they finally got my airplane fixed.

"We got up in the air and headed out and [I] was just at the far reach of my assigned sector when word came through on radio, a recall for all airplanes. The rest of the B-17s were fairly close in by that time, and they landed. When I finally got back, all the other airplanes were on the ground.

We came down through the clouds out over the mountains and one of my crew said, 'Look there, there is a big thunderstorm right over Clark Field,' and sure enough there was this big thunderstorm. Only it wasn't a thunderstorm. All our airplanes on the ground were burning, and this was the smoke going up for all the world like a big thunder-bumper over the airport.

"About that time we began to get word over the radio . . . an officer had climbed up in the control tower and called. My airplane and another were circling east of the field. The other plane—a fellow named Earl Tash—had come up from Mindanao and was going to land for repairs that couldn't be accomplished at Del Monte. The tower said, 'We are under attack. Better go elsewhere to land.' Tash managed to get his gear up when the Jap fighters jumped him. He got away and headed on to Mindanao. He had enough gas but I didn't have enough to make it.

"We had a standard approach procedure where we would come in on a heading from Mount Arayat on the east of Clark. With your gear down, the ack-ack weren't suppose to shoot at you. We had an Army National Guard outfit from Albuquerque just recently transferred over there, and they couldn't tell a four-engine airplane from a single-engine one and would fire on anything that approached the field. We had to be very careful to return in accord with proper approach procedure. Here we were with gear and flaps down headed into Clark below 500 feet. About that time the Jap fighters hit us. We thought all the Jap aircraft were gone but heck no. Their bombers had been over and done all the damage, and then waves of fighters hit the place, one after another. Here we were gear and flaps down, guns stowed—fat, dumb, and happy—between two of the waves. I was worried I didn't have much runway, only about 1,200 feet undamaged, and concentrated on setting it down on the edge of the field and here came these fighters.

"First we thought they must be P-40s out of Nichols Field and then all of a sudden we realized those little red lights that were flashing on the front end of the wings weren't playing. About that time a fighter went by, and I could see the Rising Sun on his wings. We threw everything to the firewall, got the gear and flaps up, and fortunately nobody was hit in my airplane. We took a few bullets and headed back up into the clouds. We knew that Nichols had been bombed and I didn't have fuel to go anywhere else. We hid in the clouds over on the other side of Mount Arayat until I was just about empty and then came in and landed at Clark. Fortunately, the air raid was over for the moment."

With the only airplane that could fly at Clark, Carpenter was ordered to undertake a reconnaissance flight toward Formosa. "My job was to go up and see if we could take pictures of what was going on. About halfway up my generators went out and I had to abort. I would never have made it to Formosa. They would have murdered me, single airplane all by itself. The briefing officer, the group operations officer, said, 'I want you to go up there and take some pictures. You had better stay up around 20,000 feet. I don't think they can get you up there.' Every fighter they had was very active at that altitude and higher," noted Carpenter, who remembered that as squadron intelligence officer he agreed with his briefer. "From all the information we had, they had a bunch of old fixed-gear airplanes that could hardly fly above 10,000 feet."

Carpenter said, "We had talked about possibilities and felt something like this was coming. We were convinced with our B-17s we could fly back and forth across the China Sea and sink anything the Japs could send down with just our one group of bombers. Our esprit was high. We knew we could do the job. We were also convinced that immediately after the Japs attacked, the biggest convoy you ever saw in your life was starting out from San Francisco to come over and reinforce the Philippines. We were going to take care of this thing in short order. It was not just a hope. I think it was really a belief on the part of most of our people in the Philippines."

Major Alva Fitch, commander of a battery for the 23d Field Artillery Regiment, a Philippine Scouts outfit, on the morning of 8 December was at his Fort Stotensburg post near Clark Field. Although aware of the news, Fitch and his battery received no orders, but busied themselves with digging in for protection against air raids. "We were just sitting down to luncheon when Johnny [an aide], hearing a suspicious noise went outside. I looked at my watch. It was 12:48. Johnny called to us. We saw a flight of fifty-three bombers very high. We speculated as to their identity for a very few seconds, and took to the ditch. About one minute later, Clark Field exploded. The entire Clark Field area erupted in a column of smoke and dust and with an awful and impressive roar.

"I ran for the barracks where I found the battery engaged in antiaircraft operations with Springfield rifles, with far more danger to themselves than to the airplanes. The rifles had been recently issued and only a few of the men had ever fired them before. I stopped the rifle fire, and put the men in the trenches we had dug earlier. By this time, attack planes were strafing the airplanes on the ground, and the AA installations in the vicinity. They passed low over the battery and turned back into the smoke. This started the troops firing again. I am still surprised that none of them were killed by their own barrage."

Colonel Irvin Alexander, in charge of supply matters at Fort Stotsenburg, who learned by radio of the war's opening blast, recalled, "As we went about our duties that morning we had little more information but heard a rumor that Baguio had been bombed. At lunch I turned on the radio at 12:30 P.M. to hear the news from Don Bell, our favorite Manila announcer. He reported Baguio had been bombed that morning and there was an unconfirmed rumor that Clark Field had also been initiated. Clark Field being less than a mile from where we were sitting, I laughed, as I started to say, 'Another example of the accuracy of the news.'

"In the middle of the sentence my face froze, for I became aware of the whistling approach of hundreds of bombs. This shrieking was followed by terrific explosions that made our house shake and groan like it was in the midst of a violent earthquake. We rushed out to the parade ground to see columns of smoke and dust rising from the airfield. Searching the sky, I discovered the attackers, a Vee-shaped formation of fifty-four bombers, high up, perhaps 20,000 feet, heading for home. The war had begun for us."

The action at Clark Field lasted only about forty-five minutes, but when the Japanese withdrew, almost nothing usable remained of the best of the American air stations in the Philippines. Not a single plane that had been on the ground could fly. Bomb craters pockmarked the strips. Fires raged in the gutted hangars and buildings. Casualties numbered fifty-five dead and more than a hundred men wounded. MacArthur and his people now faced a defense of the Philippines with half of their B-17 arsenal gone, and a similar situation with available fighters. Furthermore, the damage to Clark meant the remainder of the Fortresses would have to operate from Del Monte in Mindanao, 1,000 miles south. Longer flying distances meant additional stress on engines and crews.

What happened to Clark Field was a miniature replica of the disaster at Pearl Harbor. An outraged Gen. Hap Arnold, as chief of the Army Air Forces, and Brereton's boss, chewed out the commander of the Far Eastern Air Force, demanding "how in hell" he could have been caught with his bombers down a full nine hours after hearing of what happened at Pearl Harbor. General George C. Marshall, as MacArthur's superior, soon afterward remarked to a correspondent, "I just don't know how MacArthur happened to let his planes get caught on the ground."

Early in December, Adm. Thomas Hart, with tens of thousands of square miles of ocean available for dispersal of his fleet, prudently had dispatched much of it out of immediate reach of any attack. Only five destroyers—two of which were under repair—plus the bulk of his submarines cruised the waters in the Manila Bay area. The remainder of Hart's forces hung out well south, and once the news of Pearl Harbor reached Hart, he ordered his vessels even farther beyond harm's way, to the neighborhood of the Dutch possession, Borneo. The first and second days of the war thus passed with no significant consequences to the U.S. Asiatic Fleet.

Although Admiral Hart had assigned most of his ships to more southern seas, points well away from the base in Manila Bay, on the day of this attack, two destroyers were in the navy yard undergoing repairs, and the *John D. Ford*, the four-stacker with William Mack aboard, hovered nearby, awaiting its annual overhaul. "[When] we received a message from Pearl Harbor," said Mack, "we immediately activated our explosives systems and ripped down the awnings and we were all ready. We knew we weren't going into the yard but we didn't know what to do until somebody told us, so we were lying off Cavite."

The ship remained on station and on the morning of 10 December, the crew saw a few Zeros fly by but nothing happened until noon. "Then," Mack continued, "fifty-four high-level bombers came over at about 10,000 feet and made practice runs on the waterfront of the Philippines and the ships in the harbor and on the Cavite naval yard. They made three dry runs; they were actually unopposed; there were no P-40s anywhere in sight. We were sitting there thinking that was going to be a great show when all our P-40 pilots got away from the country club and went up there and showed them a thing or two. But not one P-40 showed anywhere.

"These fifty-four aircraft were bombing first the Philippine waterfront and then Manila, and they devastated that. Then they went around in a sort of triangular circle and devastated the shipyard where the *Pillsbury* and *Perry* were frantically trying to get themselves back together and get out. They [the planes] came across where the *John D. Ford* was [and merchant ships] and dropped bombs on all of us, but we were not hit."

Also undergoing overhaul at Cavite were a pair of submarines, *Sealion* and *Seadragon*, skippered by Comdr. Dick Voge and Comdr. Pete Ferrall, with Norvell Ward as one of Ferrall's junior officers. Tied up alongside each other, the two captains, and some of the crew, like Ward, scanned the skies. Ward remembered, "We watched the Jap bomber formation go over at about 22,000, 25,000 feet, watched them make a practice run from west to east, then turn around and come back and make their first bombing run from east to west. We saw the bombs drop on the pier and other buildings up in the shipyard. We saw them release, we saw them coming down, but we knew on that run that they were going to miss us, just a little bit, and they did." The absence of fighters to interfere or effective ground fire gave the Japanese the leisure to make dry runs before the actual attacks, thereby enabling them to enhance their effectiveness.

"We manned our .50-caliber [machine] guns. We manned our three-inch gun, as did the *Sealion*," said Ward. "Dick Voge turned to Pete Ferrall and said, 'I think we're damn fools staying up here on the bridge.' Pete said, 'I agree with you.' Dick cleared his people off the topside and we cleared ours. Voge had all of his go down below into the control room, whereas on the *Seadragon* some of us stayed up in the conning tower. I stayed there and so did Sam Hunter. Diaz, our chief pharmacist's mate, remained up in the conning tower among two or three others. Pete Ferrall went down to the control room.

"On the next run the *Sealion* received two bomb hits, one right on their conning tower and the other in the after engine room. If anyone had been in the conning tower of the *Sealion* they would have been wiped out. The *Sealion* lost three men, I believe, who were in the after engine room when the bomb hit. Shrapnel from the *Sealion*'s conning tower went through ours. It took off the back of Sam Hunter's head and shattered Diaz's arm. I was standing there with my hand on Sam's shoulder, and I was fortunate in that I got scraped across the belly by some shrapnel. Sam was killed instantly; Diaz was able to walk to the hospital, and I had a superficial wound."

Lieutenant John Bulkeley's Motor Torpedo Boat Squadron 3 responded to the air raid warning and sped out into the comparative safety of Manila Bay. "The admiral sent us a two-hour warning that they were coming—from Formosa, and were headed on down in our direction across northern Luzon. So we hauled our boats out into the bay. They kept beautiful formations . . . and they came in at about 20,000, with their fighters on up above to protect them from ours— only ours didn't show! I kept thinking," said Bulkeley, "wait until those Army pilots leave the officers' club and go after them. We knew we couldn't get appropriations for the Navy; all the money was going into those P-40s. I hadn't heard anything about the destruction of Clark Field and the other airfields." Bulkeley and the rest of his squadron quickly discovered they were among the targets. "They swung over Manila and began to paste the harbor shipping. It was a beautiful clear day, and I remember the sun made rainbows on the waterspouts of their bombs. They were 150 to 200 feet high and it made a mist screen so dense you could hardly tell what was happening to the ships.

"But then that beautiful Vee pivoted slowly and moved over Cavite—began circling it like a flock of well-disciplined buzzards. They were too high for us to see the bomb bay doors open, but we could see the stuff drop slowly, picking up speed; only as we watched we found we had troubles of our own. Because five little dive bombers peeled off that formation, one by one, and started straight down for us. When they were down to about 1,500 feet, they leveled off and began unloading. Of course, we gave our boats full throttle and began circling and twisting, both to dodge the bombs and get a shot at them. Our gunners loved it—it was their first crack at the Japs. . . . They'd picked out one plane and were pouring it up into the sky, when we saw the plane wobble, and pretty soon she took off down the bay, weaving unsteadily, smoking, and all at once, two or three miles away, she just wobbled down into the drink with a big splash."

Bulkeley said of Cavite after the enemy finally ended its

two-hour rampage: "They'd flattened it—there isn't any other word. Here was the only American naval base in the Orient beyond Pearl Harbor pounded into bloody rubbish. . . . We began loading in the wounded to take them to Cañacao Hospital. . . . There was half an inch of blood on the landing platform at Cañacao—we could hardly keep on our feet, for blood is as slippery as crude oil—and the aprons of the hospital attendants were so blood-spattered they looked like butchers."

After confirmation of the start of hostilities, Lt. Madeline Ullom at Sternberg Hospital read a red-bordered form labeled IMMEDIATE ACTION that directed the staff to "discharge all patients who could possibly go." A very few helpless patients remained on the wards. Foxholes were dug on the lawns of the hospital for protection. When air raid sirens wailed several times that first day, the cries of "Hit the dirt!" showed the disadvantages of white uniforms. A warehouse issued fatigues ordinarily worn by men but quickly tailored to appropriate sizes. Ullom and the others received gas masks and helmets.

"Filipino troops and the constabulary were armed and patrolled the streets," Lieutenant Ullom said. "Manila was in blackout. Heavy curtains hung over the windows. Blue paper covered flashlights. Rumors were abundant. Rumors were believed because we could not comprehend that Americans were not capable of the almost impossible." The impact of war closed in upon the nurses. "Casualties flowed into Sternberg. Huge abdominal gashes, an arm or a leg almost severed, a hunk of buried or protruded shrapnel were common sights. The dead and dying were interspersed among the wounded. Facilities were taxed beyond capacity to adequately and immediately operate and treat the multitude. The waiting section extended to the lawn between the wards and surgery. Patients were lined up side by side, on stretchers and blankets. Big bloody dressings reflected the hues of magnificent poinsettias. Hypodermics were injected to take the edge from severe pain. A colored mark on the forehead provided quick reference to determine time of medication. The Emergency Medical Tag fastened to the top pajama button kept records. Considerate men often implored us to care for a fellow soldier they felt was more critically injured, although they were next in line. Chaplains Oliver and Tiffany along with others moved among the casualties to administer the Last Rites, to console the injured. With religious duties completed, they carried litters, acted as messengers. Many former army nurses, stationed at Sternberg before marriage, hastened to volunteer their services.

"Everyone was on duty, time meant nothing. Many took turns sleeping on the operating tables, on the floor between raids. When the first bombs fell near Sternberg I was so scared I felt petrified. A patient's abdomen had just been opened when an air raid alarm sounded. We continued to operate. The thin galvanized roof above surgery rattled. We were so busy that outside sounds seemed far away. After that session, my fears left me."

Admiral Hart, with an eagle's eye view of the destruction of Cavite from atop the Marsman Building, which housed naval headquarters, lost only one docked submarine, but the raid cost the Navy a major source of maintenance and supply, including more than 200 torpedoes stored at Cavite. Without adequate facilities, with no protection against a Japanese thrust from the air, and badly undergunned in any surface encounters, the Navy wrote off the Philippines. Except for the submarines, the six-boat PT squadron, and a few PBYs, the Asiatic Fleet abandoned the local waters. Within three days, MacArthur had lost not only two potential offensive weapons; he was also bereft of the vital means for any defense of the beaches.

5

Early Engagements

OBEDIENT TO THE TERMS OF THE TREATY SIGNED WITH THE Japanese, the Third Reich, on 11 December, declared war on the United States. Some Americans, hostile to Germany for its persecution of Jews, its conquests of neighbors, and out of affection for the Allied opposition, had entered the conflict well before December 1941.

James Goodson, a nineteen-year-old student at the University of Toronto, torpedoed while aboard the steamship *Athenia* a day after war broke out in 1939, and with an English mother, quickly enlisted in the Royal Air Force. Sent to Canada for training, he returned to the United Kingdom as the Battle of Britain was winding down, flying first Hurricanes and then Spitfires. The RAF operated mixed squadrons made up of Canadians, Aussies, New Zealanders, South Africans, East Indians, and Americans. After the fall of the European allies there were also French, Poles, Czechs, and Norwegians. In September 1940, in what was more likely a politico-propaganda move rather than a tactical one, the RAF created the 71 Squadron, an all-American unit under the nominal leadership of a former U.S. Marine pilot, William Taylor. Actually, a Briton ran operations because the top RAF officer, Air Marshal Trafford Leigh-Mallory, objected to a squadron composed of American volunteers whom he believed lacked discipline. Four months passed before the first Eagle Squadron began to function.

Leigh-Mallory's opinion, one shared at the time by Hap Arnold, initially proved correct. In its first sorties, the 71 Squadron performed poorly and an RAF officer replaced Taylor with the assignment to whip the bunch into shape. Subsequently, two more Eagle Squadrons were formed, the 121 and the 133. Among the members of the 71 was Bill Dunn, a refugee in June 1940 from the life of an infantryman trapped with the British Expeditionary Force in France.

The tales of an uncle who flew in World War I and a stepfather who also piloted a plane in that conflict motivated Dunn to join the RAF. Dunn had acquired 150 hours of flying when in 1934 he went to Fort Lincoln [Texas] and told the recruiting officer he wanted to enlist in the Army Air Corps. "Recruiting people will promise you anything to get your name on the dotted line and I found myself in the infantry with a musket. The pay was supposed to be $21 a month but, in 1934 with the Depression on, Roosevelt cut all government employees' wages 20 percent. As a buck private I got $16.85 a month. Every so often some local restaurant would put a sign in the window, NO DOGS OR SOLDIERS ALLOWED.

"I finished my army service and when the war broke out I thought I'd whip up to Canada and join the RAF. I couldn't get into a flying outfit but the Seaforth Highlanders were taking volunteers. A sergeant major asked me where I came from and I said the U.S. He said, 'Sorry, we can't take you, no American citizens. However, if you walk around the block and come back in maybe you can decide you're from some place in Canada.' I went out and came back and said, 'Moose Jaw.' He asked, 'Where is that?' I said, 'How the hell would I know, I just thought of it.' He told me, 'It's in Saskatchewan and don't forget it. You're enlisted.' "

On 10 May 1940, when the German offensive started to roll through Holland and Belgium, Canadian specialists were chosen to assist the British Expeditionary Force. "I was a mortar platoon sergeant," recalled Dunn, "and they needed mortars, Bren gun carrier people, machine gunners. We were taken to France as part of the 61st Highland Division. On 14 or 15 May, when Germans broke through Belgium and were coming toward us, we were ordered to retreat to better positions. We fell back several times and followed the railroad all the way down to Saint-Omer and then back to the coast to Calais until they evacuated about 1,000 of us.

"After the Battle of Britain, the British were very short of pilots. The air ministry sent around a message that anyone with at least 500 hours flying time could transfer to the RAF. I didn't have 500 but when I wrote 130–150, somehow the pencil slipped a little, my ones looked like fives. German Stuka bombers bombed our camp at Borden and I shot two of them down with a Lewis machine gun and I think that helped my being accepted. I was awfully tired of carrying the damned mortar around the countryside. It was good to be out of the infantry.

"I went to flying school and had a total of sixty-five hours before going operational as a Hurricane pilot. The Hurricane was reasonably fast, a good climber and very maneuverable. During the Battle of Britain there were nineteen RAF squadrons equipped with Hurricanes, seven flew Spitfires. The real load fell on the Hurricane pilots. I don't mean to shortchange the Spit boys. They did an excellent job in taking the 109s off the backs of the Hurricanes while they were knocking the bombers about. It annoys me when the Spit gets all the credit and the hard-working Hurricane is forgotten by the historians."

Goodson, Dunn, et al., had been preceded by a trio of accomplished American pilots, Shorty Keough, Gene Tobin, and Andrew Mamedoff, all of whom, frustrated in an effort to form a replica of the Lafayette Escadrille of World War I for the French, reached England in time to serve in the 1940 summer campaign known as the Battle of Britain. When Dunn entered the 71 Squadron, the three were already on hand. "Shorty Keough was killed by a bomb. Red Tobin was shot down and killed. During bad weather, Andy Mamedoff ran into a hill. Another American, Mike Kolendorfski, was shot down by two ME 109s.

"The Eagle Squadrons weren't the greatest outfits in the world," said Dunn. "They were more of a propaganda idea. The 71 did a fair amount of combat work, the 121 did a little bit but the 133 never got into any to speak of. There was a lot of reluctance among the Americans in the RAF squadrons. They were happy where they were in the mixed squadrons. They already had their buddies. The squadron leaders—flight lieutenants—the intelligence, maintenance, and armament officers, and the ground crew were all English. The fighter pilots were Americans, about eighteen of us. We were formed about March or April 1941. The first fighter sweep I ever went on, a German squadron came up to meet us and suddenly our squadron leader said, 'Let's go get them.' First thing I know I'm sitting up there in the sky all by myself. There wasn't a soul around me. I looked below and there was everybody milling around, a big gaggle squirting at one another. I thought I'd better get down there and see what's going on and join the fight.

"When I got down there in that milling mess, a bunch of tracers went flying over my canopy and another bunch of tracers went flying across my nose. I shoved the throttle full forward and headed my aircraft back toward England. I went straight home, flat out. Scared? You bet I was. On the way back I noticed that the fingers on my right hand were numb. I finally realized I was holding the control column so tight that I had cut off all the circulation in my fingers. I kept thinking, 'What the hell am I doing up here? I should be back in the Seaforths with my 3-inch mortar.' I think that if I had landed and somebody asked, 'Do you want to go back to the infantry?' I might have said yes. But luckily there wasn't anybody there to make the offer.

"No one in the squadron seemed to have noticed my sudden departure from the fight. At least nobody said anything about it. I had never fired my guns in anger before and I had less than a hundred flying hours in the RAF, probably about twenty hours in a Hurricane. It suddenly scared the hell out of me because it dawned on me that I wasn't quite ready for that sort of thing. I really went to work learning how to fly my aircraft and when I wasn't on alert duty I did a lot of air-to-air and air-to-ground firing practice. Most important, I had to condition my mental attitude toward aerial warfare. I used to tell myself the other guy was no better than I was and he was probably just as scared. So I calmed down and I decided to use a tactic of strike fast, fire at close range, and get the hell out. My limited skill as a fighter pilot in those days wouldn't permit me to stay and mix it up with some Kraut pilot."

Shortly after he resolved to teach himself how to fight, Dunn put his practice to the test during an encounter with an enemy Messerschmitt. "I dove behind a 109, seventy-five feet behind him. He filled up the whole windscreen. It's hard to miss when you're that close. I started firing at him, chips flew off his aircraft. He caught fire and started down. I watched him go all the way in. He crashed near a crossroads in France. A fellow in our squadron confirmed the victory for me. The feeling was one of elation. Shooting down the first one gives you confidence in yourself. Shooting down an airplane you don't really think of the guy who was in it. You must remember it could have been the other way around. You're happy that it was him and not you. My old wing commander Paddy Donaldson used to say, 'Kill the bastard before the bastard kills you.' "

Dunn developed into one of the more accomplished members of his outfit. "I preferred the element of surprise on my side. Give them a bounce; get in a good long squirt, and get the hell out. I saw guys as soon as we lost the element of surprise tangle with the Germans in a dogfight. That was stupid. He might be a much better acrobatic pilot. The only result would be to get your rear end shot off. I [wanted] to close in on him until his aircraft just about filled my windscreen, give him a good blast at short range, 150 to 50 yards, and get out fast. If you missed, no big deal. Come back tomorrow and try again."

As the war continued, Dunn switched to the Spitfire. "It was the best. It had absolutely no bad habits. You couldn't even scare yourself in it. It had a very high rate of climb, great maneuverability, fast, so fast you could almost close the throttle and still feel yourself sliding through the air. It was very light and I flew as high as 32,000 feet and it flew very well. We did convoy duty toward France hoping to get something to come up. Then they started doing fighter sweeps which would get them to scramble for a fight but then the Germans figured out there wasn't any point in going up there and wasting a lot of ammunition on fighters because there was no damage we could do. So we escorted Blenheim and Stirling bombers on what we called 'circus operations.' Then of course the enemy would come up in droves and we'd get in some pretty big fights. The biggest involved 300 aircraft. You spent more time trying not to run into the other guys than shooting at one another.

"After a while we started carrying bombs on our fighters and the Germans didn't know whether our fighters were coming over France as just fighters or fighter-bombers so they'd have to engage us. We carried bombs for selected targets, marshaling yards or airdromes. We'd do things like fly over a seaplane base in Holland, trying to arrive at dawn, shoot up the seaplanes, then turn and cut across a German 109 base and catch the 109s being scrambled. We'd be long gone by the time they were getting off the deck to chase us. We always caught them flatfooted. These were all volunteer operations. A couple of guys would plan something, get group approval and we'd go. We never took more than four aircraft on an intruder operation. After we hit the target it was every man for himself getting home."

As a Spitfire pilot, on 27 August 1941, Dunn flew escort for Blenheims raiding a steel mill at Lille, France. "I shot down two ME 109Fs. I also got shot up by a third ME 109. The front of my right foot was shot off, two machine gun bullets hit my right leg and one creased the back of my head." Dunn told writer Vern Haugland (*The Eagle Squadrons*) "I dived on one of two ME 109Fs, fired from a distance of 150 yards and fired again to within 50 yards. Pieces of the aircraft flew off, and engine oil spattered my windscreen. The plane looked like a blowtorch with a bluish white flame as it went down.

"Tracers from another 109F behind me flashed past my cockpit. I pulled back the throttle, jammed down the flaps, and skidded my plane sharply out of his gunsight. The German overshot me by about ten feet, as he crossed overhead I could see the black cross insignia, unit markings, and a red rooster painted on the side of the cockpit.

"The 109 was now within my range. With a burst of only three seconds I had him out of commission. A wisp of smoke from the engine turned almost immediately into a sheet of flame. The plane rolled over on its back. As it started down, the tail section broke off. . . . I fired at another ME 109 and saw smoke coming from it. Just as I started to press the gun button my plane lurched sharply. I heard explosions. A ball of fire streamed through the cockpit, smashing into the instrument panel. There were two heavy blows against my right leg, and as my head snapped forward I began to lose consciousness.

"My mind cleared again, and I realized that the earth was coming up toward me. I tugged back on the control column and pulled back into a gradual dive toward the English Channel, fifty miles away. I checked the plane for damage. The tip of the right wing was gone. The rudder had been badly damaged. The instruments on the right side of my panel were shattered. There was blood on the cockpit floor. When I looked at my right leg I saw that the toe of my boot had been shot off. My trouser leg was drenched with blood. I could feel warm, sticky fluid seeping from under my helmet to my neck and cheek. I gulped oxygen to fight off nausea.

"Releasing my shoulder harness, I started to climb out of the cockpit. For some reason I paused. The engine was still running all right and the plane seemed flyable. I slid back into my seat. I would try to make it home. . . . Crossing the

Channel, the engine began to lose power. I switched on the radio telephone and called May Day. Within a few moments I had an escort of two Spitfires. They led me across the coastal cliffs to the grass airfield at Hawkinge, near Folkestone. The escorting pilot signaled that my landing gear had extended.

"I dropped smoothly onto the newly mowed turf and taxied to a waiting ambulance. An airman climbed up on the wing and shouted at me that I was in the wrong area and must taxi over to the dispersal hut if I wanted fuel and ammunition. Then he saw my bloody face and helmet and called the medical officer." Dunn spent three months recuperating at RAF medical facilities. By the time he was ready to fly missions again, the U.S. had entered the war. "Both victories are classified as unconfirmed for several days but then the German Air Force released some info about their boys who got shot down the same date, time, and place." With these two 109s, Dunn had now accounted for five enemy planes and became the first American accredited as an ace.

The Eagle Squadrons finally passed into history in September 1942, dropping their RAF designations to become American outfits with appropriate insignia and uniforms. During eighteen months of operations the three units racked up 73 confirmed enemy planes destroyed.

In a different capacity, fighter pilot Johnny Alison, under the Lend-Lease Act in which the United States supplied Great Britain with arms in return for the use of bases, in 1941 traveled to England as an advisor. "Hub [Hubert] Zemke and I took P-40s to England to demonstrate the use of the P-40." Alison, a graduate of the Army flight school in 1937, added, "My job was to visit RAF units, tell them the experiences we had with the P-40, and help them in tactical use of it. The British were not entirely satisfied with the airplane; they said it was a good airplane but that it was lacking in performance characteristics and they didn't want to use it in England. They sent them to Russia and the Middle East.

"At the time there were a great many arguments about the relative merits of British equipment and ours. The British were not satisfied with the armament of the B-17. They said it didn't have enough turrets in it. Our boys insisted they could use it and it would be a mighty good ship because it could run away from the Germans. One of our boys wrote a letter, 'The Godamned British are so turret-minded that if Winston Churchill died, they would fix a tail turret to his ass before they let his soul go to heaven.' " Actually, Alison was more aware than most of the vulnerability of the early models of the Flying Fortress. He remembered, "When they first introduced the B-17, fighter pilots found it easy to get up and stay with it because there was no tailgun. You could get right in the cone and shoot it down without any trouble. But nobody in the Air Corps was going to listen to a second lieutenant pursuit pilot who said, 'I can shoot these things down very easily.' " The British actually had accepted twenty B-17s for use in daylight raids, while the bulk of the RAF bomber force operated during the darkness. The brief experiment ended after poor bombing results and a failure to knock down a single enemy fighter.

The surviving B-17s were returned to their original owner and the P-40s committed to England instead went to the Soviet Union. Alison accompanied them to help acquaint the Red Air Force with the machines. In an account, Alison reported, "We assisted the Russians in putting them together at Archangel, checked out the Russian pilots, and had a turn amongst the Russian squadrons. That was behind the front.

The German observation planes were coming over at that time and the Russians had nothing fast enough to intercept the JU-88s. After we had completed putting the P-40s together, they were very reluctant to let us see anything or do anything. I stayed five months, during which I was unable to get in any flying time."

Even earlier than those from the States rallied to the British cause, a handful of American airmen had begun to confront the Japanese in China. The founding father and leader for what stretched into an eight-year campaign was Claire Chennault, a college dropout, onetime factory worker, English teacher, and an old man of twenty-eight when as a reserve officer courtesy of the 1918 version of OCS he pinned on his Army wings. As a fighter pilot and instructor he innovated tactics. Chennault argued against individual dogfights and stressed that maneuvers and attacks in formation made the most effective use of fighter firepower.

Bluntly outspoken, Chennault criticized the hidebound tactics taught in Air Corps schools and argued vociferously for a greater role for fighters. An unwelcome scold to his superiors, Chennault, with his limited formal education, and never having been invited to attend the Command and General Staff School, a prerequisite to advancement by the mid-1930s, reached a dead end in the Air Corps. His treatises on air combat, however, had caught the attention of Chinese leaders desperately seeking help in an escalating struggle with Japan. In 1937, plagued by poor health, as a forty-seven-year-old captain about to be grounded for medical reasons, Chennault retired from the U.S. Air Corps and accepted a three-month contract at $1,000 a month plus expenses from the Chinese government for a study of its Air Force. Instead of ninety days, he would spend eight years in China battling the Japanese through the air.

Only a few months after Chennault set foot in Shanghai, the smoldering conflict with Japan burst into a full-fledged war. Chennault volunteered his services, not only because of his sympathy with his hosts but also because, "I wanted to give [his theories on aerial tactics] an acid test in combat." Generalissimo Chiang immediately accepted the offer, commissioning Chennault to oversee training of several squadrons of fighters and bombers. The actual command of the Chinese Air Force belonged to Gen. Peter Mow [Mow Pan-Tzu], a Soviet-trained flier. Chennault discovered his fliers unqualified, and worse, they viewed practice missions as beneath them. When he set up a raid the pilots dropped their bombs among civilians rather than the targeted enemy naval vessel. A day later the Chinese by error attacked a British cruiser in the Yangtze River.

Nevertheless, he started to achieve some results. Chennault launched his pilots against enemy attacks on Nanking and in five days they knocked down fifty-four planes. Although it was rumored that in these days Chennault himself engaged in the fighting, there is no evidence that he ever actually participated and even less confirmation for any planes shot down. Because of the Chennault tactics, the Japanese now tacked on fighters to escort bomber missions.

Madame Chiang persuaded Chennault against his better judgment to create an international squadron. Chinese pilots balked at taking orders from the outsiders, many of whom were undisciplined adventurers, boozers, and devotees of brothels when not in the air. After a few successful sorties, the enterprise literally went up in smoke. Perhaps because of careless talk during their carousing, the enemy got wind of a forthcoming raid. The U.S.-built Vultee bombers were gassed, armed, and all lined up on the airfield when the Japanese hit them at sundown. "What was left of the Chinese bombing force," said Chennault, "vanished in five seconds of flame and dust. With it went the jobs of the International Squadron pilots."

Discouraged, Chennault returned for a brief stay in the States where he sought to rejoin the Air Corps and contribute his considerable knowledge of Japanese tactics, pilots, and aircraft. The authorities showed no interest in him nor in his materials. Rejected at home, Chennault went back to China where all he could do was observe the Japanese take total control of the air. The Soviet squadrons had departed. The planes they sold to China proved no match for the enemy. Frustrated, the American continued to gather data and build his intelligence net. In October 1940, the Generalissimo asked Chennault to meet with T. V. Soong, the official arranging to buy military supplies in the States. Together they were to approach Washington in an effort to beg, borrow, or recruit the elements of an effective air force. Chennault sought to curry favor when he passed along to Army intelligence specifications for the latest Japanese fighter, the Zero. American aeronautical experts pored over the documents and then appraised the fighter described in the documents and its performance as impossible. The Air Corps itself never received a copy of the papers, thus making it understandable why pilots like John Carpenter were so ignorant of the enemy's capability. Henry "Hap" Arnold, head of the Air Corps, had nourished a grudge against Chennault ever since 1932 when he criticized maneuvers directed by Arnold. To others the former airman was an unknown retired captain in the pay of a foreign government.

On the other hand, T. V. Soong had access to top political circles. He deftly influenced movers and shakers already sympathetic to China and, spurred on by increased British anxiety over pressure on crown colonies in the Far East, he found willing audiences. With President Roosevelt's backing, 100 early model P-40s, originally destined for the British, who agreed to accept a later version, were shipped to China. There were problems with spare parts, ammunition, gunsights, radios, and other gear, but, more important, the plan included Americans with military aircraft experience. Recruiters circulated through the Marines, Navy, and Army, much to the outrage of local commanders as well as high brass unhappy at the loss of skilled people. Salaries for volunteers to maintain and fly ranged from $250 a month to $750 for a squadron leader, with some extra benefits such as a ration allowance and an unwritten agreement of bonuses for planes shot down. Pilots were guaranteed $600 a month over a one-year contract as employees of the innocent-sounding Central Aircraft Manufacturing Corporation (CAMC), a subsidiary of a Chinese military purchasing operation.

In June and July 1941, the first members of the American Volunteer Group (AVG), a mixed bag of pilots and ground personnel, with P-40s and spare parts, sailed for Rangoon, the Burmese port of entry to the Far East. From there they traveled to Toungoo, a former RAF field, to begin their indoctrination in the P-40 and the science of aerial warfare authored by Claire Chennault. When he finally reached Toungoo on 21 August Chennault's tiny air force seemed about to fall apart. In the midst of jungle and teak plantations the shabby town of Toungoo sweltered under 100-degree days laced with excessively high humidity. Insects gorged themselves on humans living in screenless barracks. Burmese cooks fed the Americans an unappetizing menu of fish and rice. Electricity flowed intermittently and while the men waited for airplanes they stewed in disillusion. Several pilots and ground crewmen handed in their resignations to

Chennault on the grounds of misrepresentation by CAMC. Shrewdly, the commander terminated these individuals. Once rid of them, he set hard rules. The contracts provided fines and dishonorable discharges for anyone who quit. He outlined a program of regular flight training, ground classes, and physical-fitness routines. Order was restored and as airplanes arrived, sagging spirits revived.

In March 1941, David Lee "Tex" Hill, son of a missionary in Korea, was a Navy pilot on the carrier *Ranger*. He recalled, "We were in Norfolk, Virginia, and we came down from a flight one day and a shipmate grabbed Ed Rector and me, took us to a room, and told a man there [retired Navy commander Rutledge Irvine], 'Here's a couple of guys who will go with you.' We didn't know what he was talking about. [Irvine] had a map and it showed Burma and where they were building the Burma Road and said they were looking for pilots to patrol this area. That sounded real good to us, adventurous. It was a fast deal—he explained it real fast. 'You'll get $600 a month and all you'll be doing is patrolling the Burma Road.' I don't think any in our group realized until we got there that our job would be any more than patrol work for the Burma Road.

"I'd always wanted to go to the Orient because I happened to be born in Korea. I'd sought to get an exchange from the carrier to one of the ships in the Far East. The thing that motivated me to go to China was more or less adventure. I knew Chennault was running the show but I knew nothing about him. We signed these contracts. Our skipper flew to Washington to see if he couldn't stop it because our particular squadron on the *Ranger* and the ship itself were operational, ready to go. Bert Christman, Ed Rector, and myself all had key positions. Eddie was in operations, I was assistant gunnery officer, and Christman was on the administrative end. When our skipper came back from Washington, he said, 'I don't know what's going on, fellows, but this is bigger than me.' He gave us all a big party.

"We landed in Rangoon in July 1941. I met Chennault there. I think anyone meeting him for the first time would definitely get the impression that he was a very dynamic, strong person and would get confidence in him. Chennault had wanted to recruit 100 pilots with 500 hours' experience. He went to Hap Arnold and asked for this and Hap said, 'Hell, we give you 100 pilots with that kind of experience, you'd fold up our whole pursuit section.' Chennault said, 'You can't spare me 100 pilots with that kind of experience, you don't have any pursuit section to begin with.' That kind of thing always got him in trouble with people."

In 1937, Jasper Harrington, son of an Alabama farmer, who enrolled in the Air Corps to become an airplane mechanic, saw a priority message from Air Corps headquarters about an opportunity to become part of a flying combat group in China. Harrington and several others signed contracts with CAMC. Harrington recalled arriving in Rangoon where the P-40s were off-loaded and assembled for flight to Toungoo. "The ship with the spare parts was sunk before it reached Rangoon. We received the 100 P-40s but one of them was dropped in the drink so we wound up with 99 and no spare parts." To keep AVG flying meant scrounging from the British, salvaging from the training crackups, with repairs not always as prescribed in manuals.

Hill remembered, "We went immediately up to Toungoo [Burma], which was the base where we were going to have training. I had never seen a P-40. This was the first in-line engine I'd seen. On the takeoff, that nose seemed big and heavy out front but once I got airborne I quickly got acquainted with the airplane. You never forget the basic things.

You crawl in an airplane and it takes you an hour or two, you feel at home. You get confidence in your plane, you have complete confidence you can do anything with it you need. The old man made me feel there wasn't anything we couldn't do in it, that we could handle the situation with the equipment we had, if we used it properly. Chennault conducted tactical lectures and then we would go out and practice in the air. He tried to get us around fifty hours in these planes.

"He had blackboard and chalk. He exhibited the type of formation that we would fly and the tactics that we would use against the Japs. It was a two-ship element, the basic formation, and that was the first time I ever heard of it. In the Navy we flew three ships [the Vee] and that was basic in the Air Corps, too. He believed the basic element being two ships, he could build it on up—four, six—always working in pairs. As long as you have two, you have a combat team. I think this was his innovation. Later, everybody went to it. In the Navy they called it the Thacweave. I was on the same ship with Jim Thach when, hell, we were still flying three-ship elements.

"I got the very distinct impression from his lectures that he had actually engaged the Japanese Zero. A man couldn't talk about just exactly how this plane was going to react unless he had encountered it, and how we would use our equipment to the best advantage against it." For the heavy P-40 that amounted to speed while diving rather than maneuvers in tight turns. "That was the secret to the whole thing, as long as we followed [what Chennault taught] we had no problem. Everything he told us in his tactical lectures happened. When we made our first contacts with these enemy Zeros they behaved as he said they would."

Chennault brought to the table more than personal observation. He relied on captured manuals and lectured that the enemy were well trained but lacked initiative and improvisation. "They have been drilled for hundreds of hours in flying precise formations and rehearsing set tactics for each situation they encounter. Japanese pilots fly by the book, and these are the books they use. Study them and you will always be one step ahead of the enemy." He counseled his fliers to make a pass, shoot, and then break off. "You need to sharpen your shooting eye. Nobody ever gets too good at gunnery. The more Japs you get with your first burst, the fewer there are to jump you later. Accurate fire saves ammunition. Your plane carries a limited number of bullets."

On the cusp between training and operations against the Japanese, several pilots thought up the idea of decorating their dull, olive-drab P-40s with nose art. Chennault, aware of the need for boosts in morale, agreed for mechanics to paint a malevolent eye over sharklike teeth. Later he remarked, "How the term Flying Tigers was derived from the shark-nosed P-40s I will never know." Nevertheless the sobriquet soon became popular.

During the first months of the outfit's life, morale dove and soared. Beset by wretched living conditions, substandard equipment, and inadequate supplies, it was not a well-disciplined collection of men. Rather it was a mixture of idealists, soldiers of fortune, and hard-living types like Greg "Pappy" Boyington, who subsequently won renown as a Marine pilot. Over the years, the AVG people developed an élan, a spirit derived from their commander. Bruce Holloway, USMA 1937, who joined the Flying Tigers early in 1943, offered an objective view of Chennault. "As far as being a tactician is concerned, and particularly as being able to practically read the minds of the enemy, the Japanese over there, he was unequaled. He could tell you what they were going to do the next day almost 100 percent. He would back you to the hilt. His two biggest faults were related. He was about the poorest loser that I have ever seen.

"We would play softball and he was the pitcher on my ball team. He was a pretty good pitcher except he would get tired after about the third or fourth inning. We would always be ahead then and we would always lose the game, couldn't get him out of there. He would sort of sulk off. That night, he would want to play badminton. Any one of us could beat him at badminton. Then he would want to play Ping-Pong. Any one of us could beat him at Ping-Pong.

"He would get lower and lower and if we had any whiskey, we would drink that. He would sometimes end up wanting to wrestle somebody and he would usually challenge Casey Vincent, who was the biggest guy. Casey would stave him off, usually until he went off to bed or we ate dinner. But once in a while he would grab Casey and end up getting thrown over in the corner. He was just a terribly poor loser. The related part is he couldn't get along with anybody above him unless they absolutely agreed with him. He didn't know the meaning of the word compromise. . . . He would go out of channels. He made a mission back to the States once because the president wrote him a letter and said he would like to see him. He went all the way back to Washington and saw the president, just bypassed channels. You just don't do things like that."

Chennault organized the group into three squadrons, "Adam and Eve" led by Robert Sandell, "Panda Bears" under Jack Newkirk, and "Hell's Angels" commanded by Arvid "Oley" Olson. The primary mission of the AVG was to protect both ends of the Burma Road, China's only access to supplies. Chennault stationed Hell's Angels in Rangoon and the other pair at Kunming. As the Flying Tigers entered the final stages of preparation to intercept the almost-daily raids of Kunming by Japanese bombers, a dispatch from RAF headquarters in Rangoon advised Chennault of Pearl Harbor.

The actual baptism of fire for the new air force began on 20 December, as the early-warning system alerted Chennault of ten enemy bombers headed toward Kunming. A total of twenty-four P-40s in three elements scrambled in midmorning. A section of four shark-toothed fighters spotted the twin-engine raiders. Buck fever momentarily slowed reaction. The enemy jettisoned their ordnance and slipped into cloud cover. Chennault, alerted by radio to the situation, quickly calculated the most likely course of retreat and directed the other interceptors accordingly. The overanxious Americans forgot about tactics and fell on the planes haphazardly. Nevertheless, they closed sufficiently to pour .50-caliber bullets into the targets, sending six crashing to the ground with smoke pouring from the badly damaged survivors.

In Rangoon, three days later, Americans and RAF pilots took off with reports of a formation of fifty-four bombers advancing on the city. Oley Olson led the fifteen P-40s and eighteen British Brewster Buffalo fighters circled at 18,000 feet as a reception committee. The enemy approached from the east, at an altitude of 16,000 feet. The hosts dived on the formation of bombers, ripping up gas tanks, wings, and fuselages. Even as a number of the enemy smoked, burned, and exploded, others bore down on the Mingaladon Airfield blasting barracks, the operations building, and the radio shack while strafing runs shot up ground crews. Some attacked the docks and shipping, inflicting heavy damage.

One of the Americans, Robert "Duke" Hedman, a former Army flyer, hitherto regarded as a by-the-book aviator who had outrun another Flying Tiger to take off in an available

P-40, astonished everyone by achieving ace status with the knockdown of five enemy planes in that one day. In contrast to his reputation, Hedman had been described by an RAF pilot over Rangoon as "a ruddy idiot" when he observed him amidst the swarm of Japanese bombers fleeing toward Thailand. The final count for the day confirmed 25 planes shot out of the sky by the AVG, and the British recorded 7 more. Losses to the Americans were 2 pilots and 3 planes, while their allies suffered 5 KIA and 11 Buffalos wrecked.

Two days later, on Christmas Day, a force of nearly 100 Japanese bombers and escorts zeroed in on Rangoon. The outnumbered defenders could muster only a dozen P-40s and sixteen Buffalos. Four enemy attacked Hedman while he busily pursued a Nakajima I-97 fighter and blew off his canopy, forcing him to set down at a satellite airstrip. British ground forces confirmed 28 Japanese downed, with the AVG claiming 17 of the victims. No Americans were lost.

Chennault dispatched the Panda Bears to relieve the battered Hell's Angels in Rangoon. Tex Hill's introduction to combat occurred over Tak, Thailand. "Jack Newkirk was my squadron leader, and there was Jim Howard, Bert Christman, and myself. Newkirk had Christman flying his wing, Howard was leading my element, and I was flying his wing. We took off early one morning and went over to this airdrome. Christman developed engine trouble and had to come back. We went over at an altitude of 10,000 feet, dropped down on this airdrome. When we made this run on the field, the first thing I know when we pulled up—hell, there are more of us in the circle.

"When we pulled up there was a Jap coming toward Newkirk. He just turned into him head-on, just as Newkirk pulled off his first strafing pass. He just disintegrated. Then I looked around and here was this Jap on Jim Howard's tail, just sitting back there. I hate to say this, but I don't think that Jim even knew that we had been attacked from above on this trip until we got back. I shot the Jap off his tail because I was so nervous. I was so excited, hell, I wasn't even looking through the gunsight. I was just looking through the windshield. Of course, we had tracer bullets. It was just like putting a hose on a man. I just flew right up the guy's tail and brought around on him. I saw it set on fire and it went down.

"In the meantime, a fellow had made a pass on me from overhead that I didn't see. Why I didn't get it, I don't know, because when I got back I had thirty-three holes in my plane. I felt it when it hit and looked back down. I could see the metal on the wings turn back. I don't know whether it was the way his guns were bore-sighted but it was just at the critical point where they intersected and began to spread. The holes were on either side of my wings. I began learning fast from that time on. I think my neck size increased about an inch, keeping my head on a swivel, looking around."

As enemy forces pushed through the Philippines and the Asian mainland, while German armor rolled on in North Africa, U.S. sources, desperate for any good news in the early months of the war, pumped up stories about the AVG in action. Winston Churchill cabled the governor of Burma: "The magnificent victories these Americans have won in the air over the paddy fields of Burma are comparable in character, if not in scope, with those won by the Royal Air Force over the orchards and hop fields of Kent in the Battle of Britain."

The successes of the AVG and of the RAF notwithstanding, the Japanese Army relentlessly pushed toward Rangoon and all along the coast. Mitsubishi bombers and Zero fighters continued to smash at targets in Burma and China. Fearful his command would become a subsidiary of the British in Burma, and perceiving the imminent loss of the country along with the entire Malay Peninsula, Chennault contrived to withdraw his tiny armada to China. He also started to bill for the $500 bonuses China had verbally agreed to pay per shot-down enemy plane.

While that bolstered his pilots' morale, Chennault coped with his precarious position. Ostensibly on the grounds of efficiency, he pleaded to keep the AVG as an independent duchy under contract to China. The Air Corps, intent upon setting its chain of command in order, began steps to restore him to active duty with the eventual goal of installing more tractable officers over him. The harsh air war in the China-Burma-India (CBI) Theater would be accompanied by nasty strife among those running the show.

6

Retreat

HAVING SUCCESSFULLY RAVAGED THE AMERICAN FLEET AT Pearl Harbor, Imperial Japan focused on demolishing the remnants of the first lines of U.S. defenses in the Far East. Guam, a U.S. possession dating back to the Spanish-American War and a lone outpost amid the otherwise Japanese-held Marianas, succumbed after a twenty-five-minute token defense on 10 December. But when the Japanese, on 11 December, attacked a second chunk of American turf, Wake Island, roughly halfway between Hawaii and Guam, they encountered dogged resistance from a small band of Marines backed by a few airplanes and former naval guns installed as artillery. Not until 23 December did the defenders run up a white flag. In their zeal to boost U.S. morale, the military flacks claimed the Wake Marine commander, Maj. James P. Devereaux, at the onset of the assault responded to a query of what he needed: "Send us more Japs." Undoubtedly aware of the overwhelming forces arrayed against Wake, Devereaux never issued any such statement.

And as these two puny bastions fell, the Imperial ground forces struck at the heart of the U.S. interests in the Philippines. The badly rattled members of Sam Grashio's 21st Pursuit Squadron regrouped at Nichols Field, minus a number of their planes and pilots, early casualties, on the afternoon of 8 December. Under orders, Ed Dyess gathered the remnants of his flock and led them back to Clark Field where, according to Grashio, he guided them safely down to a field pitted with craters and covered with several inches of dust as fine as flour.

"That night we survivors," recalled Grashio, "still half-dazed, slept in the jungle. When we awoke at dawn, somewhat recovered from the shock of the previous day's disaster, it occurred to someone that we might be caught napping again, so we were ordered to take our P-40s up to 15,000 feet and get into position ready to attack. When a plane taxied to takeoff position, the cloud of dust that rose exceeded in size and density anything I had ever seen prior to the clouds caused by the bombing of the day before. Moreover, the field was full of bomb craters. Thus, three-minute intervals were prescribed between takeoffs.

"Even so, there were several accidents. One pilot lost his engine, careened madly into the jungle, and was killed. I got airborne without mishap but Bob Clark, who followed me, did not allow enough time for the dust to settle, lost his way, and crashed blindly into a parked B-17 bomber. There was a sudden flash of light, a violent explosion, and hail of bullets all over the area as flaming gasoline from the plane's ruptured tanks set off the six loaded .50-caliber machine guns it carried. Bob was killed instantly.

"My own promising start was short-lived," Grashio continued, "At about 9,000 feet, my engine started cutting out and losing power. Down I came, trying desperately to identify the problem and to restrain my panic. Soon the engine cut in again, then went out, then cut in once more. Gradually I gained control of the plane in the sense that I felt reasonably sure I could land, though it was clear I could not maintain flying speed. The sticking point was that there was a certain identification procedure for landing that specified entry corridors. This I would have to ignore if I was to get the plane down at all. So I came in from an unexpected direction. Our antiaircraft batteries, understandably trigger happy after the events of the day before, promptly opened fire on me. Fortunately, their marksmanship had not improved overnight. I got down unscathed." Mechanics went to work on Grashio's P-40 and that afternoon, another pilot tried to take the plane up. The engine quit during takeoff, causing a fatal crash.

For Alva Fitch, with a battery of 2.95-inch mountain guns, the commotion caused among his troops by the raid at nearby Clark Field on 8 December remained his only glimpse of the war, as nearly two uneventful days passed. A short distance from Stotsenburg, Fitch had posted sentries at a jungle bivouac. A rumored parachute assault brought a summons for Fitch's unit to protect Stotsenburg. "The Battery looked ridiculous with the guns dug in in front of Post Headquarters, astride the flagpole, shooting toward the hospital. On the morning of the tenth, a flight of twenty-seven bombers raided Stotsenburg without much damage. They bombed the stables and the utilities. Several cavalry horses were killed or wounded. The ice plant was put out of order."

Major Philip Fry had seized an opportunity to volunteer his services to the 57th Infantry, the well established Philippine Scouts regiment. "This decision cost me an immediate promotion to Lt. Colonel but was well worth it. The CO of the 57th, Col. George Clarke, was visibly pleased to have a few senior officers assigned. The 57th had been badly depleted of senior people by the organization of the Philippine Army. All they had left were a bunch of youngsters. My rank entitled me to Ted Lilly's job as executive officer but I wanted my own command of combat troops and asked for a battalion. I was assigned the 3d, Frank Brokaw the 2d Battalion. We were given guides and staff cars and off we went to locate our new commands.

"The 3d Battalion position was located in a draw between officers' row [housing designed for commanders] and Guadaloupe. The units were badly congested and a beautiful target for the bombing attack I expected in a few minutes. I assembled the officers and informed them of my assumption of command. They were all so young, and a bit dazed by the speed of events. We started preparations for a move that night. We had sufficient weapons carriers but needed buses to move the men. I was given thirty-three civilian buses and two Ford sedans for me and my staff. At dusk we started out and it was a terrible nightmare. My orders were changed so many times they had me dizzy. Our convoy of about sixty vehicles was turned around. The roads were jammed; every mile there was a traffic jam. On both sides the rice paddies were flooded. There was absolutely no cover of any kind. All officers were on foot, trying to make our way through. We were in a helluva fix and the Philippine defense could have been given a mortal blow that night, but the Nips were busy working our airfields.

"We broke through and headed for San Fernando. Our position was regimental reserve near Florida Blanca. We were the first battalion to arrive and were completely under cover by daylight. Poor George Clarke was there and frantic about the remainder of the regiment. He kept bothering me about them until I suggested he go look for them because we were busy. Not a nice gesture but I was provoked beyond endurance."

On a map, the island of Luzon has the rough shape of a mitten, with the thumb at the left as it narrows toward its southern end. From the northern tip, about 275 miles from Manila, extend several rugged mountain ranges that peter out into the central plains just above the city. An invasion force striking at the fingertips would have a long, difficult line of march toward Manila, particularly against a well-orchestrated defense. However, the space between the thumb and the rest of the glove approximates the Lingayen Gulf, an indentation from which a network of highways and roads led to Manila and an attractive route for conquest.

General Jonathan Wainwright commanded the forces assigned to wall off all of northern Luzon. Under him served three Philippine Army divisions, a Philippine Scout cavalry regiment, an infantry battalion, a single battery of field artillery—Alva Fitch's outfit—and a supply unit. On paper it was a formidable number of soldiers, but the territory stretched over thousands of square miles including mile upon mile of beach. The steep mountains, thick vegetation, and lack of many suitable roads restricted communication and movement. Wainwright's army was little more than a paper organization. The Filipino divisions expected to halt any enemy incursions were of the ilk described by Glen Townsend and Clifford Bluemel: reservists summoned to duty in September, most of whom had little instruction in the art of war. The problems of supply storage loomed larger in light of limited means of transport. After Rainbow Five supplanted War Plan Orange, ammunition, foodstuffs, and other necessities had been moved to sites spread around Luzon.

The Japanese came ashore at two ports, Aparri, located at the tip of what would be a ring finger in the Luzon mitten, and at Vigan, along the western shore. So thin were Wainwright's forces, he had only a single company of infantry in the vicinity of Aparri and not a man at Vigan. The initial troops splashing ashore at Aparri probably numbered about 2,000. To the eye of the U.S. officer in charge, however, the invaders seemed five times as many. Since he had less than 200 untrained and ill-equipped defenders he ordered a retreat without firing a single shot.

From Del Carmen, Lt. Samuel Marrett led his squadron on a mission. "After takeoff," recalled Tom Gage, "there were conflicting orders to change the destination." Marrett chose to intercept at Vigan rather than Aparri. Deteriorated engines forced nine of the sixteen P-35s to abort and scramble to turn back. P-40s that preceded the 34th to the area had been able to work over the landing forces with fragmentation bombs and strafing runs after Japanese air cover had left.

With only pairs of .30- and .50-caliber machine guns, the remnants of the 34th dove on the beachhead, the barges, and some larger vessels near the shore. Marrett led the attack, picking out for himself a 10,000-ton vessel. He made several passes at it and then bore in at almost masthead height while surrounding cruisers and destroyers threw shells at him. Just as the squadron commander began to pull out of his dive, his target blew up; he apparently had ignited an ammunition cache. The blast ripped away the wing of Marrett's aircraft. Other pilots saw his plane crash into the sea even as debris from his victim started to splash down into the water.

"The squadron came back to Del Carmen just before noon," says Gage. "I remember one of the pilots remarking how machine gunning the troops landing on the beach made him sick at his stomach because of the slaughter." But there was neither time to mourn Marrett nor listen to war stories at Del Carmen. "We had some P-40s there fueling up. As the P-35s came in and landed, some Zeros came right in with them. They proceeded to beat up the base camp and shoot up the line. Myself, my two clerks Robert Reynolds and Dermott Toycen, Lieutenant Jennings, and several pilot officers ran over the hill away from the line and lay down flat. We couldn't see but could sure hear. Spent bullets buzzed around. One clanged off the edge of Reynolds's tin helmet.

"The attack only lasted a few minutes but it seemed like hours. After the enemy left, it was real quiet—then we could hear the flames crackling. We could see a P-40 hooked to a gasoline truck, both on fire. One of our men had been caught in the open and took cover under the gasoline-tank truck. After tracers set that on fire, he slipped under the P-40. When the fire traveled down the hose and set the plane on fire, he just got up and strolled away, ignoring the strafing completely. On this day all the propaganda rubbish about the inferior Japanese material went down the drain. Those fuel wing tanks dropped by the Zeros were far better than ours."

As the Filipino infantry hastily backed off, the one blow aimed at the incoming troops near Aparri came from the sky. Remnants of the Air Corps in the shape of a pair of B-17s attacked the landing fleet. Captain Colin Kelly piloted one of the two ships. With Clark patched up enough to service B-17s, Kelly, and several others, arrived from Mindanao on the morning of 10 December to carry out missions against an aircraft carrier reported in the neighborhood. In the air, Kelly, toting three 600-pound bombs in his racks, became separated from the others as he headed north. From almost four miles up, the crew gazed down on the enemy ships, some of whom blasted away at the coastline while others ferried in men and supplies. Kelly ignored these targets for the moment and searched for the aircraft carrier but, although the hunt went almost to Formosa, the target was never spotted. Returning toward Luzon, the airman picked out the biggest vessel off the coast, what they believed was a battleship.

Bombardier Meyer Levin, a corporal in an Air Corps era when the job did not carry a commission, tracked the target and at the appropriate moment released the bombs. To the men in the Fort, it appeared as if they scored two near misses and one direct hit. Kelly headed for home but not before his navigator Lt. Joe Bean noticed far below a half-dozen Japanese fighter planes taking off from the Aparri airfield now possessed by the enemy.

The Americans, descending through the clouds, prepared for touchdown at Clark. Suddenly the navigator's dome exploded into pieces and the instrument panel shattered. A burst of fire beheaded the radio operator stationed at the left waist gun and wounded another gunner. Fighters had tracked them more than 100 miles and closed in for the kill. Bullets ripped into the left wing, fire enveloped the ship; the fuel tanks of the earliest B-17s were not self-sealing.

Kelly consulted the crew on the damage, ordered them to bail out. Levin and Bean frantically worked to pry open the bottom escape hatch, whose pins were corroded. Levin went first and then Bean, who saw the copilot Lt. Donald Robins moving toward the top escape hatch. The aircraft disintegrated with a mighty blast. Dangling from his parachute, Bean saw four others swinging in the air. Still not finished, the enemy fighters swept by to strafe the men floating down. A bullet chipped Bean's ankle but the others escaped unscathed. Search teams from Clark found the badly burned copilot, who had been blasted free of the ship when it exploded. Somehow he managed to yank his ripcord and reach the ground alive. But Kelly's body was discovered amid the wreckage. He was the first graduate of the USMA to die in the defense of the Philippines.

With only defeats to announce, the authorities quickly proclaimed Kelly a hero and awarded him a posthumous Distinguished Service Cross for allegedly sinking the battleship *Haruna*. Post–World War II research revealed no battleship ever was in the area nor did the attack sink any Japanese ship. Samuel Marrett, who probably struck a more effective blow for the cause and with greater disregard for his own survival, received a Distinguished Service Cross, but none of the fame and glory accorded Kelly. Marrett, as a mustang, or former enlisted man elevated to the ranks of the commissioned, struck his chief clerk, Tom Gage, as a "bitter" man. For reasons of personality, background, or misperception of the events, the publicity focused on the West Pointer.

John Carpenter, as a B-17 pilot whose suicidal mission to Formosa fell through only after his generators failed, during the first few days flew missions from the patched runways at Clark. "On the third day of the war, I had been up to Lingayen Gulf and I was briefed for the next mission while my airplane was being serviced. We were just ready to go, walking over to the airplane and a flight of three P-40s was taking off. It was in the dry season and it was a sod field. It was pretty dusty. The third guy in the [P-40] element got disoriented in the dust and got off course on his takeoff and ran right through my B-17. He hit just outboard of the outboard engine, took off the wing, went right through, and broke our back halfway down the fuselage.

"He turned around 180 degrees facing the other way. We ran over. I expected it to burst into flames and we thought we would pull him out. There wasn't anything left of that fighter except the pilot's seat, and he was sitting strapped in it. His right hand was on the stick; his left on the throttle. There wasn't anything else left of that airplane. He looked at us; we looked at him. He reached down and undid his safety belt, got out, and said, 'Goddamn,' walked away. He ruined my airplane and that was serious because that was my means of escape from the Philippines.

"We had moved our ground echelons out from Clark and set up a camp on the Bamban River. The Japs used to come by and strafe us about three times a day. But we all had pretty good slit trenches and we didn't lose many people. But every time an airplane came in to be repaired, serviced, or whatever, my crew and I were on hand saying, 'Aren't you very tired? Don't you want to rest a while and let us take this next mission?' We want to get our hands on an airplane but you can bet your boots they all said, 'Oh, no. I am not tired.' They might have flown five missions that day but they weren't going to get out of their airplane because they knew what was going on."

The Air Corps had succeeded in disrupting the beachhead at Vigan with the early morning raid by five B-17s accompanied by P-40s and then the 34th's P-35s. The attacks damaged and beached a pair of transports, sank a minesweeper, inflicted some damage to a pair of warships, and chewed up a number of soldiers. But it was the last well-choreographed effort by the FEAF (Far East Air Force) as successive waves of enemy planes reduced U.S. Philippine air operations to spasms of little import. The run at Del Carmen had destroyed twelve P-35s, damaged the remaining six so badly that the 34th to all intents and purposes was grounded. Conditions were almost as bad with other squadrons. At nightfall 10 December, the defenders could count only thirty airworthy fighters.

Americans in Manila began to appreciate the situation. On duty at Sternberg General Hospital, Madeline Ullom recalled, "A large formation of silver planes were silhouetted against the blue sky. The rumor must surely be true. We smiled. Reinforcements had arrived. Bombs suddenly began to drop on the nearby Pasig River. Shell windows fell from the eye-ear-nose-throat clinic. Crystal chandeliers in the officers' ward dining room swayed from the ceiling. The sound of the bombs hurt our eardrums. The feeling pierced our hearts. The truth was apparent. We were soon to remark, 'If you see one plane flying in formation, you know it is ours.' "

The defenders were confused and back on their heels. One American officer with the 21st Philippine Division said that after some dark shapes hovered near the mouth of the Agno River, a field artillery unit opened up. "It was like dropping a match in a warehouse of Fourth of July fireworks," he remarked. "Instantly Lingayen Gulf was ablaze. As far as the eye could see the flashes of artillery, shell-bursts, tracer machine gun bullets, and small arms . . . Thousands of shadows were killed that night." Townsend recalled, "On the night of 10 December, I heard a fusillade of rifle and machine gun fire on a nearby river."

In the morning, the only evidence of anything amiss was a single life preserver which may not even have been Japanese. Neither sunken vessels nor corpses of blasted bodies were found. "Later," said Townsend, "we read in the Manila papers that the Japs had landed at Lingayen but after a terrific battle they had been annihilated." The erroneous report of the victory originated with a Filipino commander who insisted his forces repulsed an enemy landing. Investigation after the war revealed a single enemy motorboat had ventured into the area on a reconnaissance.

Alva Fitch noted, "In general things were fairly quiet. A tremendous amount of false information continued to come by telegraph. This kept the staff in turmoil. Apparently there were a lot of fifth columnists in the telegraph system. It was so bad that all information and even orders received by telegraph were suspect and had to be verified. A few days after the landing at Vigan, we received a telegram from a 'Colonel Jones' of the constabulary saying that a column of 40,000 Japs with some mechanized equipment was marching south from Vigan to Damortis. It was fairly routine to hear of fictitious landings in force, of parachute landings, and of large Jap convoys. The telegraph service became so unreliable that eventually motor or airplane couriers were used for delivery of most important orders."

The confusion created by poor communications, misinformation, and unwillingness to digest bad news affected MacArthur's judgment. Even *after* the war was over he would write in his *Reminiscences*: "On December 10th . . . Twelve transports with naval escorts landed troops at Aparri in the north and Vigan on the west coast. Our air force attacked these transports sinking four and damaging three others. [Actually, the foe lost only three of its troop and cargo carriers.] . . . At the end of the first week of war there had been many widely scattered actions, but the all-out attack had not yet come. The enemy had carried out fourteen major air raids, but paid dearly in the loss of transports, planes, and troops, and at least two major warships damaged. He had attempted a landing in the Lingayen area, but was repulsed with severe loss by a Philippine Army division. At Aparri, Vigan, and Legaspi there had been only local activity."

In fact, the Japanese at Clark Field lost only seven fighters compared with the horrendous damage done to American planes, personnel, and installations. Americans were credited with four kills at Del Carmen but lost an entire squadron. The enemy casualties at other airfields, at Cavite, and other navy bases were similarly negligible when weighed against the damage inflicted. The Lingayen defeat was sheer fantasy and the "local activity" at the three Luzon sites amounted to a firm foothold on the island. As Wainwright put it, "The rat was in the house."

What was true was that the main body of MacArthur's army had yet to engage the enemy. The Japanese units, under Lt. Gen. Masaharu Homma, Fourteenth Army commander, rapidly trekked south in a strategy designed to pinch off northern Luzon. The objective of the invaders from the west was control of Lingayen Gulf. With that site in hand, large numbers of troops and their supplies could be aimed at Manila. Meanwhile, another unopposed landing on the southeastern coast at Legaspi on 12 December confronted the defenders with an enemy at the backdoor.

The booty for the Japanese included an airstrip near Legaspi. Three B-17s, operating from the Del Monte base, attempted to attack the occupants only to discover themselves overmatched against the now-resident Japanese fighter planes. Only one Fort managed to escape unscathed to the home base; the two others crash-landed. Further operations by the big bombers from Del Monte were in jeopardy. MacArthur agreed with Brereton's decision to move the remainder of the B-17s to Darwin, Australia. They flew off on 15 December, four days before a series of heavy assaults from the air upon Del Monte. Among those left behind was John Carpenter.

Whether MacArthur at the time of the first Japanese landings truly believed he still had a shot at denying the enemy the Philippines, he early on realized the shakiness of such an ambitious strategy. On 12 December he sent word to Que-

zon, the Philippine president, to ready himself for movement to Corregidor on four hours' notice. "Startled" by the
ominous import, Quezon conferred with MacArthur that
evening. MacArthur said there was no immediate concern
but only that he was "preparing for the worst in case the
Japanese should land in great force at different places."
Under these circumstances, explained MacArthur, effective
strategy would require a concentration of Fil-American
units and the site would be Bataan.

And to the horror of Quezon, MacArthur added that the
plan would require shift of his headquarters, the high commissioner's office, and the Commonwealth government to
the rocky fastness of Corregidor. In this event he would declare Manila an open city. An incredulous Quezon asked,
"Do you mean, General, that tomorrow you will declare
Manila an open city and that sometime during the day we
shall have to go to Corregidor?" MacArthur reassured Quezon that this was just contingency strategy and he merely
wanted the president to be aware of the possibility.

At the start of hostilities, Wainwright assigned Clifford
Bluemel and the 31st Philippine Army Division responsibility for defending the South China Sea coastline near
Zambales, perhaps sixty miles south of the Lingayen Gulf
landing zones. Nearly a week of war had passed when
Bluemel discovered that his latest additions, artillerymen
who had undergone basic training, had never fired their
75mm guns. Under his instructions, each battery expended
two rounds per gun because that was all he felt he could
spare. Bluemel, outraged by the responsibilities thrust upon
an "untrained rabble," was equally vehement in his dispar-
agement of the revised Rainbow Five that expected units
such as his to repulse the Japanese. "MacArthur and Sutherland were trying to draw up a plan in a few days after dis-

carding the one that had been worked on for twenty-five years, which to me, shows inability to command." He criticized his commander for a strategy that ignored the peculiarities of terrain and roads. "MacArthur practically had no transportation for us. He was too busy thinking about meeting them at the beaches. The artillery was old wooden-wheeled artillery and I had nothing to tow it. We had to portage it. I sent a young officer to a mine and he confiscated some fifty trucks and brought them to me. We pushed the guns up on the trucks to portage them. We couldn't tow them because the wooden wheels would fall off if we went at truck speed. We could not even have run three or four miles an hour with them, the way we moved horse-drawn artillery. It's something MacArthur should have known."

The 31st Division area included the now-destroyed airfield at Iba. According to Bluemel, some of the American enlisted men "took to the hills" after the air raids blasted their base. "A Filipino came to me with a note from them, 'We won't come in unless we get a note that it's all right.' They thought the Japs had landed." A handwritten message from Bluemel convinced the fugitives that Americans still controlled the territory and they returned.

Bluemel had the habit of riding his horse up and down his zone during the night. He said, "I came in from reconnaissance on the morning of the 24th of December. I had a Filipino officer, Pastor Martelino, who was a graduate of West Point and a very intelligent man who said, 'There's a message in code.' But I had no code; we had no code book. I got on the phone and found somebody who had a code book. He sent it out to me, and I translated it: 'You will move your division to Bataan immediately.' I started the movement with buses of the Trytran Bus Company [which I confiscated]. A fellow named [Ramón] Magsaysay was the manager; he later became president of the Philippines. Magsaysay went with me in charge of the buses."

As early as 19 December, signs of a reversion to War Plan Orange—retreat to Bataan in hopes of preserving a presence until relief could arrive—showed up in the deployment of the Fil-American forces. The 26th Cavalry, a Philippine Scout regiment, had traveled north to meet the invaders and Fitch's guns accompanied them. But while in bivouac Fitch received word consigning his battery to Bataan. The artillerymen marched south for three nights where Fitch heard the disquieting news to continue their retreat.

"The Philippine Army was withdrawing into Bataan," Fitch said. "General Bluemel's division from Zambales was coming in the night. Time was of the essence. The only road would be no place for mules [used to pull the pack artillery pieces] with a division of the Philippine Army using it. There was no other course but to go on to Balanga in the daylight. This was no pleasant prospect. To move my mules down a narrow road, entirely flanked by impassable fish ponds, in daylight through heavy traffic, and with Jap planes swarming overhead, would not be pleasant.

"The Battery had marched all night with full war loads and the men and animals were dead tired. We began arriving about dusk. The animals were strung out at long intervals. I rode my horse off the road into a grass plot in the public square to watch them pass. A couple of policemen came rushing out of the municipio to tell me of my outrage and to save their lawn. I hadn't the heart to tell them their damned town would be blown off the map in a few hours. We made bivouac that night in a semiexhausted state. We had marched from Tarlac in three days, and more than thirty-five miles in twenty-four hours."

Fitch said that several nights after he reached Bataan a

commotion that included artillery fire awakened him to a possible surprise assault. He and an associate reconnoitered and discovered his fears were groundless. But enroute to his bivouac area he stalled in a traffic jam. "While we were waiting," reported Fitch, "a man stuck his pistol against my ear and told us to get moving or he would kill us. It was General Bluemel. He had been reduced to a state of semi-insanity by the task of moving his division from Zambales to Bataan, and was trying to clear the traffic jam before daylight. We helped him and got home before morning."

Philip Fry, with the 3d Battalion of the 57th Infantry, also initially moved to block the Japanese advance. "On December 19, because of probable landings at Subic Bay near Olongapo, orders came to move there and defend the Zig Zag Trail in that sector. This being a daylight move, I instructed all units to maintain thirty seconds between any vehicles to avoid any tendencies to close up on straight stretches."

The troops reached their designated spot and started to dig in and prepare defenses covering the trails. But as Fry and the others in the outfit readied themselves for battle once again they received new instructions and shifted their location. By the end of December, the 57th had withdrawn to Bataan, to occupy the right flank of defenses from Mabatang on the shore of Manila Bay and behind the Balantay River in a line that extended westward for about three-quarters of a mile.

There were no significant Air Corps resources available to ravage the fleet in the Lingayen Gulf, but the U.S. Navy still had one seemingly puissant weapon, its flotilla of submarines. Admiral Hart dispatched three undersea boats to strike the enemy ships. The USS *Stingray*, USS *Saury*, and USS *Salmon* all slipped in among the covey of troop ships, freighters, landing craft, and warships debarking men. The invasion force was already in the shoal waters near the shore by the time the three subs got into position to make their forays. But they sank only two vessels.

Charles Adair, a member of Admiral Hart's staff, remarked, "These people would fire. They could see the torpedoes and knew where they were going. They could hear them hit, bounce off, and nothing happened. Then they would get a terrific depth-charging, for the Japanese destroyers would chase them, drive them under, and depth-charge them. The Lingayen Gulf is not very deep anyway—in some places about 120 feet or even less. When they came back and Admiral Hart wanted to know what happened they'd tell him they hadn't sunk anything. He would want to know why and they were unable to tell him. General MacArthur would want to know why the submarines hadn't been able to sink any ships with the torpedoes and I'm sure Admiral Hart had no answers to give him. He couldn't believe that such well-trained submarine officers could be so ineffective. That went on until morale was very low so far as the submariners were concerned."

How many of the invaders at Lingayen and elsewhere were framed in the periscopes and had torpedoes unloosed at them is unknown. But the consistently disappointing results underscored a miserable failure in Navy weaponry. In an effort to conserve funds, the standard Mark-14 torpedo, at $10,000 apiece, was considered so expensive that it had never been tested with a live warhead. Instead, during peacetime submarines and destroyers fired missiles armed with water-filled warheads. Once the war began, the Mark-14 more often than not failed to hit the target or to explode when it managed to home in. Not until 1943 would Bureau of Ordnance experts finally correct problems with the depth mechanism and exploders.

The ill-prepared pair of Philippine Army divisions assigned to block entry at Lingayen folded quickly, although an occasional unit fought bravely before being overrun. The Filipino soldiers streamed backward in an ever-deepening rout. The chief resistance to the advance came from Fitch's former associates, the 26th Cavalry, Philippine Scouts, mounted on horses, "a true cavalry delaying action, fit to make a man's heart sing," commented ex-cavalryman Jonathan Wainwright.

But two days after landing, as Christmas Eve approached, the Fourteenth Army under Homma grasped the best roads in the islands, daggers pointed at Manila. Although Homma's forces that came ashore at the Lingayen sites added up to 43,000 men, MacArthur informed Marshall that the invaders numbered from 80,000 to 100,000 and he could only field about 40,000, "in units partially equipped." In fact, MacArthur actually had probably double the number of men in uniform commanded by Homma. The reinforcements aboard the *Pensacola*-led convoy, however, including a light bomber squadron and more P-40s, detoured to Australia. The general himself traveled by Packard automobile into Luzon to confer with Wainwright, who now asked permission to retreat. A message from Gen. George Parker, the Southern Luzon commander, reported that 10,000 Japanese from the Lamon Bay landings were advancing on Manila. When all this had been translated onto a map, MacArthur read its import: His Luzon forces were in imminent danger of being trapped in a standard pincers strategy.

Quezon's worst fears took tangible shape. On 23 December, the USAFFE commander advised all his subordinates, "WPO is in effect." On the afternoon before Christmas he drafted an announcement: "In order to spare Manila from any possible air or ground attacks, consideration is being given by military authorities to declaring Manila an open city." On 26 December the two big Manila newspapers bore the same headline: MANILA ES CIUDAD ABIERTA.

Until the very last days of the crisis before the shooting war commenced, contact between the Army and the Navy had been tenuous. Robert Lee Dennison, whom Admiral Hart deputized as his liaison with MacArthur, recalled, "There was no personal contact between Hart's staff, MacArthur's staff, or MacArthur and Hart. MacArthur didn't know what we were up to in terms of ship movements or what our war plans were, nor did we know what his were. That was the purpose of my being in this particular capacity. It wasn't much use until the war did break out."

According to Dennison the lack of coordination and communication was not because MacArthur was unwilling to share matters. "MacArthur was completely open with me. When I first reported to him, he called his staff in and instructed them in my presence that they were to show me all the dispatches that were exchanged between themselves and Washington and he intended to do the same. And this was whether I asked for [the material] or not, because how could I ask for something I didn't know existed. I was appalled to find [Col. Charles] Willoughby, the G-2, telling the G-2 in the War Department things that were completely different from what MacArthur was telling the chief of staff of the Army. There was no communications intra-staff worth a damn."

According to Dennison, he went to MacArthur's headquarters one morning around nine. "He said, 'Before I talk with you, I want you to hear what I'm going to tell my staff.' He called them in and he said, 'Gentlemen, I'm going to declare Manila an open city as of midnight tonight.' " Dennison claimed, "This was the first anybody had ever heard of it. After he [finished] I said, 'May I go back and talk to Admiral Hart?'—which I did. Hart didn't usually show much emotion but he said, 'What!' Then he got up out of his chair and said, 'Sit down and write that down!' I wrote a simple sentence, 'At 9:10 this morning, General MacArthur told me and so on.'

"Hart read it and still couldn't believe it, because he'd been making preparations to operate out of Manila. They'd moved the submarine tender *Canopus* alongside the seawall in the port district. We'd taken off warheads, torpedo exploders, and distributed them all over that general area so they wouldn't be concentrated in one place, and put camouflage over the tender. She was in shoal water so that if hit she wouldn't submerge. We were planning on continuing submarine operations. We had barges of fuel oil all around the Manila area and all kinds of supplies that we couldn't possibly get out. We needed more than a few hours, which meant we couldn't back up this concept of an open city because we had to have those supplies. It was an example of complete lack of consultation or accord between two senior commanders—MacArthur didn't comprehend what this would mean to us."

Indeed, without Manila and its facilities there was no place from which the navy could effectively operate in the Philippines. Hart left aboard the submarine *Shark*, turning over command of those Asiatic Fleet forces still in the Philippines to Adm. Francis Rockwell. The miasma of disorder that afflicted MacArthur's staff and its relationships with other organizations marked the Navy as well. Dennison, on instructions from Hart, traveled to Corregidor, the new headquarters for the American defense, to meet with Rockwell. "Hart, typically, hadn't briefed Rockwell on what his war plans were, what his thoughts were. When I put Hart aboard the *Shark*, he told me the gates to the south were closed, the Japanese fleet is there; we can't get any more ships out. This was just stupid. The destroyers didn't have any torpedoes, they were running short of fuel oil, and they had to get out, or sit there and have everybody killed. I told Rockwell I didn't agree with Hart and why. And we did get the ships out."

Near-chaos developed with the designation of an open city—the defenders would not use Manila for military purposes and therefore the enemy should not bomb or attack it. Thousands of soldiers with their weapons in "retrograde maneuvers," or retreat, to Bataan could only reach there by passage through Manila over a number of days after it was named an open city.

Submarine commander S. S. Murray, after receipt of the word on Manila's status, recalled returning to the Army-Navy Club where he spent his few off-duty hours. "I went down in the bar of the club and met the Army officers coming in from the east coast of Luzon. Their troops were just arriving in the outskirts of Manila and they had until midnight that night to start moving by foot to Bataan. They were supposed to be there the next night [a distance of perhaps sixty miles].

"They had been on a forced march ever since the Japanese had landed on the east coast and I've never seen such a bitter, frustrated crowd in my life. Most of them were weeping because they said, 'They wouldn't even let us shoot once at the Japs and we had twice as many troops as they had.' " The laments notwithstanding, although the terrain may have favored the defense, MacArthur's strategy recognized that the Southern Luzon Force could not have remained viable once the Northern Army was overwhelmed.

Paul Carpenter, a bomber pilot without a plane, ate the traditional Christmas turkey dinner on the eve of the holiday. On Christmas Day he served as train commander for the evacuation of all ground troops at Clark Field. Their destination was a stop on a highway that led into Bataan. "There wasn't anybody in charge except the engineer, the fireman, and me. We pulled into a station and we stopped. The engineer said, 'This is as far as I go. I unhook and another engine picks you up.' This happened about three times and I began to get suspicious. These guys were going to turn us loose in some little stop I didn't even see on the map. About midnight, the group exec and I went up and I said, 'No, we're not going to do this.'

"[The train crew said] 'Oh, yes, we have to leave.' At the point of a .45 automatic, we said, 'You're not going anywhere' except whatever the name of the place was. The two of us held automatics on these guys until we got to this stop that turned out to be the end of the line toward Bataan." The passengers debouched swiftly when they saw an ammunition train directly ahead, an obvious target for enemy planes. Before they could move out, a colonel arrived and ordered them to unload the freight cars. "It was Christmas Day and we were starving. There were two or three boxcar loads of C rations and when we finished unloading we broke up the C rations. That was our Christmas Day dinner. We headed out and the Japs came over and blew all the ammunition we had stacked." Trucks arrived and carried the airmen, now made "ground pounders," to defensive positions on Bataan.

Carpenter and his associates also constructed an airfield to handle B-17s. "We had bombs, ammunition, gas, anything you could think of that was necessary to refuel and turn around a B-17 unit. We had engineer troops with bulldozers who made a runway 5,000 feet long, 300 feet wide. We had hardstands so we could pull the airplanes off, service them. We were convinced that B-17s were going to come in any day, maybe thousands of them, and we wanted to be ready."

For many in Manila there was neither an opportunity nor a real choice of evacuation. Mary Rose Harrington, the Navy nurse posted to the medical facility near Cavite, had left that area. "It was too vulnerable out there. They made arrangements for us to work at several places in Manila. They set up a main operating center at the Jai Alai palace and took over several schools. Mary Chapman and I set up at one of the schools where we had a few patients. On 23 December, the Army doctors and nurses told us they had orders to move to Bataan. We were told we could do whatever we wanted. We had no orders. The saddest of days was when the Army left and Manila was declared an open city. We got bombed but they hit mostly bodegas and ships on the waterfront. The Red Cross offered to send our wounded by boat to the southern islands. Someone screwed up; the corpsmen and ambulances moved only army patients." Without the means or direction to flee, the navy nurses awaited the conquering army.

Madeline Ullom, the Army nurse, saw a number of her sorority receive orders to join the defenders on Bataan. The first contingent of twenty-four Army, one Navy, and twenty-five Filipino nurses left in a twelve-bus motor caravan to set up shop at Hospital Number One at Limay in the peninsula. "The drivers waited about ten minutes between every departure to provide a greater safety factor and to try to dispel the convoy idea. Many stops were necessary to seek roadside shelter from the planes which bombed and strafed most of the day." A second batch of twenty-five nurses embarked on Christmas night to sail for Corregidor, and another group boarded a boat that evening for a trip to Mariveles on the southwestern tip of Bataan. Successive shipments ferried the remainder of the Army and Filipino medics to Corregidor and Bataan.

The authorities, however, ordered Ullom and some colleagues to stay in the city to treat wounded. "Manila was declared an open city," she remembered. "The American flag was not hoisted to the pole above Sternberg General Hospital's entrance. A desolate, helpless, and unrealistic sensation gripped me. So many of my close friends departed. Officers no longer carried arms. Japanese prisoners were released. Lights of the city shone at night, although not as extensively as before the first week in December."

But on 29 December, Ullom and others received word to prepare for evacuation. "Surgery was quiet. I packed some instruments which I knew were the only ones in the department. I went to bed early. After midnight, Josie Nesbit [one of the senior staff] awakened me. She whispered to come quietly. I slipped into the fatigues, gave a parting glance to the mementos on the dresser, to the dresses hanging in the closet, slung the gas mask and helmet with the musette bag on my shoulder to tiptoe down the stairs.

"Some tanks rolled by the quarters. We moved to the door to better see them. Hope continued to exist. Josie cautioned us to keep back from the porch in the darkness. We were not certain whose tanks were rolling along Arrocerras Street." Ullom climbed into a field ambulance. The driver skirted huge bomb craters as the vehicle, without headlights, bumped along the pitted roadway to the port area. "Ships were blazing in the Bay. Buildings were burning along the waterfront. Structures of jagged concrete were still visible. Heaps of wreckage and crumbled ruins were everywhere. The sky was more vivid toward Cavite than the spectacular and vivid sunsets we often watched from Dewey Boulevard.

Loud blasts punctured the quiet. A stretching flame, an exploding substance colored and streaked the horizon."

As the interisland steamer *Don Esteban* left the pier, Japanese planes hovered in the sky before bombing and shooting up the port area. Ullom saw that the pier on which she had stood shortly before was now a blazing mass. At dawn, the *Don Esteban* increased its speed and lessened the danger of blindly colliding with a mine. After a "big, delicious breakfast," the steamer docked at Corregidor. Ullom felt secure again. "The Rock, the Eternal Rock, were the terms for the fortification. Phrases of conversation mysteriously linked its features to an unconquerable entity."

On Christmas Eve, the *Don Esteban*'s passenger list was substantially more imposing than a collection of medical personnel. When MacArthur abandoned Rainbow Five and reverted to War Plan Orange, he moved his headquarters to the Rock and the office opened for business on Christmas Day. "Manila," said MacArthur, "because of the previous evacuation of our forces, no longer had any practical military value. The entrance to Manila Bay was completely covered by Corregidor and Bataan and, as long as we held them, its use would be denied the enemy. He might have the bottle, but I had the cork."

Actually, the evacuation of MacArthur's army was very much in progress and its success still in doubt when the general announced his new location. It was not a single but a double retrograde operation if the bulk of both the Northern and Southern Luzon Forces were to withdraw into Bataan. Wainwright, confronted with a steady erosion of his army from casualties inflicted by the enemy and desertion by the untrained, undisciplined troops, withdrew behind the Agno River, a natural barrier for anyone seeking access to Manila from the north. Wainwright actually talked of a counterattack if his boss would order up the most effective fighting force in the entire defense, the Philippine Division with its Philippine Scouts, and the U.S. 31st Regiment.

However, not only did MacArthur not accede to the request for the Philippine Division but he now informed Wainwright that Orange was in effect and that Wainwright's soldiers must fight delaying actions that would allow the bulk of his army to escape to Bataan. Although supported by the 192d and 194th Tank Battalions, a pair of U.S. National Guard units, Wainwright's army continued to recede under pressure from Japanese infantry supported from the air.

One of the strong points for a Bataan defense lay in the limited access to the peninsula. But while the choke points favored the forces established there, they posed a threat to the moves by Wainwright's North Luzon Force and the South Luzon Force under Brig. Gen. Albert Jones. The route to Bataan for both required passage across the Pampanga River over the Calumpit bridges, one of which handled highway traffic and the other served the railroad. Military vehicles, soldiers on the march, and a thick stream of Filipinos with wagons, animal-drawn carts, a few cars somehow not commandeered by the military, and civilians on foot packed the route to the bridges. In the sky, flights of Japanese planes continued to bomb and machine-gun military targets and portions of Manila. They ignored the long column snaking toward Bataan but resolutely attacked designated targets. Unlike the Germans in Europe, who understood that disruption of road traffic often prevented an effective retreat, the Japanese hewed to the prescribed plans and, as they demonstrated through the war, lacked an inclination to improvise and exploit unexpected opportunities. Indeed, General Homma, had he elected to concentrate his army upon the elements bound for Bataan, might well have destroyed the forces of Wainwright and Jones. But he, too, stuck to the script that made the capture of Manila top priority.

With some desperate defensive efforts delaying those Japanese units that were approaching the Pampanga, Wainwright himself crossed the bridge. At 1:00 A.M. on New Year's Day 1942, he heard a rumbling that signaled the approach of tanks. The anxiety eased as the armor from the 192d and 194th Tank Battalions rattled through the darkness and across the river. The main remnants of both the NLF (Northern Luzon Force) and SLF (Southern Luzon Force) continued to make their way toward Bataan. Around 6:15 A.M., twin four-ton dynamite charges dropped both spans into the deep, unfordable current of the Pampanga. For the moment, the Fil-American Army was intact and secure.

Much worse than the shrinkage of the turf controlled by the U.S., and loss of 40 percent of the troops because of casualties and desertion, was the loss of vital supplies. As part of MacArthur's strategy, the troops evacuated Fort Stotsenburg; up in smoke went as much as 300,000 gallons of gasoline and large amounts of high-octane fuel. Tons of food, clothing, and other military gear were discarded.

John Olson, a West Pointer and adjutant for the 57th Regiment, Philippine Scouts, a component of the Philippine Division, while delivering a message learned of Stotsenburg's abandonment and of the vast stores left behind. Olson reported the news to his superior and said, "Major Johnson directed Captain Anders to investigate. He did so and returned laden with soap, toothpaste, candy, film, cigarettes, and a number of other items from the Post Exchange. Colonel George Clarke, the regimental commander, denied Major Fisher permission to send men and vehicles into the post on the grounds that they 'might be hit by fragments of Japanese or American bombs.' [Engineers at Clark detonated ordnance they could not carry off.]

"Major [Royal] Reynolds, whose patrols had ventured into the post, sent all the vehicles he could get his hands on to salvage whatever they could. From this trip they got large quantities of clothing and food. Among the clothing were winter overcoats that members of the 31st Infantry had worn when the regiment was sent to Siberia in 1919. Though of interest, they were left for the Japanese in favor of more usable items. The salvage party did bring back thirty-six Smith & Wesson .45-caliber revolvers. The most valuable acquisition was enough Class C rations to fill two buses. They were to be worth the equivalent of gold later in the campaign when food became scarce. In spite of the haul, there was much more that could have been saved. But the timidity of the regimental commander prevented any further exploitation of the abandoned supplies."

The items written off at Stotsenburg can be attributed to panic, but a much more basic logistical difficulty arose from the substitution of Rainbow Five for Orange late in the game. To feed the army that would deprive the invaders of a foothold in the Philippines, quartermasters deposited huge stocks of food in the central Luzon plains where they would be accessible to Wainwright's forces. According to Bluemel, a Filipino captain told him that one million pounds of rice had been left at the Cabanatuan storage area. From the commander of the depot at Tarlac, Bluemel heard that 2,000 cases of canned food and clothing could not be taken by the retreating army because it belonged to Japanese companies. The refusal, allegedly from MacArthur's headquarters, to allow confiscation of items owned by citizens of the invading nation would seem to carry the rights of private property to an extreme. To further complicate supply problems, commanders of many units refused to return precious vehicles that brought materials to them, retaining trucks and cars for their own use or for use in an emergency. The law of the jungle infected some units that hijacked and commandeered transportation, wrecking any systematic efforts by the quartermaster organizations. No one stepped forward to halt this anarchy. Richard Sutherland commented that his boss never had any interest or understanding of logistics and that flaw would be crippling. The theory for WPO's premise of resistance to conquest by an army defending in the Bataan redoubt rested on critical logistical assumptions. The strategists expected a force of perhaps 40,000 troops with appropriate equipment and other necessities to be able to withstand the estimated Japanese army for six months.

MacArthur's plan to prevent the Japanese from overrunning Luzon had upset the schedule for stockpiling the munitions, food, and other vital items on Bataan. When he reinstituted the concept of a defense built there, the supply system, like some great ocean liner forging in one direction, could not instantly reverse course, but shuddered as it sought to halt its momentum. The confusion and absence of a disciplined system might have been overcome by a forceful attention to the problem, but a monumental miscalculation overrode whatever anyone did.

Instead of the compact, well-commanded, skillful body of 40,000 troops envisioned, tens of thousands more men reached Bataan. Some arrived as members of the intact but unreliable Philippine Army divisions; others from shattered units seeped through the jungle. Along with the Filipinos came a horde of air corps and navy men, their primary mission in the Philippines now vanished with the disappearance of the planes and ships. They now became ground forces. Under the authority of WPO, the military expected to evacuate civilians on the peninsula. With the Japanese rushing forward and the Fil-American forces in retreat, no one attempted to reduce the local population. Furthermore, refugees, who feared Japanese occupation of their home areas, swelled the numbers of noncombatants on Bataan. With as many as 80,000 uniformed men on Bataan and an extra 10,000 civilians added from the start, the food and medical supplies on Bataan were pitifully inadequate.

7

The East Indies

ADMIRAL THOMAS HART HAD ACTED UPON A 27 NOVEMBER 1941 message from chief of naval operations Adm. Harold Stark that said, "This dispatch is to be considered a war warning. . . ." Hart had sent much of his Asiatic Fleet to sea before the raids smashed the ships at Pearl Harbor and then devastated the Manila base at Cavite. Among the vessels temporarily removed from harm's way was the heavy cruiser USS *Houston*. Otto Schwarz, a refugee from the Great Depression in New Jersey and an alumnus of the Civilian Conservation Corps (CCC), at age seventeen had enlisted in the Navy eleven months before the war began. Originally assigned to the *Lark*, a minesweeper, Schwarz was transferred to the *Houston* in June.

As 1941 dwindled down, Schwarz said he and his shipmates groused about the frequency of long gun drills. The procedures at the time stored a number of 150-pound projectiles for the eight-inch guns on the deck, with more shells stashed on a shelf five feet above the deck. A hoist with a chain theoretically brought down the reserve ammunition. "We used to ask old-timers how we were going to get those shells down during battle and they always told us, 'Don't worry about it, because there has never been a naval battle more than twenty minutes and you'll never use the shells on the decks.' The first time we went into battle, we used every shell on the deck, and the guys were lifting the ones off the shelf by hand. It was quite a difference between what you had been taught and what you ended up doing.

"A week or ten days before Pearl Harbor, we were over in Cavite Navy Yard undergoing repairs. We had some of our boilers dismantled and parts all over the deck. All of a sudden we received orders to weld up all of the portholes. We took all the parts off the deck and threw them up on the ship and took off. At sea we hurriedly put everything back together again. From that moment on we were at general quarters and Condition Two with the guns manned all the time. On 8 December we were in condition of readiness and general quarters sounded. We all went to our battle stations and a short message over the p.a. system said the Japanese had attacked Pearl Harbor and we were in a condition of war. We were already in a frame of mind that we wanted to get at the Japanese. There was no doubt that they were an enemy of ours, embarking on a campaign to gobble up territory. It seemed to me that we were almost jubilant about the war starting. That soon changed after we got our noses bloodied and found out what life was really all about. We were all rather young, ready to go."

He remarked that he and his colleagues stereotyped the Japanese as "about four feet tall, wore round glasses, were not too intelligent, and ate women and little children for breakfast. [The war] couldn't possibly last more than five or six months after we got involved."

Japanese airmen had dealt the Allied naval forces a stunning blow on 10 December by sinking the British battleships *Repulse* and *Prince of Wales*, the two biggest warships in the Far East. Meanwhile, for almost two months the *Houston* engaged in convoy duty, traveling to Borneo and Australia without coming in contact with the enemy. The American-British-Dutch-Australian (ABDA) Command, activated in mid-January, cobbled together a paltry naval strike force to disrupt the Japanese campaign against the Dutch East Indies.

The Dutch and Americans anted up four destroyers each and two cruisers apiece, including the *Houston*. On 4 February, operating without aerial cover, the ABDA force came under attack from fifty-four bombers and torpedo planes. "I was down below the waterline," said Schwarz, " and I knew nothing about what was going on except from putting two and two together. For instance, if the 5-inch guns went off, we knew that the bombers were at a high level; if we heard the .50-caliber machine guns go off, we got a little worried because they were pretty close. I was in the powder magazine of the 8-inch guns, which do absolutely nothing during an air raid. We were just manning our battle stations. We really didn't get to see anything, only hear noises."

When a 500-pound bomb struck the *Houston* squarely on its aft 8-inch turret, Schwarz said it shook the entire ship but his area remained undamaged. A Dutch cruiser and the other American one, *Marblehead*, incurred severe damage, forcing the ABDA flotilla to flee the Java waters. "After we secured general quarters," noted Schwarz, "I went aft to see what was going on. There was a lot of feverish activity, attempting to get the bodies out of the turret. I did have a couple of friends in that turret and when I got there, they were screaming for someone to go inside the turret to try and get out a couple of bodies. There was a tiny room where the shells and powder come up from below with a little window entrance or exit. They needed somebody small enough to go in there. I was pretty small and thin so I was chosen. The two bodies were fused together and I had to break them apart and pull them out. That's when I first found out that it was not going to be fun and games. It finally hit me that we were in for something distasteful, that war was not all the glory of finishing the Japanese in five weeks. We buried something like forty-eight men and went about putting the ship back in order."

Walter Vogel, who was on deck, said, "We were attacked by some fifty land-based bombers. We had no air support and to our surprise our five-inch AA shells were duds. That left us sitting ducks and they attacked our group for about three hours. I had my head cut open by shrapnel. At Tjilatjap I went to the hospital for seven stitches and a plaster pack on my head. While I was there, the *Houston* departed because Japs were reported making a landing. I went down to the dock and was ordered to get the hell out the best way I could. I went aboard the USS *Gold Star* [a freighter which was among the vessels the *Houston* guarded on the way to Java]. It had no guns and could do only ten knots but we made it to Darwin, Australia."

While the British Empire and the Netherlands fielded the ground forces in Southwest Asia, the United States committed its available resources in the air as well as at sea. Bomber pilot Paul Carpenter, whose B-17 had been wrecked in an accident at Clark Field, had retreated into Bataan by rail, truck, and on foot. Early in January, he and other grounded pilots were evacuated to the island fortress of Corregidor in Manila Bay. "We were at Corregidor for two or three days. In the middle of one night, they took us through the tunnel and put us on the old *Sea Wolf* submarine and away we went for Java. The submarine looked mighty good to me. It was a big old black thing, long as a football field, and it was a way to get out of the Philippines and I was delighted. There were twenty to thirty Air Force types aboard, eight or nine from the 19th [his group]. All were aircraft commanders. There was a dive-bombing outfit with five or six of its pilots, some specialists, bombsight or electronics men. The submarine also had aboard a great amount of the gold that belonged to the Philippine government and quite a supply of quinine seeds [extracts from the plant were used to treat malaria].

"We came right down through the Battle of Makassar Strait [where the *Houston* took a bomb on its after turret]. The submarine commander had orders not to engage in any hostilities because of all this junk he had aboard—the people, the gold, quinine seeds. His job was not to fight but get us down to Java. That made the submarine crew very unhappy because of all this activity going on around them. We got picked up [by enemy ships] on two or three occasions and I am sure they were all Japanese tin cans [destroyers]. That really shakes you up on a submarine when those depth charges come."

Running on the surface with diesel engines while charging the batteries, the voyage of the *Sea Wolf* from Corregidor to the Javanese port of Surabaya lasted eight days. "They were beginning to get B-17s for replacement through the Africa route. They flew down to Brazil, to Belem, across to Africa, then to India, and on into the East Indies. The pilots that brought those airplanes over just had a trip around the field, a pat on the back, and away they went. They had never seen a B-17 more than a week or so before they headed out for the Southwest Pacific area. They [the command] were eager to get those of us who had some experience in the airplane to get down there and fly. So we did.

"We attacked Jap shipping," Carpenter continued, "and primarily the Jap Navy who was at that point coming down from the Philippines and engulfing all of the East Indies. The Japs knew where we were, and they attacked us once or twice a day. We would try to get a flight off in the interim and you would generally land, and here the Japs would be with their fighters strafing the place when you got there. It was a dicey time. We generally managed to get about six to nine airplanes airborne every day for the month I was there. Our bombardment wasn't very effective because we didn't have much to work with. We were more an annoyance to the Japanese than anything else. Every once in a while we would make a good strike, but I am sure it didn't bother them very much."

Along with the bombers, there was a small fighter-plane force. Tommy Hayes, a member of the 35th Fighter Group, who had pinned on his wings and second lieutenant's gold bars in February 1941, had been posted for Clark Field. "On December 7th, the 35th was spread a bit. About one-third had arrived in the Philippines at the end of November. One-third were in mid-Pacific and turned around to head for Hawaii, and the last third had not left the States. The plans were to move fifty-five crated P-40Es, along with a like number of pilots, crew chiefs, and armorers. We sailed in mid-December and were diverted to Brisbane, Australia.

"The planes were reassembled and flown to a base prepared for us at Surabaya, Java. When we had arrived in Australia, we were met by ten or twelve veteran fighter pilots from the Philippines. They were the leaders and we, yet to be baptized, were the wingmen. Against the Japanese, who had been fighting in China for four or five years, we had leaders who had a few weeks of war and the majority of us had not even squeezed the triggers of our machine guns.

"Aboard the ship to Australia we had a Navy intelligence officer who briefed us on the Japanese air force—a collection of fixed-landing-gear, biwing aircraft. The P-40 pilots on board were sure we would be home in six months. Yes, they had a few of those obsolete planes, but they also had the Mitsubishi Zero and the Betty two-engine bomber. Their navy had better fighters and bombers than their army. And their disregard for human life contributed to their success over the British, Dutch, and the U.S. in initial air battles. They deployed their equipment very well. Their weakness was a lack of self-sealing fuel tanks.

"The guys from the Philippines explained, 'You don't turn with a Zero.' It's hit and run and the P-40 had speed and was fast in a dive. We overcame our fears and anxieties and gained experience. The Flying Tigers in China with P-40s did a great job, thanks to their early-warning system. In Java, and later in New Guinea, without early warning, P-40s were always below the Japanese, losing the advantage of being on top where you can pound and add or subtract for your rate of climb. Learning was costly."

The *Houston* escorted a convoy of four troop transports to the besieged garrison on the island of Timor. Enroute the cruiser valiantly protected its flock as marauders off Japanese carriers and land-based bombers from the conquered Celebes Island swooped down near Darwin, Australia. "When we were attacked Captain Rooks put on a display of seamanship and guts. He used the *Houston* as a one-man defense of the four ships. Moving the ship rapidly in and out of the convoy and firing constantly we soon became the target, which is what he wanted, I suppose. The bombers really went after us. There were a couple of times when people on other ships told us later they thought we had just disappeared from the sea. Large numbers of bombs would explode, and the ship would just disappear and then come back up. We drove off the bombers without a single direct hit. There was only one near miss on one transport. After we had defended those four ships, we aborted the mission and went back to Darwin. We let the four transports go in the harbor and then the *Houston* went between them and they lined the rails and cheered at the top of their voices . . . they were so thankful for us actually having saved them."

The Japanese had reported the *Houston* sunk on several occasions and the sailors began to refer to their ship as the *Galloping Ghost*. But while it evaded hits at Darwin and the four ships shielded by the cruiser were spared, the enemy blasted a number of other vessels, shot down Allied aircraft, and wrecked Darwin's port facilities. The string of defeats weakened an already rag-tag assemblage of battered, aging ships, and even the *Houston* lacked radar. The American high command conceded the loss of the Dutch East Indies and in a bit of save-face, sleight of hand, Admiral Hart yielded the leadership to a Dutch counterpart.

The Imperial Navy now set its sights on the main prize—Java, with its vast oil stocks and its strategic location. A mighty armada of carriers, battleships, cruisers, and a swarm of lesser but still deadly warships accompanying a large invasion force, bore down upon the Dutch-controlled island. To intercept this fleet, a motley formation of five cruisers, including the *Houston*, plus a few destroyers, sallied forth. David was off to meet Goliath without even a slingshot.

In the Battle of the Java Sea, on 27 February in the late afternoon, the Japanese spotted the small Allied force and attacked. The outgunned ABDA vessels raced for safety. Enemy shells disabled the Royal Navy's HMS *Exeter;* a

Dutch destroyer sank after a torpedo hit. The *Houston*, with its after turret still unrepaired, maneuvered to defend itself with the six forward guns. That night star shells illuminated the battle scene and long-range torpedoes accounted for two Dutch cruisers. The Australian Navy's *Perth* and the *Houston* escaped momentarily. A day later, they headed into the jaws of destruction, blundering into the convoy unloading troops and cargo at the northwestern tip of Java. Although the Allied cruisers sank four of the fifty-six transports, heavyweight Japanese warships surrounded the pair and blasted them with torpedoes and shells.

"We had very little ammunition left after the Java Sea battle," said Schwarz. "We had taken all of the ammunition out of the disabled turret and dispersed it. We were firing star shells—ones that you normally use in practice—giving them everything including the kitchen sink. General quarters had been called so quickly that night that the only clothing I had on was a pair of khaki pants. The speakers on the telephones would say, 'There's another cruiser over there; we hit one!' It was pandemonium. The ship was moving at great speeds and making all kinds of maneuvers. The *Perth* went down first and rather quickly. We were shooting everything, including .30-caliber machine guns. It became obvious we were in trouble. We knew we were being hit because we could feel all of the jarring and the explosions.

"We got word to abandon ship and there was a problem. There is supposed to be a repair party to open the hatches that were battened down very tightly. No repair party was there. Either they'd been killed or were busy elsewhere. We had a mallet which we could use in an emergency to undog the hatch from our side. We let the crew out of the powder magazine inside into our compartment.

"I led the group. I had the mallet in my hand and I opened

up the dogs. When you open up the hatch, you don't know what's on the other side. Maybe that compartment has been hit and it's on fire. Maybe it's flooded. Each time you open up another hatch, you go through this trauma of not knowing whether you're going to be alive in the next instant. We got up on the next deck and started forward. Everything was filled with smoke. You could hardly breathe. You couldn't see at all; it was pitch black. I hollered back, 'Okay, everybody put one hand over your nose and mouth and one hand on the shoulder of the guy in front of you and we'll try to get out!' I led.

"Going up on another deck," Schwarz went on, "I felt the guy's hand behind me leave my shoulder. For whatever reason, he went left toward the port side and I continued through the compartments on the starboard side. A short time later, a torpedo hit on the port side. It knocked me off my feet and unconscious. I found out later that the entire group behind me that had let their hands go off my shoulder were killed by the torpedo.

"When I came onto the deck, it was like the Fourth of July at an amusement park. We were dead in the water, just drifting or floating. The Japanese seemed to be ten feet away with searchlights on us and stuff was coming at us like crazy. Shells were exploding all over the place. [Machine-gun fire raked the deck as well.] It was a duck shoot. They had us surrounded and were just sitting out there shooting. Guys were running all over the place.

"I had no life jacket and started forward to my Abandon Ship station. Some guy passed me, running. He stopped and said, 'Don't you have a life jacket?' I said no. He said, 'Here, take this one.' He had one on and one in his hand. I took it and went up forward where the rest of the guys from my division, those that were still alive, were forming. Orders came to cancel the Abandon Ship order. By then a lot of guys had bailed out already. I saw some run past me and go right off the bow, which was darn high. I looked down at the water, watching them dive in and then go past the ship like little corks.

"I went forward to await orders," said Schwarz, "and Ensign Nelson jumped on top of number two turret and ordered us all back to our battle stations. Everybody said, 'What battle stations?' We had none. Our compartments were flooded, on fire. We had no more shells left. Shells exploded all around us. Pieces of teakwood deck were flying in the air. Very shortly, we got word to abandon ship. I went to the port side of the bow where there was a boat boom that is let out when you're at anchor and your boats tie up to this boom. It is a few feet below deck level. I lowered myself onto the boom and then jumped. I started to swim as rapidly as I could away from the ship. Shells were exploding in the water; my stomach kept bouncing back and forth from my backbone. I had one objective and that was to get away from the ship because the suction would take me down. I didn't look back. I headed out, as fast as I could. Swimming with the life jacket was very difficult because they were not the modern Mae West inflatable ones but old-fashioned kapok canvas jackets that completely enveloped you.

"I kept swimming and everything started to quiet down. The ship had sunk and the ocean was dark and silent. I could hear occasional screams from some of the guys in the water. In an attempt to save my life and reach land, I swam for hours. I didn't meet a single soul. I saw a boat approaching me and became very frightened. I could hear the Japanese were machine-gunning the water, so I decided to make them think I was already dead. I tucked my face up underneath the collar of my jacket, got an air pocket there and just bobbed up and down.

"I heard the boat come up to me. They shut the motors down to an idle. I could hear a foreign language being spoken, I could hear them jabbering away. I could 'feel' a searchlight on me. I felt myself being poked with a hook or pole and the jabbering went on. I felt the searchlight go out. The boat started up again and left me. I had been born and raised Roman Catholic. I had been an altar boy and a choir boy. I was very church-oriented as a child. I found out that at my time of need, my orientation had been one of a God that I feared. I tried to pray that night and seek help but I didn't find any feeling of association. I prayed a lot, but didn't feel it did any good."

For a brief period as he struggled toward the shoreline of Java, Schwarz swam in the company of another sailor. But when Schwarz flagged because of leg cramps the other man paddled off. "Just before dawn, a Japanese landing boat came up. They pulled me out of the water. I was glad to be out of the water. They threw us down in the bottom of the barge but did not mistreat us at that point." Taken to the beach, Schwarz joined a group of seventeen or eighteen survivors from the ship. His new ordeal, life in a prisoner of war camp, was about to begin.

The Americans still in the battle lacked the resources to carry on an effective war from the air. When the Japanese occupied Bali, the always-tenuous supply line between Australia and the bases on Java broke down. By then Tommy Hayes had shot down a pair of enemy planes but on 20 February a Zero hit him from the rear. "The tail was damaged and the canopy dislodged from its track. On landing, coming in over a coconut plantation, turning and slowing to land, the tail dropped and the P-40 fell into the trees. It stopped quickly, the tree trunks ripping the wings off. My head hit the gunsight. I was taken to a hospital with a concussion. About a week later they started evacuation for Australia. I was on a Dutch ship, the *Aberkirk*, along with about 2,000 U.S. and British from Malaysia and Singapore. The ship had about twenty staterooms for the crew but these were given over to badly burned sailors from the *Houston*."

Because replacement parts needed to maintain the bombers were scarce, only two or three in Paul Carpenter's entire B-17 group could operate at high altitudes. Toward the end of the March, as the enemy advance inexorably swallowed the East Indies, the air fields became untenable. "We got word to evacuate to Australia," he remembered. "At that time, I again had no airplane. I was just extra crew and came out in the back end of one of the last B-17s that left. We could see the Japs coming down the road as we took off. They fired at us, and we fired back." With the remnants of planes and crews, the refugees from Java waited for reinforcements and to regroup.

The Allied efforts in the Dutch East Indies did nothing to relieve the pressure brought by the Japanese upon the hapless American and Filipino forces in Philippines. Tom Gage, among the airmen refugees fleeing into Bataan, recalled a hellish bomb attack. "The strike came just at lunch time. I remember getting into one of the slit trenches with my mess kit in my hand. To the best of my knowledge I finished the meal. General opinion was they were trying to hit the highway bridge over the river at Orani, which they missed completely. However, they did get two direct hits on the gasoline tanker trucks that were parked in the village. The drivers, not from the 34th, were killed and the town was set afire.

"We continued at Orani until January 7th. During this time I went back in the direction we had come from with a small truck convoy to scavenge anything we could get in the way of supplies. We moved at a snail's pace, bumper-to-bumper with trucks, and overhead, flight after flight of Japanese bombers. Luckily for us they had no bombs to spare and also equally lucky no fighters were interested in us. We had no place to hide in the rice fields."

While Americans and Filipinos alike had struggled and straggled toward Bataan, General Homma savored a triumphant entrance into Manila. The soldiers moved into public buildings, hotels, university and school buildings. Japanese officers, prepared with occupation pesos, bought up souvenirs wherever they found an open store. All British and American citizens, including Navy nurse Mary Rose Harrington, were incarcerated on the campus of Santo Tomas University.

With control of the big city established, General Homma unleashed his armies on the last line of American and Filipino troops blocking access to Bataan. The available defenders considerably outnumbered the fighting men fielded by the Japanese commander, although the American commanders continued to insist the enemy had far more troops at his disposal. For their part, Japanese intelligence undercounted the defenders, figuring MacArthur could call upon roughly 40,000 or so underfed, poorly trained, and dispirited soldiers.

Only the support of artillery and heavy fire from the two American tank battalions prevented swift progress by the enemy. But the longer-range Japanese artillery blasted holes in the defensive lines and the last of the Luzon armies retreated into Bataan. Officially, defense of the peninsula began on 7 January 1942 as Wainwright assumed command of the west sector while Gen. George M. Parker received responsibility for the east sector.

The relatively easy initial success against the armies arrayed for the defense of the island had persuaded the Japanese High Command that conquest of the remnants on Bataan would not require as much force as originally planned. To consolidate and expand the control of Southeast Asia, the Japanese army command had snatched away some of Homma's best ground and air troops for the invasion of Java. In place of these experienced and effective soldiers, the 65th Independent Brigade, with 6,500 men, landed on 2 January. The enlisted personnel, all conscripts, had only a month of training and the commander, Lt. Gen. Akira Nara, a graduate of the U.S. Army Infantry School in 1927, described his organization as "absolutely unfit for combat."

The consequences of hurling men with little more knowledge than how to march into the inferno of battle showed immediately. On 8 January, advancing toward Mabatang near Manila Bay, elements of the 65th Brigade tramped along a road in a column of fours with their horse-drawn artillery trailing. Observation posts on the slopes of nearby mountains spotted them and called in the 155mm artillery, already registered for targets on the highway. A torrent of shells burst among the Japanese soldiers, killing and maiming many. Whenever the barrage slackened, the troops dutifully reformed into their columns and renewed their trudge toward death and destruction, for what the defenders could only describe as a "turkey shoot." First blood in the battle for Bataan spilled mainly from the offensive forces.

Nevertheless, the invaders continued to attack. The 57th Regiment, Philippine Scouts, with Philip Fry, recently promoted from major to lieutenant colonel, as CO of the 3d Battalion, opposed the thrust. "On the afternoon of January 10th, our patrols reported contact with strong Japanese combat patrol. Companies were notified to be on the alert and increase their local security. About 2:00 P.M., rifle and machine-gun fire commenced in the I Company sector. We had these flare up before when stray carabao wandered into minefields and set off mines. The men, on edge, would immediately fire a few shots into the darkness. As soon as the firing started, I called Captain [Herman] Gerth, I Company CO, and was informed he was on the front line. I managed to get Captain Haas, Company K, on the phone, who said his sector was quiet. I told Haas to send a patrol to look over the I Company sector and find out what was going on. Not satisfied with the information available, I started out for the observation post.

"On my way up, the firing became more severe. One of the runners was shot through the arm. In spite of his pleading and tears, I ordered him back to the first aid station, as our first casualty. By the time we arrived at the OP the firing had become even more severe and the machine guns had joined in. In fact, the entire left sector was violently active. Gerth was on the OP phone waiting for me. He told me that his entire company was engaged and the Japs were advancing through our minefield. I could see and hear the flash of the mines going off. They were supposed to withstand 600 pounds pressure, but many were homemade and went off at the slightest provocation. I told Gerth to pour it on them and help would be forthcoming if needed.

"A great shout of 'Banzai!' came from the front and the Japs started an old Civil War charge. I got Haas on the phone and told him to sweep Company I's front with his machine guns. It was slaughter. All of our guns had been carefully sighted for mutual support and the Japs were caught by terrific fire, both frontal and flanking. Even now I can't understand why the Japs launched an attack of this kind against modern weapons. My only explanation is they had not faced trained troops before and thought that if enough noise were made the opposition would simply fade away. The attack was smashed before it got underway. The Scouts were jubilant. I made a hurried trip to the front lines and warned them to expect another more serious attack soon. Our casualties were only five wounded including my runner.

"The second attack began about one A.M. It was preceded by considerable small arms and mortar fire. Our lines were smothered and the OP came in for its full share. The entire battalion front came into action. This time the enemy brought up his tanks and hit us hard. Once again the main effort was against Company I. We were forced to put our fire back along the final protective line. A few of the enemy started filtering through and circling behind the Company I sector. As soon as Gerth sensed this he very properly asked for help. I just couldn't afford to commit my reserves so early in the game.

"Captain Coe, the artillery liaison officer, was with me and designated the cane field [to the front of the defenders] as the target and asked immediate fire. Captain Grimes, the heavy weapons company commander, was nearby and directed to concentrate all mortars in the same place. The concentrated fire of these mortars alone would have been terrific. But we had World War I ammunition and averaged about six duds out of every ten rounds fired.

"We abandoned the new light mortar guns at Fort Mc-Kinley because the ammunition for them had never arrived. We were badly handicapped without our own protective weapons and forced to rely heavily on the artillery. Captain Coe had Colonel Luback on the phone and asked me to talk to him. Luback said the regiment had taken control of all artillery support, and out of the hands of battalion commanders. This was incredible. I believed some mistake had been made. My only reaction at the time was irritation.

"I asked Luback to keep his line open while I contacted the regiment and got Major Johnson, regimental S-3. I explained the situation and asked him to authorize a barrage. Johnson was evasive so I asked him to put George Clarke [the 57th's commander] on the phone. Once again I went over the situation with Clarke. He had the same line of conversation as Johnson and we ended in a furious exchange of words but no artillery!" The supposed excuse for Clarke's behavior was his fear that any use of artillery would bring retaliatory fire upon his headquarters. Harold Johnson, who also served under Clarke, described him as "phobic" about air attacks.

Outraged and frustrated, Fry rallied his forces. "Company K as well as Company I was now heavily engaged with more and more snipers, armed with Tommy guns, filtering through the lines. They were coming mostly through the 41st Infantry [Philippine Army unit manning the left flank] and circling behind us. Both Gerth and Haas were asking for supporting fire and they were badly worried. They didn't have a thing on me. The Scouts were willing fighters but after all it was their first combat experience. They were bound to be affected by fire into their backs."

The men under Fry pulled back and reestablished their lines. But the enemy seemed relentless in purpose and heedless of losses. Fry recalled, "January 11 about 10:00 P.M. there were signs of formation for a coming mechanized attack from the Nip side. The sounds of tanks couldn't be mistaken. We took preparatory countermeasures. Our mortars and artillery went into action at once. The antitank weapons, 37mm cannons, .50-caliber machine guns, and a battery of 75mms, were silent. They had strict orders not to fire a sin-

gle shot unless tanks were seen approaching. Otherwise they
would give their positions away.

"The attack was broken up before the tanks could be used.
The Japanese opened up with heavy and light mortar fire
against our front lines. Not much damage was done thanks
to excellent foxholes. Soon everything we had was in action.
The firepower of a battalion armed with modern weapons is
something. The Garand rifle is beyond my descriptive powers. It is a mystery to me how anyone can come through it
[the battalion firepower] alive. But they do. And they came
with the now familiar cry of 'Banzai!' The fight was on.
Once again the filtering tactics, but on a much larger scale.
We had men stationed in commanding positions waiting for
them. Here at least, there was plenty of individual combat.
The Nips poured men into the battle. They had face and
prestige at stake. This battalion of Scouts, though badly outnumbered, were desperately eager to place the number of a
new American-Filipino Regiment among the war great."

Lieutenant Alexander "Sandy" Nininger, a Georgia-born
youth and West Point graduate, fresh out of the infantry
school at Fort Benning, had only come to the Philippines
and the 57th Regiment in November 1941. According to his
superiors, Nininger volunteered to accompany one party of
Scouts bent on rooting out infiltrators. His company commander gave Nininger the names of six or eight of the best
marksmen in the outfit but specified they must all be volunteers. The heavily armed patrol set out. Those behind them
heard intense exchanges of gunfire and explosions. The
party returned intact with their ammunition expended.
Nininger insisted on another expedition but this time he selected only three Scouts for the mission.

"After some time," wrote John Olson, "they came running back. Shouting to his men to remain, the lieutenant

grabbed some more grenades and a bandolier of ammunition and raced back into the trees. He was never seen alive again. His body was found later leaning against a tree. Lying around him were three dead Japanese, one of whom was reported to have been an officer."

Subsequently, Nininger was posthumously awarded the nation's highest military decoration, the Medal of Honor. He was the first American to receive the congressional medal during World War II. Nininger seems to have demonstrated genuine valor, although the eyewitness testimony that is a prerequisite for a Medal of Honor is murky. Encomiums, like that of his regimental commander, Clarke, in the forms of letters to the dead man's family, seem inspired more by desires for reflected glory than for drafting a factual record.

While Nininger and the embattled Scouts of the 3d Battalion sought to repulse the onrushing Japanese, a renewed appeal for artillery support was not denied. Major Johnson, instead of consulting Colonel Clarke, arranged for barrages in the canefields directly in front of the Scouts. The defenders momentarily halted the offense. Captain Gerth personally went among the front-line platoons, leaving Lt. Arthur Green in his command bunker. A bullet struck the company commander in the groin at 0330. Carried to the command post, Gerth tried to carry on, reporting the situation to higher headquarters. The battalion supply officer, Capt. John Compton, hearing about Gerth, received permission to go forward and aid him.

According to Fry, "A portion of the line was penetrated. Green was telling me this over the telephone when all of a sudden he exclaimed, 'They got Johnny [Compton]! There he goes down.' I told Green to hold on and I would send help to him right then. I turned to Brown who was standing right beside me and ordered an immediate counterattack in the I

Company sector. I had one more call from Green, his last
one, stating his company was being forced back, casualties
heavy but the remainder was fighting hard. I told him of
Company L entry." While Gerth continued to pass on details
to Fry, Lieutenant Green, leaving the safety of the dugout,
headed for the forward positions of the I Company troops.
As he consulted and advised, he incurred a fatal wound to
the head.

Fry continued, "Haas reported his left flank exposed,
Company I shot to pieces, and his company being out-
flanked. I told him about Company L's entry and for him to
give all possible assistance. I believed the enemy had shot
the works and was hoping for a breakthrough with Brown's
Company L being timed correctly. I called regiment and informed them of the situation and that my reserve had been
committed. I asked that at least one company of the regimental reserve be placed at my disposal. Company E was
assigned to me and ordered to report to my battalion support
line and there await orders. This action on the part of regiment was a very generous one and paid big dividends. Company L under Captain Brown hit the hole in the I Company
sector hard. He established contact with Haas, relieving the
strain there, but failed to contact the 41st Infantry. Things
quieted a bit."

Although a lull fell over the front, Fry remained aware of
threats to his sector's positions because of an exposed flank.
"The stage was set and it was a question of who would get
there fustest with the mostest." [Employing a quote attributed to the Confederacy's Nathan Bedford Forrest.] Company E, borrowed from regimental reserve, and some added
men would carry out the mission. Other companies set up
machine guns to hammer the foe if he tried to pull back.

"The attack was a beautiful one," wrote Fry, " an inspiring sight to see. The Scouts had been trained for years in the company-in-attack and it was a model of precision and played for keeps. The reward of perfection was retention of one's life. If this attack had been staged at Fort Benning to show visiting firemen the mechanics it would not have been improved upon. I knew the outcome at once. With such leadership as [Capt. Don] Childers [E Company commander] was showing and such trained fighters as these Scouts, it couldn't fail. The Japanese were trapped. They fought bravely and tried to withdraw in orderly fashion but they were caught by the machine guns positioned for the purpose."

John Olson, as the adjutant at regiment, described the scene at daylight: "The picture that greeted the sleepless eyes of the surviving Scouts as the sun rose, was one of utter chaos and devastation. Broken and bloody bodies were sprawled all over the foxholes and open ground throughout the I and left of K Company sectors. Forward of the front lines, mangled Japanese corpses were strung on the barbed wire like bags of dirty laundry. Abandoned weapons were strewn everywhere. The occasional bursts of fire from enemy-occupied holes, while sometimes provoking retaliatory fire from the Scout strong points, served to keep down any friendly movement. . . . Everyone, even the enemy, seemed content to desist temporarily." The losses to the Scouts added up to more than 100.

Harold Johnson, as executive officer for the 57th, coped with the importunings for aid from Fry, replacements for the high number of casualties among the American officers and Scout noncoms, and strove desperately to provide additional ammunition and supply. His by-the-book superiors flatly refused on the grounds that all allocations of artillery shells would be based upon a calendar basis. The schedule re-stricted batteries to less than one hour of fodder per day.

Johnson went over the heads of the commanders to reach MacArthur's deputy Richard Sutherland. The chief of staff, having visited the 57th two days before the opening of the attack, agreed with Johnson and forthwith directed ordnance to replace each day's expenditure of ammunition as it was consumed rather than hewing to a calendar. Furthermore, Sutherland recognized the failings of George Clarke and started a hunt for a new regimental leader.

As dawn lit on 10 January, the same day that Fry and his outfit met the Japanese attack, a PT boat carried MacArthur and Sutherland from Corregidor to Bataan for an inspection of the terrain and defenses. In his *Reminiscences*, MarArthur said, ". . . I had to see the enemy or I could not fight him ef-fectively. Reports, no matter how penetrating, have never been able to replace the picture shown to my eyes."

This visit, the only one made by the general to the penin-sula during its three-months' siege, covered an area south of where Fry's embattled forces in II Corps repulsed the initial assaults on the eastern edge of the front lines. Driven west, MacArthur conferred with Wainwright, the I Corps com-mander, who offered to show his boss where his 155mm guns awaited the enemy. MacArthur supposedly replied, "I don't want to *see* them. I want to *hear* them."

According to Clifford Bluemel, the CO of the 31st Divi-sion, then part of the I Corps, Wainwright summoned all of the generals to meet with their supreme leader. "We spoke to him and shook hands," recalled Bluemel. "He said, 'Help is definitely on the way. We must hold out until it arrives. It can arrive at any time. [Maj. Gen. George] Parker [II Corps commander] is fighting the enemy on the Manila Bay side [site of Fry and the 57th Regiment battle] and he'll hold them. He'll throw them back. We've just got to hold out until help arrives.' " Bluemel did not dispute the general's optimism then, nor did he criticize him for misleading his subordinates. To have talked in terms of defeat could only have led to a quick collapse of resistance.

The week before the 57th engaged in its fierce series of battles with the enemy and he toured part of Bataan, MacArthur became aware of the meager food stocks available for both civilians and troops. An inventory indicated only enough to feed 100,000 men for thirty days. On 5 January MacArthur approved a recommendation of his quartermaster that placed all troops and civilians on Bataan and Corregidor on half-rations. The diet amounted to roughly 2,000 calories daily, adequate for sedentary individuals but far below the needs of troops working or fighting for twenty hours a day. Furthermore, vital nutritional elements were missing from the reduced fare. Some units temporarily supplemented the short rations with items scrounged from depots during the retreat. The troops in the field also hunted for their meals, killing a number of carabao, the domestic cattle.

"I got a call one night to come up to Wainwright's headquarters," said Clifford Bluemel, whose 31st Division protected the unchallenged section of the west coast of Bataan. "He said, 'Your division's going to be moved over to the Manila Bay sector.' I said, 'My God! I haven't reconnoitered anything over there. All my reconnaissance has been on the China Sea side and out in Zambales.' " Poor mapping, few roads, and spotty trails through thick vegetation fomented Bluemel's anxiety. Any shift of men and equipment entailed the possibility of being lost.

"There was to be a guide to show me how I was to get to Guitol [a hamlet four or five miles behind the front lines]. I was to be in reserve. General Parker told me on the telephone, 'You follow the road. There is a wire that leads up there. All you have to do is follow the wire.' But there were dozens of wires. I was in a car and I followed this wire and that wire. I ran into an artillery battery and finally someone showed me where Guitol was. I got the troops up there, but we were bombed on the way up. That was the first time the division had been under fire."

With the bulk of his soldiers in reserve, Bluemel dispatched one regiment to support the Philippine Army's 41st Division, commanded by Gen. Vincente Lim, a Filipino alumnus of the USMA. "I went up to see how they were getting along," said Bluemel. "On the way back, I ran into a Japanese patrol behind the lines. There was a truck trail through a sugarcane field. I wanted to go up through the trail to get back to my command but was cut off by the Jap patrol.

"There was a Philippine Scout engineer detachment with one machine gun and a lieutenant. I said, 'You form up a point of an advance guard here, and we'll go up that trail.' But, by God, he wouldn't move. About this time I saw a captain with thirty Filipino Army men. He said, 'General, I think the Japs are there. I'll tell you what we'd better do. Comb that tree and all that area with a machine gun. Then I'll go into the sugarcane and you can go up the trail.' He made a remark to those Filipinos. 'Go on in there. What the hell's the matter with you! Goddamn you, you can't live forever!' They went in and drove out the Japanese patrol. I started up but those engineer Scouts wouldn't move. There was a little Filipino soldier there and after that he became my bodyguard. Nobody would go up the trail but he said, 'General, I'll go.'

"I said, 'All right, we'll go. You go ahead and I'll go with you.' Then I turned to those Philippine Scouts and said, 'I'm a brigadier general. I'm going up this trail, all of you goddamn yellow sons of bitches that are cowards stay there.' They came. From then on I found I could get them to obey orders by cursing."

Even though the enemy was apparently driven off, Bluemel soon found himself under attack. "Some of my own troops opened fire on me. I got off the trail into the sugarcane field. I lay down on my stomach and I could hear the bullets cutting through that sugarcane over my head. Finally they stopped. I went to the trail and waved my hat. There were some Filipino soldiers who belonged to my division. I said, 'What the hell do you mean by shooting up your own division commander!' "

While the body of the Fil-American defense futilely sought to contain the enemy on Bataan, the brain directed movements from the 2.74 square miles of Corregidor, the Gibraltar of the Pacific. Tadpole shaped, the island's head lies two miles south of Bataan while the tail points toward Manila Bay. The bulbous end of Corregidor thrusts 600 feet above sea level and on Topside, as it was known, stood the basics of an army post, headquarters, barracks, and officers' quarters all grouped around a parade ground. A small golf course adjoined the parade ground. The cliffs of Topside, cut by a pair of ravines, dropped precipitously to the water.

Adjacent to Topside, more quarters for officers and noncoms, a hospital, service club, and schools for children occupied a small plateau, Middleside. East of this area the land fell away to almost sea level and was only 600 feet in width. Known as Bottomside, the low area contained docks, warehouses, a small barrio, San Jose, and a vital power plant. Life upon Corregidor depended heavily on the energy generated on Bottomside to pump fresh water from wells, to refrigerate perishable foods, to move the electric railroad that supplied military installations. The topography changed radically as one continued from Bottomside toward the tailend. Another hump, Malinta Hill, almost 400 feet high, rose above the water. Beyond this outcropping, on the extreme eastern edge, lay a small air strip and a Navy radio station.

It was from Malinta Hill that MacArthur and his staff directed the struggle to preserve the American presence in the Philippines. To protect the nerve center for a War Plan Orange strategy, engineers had burrowed deep into the side of Malinta Hill to construct a 1,400-foot-long, 30-foot-wide tunnel. From the main shaft, with its railroad track running through it, extended twenty-five laterals, narrower 400-foot-long branches. A separate network of tunnels with a connection to the main passageway served as an underground hospital.

Blue mercury-vapor lights pierced the gloom of Malinta Tunnel, reflecting off the six-foot-high, endless line of packing crates with supplies. Signs that denoted organizations identified the province of the laterals. Within the confines of stale, hot air, insects, including bedbugs, tormented the residents. People intent on their business constantly jostled against others; solitude was impossible. The claustrophobic ambience drove some to stay outside even though exposed to enemy shells. Others developed "tunnelitis," unable to leave the seeming security of underground.

To maintain fortress Corregidor, a seemingly formidable array of heavy guns, principally coast artillery, housed in concrete bunkers, menaced anyone who approached by sea. But there were acute deficiencies. The big sticks all were of World War I vintage. They were geared for action against ships, not in support of ground troops. The antiaircraft weapons lacked the best ammunition for use against planes. And although emergency generators could operate the big guns, long-term efficiency required the services that only Bottomside could provide.

Three smaller islands bolstered Corregidor's control of Manila Bay. Tiny Caballo (Fort Hughes), only a quarter-mile square in area, lay due south. It bristled with eleven batteries of artillery including antiaircraft. Also blocking access through the south channel to the bay were Carabao (Fort Frank) and El Fraile (Fort Drum), a pair that contributed another thirty-two heavy pieces to the arsenal. Carabao's own heavy weapons, beach defenses, and 100-foot-high-cliffs made it an uninviting target for invasion.

Life on Corregidor during the first few weeks after the evacuation of Manila was subdued, broken only by the start of air raids. Food rations were more of an inconvenience than a severe hardship as boats from the southern islands ran the tightening blockade by the Japanese Navy. The vessels that reached the Rock brought fresh fruit, vegetables, and even candy along with other supplies. The population continued to grow. The 1,000 leathernecks of the Marine 4th Regiment, stationed first at Olongapo and then Mariveles, the port on the southern tip of Bataan, on 26 December boarded vessels that ferried them out to the Rock. According to one of their officers, "There was much talk among the men about its big guns and underground system of defense. Inspired by the memory of photographs of the Maginot line, they conjured up pictures of underground barracks and supply lines direct to gun positions. We watched Jap bombers steer clear of the antiaircraft barrages. It was pointed out that Corregidor's antiaircraft was so good that the Japs had not even dared to bomb it yet!"

On 29 December air raid sirens sounded on Corregidor, as

they had so often in the past without incident. Convinced this was one more false alarm, the denizens of the Rock paid little attention to the planes. But then bombs rained down upon portions of the island, with several striking at Middleside. Most of the Marine 4th Regiment dropped to the floors of their buildings as the explosions testified to the limits of Japanese fear of Corregidor's defenses.

"An army officer came in the room in which we were," said one leatherneck, "and informed us that there was no need to worry because the barracks roof was bombproof. A few minutes later, a Jap bomb had penetrated the roof on the other end of the barracks." The Marines moved outdoors to tents set up near the beach areas they would be expected to defend.

With the Marines now in residence, the number of people on Corregidor added up to 5,500 men, plus assorted civilian refugees connected with the uppermost echelons of command—the families of MacArthur, Quezon, Sayre, and some Filipinos acting as houseboys. The abundant portions of butter and eggs disappeared. On the 29 December raid, the twin-engined bombers maintained an incautious level of only 18,000 feet. The 60th Coast Artillery, throwing up three-inch shells and some .50-caliber machine-gun lead made the Japanese fliers pay for their insouciance. Several planes began smoking and the enemy formations, recognizing the error in judgment, climbed to a safer height. The bombardment scored heavily against barracks, warehouses, and other unshielded surface installations. It killed twenty-two and wounded another eighty, but tallied insignificant damage to the essential defensive armament of the Rock. Further aerial punches over the next week or so shattered more buildings, gouged ugly craters in the once-lush greenery but left the fortress intact. The residents, now aware of the deadly consequences if caught in the open, learned to either dig in or take shelter in places like the Malinta Tunnel.

General George F. Moore had named Col. Paul D. Bunker, nominally in charge of the 59th Coast Artillery manned by Americans, to run the seaward defenses of the Rock. At the start of the war, Paul Bunker had already worn an army uniform for thirty-eight years. A classmate of Douglas MacArthur at the Military Academy and an athletic star, he was an opinionated man freely given to the prejudices of his era. Bunker exuded spit and polish. "He appeared to walk at attention as he made his daily inspection of various batteries under his command," said one account.

Bunker jotted down his record of life on Corregidor. A 3 January entry noted: "Awoke early and went down to relieve the watch officer. Breakfast and then [for] bath and shave as usual. . . . They sprang the usual Air alarm on us which usually occurs when that lone Jap observation plane comes over every morning, thus wasting an hour. . . . Bought toothpaste and shaving cream in the heap of ruins which was once our Post Exchange. Lunch at Wheeler [a battery] on Topside. . . . As all was quiet went to my dugout to arrange its contents when Wham-o! She started. This was our second dose of Jap bombing, composed of four courses across the rock, said to be by two flights of six and eight planes, some of them the largest of the Jap bombers.

"Got into my car for a tour of inspection. Arrived at barracks at 2:35 and what a scene of devastation met the eye! Huge patches of corrugated roofing missing and scattered in painfully distorted shapes all over front and rear parades [grounds]. Captain [Harry] Julian met me and smilingly reported, 'Colonel, I have no office now.' A huge bomb had landed just across the car track in the rear of his place and blew out a crater twenty-five feet deep and forty feet across, cutting rails and trolley wires and shattering every window on the rear face of barracks. A smaller direct hit on [the] Mechanic shop where the Mech had practically finished making me a filing cabinet! Our regimental workshop [was] burning fiercely and, of course, no water at Topside.

"One could see, from the direction of wind, that it would also burn the other buildings, including the 'Spiff Bar.' I went up into my library and found utter chaos. Glass case containing my shell collection blown to smithereens and thousands of books littering the floor everywhere and even some outside. Going downstairs I found soldiers already looting the PX like ghouls. . . . Stationed a sergeant as guard temporarily."

In his diary, the coast artillery officer disparaged the Filipino soldiers. "It is an obvious fact that the Philippine Army is worthless because the Filipino will *not* fight under Filipino officers. And there are practically no Filipino officers who are worth a damn. The graduates of the 'Philippine West Point' at Baguio are sometimes pretty fair but others are political appointees whose only idea is to line their pockets. They have no control over their men."

The one resident of Corregidor who seemed totally unconcerned about the air raids was MacArthur, who, as navy officer Robert Lee Dennison previously observed, refused to seek shelter. As the siren sounded everyone headed for the safety of the tunnels. But MacArthur insisted on walking outside to watch the attack without even a helmet to protect him from debris or shrapnel.

High Commissioner Francis Sayre recalled an incident where he was among a group outside the shelters with MacArthur when a sudden bombardment exploded. Everyone except the supreme commander dropped to the dirt. "Anyone who saw us," remarked Sayre, "must have had a good laugh—at the General erect and at ease while the High Commissioner lay prone in the dust. I have often wondered whether he was as amused as I. In any event, his expression never changed." Sayre also remembered that MacArthur once remarked "he believed death would take him only at the ordained time." The nickname of "Dugout Doug," bestowed at a later period when MacArthur escaped from the Philippines and capture, was singularly inappropriate to describe his behavior on the Rock or, for that matter, other instances when he came under fire.

Seemingly oblivious to danger, MacArthur also exhorted his flagging troops. He issued a letter on 15 January: "Help is on the way from the United States. Thousands of troops and hundreds of planes are being dispatched. The exact time of arrival of reinforcements is unknown as they will have to fight their way through Japanese attempts against them. It is imperative that our troops hold until these reinforcements arrive.

"No further retreat is possible. We have more troops in Bataan than the Japanese have thrown against us; our supplies are ample; a determined defense will defeat the enemy's attack. It is a question now of courage and determination. Men who run will merely be destroyed but men who fight will save themselves and their country. I call upon every soldier in Bataan to fight in his assigned position, resisting every attack. This is the only road to salvation. If we fight we will win; if we retreat, we will be destroyed."

The message adds further mystery about the workings of the MacArthur mind. This was the only occasion on which he indicated numerical superiority for his own army; his reports to Washington and his memoirs constantly spoke of the greater strength of the foe. The statement "thousands of troops and hundreds of planes are being dispatched" was ambiguous if not deliberately deceptive. Any men and equipment moving to the Pacific were bound for Australia, not the Philippines. In his *Reminiscences*, MacArthur claimed, "A broadcast from President Roosevelt was incorrectly interpreted because of poor reception in the Philippines, as an announcement of impending reinforcements. This was published to the troops and aroused great enthusiasm, but when later corrected, the depression was but intensified." It is hard to believe a radio broadcast would be the means to inform the Pacific War's top commander that vital reinforcements were on the way.

Paul Bunker greeted the exhortation with reserve. Of the expected additions of men and machines, he noted, "If the Navy is responsible they'll never get here! Rumors are persistent that instead of six months' reserve of food, we have only three months!"

Army nurse Madeline Ullom says she took MacArthur's statement at face value. "Every morning, before breakfast, I walked to the top of Malinta Hill to see if the promised convoy was arriving." A month would pass before she realized help would not come over the horizon.

8

The Fall of Bataan

AT THE START OF THE THIRD WEEK IN JANUARY, ALVA FITCH with his artillery battalion feared an imminent and dangerous thrust from the enemy. Fitch's direst expectations proved well founded. When he reached headquarters, he recalled, "The CP was in a stew. The gooks were chattering like so many monkeys. A force of Japanese had gone around our right flank and cut our communications exactly at the rear echelon of the Pack Battery, five kilometers back. All forms of communication were cut. [Col. Halstead] Fowler [his commander], when he heard about it, had gone back and tried to drive them out with an automatic rifle. He had been hit twice in the back and lungs, but had escaped and returned to the Regimental aid station.

"About 4:00 p.m.," said Fitch, "a gook lieutenant, unknown to me, told me the road was open. I relayed the information to Colonel Berry. He sent an ambulance loaded with wounded to the rear. The road was not open. The Japs shot up the ambulance. Colonel Fowler and one other man who could walk, escaped. The Filipinos decided the Japs were using the ambulance as a machine gun and literally tore it apart with rifle fire. Of course the wounded were still in it.

"I found myself with 700 men who had not eaten for twenty-four hours. I got a sack of rice from the Philippine Army Infantry, and found a carabao during the night; each man got a little to eat. On the 22d, the Japs began closing in on us from all sides. We had no reserves after we had committed Laird's battalion in the rear and it was rapidly tiring. During the afternoon I called a conference of all of my battalion commanders and gave instructions for the destruction of guns and other materiel when the position should fall.

"We had received no word from General Wainwright and had no communications. Our position was extremely precarious. The troops had received only one meal since the interruption of communications and the capture of our rear echelon. Our ammunition was about gone, and we knew that a heavy battle was under way on the other side of Bataan. The principal reserve of General Wainwright's Corps had been moved to support the other battle before our communications had been cut. We could expect very little help and our force was exhausted."

Strategists plotted a new defensive position. But what looked good on a map proved extremely difficult to achieve. Access to the designated position depended upon a trail that deteriorated into an impassable path for vehicles. "As in many situations during the early days of the war," said John Olson, "no one on the higher staffs had taken the trouble to verify all of the facets of WPO-3. So no provision had been made to ensure that supply and evacuation could be effective for the organization given this portion of the line to defend."

For engineers to hack a road through the thick growth would require five days, an unacceptable delay. Regimental supply organized mule trains to pick up supplies dropped by vehicles at the point where the trail became inaccessible for trucks. Harassed by Japanese planes, the troops still managed to transport enough to sustain the infantrymen for several days. The planners worked out an intricate choreography—trucks or buses to haul soldiers as far as possible, and night marches to avoid the threat of air attacks. Military police patrolled the roads and trails but only partially prevented traffic jams. Periodic salvos of Japanese artillery rained upon critical sites under enemy observation during daylight hours and added to the difficulties.

A runner brought a message from Wainwright, directing units to "Hold your positions. Plenty of help on the way. Food will reach you tomorrow." The besieged troops hunkered down and employed what means they could to consolidate their position. A Japanese cavalry unit slipped into the area and triggered a firefight. Far worse, the battalion committed to an attack against the enemy in the rear slipped away. Their escape left the men with Fitch vulnerable.

Said Fitch, "We discovered [this] defection the next morning when Japs began arriving in the vicinity of our CP in buses. By 9 A.M. on the 23d our position had become untenable. All wire communication was broken. I lost all but one of my OPs. Rifle fire was coming through my CP from the front and the inland flank. About 10 o'clock, I gave the order to destroy all guns, except the 2.95" pack guns which were to be carried, and ordered all battalions and batteries to assemble about a kilometer to the rear of my CP. When I arrived at the assembly area, I found that Lieutenant Platt had been wounded. He had received bullets through one foot, and his testicles, and couldn't possibly walk. Colonel

Fowler was also there. I found myself with 700 men, of which 80 were Scouts from the Pack Battery, the remainder untrained and undisciplined P.A. artillery. I had four unwounded American officers."

Not only were Fitch and his companions in dire circumstances but the entire Bataan defense was threatened by a clever maneuver instigated by General Homma. The Japanese loaded a battalion of infantrymen aboard barges and set out for Caibobo Point, one of a series of finger-like protrusions along the western shore of Bataan behind the bulk of Wainwright's I Corps. Hastily mounted, the amphibious operation miscarried during a series of misfortunes. A lack of proper maps misled the navigators. Treacherous tides and a cranky sea sickened soldiers. But the worst to befall the ill-fated troops was their discovery by PT-34, skippered by Lt. John Kelly, with squadron commander John Bulkeley also on board. "We were returning to our base on Bataan early in the morning," said Bulkeley, "from a patrol off Subic Bay. We saw these barges and charged in among them, strafing them with .50-calibers and raising general hell but without very decisive results." In the darkness, a dim light, low in the water, had appeared. When PT-34 came within twenty-five yards of what was now perceived as a boat very low in the water, Bulkeley hailed it with a megaphone to determine friend or foe. A burst of machine gun fire and a stream of tracers established the relationship. Bulkeley himself took up an automatic rifle while the four machine guns on PT-34 pumped bullets at the craft now headed for the shore.

An enemy bullet ripped into the ankles of Ens. Barron Chandler, Kelly's second in command. But the enemy barge had taken too many hits to remain afloat and soon sank. According to the stripped-down narrative of Bulkeley, "We concentrated, after a general dispersion, on two barges that appeared to be crippled and sank them. The last one was boarded before sinking by myself and two live prisoners were taken with a lot of papers which were delivered to Corregidor. That first gave the news of the strength and force of the attempted landing. The Japanese barge sank with me and I was in the water hanging on to the two Nips till Kelly rescued me. It was a good thing that I had been a water polo player."

The interruption by PT-34 completed the disarray of the small flotilla. Not a single man reached Caibobo Point. Instead a third of the men came ashore at Longoskawayan Point ten miles southeast of the objective and the rest of the battalion landed about three miles from Caibobo. Guarding the beaches where the latter group came ashore were the Air Corps comrades of Tom Gage in the 34th Pursuit Squadron. The official U.S. Army history, *The Fall of the Philippines*, noted, "the airmen failed to make proper provision for security, for there was no warning of the presence of the enemy. The gun crews, awakened by the sound of the Japanese coming ashore in pitch blackness and unable to fire their .50-caliber machine guns, put up no resistance. After giving the alarm, they, in the words of an officer 'crept back to their CP.' "

Tom Gage offered a somewhat different version. "For several days," remembered Gage, "we could see mast tops just over the sea's horizon, coming down from the north to even with our position and then patrolling back and forth. Rumors said it was a battleship, mine sweeper, cruisers, tug boats pulling barges. No matter, during the night of the 22d, barges did land in a ravine or gully that ran down to the seashore. Our furthest northern point was a machine gun (.50 caliber) placed inside a rock barricade. In the early morning of the 23d, Japanese soldiers climbed out on top and approached the gun position. Some men thought they were Filipino soldiers, even called a greeting to them that was answered with rifle fire. Private first class John W. Morrell from Ohio was killed. The remaining men of the gun crew withdrew. Lieutenant Jack Jennings took a patrol later in the day into this area and came under heavy fire. He was wounded in the knee and Sgt. Paul Duncan was hit in the thigh by something of a large caliber. Paul died during the night in the squadron aid station. Others from the 34th incurred wounds from tangles with the invaders."

The Japanese who did reach the shore threatened Mariveles. Defense of the port depended upon one of the many improvised units, the Naval Battalion, with men drawn from the PBY Patrol Wing, the *Canopus* crew, shore personnel from Cavite Naval Base, and Battery A and Battery C of the 4th Marines. It was a collection of former shore-based torpedomen, storekeepers, yeomen, a motley crew of naval rates, and some marines under the leadership of Comdr. Francis J. Bridget—"Fidgety Francis" to some of his men because of his relentless insistence for them to "get war conscious." An Annapolis graduate, Bridget flew PBYs and had served as a squadron commander in the Philippines. But after air raids destroyed all nine planes, Bridget volunteered to form a security force that would defend the Naval Station at Mariveles.

During the week or so after the creation of the Naval Battalion, the new foot soldiers began courses in such unfamiliar subjects as marksmanship, squad tactics, and the use of the bayonet under supervision of Marines. Aware that their ordinary Navy whites made the men easier targets, the novice foot soldiers desperately attempted to dye their uniforms khaki but instead produced rather bright, mustard-colored garb. Sometime after eight on the morning of 23

January, Bridget listened to a frightened call from the lookout. "Longoskawayan, Lapiay, and Naiklec Points are crawling with Japs," supposedly shouted the observer. "We're getting the hell out of here, right now!" After those few words, in spite of requests for further information, Bridget heard only the ominous sounds of rifles. Bridget briefed and then dispatched two separate outfits to deal with the enemy until he could round up more men. He failed to advise either that a second friendly force would be active in the vicinity. The two units marched off into the wilds leading up to Mount Pucot.

One platoon blundered into a small group of enemy and a firefight ensued. The Navy ensign in charge and his senior Marine noncom both incurred wounds but the invaders took off. The untrained Navy troops kept firing long after the foe vanished into the jungle. Another platoon routed a handful of Japanese with more bursts from their rifles. The first effort of the novice infantrymen wiped their sectors clean but the main element of the amphibious force was still on the scene. Still, by nightfall, Bridget's ersatz infantry had control of Mount Pucot. A dead Japanese soldier's diary reported the presence of a "new type of suicide squad" dressed in brightly colored uniforms. He marveled at their tactics. "Whenever these apparitions reached an open space, they would attempt to draw Japanese fire by sitting down, talking loudly, and lighting cigarettes."

Bridget's makeshift army, reinforced with some soldiers from the Air Corps, a chemical unit, and the Philippine Army, sought to displace those Japanese still on Mount Pucot and the Longoskawayan peninsula, but most of the seaborne force had advanced into Quinauan Point after passing through thin beach positions of the 34th Pursuit Squadron. Brigadier General Clyde Selleck, required to defend the ten

miles of the entire southwestern Bataan coast between Caibobo Point and Mariveles, ordered Lt. Col. Irvin Alexander
and his regiment to drive the invaders into the sea. After his
initial mission of surveying the turf to be manned by the 71st
Infantry Division, Alexander now led the 1st Philippine
Constabulary Regiment.

Inducted into the Army only in December, the constabulary ordinarily served as an indigenous police force. Their
background did not include infantry training. Alexander
hurriedly mobilized his 3d Battalion and set out to block the
enemy. Rugged terrain, overgrown trails, and a single pass-
able road delayed movement long enough for the Japanese
to dig in. Alexander ordered an attack that faltered. He recalled, "The battalion commander explained that he had attacked frontally without making any attempt to explore
either flank. After I had moved to try to start the envelop-
ment myself, the Nips must have spotted me for they opened
up with a heavy machine gun which snipped off many
leaves uncomfortably close to my head. I lost no time hitting
the dirt, but before my head got there, a bullet struck the
ground where my head hit an instant later. Wiping the dirt
out of my eyes, I realized I was badly scared, my brain
seemed paralyzed.

"I explained to the battalion commander the necessity for
a flanking attack and assured him I would go with it. A Filipino corporal who saw the logic, jumped up shouting and
kicking at his men to get them moving. It was difficult to get
the men started, but we had to get results when the Nip machine gun opened up again, killing the corporal and several
men, thereby putting a stop to our attack. That corporal was
a gallant man who deserved recognition, but later, when I
tried to find out his name, I was unable to locate anyone who
remembered the incident."

MacArthur's chief of intelligence, Col. Charles Willoughby, accompanied by a member of his staff, showed up for a firsthand look at the problem. Along with the dismayed Alexander they kept meeting soldiers straggling away from the front. The Americans sent them back to their posts. But, noted Alexander, "Finding a number of officers standing behind trees, we tried to get them to take some tactical action; we had no success." Alexander said he made another determined effort to launch an attack. "There were no Filipino officers present, and the men were not going to be pushed, so I saw I had to lead them. I crawled ahead of the line about ten feet. By shouting and waving my arms, I managed to get the line to crawl up to me. We moved a couple of times more, while [an American officer] kept shouting a description of what he could see from the flank. He said we were very close to the Nip line that was made up of individual foxholes, except for a machine gun position that had two or three men in it. He announced that he could see a Nip sticking his head up, to which I answered, 'Shoot the son of a bitch!'

"His voice suddenly sounded very excited as he yelled, 'Look out! They are turning the machine gun in your direction!' I could not see a thing as I raised up on one knee, holding my rifle in front of me with both hands. Something struck the rifle with a metallic sound, jarring my hands pretty severely. Feeling an additional jolt on my right thumb, I turned it up to see a phosphorus core of a tracer bullet burning into my flesh. Before I became aware of any pain in my right hand, I had started jerking it violently. At last the phosphorus came off, leaving the top half of the thumb almost as dark as a piece of charcoal. Not until the pain eased up did I notice that one finger of my left hand had been shot away, and another one had been considerably mangled.

"After I recovered my wits, I ran a little to the left rear of where I was hit so that my location would not be the same when the Nips fired again, and then I was sick. For thirty-six hours, with the exception of four hours of sleep, I had been going at top speed. I had made countless decisions, some of which might have been of sufficient importance to influence the critical situation and I had one scanty meal during the action while working so hard to get results with poorly trained and poorly equipped soldiers who did not even understand my language. I was in doubt as to the results of the engagement, and I was suffering somewhat from the shock of my wound."

Willoughby bandaged Alexander's hand and led him to a first aid station. A surgeon discovered a sliver of metal in his breast bone. Driven to the Bataan hospital, Alexander admitted, "I had [a] feeling of relief . . . a mixture of thankfulness for being practically still in one piece and of pleasure at the opportunity to go to a place of comparative safety and comfort. On the other hand, I had a small guilty feeling that I was running away from the boys."

General Parker ordered the U.S. 31st Infantry and the 45th Infantry, the other Philippine Scouts regiment, to counterattack. The troops moved out with less than precise coordination as the Americans jumped off well before their Filipino comrades. The GIs achieved some good gains but then the attack stalled against a stiffening and increasingly numerous enemy. Even as the strategists rearranged their front, the hazard of the Japanese presence on the Points between Mariveles and Bagac required quick action. Not only had USAFFE strategists thrown General Selleck's forces into the fray alongside Bridget but, also, after Col. Paul

Bunker pleaded the case, Battery Geary, crewed by Philippine Scouts on Corregidor, blasted enemy positions with huge shells from its guns. A Coast Artillery installation had not fired against an enemy since the Civil War.

The psychological effect of the big guns may have shattered the spirit of some of the inexperienced enemy, but the interdiction capacity of Coast Artillery emplacements on the Rock was severely limited. Most fired flat-trajectory missiles, almost useless against an enemy hugging the reverse slope of a ridge. To support the Fil-American soldiers attempting to root out the opponents on the Points, 14,000 yards from Corregidor, the big guns at Geary lobbed shells at their most extreme range. Early in the month, a hit from an airplane had collapsed a half-completed air raid shelter, suffocating most of Geary's top noncoms. Their replacements were still learning their jobs. While a forward observer did accompany the men on Bataan to pinpoint targets, the ragged performance of guncrews led to inaccuracy and worse, several short rounds inflicted casualties upon about a dozen sailors serving as riflemen.

On another front, an infantryman well schooled in the theories of fire and movement so basic to the foot soldier, in jungle tactics, and coordination with artillery, Lt. Col. Hal Granberry, with his executive officer Maj. Robert Scholes, expertly directed the 460 men of 2d Battalion from the 57th. The Japanese fiercely resisted; some men fought hand-to-hand, but the Scouts relentlessly swept the enemy from their positions. Driven to a precipice, some threw away their weapons and hurled themselves from the cliffs into the water. They either drowned or fell victim to marksmen.

The corpses of the invaders lay exposed for several days, putrefying in the sun while Scouts busied themselves cleaning out caves along the shoreline where a few Japanese soldiers sought to hide. Not until the mopping up ended could a burial detail dig holes large enough for a mass grave to accommodate more than 100 bodies. Another 200 men were estimated to have been either blown up by the artillery, drowned, or been interred by their comrades. Casualties for the Scouts numbered eleven dead and about forty wounded.

The Japanese tried to add troops with more seaborne ventures. Sam Grashio, limited to flying reconnaissance missions from the field near Cabcaben, recalled, "Somehow our Intelligence got some remarkably accurate information: on February 1 at about 10:30 P.M., a Japanese ship would tow thirteen landing barges, crowded with 1,000 troops, into nearby Aglaloma Bay. At the appointed hour, our shore batteries abruptly shone their searchlights onto the barges, turning them into sharp, silvery silhouettes against the black waters of the South China Sea. As targets they were perfect. The other pilots and I, singly and in two-ship formations, flew back and forth over them, no higher than 200 feet, strafing every barge repeatedly, from end to end with .50-caliber machine gun bullets until we ran out of ammunition. Most of the barges sank.

"It seemed to me at the time that every last enemy soldier must have died either from gunfire or from drowning, though many years afterward I read an account that stated that about 400 Japanese troops did manage to get ashore, where all but three were killed by our troops. When it was all over, around 2:30 A.M., General George was ecstatic. He grabbed each of us in a Russian-style bearhug and recommended all of us for Silver Stars." Along with the blows struck by the four P-40s in Grashio's flight, the unfortunate Japanese reinforcements reeled from a rain of shells fired by field artillery outfits and small arms fire from Scouts on the shore. Among the participants in the ground fighting was Ed

Dyess, Grashio's former squadron commander. He led infantrymen manufactured out of former Air Corps men, some of whom, according to Grashio, could be heard inquiring how to fire their weapons even as they moved into combat.

While denying reinforcements to the enemy, hundreds of the original invasion force continued to present a risk for the defense. Poor coordination marked the first experience of the Scouts with tanks dispatched to their aid. The foot soldiers, instructed to keep 100 to 150 yards behind the armor, could not protect the hapless tankers from mine and grenade attacks. Individual Japanese soldiers dashed from the thick cover beside the trails, plastered a magnetic mine against a tank and then scurried into the jungle before the device exploded. On other occasions, they simply pulled a contact mine by string across the path of the tank. The Scouts, however, learned quickly. Instructed to stick close to the tanks, the riflemen picked off would-be mine layers before they had a chance to place the explosives. The determined troops contained the drive designed to conquer the western half of Bataan, albeit maintenance of the Fil-American lines required a pullback beyond a stretch of major east-west road from Pilar to Bagac.

To the east, in the II Corps, the Japanese had simultaneously applied pressure, particularly at a point centered around Trail 2 that plunged into the heart of the peninsula. Responsibility for the area, known as Sector C, belonged to Clifford Bluemel, who understood he would have at his disposal his entire three regiments of the 31st Division. Bluemel, organizing in Sector C, assigned his three regimental commanders to areas and they supposedly moved into place during the night. Said Bluemel, "The next morning I got an early breakfast, picked up all my staff, and headed for the front line. I made it a rule to visit the front line before the fighting started.

"I had a hole in the line which you could walk through. I had a battalion headquarters company from the artillery, fifty or sixty men, armed as infantry." They were available because a few days before, about 2,000 recruits had reported and, when asked how many he would accept, Bluemel grabbed them all. The newcomers filled such units as the artillery battalion, but since they had no field pieces, they served as riflemen, equipped with obsolete Lee-Enfields.

Bluemel assigned this skimpy band of soldiers to plug the gap. The handful of artillerymen armed with rifles could hardly have been expected to do more than delay an attack by even a company of Japanese soldiers at Trail 2. Bluemel tossed in a chunk of the reserves. "I had a G-2 [intelligence officer], a very bright young Filipino named Villa. The 32d had two battalions on the line and they had one in reserve. I told Villa, 'You see all these foxholes?' I want you to see a soldier in each foxhole before you get back to my headquarters, even if you're there until the day after tomorrow.' When he got back about 7:00 that night, he said, 'The battalion is in.' A little later the Japs attacked us. Right in that place they made their main effort."

Bluemel rightfully boasted, "If I hadn't gone out to the front line, assuming it was there, the Japs would have walked right up Trail 2 and Bataan would have fallen. If I had stayed back in my command post, it would have been a bad state of affairs." Not only was the planned advance through Trail 2 halted but Bluemel organized a counterattack that eventually pushed the Japanese back across the Pilar River.

Initially, the Japanese benefitted from the confusion and weakened state of their adversaries. The 1st Division of the

Philippine Army, commanded by Gen. Fidel Segundo, had taken such a beating and dumped so much of its equipment during its earlier encounters with the invaders that men who had lost their entrenching tools dug holes and trenches with mess kits and cleared fields of fire with bayonets. The Japanese secured positions behind the Fil-American lines that became known as "the Pockets." They dug in with the skill and camouflage they would consistently demonstrate throughout the war. Against the Pockets, artillery proved almost useless. Forward observers could not pinpoint targets; the absence of maps to indicate ranges and topography hampered gunners; the prevalent high-trajectory weapons only shattered treetops; and the plethora of dud mortar shells limited effectiveness of the basic piece for close support.

Wainwright personally directed the overall defensive operations against the incursions and at the Pockets as much as possible. During an inspection trip, the general's car rounded a curve that exposed it to enemy gunners. Incoming shells pounded the area and the occupants leaped out in search of cover or foxholes. Wainwright noticed a captain from his cavalry days and for eighteen minutes of the barrage calmly sat atop a heap of sandbags chatting with his old comrade.

Navy Lieutenant Malcolm Champlin, that branch's liaison to Wainwright, who had accompanied Wainwright, said he asked the general why he took such a risk. Recalled the Navy officer, "He said, 'Champ, think it over for a minute. What have we to offer these troops? Can we give them more food? No, we haven't any more food. Can we give them supplies or equipment or tanks or medicine? No. Everything is running low. But we *can* give them morale, and that is one of my primary duties. That is why I go to the front everyday. Now do you understand why it is important for me to sit on sandbags in the line of fire while the rest of you seek shelter?' "

The defenders, guided by Wainwright with his local commanders, gradually marshalled their superior manpower, brought up tanks, and squeezed the foe. As usual, gains accrued from the ranks of the Scouts—the 45th Regiment. Platoon leader Willibald C. Bianchi earned a Medal of Honor, knocking out a pair of machine guns while absorbing three wounds, including a pair of bullets that struck him in the chest. Tough fighting at a significant cost in casualties annihilated the substantial number of enemy invested in the Pockets, and the entire Japanese campaign to conquer Bataan ground to a standstill.

While the Fil-American forces had begun to decline due to the effects of short rations, fatigue, and disease, the enemy had also succumbed to the brutal conditions where the temperature averaged ninety-five degrees and the terrain was particularly inhospitable to an attacking army. Instead of the customary sixty-two ounces of food daily, the Japanese soldiers nearly starved on only twenty-three ounces in rations. Malaria and dysentery ravaged the Nipponese and medical supplies ran desperately short. Most of all, the jumble of Fil-American forces slowly, but with deadly effect, battered the Japanese. General Homma, expected to declare victory by the end of January, now saw his 16th Division of 14,000 soldiers able to field only 700 for combat. The 65th Brigade, nominally 6,500 strong, could muster only 1,000.

A temporary respite gripped the war zone during mid-February. The breather allowed replacement of forces and resupply for the Japanese, but no such restoration attended the defenders. Colonel Glen Townsend, commanding the 11th Regiment, which played a principal role in reducing the Pockets, noted, "The 26th Cavalry had eaten its horses. Rations were reduced from sixteen ounces a day to eight and then to four. Twice a week we got small amounts of carabao, mule or horse meat. There was no flour, vegetables, or sugar. The quinine was exhausted; malaria rampant. Almost everyone had dysentery. The hospitals and aid stations were jammed with sick and wounded [there were as many as 7,000 patients in Hospitals Number One and Two]."

Along with the troops on Bataan, those on Corregidor endured half-rations, but food recovered from barges and sunken vessels around the island shores supplemented supplies. Even as the troops on Bataan sucked on boiled hide, Paul Bunker on Corregidor recorded eating a dinner topped off with a piece of pie. "Probably the last," he noted, "because of the flour shortage. We are now on a ration that allows only one ounce of flour and seven ounces of bread per day." Meager as it sounds, the amount surpassed that available to the soldiers on the peninsula.

Blockade runners from the southern islands or even, in a few daring forays, from Australia, increasingly ran afoul of Japanese warships. Because of their limited cargo capacity, submarines, which operated with much greater impunity, were used only to bring in munitions and remove items like gold bullion and, increasingly, personnel—code experts, pilots, naval specialists deemed essential for prosecution of the war. Some of those evacuated owed their rescue to whom they knew rather than what they knew, and that engendered some resentment. The *Seadragon* scored one of the few successes at sea, sinking a fully loaded 6,441-ton transport outside Lingayen Gulf.

The administration in Washington, D.C., had already written off the Philippines. Always a longshot, the achievement of War Plan Orange required a fleet capable of carrying massive numbers of troops and gear 5,000 miles.

Shattered hulks at Pearl Harbor and the imperatives of a two-ocean war, factors never introduced into the original planning calculus, reduced WPO to the irrelevant. Glumly contemplating month after month of defeat, the policy makers desperately seized upon MacArthur both as an irreplaceable strategist and a rallying figure. He had earned this stature more for his skills as a diplomat and public relations than for any smashing victories.

A disheartened, sick Quezon had proposed to accept a Japanese offer that would grant the Philippines independence. He dictated a cable to President Roosevelt in which he complained that the U.S. had abandoned the Commonwealth, and it was "my duty as well as my right to cease fighting." MacArthur persuaded Quezon not to transmit the message. However, as Quezon continued to grumble about the ineffective American defense of his land, Washington politicos offered only encouragement, but no material aid. MacArthur, as middleman, skillfully navigated a tricky course. Surrendering before exhausting all possible resources would be a terrible blow to U.S. morale. At the same time, the supreme commander endeavored to convince the Filipino leaders that their citizens were not being sacrificed to salve American pride but to provide breathing space for mobilization of resources in the U.S. Sergio Osmeña, Quezon's vice-president, buttressed MacArthur's argument, suggesting to his president that history would perceive him as a traitor if he capitulated. For the wheelchair-bound, tubercular Quezon's protection, and perhaps to remove him from a stage where his cries of desertion might still echo, the submarine *Swordfish* evacuated the Quezon family to the southern Philippines. (Bulkeley spirited Quezon to Mindanao and a B-17 flew him to safety in Australia.)

The orders to MacArthur stipulated resistance so long as

humanly possible and he expected to die with his boots on. To his aide, Sidney Huff, he confided, "They'll never take me alive." Wife Jean, offered an opportunity to accompany the Quezons, refused. "We have drunk from the same cup, we three [their son Arthur] shall stay together." Instead of the MacArthur dependents, the *Swordfish* stored a foot-locker with the general's medals, the couple's wills, some investment securities, their son's birth certificate and first baby shoes, and a few similar personal items.

The doughty spirit MacArthur presented to the world was not lost on his superiors half a world away. Correspondents filed stories of his fearlessness during air raids, detailed his almost daily visits to the cots of the wounded, painted por-traits of his constant sessions with his commanders to plot moves which could thwart the enemy. Winston Churchill, with only melancholy news to issue about his own nation's engagements, addressed the House of Commons: "I should like to express . . . my admiration of the splendid courage and quality which the small American army, under General MacArthur, has resisted brilliantly for so long, at desperate odds the hordes of Japanese who have been hurled against it. . . ."

American soldiers on Bataan had begun to look at MacArthur differently, however, expressing resentment at a commander seemingly safely ensconced in an impervious fortress. The GIs, increasingly cognizant no help was on the way, referred to him as "Dugout Doug" and composed the ballad "Battling Bastards of Bataan," which mocked their status. In marked contrast, the Filipino soldiers seemed to maintain their faith in MacArthur. More important, the sto-ries printed in American newspapers and magazines played him up as an authentic hero to the public.

Military and political leaders at home and abroad urged

that MacArthur be extricated from Corregidor as an essential weapon for continuance of the war. He represented a rallying figure, and his capture or death would give the Japanese a propaganda coup. MacArthur's superior, General Marshall, on 23 February instructed him to visit Mindanao, spend a few days lining up defenses, and from there proceed to Melbourne for command of all U.S. troops in the Pacific theater.

In his memoirs, MacArthur claimed, "My first reaction was to try and avoid the latter part of the order, even to the extent of resigning my commission and joining the Bataan force as a simple volunteer [an improbable fantasy]." The assembled officers, according to MacArthur, vociferously protested the idea. "Dick Sutherland and my entire staff would have none of it. They felt that the concentration of men, arms, and transport which they believed were being massed in Australia would enable me almost at once to return at the head of an effective rescue operation." The general agreed to mull over his decision. A day later, the wishful thinking of his subordinates, based on rumors and interpretation of vague messages about shipments of men and machines, apparently infected MacArthur. He agreed to leave but on his own timetable.

Over the next few weeks MacArthur recalled, "I began seriously to weigh the feasibility of trying to break through from Bataan into the Zambales Mountains to carry on intensified guerrilla operations against the enemy." Obviously, the general was once more intoxicated by dreams of ventures far beyond the capacity of his ragtag army. In light of the condition of the Fil-American forces, piercing the Japanese lines was preposterous. More urging from Washington persuaded MacArthur to schedule his departure before the foe foreclosed any escape.

On the eve of his departure, MacArthur summoned Wainwright, to whom he would turn over command of Luzon. At that moment Wainwright's control covered at most a couple of hundred square miles because the enemy now occupied almost the entire island. Separate COs were named for other portions of the archipelago—Mindanao with 25,000 men, and the Visayan grouping that had a garrison of 20,000, all under Gen. William F. Sharp. There was also a commander for the fortified islands in Manila Bay. Strategic and tactical command for the Philippines remained vested in MacArthur, about to reside in Melbourne, 4,000 miles away.

MacArthur recalled his final meeting with Wainwright: " 'Jim', I told him, 'hold on till I come back for you.' " Wainwright in his memoirs offered a much lengthier version of their remarks. In his account, MacArthur addressed him as "Jonathan" and vowed he was leaving only under repeated orders of the president. "I want you to make it known throughout all elements of your command that I am leaving over my repeated protests." He did reassure his subordinate that if he got through to Australia he would come back. Wainwright, in addition to the command of a badly depleted army in wretched physical condition, received a box of cigars and two jars of shaving cream from the departing chief.

MacArthur recalled the scene at the dock the night of 11 March. "I could see the men staring at me. I had lost twenty-five pounds living on the same diet as the soldiers, and I must have looked gaunt and ghastly standing there in my old war-stained clothes—no bemedaled commander of inspiring presence. What a change had taken place in that once-beautiful spot! My eyes roamed that warped and twisted face of scorched rock. Gone were the vivid green foliage, with its trees, shrubs, and flowers. Gone were the buildings, the sheds, every growing thing. The hail of relentless bombardment had devastated, buried, and blasted. Ugly dark scars marked smoldering paths where the fire had raged from one end of the island to another. Great gaps and forbidding crevices still belched their tongues of flame."

He said he thought of those who would stay, like his classmate Paul Bunker. "He and many others up there were old, old friends, bound by ties of deepest comradeship. Darkness had now fallen, and the waters were beginning to ripple from the faint night breeze. The enemy firing had ceased and a muttering silence had fallen. It was as though the dead were passing by the stench of destruction. The smell of filth thickened the night air. I raised my cap in farewell salute, and I could feel my face go white, feel a sudden convulsive twitch in the muscles of my face. . . .

"I stepped aboard PT-41. 'You may cast off, Buck,' I said, 'when you are ready.' "

Bulkeley later said he had full confidence his boats and he could deliver their human cargo to safety. Although he had no sophisticated instruments for navigation through the thousands of islands, tricky currents, and in the darkness, Bulkeley said, "I had been in the Philippines for a long enough time and gone through the islands many times. I never doubted success and I was damn glad to get out of Corregidor."

Racing through a stiff wind that sent water lashing the faces of all aboard—seasickness struck all of the landlubbers—forced to stop from time to time to clean gasoline strainers, changing course to make a time-consuming swing away from land after signal lights from shore seemed to inform the enemy navy, only three of the PTs reached the first stop after almost twelve hours afloat. With PT-32 unable to continue for the moment, its passengers transferred to the 34 and 41. In tandem they set out for Cagayan on Mindanao.

On the morning of 13 March, the boats docked on schedule, having traveled 560 miles through Japanese-patrolled waters with only charts and a basic seaman's knowledge of navigation to arrive precisely on schedule. B-17s from Australia picked up the entire party for the final 1,500-mile leg of the trip to Batchelor Field, fifty miles from Darwin, Australia.

The general said it was at Batchelor that he issued the most famous pronunciamento of World War II, "I shall return." Manchester's biography of MacArthur reports the statement went to the press that met him at the Adelaide railroad station while he was enroute to Melbourne. In light of the details supplied by Manchester, his account appears more likely. The use of the first person singular provoked considerable argument, with detractors citing it as damning evidence of MacArthur's egomania. However, according to the biographer, the suggestion to use "I" instead of "We" developed from Carlos P. Romulo, then a lieutenant colonel and former newspaper editor and publisher, charged by MacArthur with handling news for the USAFFE. Sutherland, foreseeing the immediate future, while on Corregidor had suggested the Allies should employ the slogan, "We shall return." But Romulo argued that while Filipinos believed the U.S. had let them down, they maintained their faith in MacArthur. "If *he* says *he* is coming back, he will be believed."

Whatever the origins, MacArthur gloried in its use. "I spoke casually enough, but the phrase, 'I shall return' seemed a promise of magic to the Filipinos. It lit a flame that became a symbol which focused the nation's indomitable will and at whose shrine it finally attained victory and, once again, found freedom. It was scraped in the sands of the beaches, it was daubed on the walls of the *barrios*, it was stamped on the mail, it was whispered in the cloisters of the church. It became the battle cry of a great underground swell that no Japanese bayonet could still."

The American propaganda machines seized upon the slogan. Only a few days after MacArthur left, Sam Grashio and several other pilots flew over Manila and other sites to drop leaflets in which MacArthur sought to explain why he had left. "He also called upon them to be courageous, and promised that U.S. forces would return soon to rescue them," noted Grashio. Later, submarines handed out cartons of supplies bearing the three-word quotation.

The looming defeat of the MacArthur defense of the Philippines notwithstanding, the general was awarded the Medal of Honor

> For conspicuous leadership in preparing the Philippine Islands to resist conquest, for gallantry and intrepidity above and beyond the call of duty. . . . He mobilized, trained and led an army which has received world acclaim for its gallant defense against tremendous superiority of enemy forces in men and arms. His utter disregard of personal danger and under heavy fire and aerial bombardment, his calm judgment in each crisis, inspired his troops, galvanized the spirit of resistance of the Filipino people and confirmed the faith of the American people in their armed forces.

For the moment, regardless of how it originated and how much the phrase "I shall return" was trumpeted or inscribed, MacArthur as a figure in the defense of the Philippines was now offstage. The problem was he did not acknowledge the fact. To the confusion of the War Department in Washington, MacArthur did not clearly spell out the legacy of his command arrangements. It was assumed that he had endowed Wainwright with power over the entire archipelago forces. Made aware that such was not the case, a flurry of messages flowed from the interested parties. MacArthur told his boss Chief of Staff Marshall he still expected to control operations in the Philippines. Marshall declared the MacArthur plan unsatisfactory, advising President Roosevelt of the difficulties in managing four separate commands in the Philippines from a base 4,000 miles away. Roosevelt promptly elevated Wainwright to lieutenant general, officially notified him he now headed the U.S. Forces in the Philippines (USFIP), and carefully explained the decision to MacArthur, who for the moment accepted the new arrangements without objection.

The reactions to MacArthur's exit by the Americans who remained varied. Irvin Alexander said, "We were electrified by the news that General MacArthur and a part of his staff had gone to Australia. Of course, there was a great deal of resentment among those left behind, and the expression 'Ran out on us' was on many tongues, but if there was a single officer who would not have given his right arm to have gone with him, at least he would have settled for his left. I can never forget my elation when [word] came to my headquarters to tell me that General MacArthur intended to send for the remainder of his staff, and alerted me to be ready to go to Corregidor at an hour's notice, . . . others were scheduled to go with the next group of staff officers. It was our great misfortune that our call never came."

MacArthur's former West Point classmate Paul Bunker initially expressed his faith in the general. "We have been at war almost four months now and so far as we can see, no slightest effort has been made to help us. From the first, knowing the Naval War College 'solution' [reference to both WPO and Rainbow Five] to the Philippine Problem, I have secretly felt that we are slated to play the part of another Alamo. However, if anybody can help us it is MacArthur. He is our only chance. It is disturbing, however, to read that our President has appointed a 'Board' of all nations to control the 'strategy of the War in the Pacific'—why hamper MacArthur."

Sam Grashio, still flying one of the paltry stock of airworthy planes, said, "His departure occasioned some bitter remarks about 'Dugout Doug' from men who had long envied the Corregidor garrison for what they presumed was the easier life of the latter or who blamed MacArthur for the inadequate defenses of the Philippines. There were also gripes that the General had taken along the family's Chinese maid and, according to 'latrine rumors,' even a refrigerator [false as was one that said the family took out a mattress stuffed with money]. I never shared that discontent. Like most GIs at all levels I felt somewhat let down to learn that the Chief was no longer with us, but it seemed to me mere common sense to save him for the rest of the war."

To John Olson, fighting with the 57th Infantry, Philippine Scouts, however, the news was depressing. He noted that a rumor had circulated of General Homma's suicide, a reaction allegedly for the disgrace in not having overrun Bataan. "Perhaps this was to counter the dishearteningly accurate report that Gen. Douglas MacArthur had transferred to Australia. While this was explained as making it possible for him to command the reinforcements that had been promised since late December, it encouraged very few who heard it. Promises and predictions were not chasing the enemy from the Philippine Archipelago."

Clifford Bluemel spoke of MacArthur as a magic talisman. "There are always soldiers who say it's nice to fight under a lucky commander. I figured MacArthur had been a lucky commander and I said to some of the American officers, 'We've lost our luck' and I think we did. I think it hurt morale all the way down to the front-line people. I had to tell them, because if I didn't, the Japs had loud speakers . . . talking to the men, telling and begging them to desert. I told them, 'Help is going to come. He's going to bring it back.' I had to lie a little bit. I didn't believe it."

Meanwhile, USFIP commander Wainwright coped with his meager resources in men and supplies. It was clear that all efforts to break the blockade had failed, that the Luzon defenders could count on only insignificant amounts of food or medicine to reach them. Already puny food rations continued to dip in February and March. The Bataan soldier, American or Filipino, by late March lived on less than twenty ounces of food a day. Rice, in barely palatable, soggy portions, replaced wheat products like bread or potatoes. Those on Corregidor ate better than the troops fighting on Bataan. Rear-echelon troops managed to siphon off some items destined for the front lines. Commanders took to inflating their roster numbers in order to draw extra rations— a division that normally counted 6,500 men, dispatched two-thirds of its men for service elsewhere, then claimed it was feeding 11,000. Squabbling over the apportionment of food stocks racked relations with headquarters, quartermasters, and those engaged in distribution. Cigarette-hungry soldiers, down to an average of one smoke a day, created a black market that pushed the price of a pack to as much as five dollars. The low-calorie diet wasted muscle, depleted fat reserves, and men acted listless after any spurt of exertion. Serious vitamin deficiencies produced scurvy and beriberi. Malaria, dengue fever, and amoebic dysentery thrived in the weakened bodies.

The progress of the war curtailed medical care. Madeline

Ullom recalled, "The supply of plasma and for blood trans-fusion was soon exhausted. Doctors and enlisted men do-nated blood. The influx of many orthopedic cases used up the supply of traction ropes. Jungle vines were substituted. Backs ached from long dawn to dusk hours of changing dressings of patients on beds about one foot from the ground. Amputees without hope of prosthesis tried to learn balance and movement in their weakened condition. Gauze was washed, sterilized, and reused. Amputees spent long hours stretching and folding gauze. The transfer of patients from Hospital Number One to Number Two could not com-pete with the increase in admission rates."

As Wainwright assumed command, he still could list just under 80,000 soldiers in his 200-square-mile fief. But a large proportion could not be described as fighting troops. Doctors rated combat efficiency below 45 percent. In outfits like the Scouts, the best ones that Wainwright could field, company strength dropped considerably. And not even re-cruitment of the most capable from the constabulary, nor the promotion of men of proven worth to upper echelon non-coms or even the ranks of officers, could compensate for the losses. Wainwright and his staff learned that reports of Gen-eral Homma as a suicide had been erroneous. Actually, Homma had added 25,000 fresh soldiers, more and heavier artillery, and, equally important, a massive influx of air ele-ments with a mission to pulverize the Bataan defenders.

"On April 3," noted John Olson, "the sun when it rose looked down upon a peninsula torn by incessant and devas-tating bombardment from virtually every tube of the avail-able Japanese artillery pieces. The artillery fires were reinforced periodically by the heavy thumps of bombs that shrieked in clusters from dive bombers that flew with almost complete impunity back and forth across the lines." According to Olson, an uninterrupted, five-hour deluge of bombs and shells literally blew a hole in the sector of the jungle defended by the Philippine Army 41st Division. An ongoing barrage prevented reserves from sealing the hole. "Except in the western portion, the defenders had been reduced to a dazed, disorganized, fleeing mob. Nothing that the American and Scout advisors tried succeeded in stopping the bewildered and terrified Philippine Army personnel. A major rupture of the line had been achieved."

Exploding missiles interrupted Easter Services at Hospital Number One. The steady flow of casualties to the battered medical units became a torrent. "By five in the evening on the next day," said Ullom, "shells were raining. Word was that the Japanese had landed at Cabcaben which was only two kilometers away." Nurses like Ullom could not handle the volume. "Beds were assigned before those who occupied them were discharged prematurely to return to combat. Front lines seemed to vanish. Most of the patients suffered from gunshot and Hospital Number Two sent buses, trucks, and ambulances to transfer patients."

Alva Fitch witnessed the same overture to the final assault. "Our own news agencies kept reassuring the troops that everything was under control. By the sixth, all of our reserves had been committed and the Japs were advancing even more rapidly. At noon of the eighth, I was told to move my battalion about fifteen miles to my rear, about ten miles from Mariveles. I started my ammunition back during the afternoon. About dusk, I was told to remain in my present position, that Mariveles would be abandoned and we would make our final stand on the west side of Bataan. There was considerable confusion and no one seemed to know what was going on."

Deploying tanks and piercing the Fil-American lines in a

number of places, the Japanese surrounded some defenders
and swept others to the rear in a rout. This was accelerated
by their air arm that blasted the trails or roads packed with
men and the few vehicles and field pieces not abandoned or
shoved into ravines and ditches when passage became ob-
structed. With the enemy about to overrun the hospitals, the
authorities forestalled the capture of the women. "Around
eight on the evening of 8 April," said Ullom, "nurses at Hospital Number One and Number Two were ordered to take a
small bag and be ready to depart immediately. It evoked
mixed feelings from the nurses. Many were reluctant to go.
They felt an obligation to nurse the seriously and critically
ill patients. But they knew orders must be obeyed. The doctors came to see them leave. Goodbyes were hasty with
promises to see each other again.

"About midnight, the nurses from Hospital Number One
were in a small open boat. It tossed about in the water as
blasts hit nearby. Guns on Corregidor were hitting the Japanese on Bataan. Shells whizzed over heads repeatedly. Men
on all sides were attempting to swim to Corregidor. At 3:30
the pier was reached finally, amidst flashes of gunfire and
blast of bombs."

Later, evacuees from Hospital Number Two endured an
even more harrowing trip. They had gathered at the Mariveles dock while in the early morning hours, defenders demolished stores of TNT, warehouses, ammunition dumps,
and storage tanks rather than allow them to fall into enemy
hands. For as long as seven hours, the nurses and personnel
accompanying them huddled in ditches, under trucks, in an
engineers' tunnel, or in a culvert. Meanwhile the orgy of destruction continued to streak the sky with streams of colored
fire and smoke. Sailors scuttled the few ships and the faithful *Canopus* backed out into fifteen fathoms of water and

then slowly settled to the bottom as water flooded the torpedo warhead locker and forward magazine. Even Mother Nature battered the hapless on Bataan and Corregidor. An earthquake shivered the ground, sent men sprawling, bounced the beds in Hospital Number Two, shook the walls of Malinta Tunnel on Corregidor, swayed the trees, panicked screaming monkeys.

The II Corps, defending the eastern side of the peninsula, ran out of space to back up in as the enemy advance from the north and on the western flank shoved troops under Bluemel toward Manila Bay. Bluemel supposedly had three regiments and a battalion of his own tied in with two more regiments under Col. John Irwin. In fact, surrenders, desertions, killed, and wounded had depleted approximately 10,000 combat troops to 2,500 who, said one officer, "were all so tired that the only way to stay awake was to remain standing. As soon as a man sat or laid down he would go to sleep."

As communications broke down and the defenders broke ranks to retreat, Bluemel could personally exercise command over only a small portion of the men. He spoke for many of the embittered at the front as he exploded to a handful around him, "Those goddamned bastards back there have been sitting on their damned fat asses for months, eating three squares a day before retiring to their comfy beds for a good night's sleep. They've had their heads in the sand like a covey of ostriches. They haven't known what is going on, what has happened, and they haven't listened. And now it's all down the drain. I can't pull their dead asses out of the fire, and I don't know of anyone else who can except the Good Lord, but I don't see Him taking the trouble." While Bluemel overstated the living conditions to the rear, the orders he received indicated at best wishful desperation and at worst woeful ignorance.

On 8 April, the troops led by Bluemel yielded along the Alagan River, the final natural barrier to the enemy advance. The haggard general, who had suffered the same extreme physical demands as his soldiers, had halted at night by a stream of water, waded out to a rock, and removed his shoes and socks to bathe his sore, swollen feet. When his II Corps commander and nemesis Gen. George Parker reached him by field telephone and told Bluemel to form yet another line of defense, Bluemel scalded his superior: "You sit back there on your dead tails in your comfortable, well-lighted CP and draw a line on a map with a grease pencil and tell me to hold it. I am lying here in pitch black dark, with no map and only a vague idea of where I am. I have been fighting and falling back on foot for the last seventy-two hours. I have no staff, no transportation, no communications except the phone I hold in my hand. My force consists of remnants of the only units that have fought the enemy, not run from them. The men are barely able to stagger from fatigue and lack of food, which we have not had for more than twenty-four hours. Yet you cannot send me one of your many fat, overworked, staff officers to show me where I am to deploy the handful of men I have. Where is the food we need to revive our starving bodies? Where is the ammunition we need to fire? Where are the vehicles and medics to treat and evacuate our wounded and disabled? I'll form a line, but don't expect it to hold much past daylight. OUT!" As Bluemel and his staff tried to organize a cogent defense they too felt the earth tremble beneath them. They first thought that hunger and fatigue had induced hallucinations but then realized it was a quake.

In Australia, MacArthur said, "Rumors reached me of an

impending surrender. I at once radioed General Marshall, informing him that under any circumstances or conditions I was utterly opposed to the ultimate capitulation of the Bataan command. If Bataan was to be destroyed, it should have been on the field of battle in order to exact full toll from the enemy. To this end, I had long ago prepared a comprehensive plan for cutting a way out if food or ammunition failed. This plan contemplated an ostentatious artillery preparation on the left by the I Corps as a feint, a sudden surprise attack on the right by the II Corps, taking the enemy's Subic Bay positions in reverse, then a frontal attack by the I Corps. If successful, the supplies seized at this base might well rectify the situation. If the movement was unsuccessful, and our forces defeated, many increments, after inflicting important losses upon the enemy, could escape through the Zambales Mountains and continue guerrilla warfare in conjunction with forces now operating in the north. I told him I would be very glad to rejoin the command temporarily and take charge of this movement. But Washington failed to approve. Had it done so, the dreadful 'Death March' which followed the surrender, with its estimated 25,000 casualties would never have taken place."

Nothing demonstrates better than this statement the fantasies that had swathed MacArthur's thinking. From his first decision to meet an invasion with an untrained, ill-equipped army through the final moments when he proposed that the starving, sick [80 percent with either malaria or dysentery], ammunition-poor, artillery-weak, and ragtag aggregation, an army largely only in name, carry out an attack against a well-led, fully equipped foe supported by an abundance of big guns and aerial supremacy, he seemed to believe he could control reality by means of his will.

MacArthur voiced his faith in this "sudden surprise attack" even after the war. Wainwright, who had dutifully echoed his superior, years later said of Gen. Edward P. King, "[he] was on the ground and confronted by a situation in which he had either to surrender or have his people killed piecemeal. This would most certainly have happened to him within two or three days."

Irvin Alexander attended the conference at King's command post while the strategists wrestled with Wainwright's notion of an attack by I Corps. Remembered Alexander, "Calling General Wainwright's headquarters again, [King] demanded to know what the decision was with reference to I Corps in view of the fact that General Jones had reported to General Wainwright exactly as he had to General King, that he could not launch an attack. . . . There was a considerable pause, during which I assumed that a discussion was going on at the other end of the line. Two or three minutes later, General King said, 'Thank you very much' and hung up. Turning to his staff, he reported that General Wainwright could not agree to a surrender of Bataan as General MacArthur had ordered him to hold on, but that if General King did surrender on his own authority, there would be no interference with any element of his command." Wainwright later would categorically deny he held any discussion with King about the option of surrender.

Said Alexander, "The general went on to say that if he survived to return home he fully expected to be court-martialed, and he was certain that history could not deal kindly with the commander who would be remembered for having surrendered the largest force the United States had ever lost." After further review of the situation with his staff officers late during the night of 8 April, King concluded he had no alternative but to submit to the enemy. He made the decision on his own, knowing full well it directly disobeyed the orders emanating from both Australia and Corregidor. King and the enemy commander, Maj. Gen. Kameichiro Nagano, met to cover the details for a formal surrender. The first hours of the session went badly. General Homma had expected the U.S. envoy would be a representative of Wainwright and prepared to speak for all Fil-American forces in the islands. King could speak only for the Luzon army. King bargained an immediate armistice, for assurances that all prisoners would be treated in accord with the Geneva Convention, and that the sick, wounded, and weary ride in trucks with gasoline expressly saved for this contingency. The Japanese dismissed the plea for an immediate halt to the shelling, saying that their pilots, already in the air for missions, could not be recalled before noon and raids would continue until that hour. Irate because King could not yield the defense of the entire archipelago, the victors demanded unconditional surrender of those under King's command. The discussion dragged on for ninety minutes before King, desperate to spare useless bloodshed, assented. Even then, his conquerors demanded that every individual and unit accept the uncompromising terms.

The chaos continued even with the cessation of hostilities. Alva Fitch recalled, "A messenger told me to report to General Stevens's CP as Colonel Hunter's representative. [Luther Stevens commanded the 91st Division supported by Fitch's artillery.] When I arrived, the staff was sitting around with long faces, drinking coffee. I was given a cup of coffee and a chair. General Stevens blew his nose a couple of times, and said: "Major, General King has gone to Japanese headquarters to surrender the Bataan forces. The terms are not yet known. Be prepared to complete the destruction of your guns and material before 6:00 A.M. [There is a discrepancy between Fitch's time table and the official record but there is no reason to doubt his memory of the experience.]

"I reported this to Colonel Hunter and assembled my battalion commanders and staff. I gave them the news and instructions as to what to do to their guns and equipment. About 4:00 A.M. I received a call from General Stevens. He said the Japs had refused to accept the surrender. And that we were to fight it out on our own. My Filipinos didn't like this much, nor for that matter did I. About half an hour later, he called again and said that the surrender had been accepted.

"The next few hours were very noisy. The sound of demolitions and of burning ammunition dumps gave the impression of a fair sized battle. . . . We had a good meal, posted guards for local security, and I went to sleep. By the time I awakened on the tenth, most of the sounds of fighting had stopped. We received orders to stack arms and display white flags. All day we heard stories of how the Japs were treating prisoners. Generally, they indicated that we could expect fair treatment. My lieutenants were in favor of taking to the hills. All had malaria, some had dysentery, and we had no medicine. I feared that it would be a year or eighteen months before the Philippines were retaken. I didn't believe we could live that long among the Filipinos without being captured or betrayed by them. Eventually they [his subordinates] all took my advice and stayed with me."

When Col. Irvin Alexander returned to the 71st Division headquarters he reported to his superior, Brig. Gen. Clinton Pierce. "I informed the division commander that most of my American officers and a number of the best Filipinos had spoken of going to the hills instead of surrendering. I suggested the possibility of the general leading a picket detail through the Nip lines. He answered, 'If the commanding general had wished that I take a patrol to the mountains, he would have told me. I have received orders from my commander to surrender myself and my command and I am a soldier who carries out orders.' I asked him if he would authorize the immediate departure of a patrol if someone else led it. He answered, 'No!' "

The upper echelon officers waited for official word of acceptance of a cease fire. Word came that the enemy had started an attack. Alexander received orders to block the Japanese, using a battalion of Scouts already on hand and another battalion that would join them subsequently. "The men had been informed before noon that the war was over, and they had thrown their arms away, substituting white flags for their guns. I tried to get them off the road into the jungle but I was not successful. The story of surrender spread like wildfire, so that the newly arrived men started to throw their arms away. I appealed to the battalion commander who did get his companies into position, but I knew there was no fight left in the men.

"General King had surrendered us, yet I had command of a defensive force that was practically useless, under order to allow no Nips to pass our position. The American officer with me tried to reassure me by saying there would be at least one man to back me up when I started shooting." To Alexander's enormous relief, he received instructions to withdraw into a bivouac at their permanent camp. "I assembled all of the Americans at supper to repeat my conversation relative to taking to the hills. I told them I was not in good enough physical condition to try to pass through the Nip lines. I [explained] I saw it my duty to stay and accept surrender but I would order out a patrol consisting of all those who felt their chances were better in the hills. Moreover, I would take full responsibility for their absence in the event they did not come back. After a brief discussion among themselves, every man decided he would stay."

By field telephone, Gen. Arnold Funk advised Bluemel to withdraw his people to an isolated position where they could escape contact with the enemy while rations would be sent to them. The general with men from his 31st Division and other units formed into a column trudging toward a safe area. Bluemel recalled, "While moving on [a] trail, [I] was leading the column with a patrol of two men and came under rifle and machine gun fire in the open at a distance of about 100 yards. The troops of the 26th Cavalry were deployed and an engagement commenced. At this time the attention of the CG 31st Div. [Bluemel] was called to the fact that head-quarters Luzon Force surrendered at daylight and directed firing to cease at that time, that it was now almost noon and a fight was commencing. If the command fought its way out of this situation, it would be to surrender at Mariveles or some other place as there was no place to go or other troops that could be reached—and that many casualties would be incurred for no useful purpose. It was decided to stop the fight and surrender."

9

The Death March
and Morale Missions

IN THE HANDFUL OF HOURS THAT REMAINED BEFORE THE Japanese overran all of Bataan, Wainwright endeavored to import as many as 7,500 men to Corregidor. He hoped to reinforce his garrison with proven units like the 45th Infantry Philippine Scouts, a field artillery battalion with its weapons, and other soldiers. He agreed to take all Navy personnel, mostly Americans, with their precious stores of food, fuel, and boats to the fortress. Transportation specialists rummaged a shuttle service employing a minelayer, interisland steamer, launches, and barges towed by powered vessels. The entire operation fell apart as gridlock on trails and roads as well as interdicting fire from the enemy prevented the 45th from ever reaching the docks. Through binoculars, a horrified Wainwright and staff watched servicemen and civilians improvise their own craft, sometimes as flimsy as a few bamboo poles lashed together. Others plunged into the oily, shark-infested water and swam toward the Rock while Japanese artillery lobbed shells among them and snipers picked off the bobbing heads. About 2,000 eventually joined 8,000 already on Corregidor. Had everyone whom the command authorized reached the island, the limited food supplies would have run out within ten days.

On Bataan, the Japanese bagged as many as 78,000 men, the largest number ever surrendered by an American commander. The volume staggered the victors, who had anticipated only about 40,000 troops opposing them. Not only were there nearly double the amount of captives but also the speed of victory far exceeded the Japanese timetable. In little more than a week they had achieved what they believed would require at least one month of operations. Under these circumstances the absence of a plan to handle prisoners is understandable. As a consequence, there were no preparations to provide food, water, or transportation for the tens of thousands. These inadequacies alone boded ill for forces taken on Bataan.

Adding to the potential for disaster was the attitude of the winners. Resentment toward those whose bullets, grenades, and shells killed friends and associates was expectable. But racism also played a role. The Japanese considered themselves a superior ethnic strain and the subjugated Filipinos, along with the Chinese, Polynesians, Koreans, and other Asians, as inferior. Their knowledge of the U.S., much of it drawn from Hollywood's gangster movies or westerns, coupled with propaganda, persuaded them Americans were crude, thuggish people bent on the destruction of the Japanese way of life. Perhaps most damaging to the esteem for Americans was *Bushido*, the warrior code that taught that death was preferable to surrender. For a foe to yield while still able to fight generated contempt, particularly among the officers.

What would become known as the "Death March" developed slowly; the men caught up in it had no inkling of what lay ahead. In the chaos neither American officers nor the captors provided direction. Tom Gage, the Air Corps clerk, remembered, "When we got the news that Bataan had been surrendered—something like jungle telegraph spreads by osmosis—everyone started gathering in the headquarters-supply area. We built a fire and began throwing the .45s into the fire. Rifle bolts went into the fire, too. Campbell came over and suggested we drift toward the supply trailer and see if we couldn't get ourselves some new clothes. I put on everything new and picked out several pairs of socks. I also put on a brand new pair of brown army shoes." Some in Gage's area had been approached by Filipinos offering to sell food. After agreeing to a deal, the Americans followed the natives. Gage recalled, "They found a mountainous food dump, and we had been starving for the past two months. Everyone could get all the milk [condensed], chocolate, corn beef [canned] they wanted. There were a lot of K rations, too.

"On April 9th, we were told to move out. I don't think a single officer stayed with the enlisted men. I think we were trucked in relays to area headquarters. Our truck wouldn't run so it was towed to Mariveles by another loaded truck. We were packed in standing. On the way down we saw our first Japanese troops. They were stringing telephone wire up the road. When we got to Mariveles we were not allowed off the trucks. In the morning, they would let a few off the back but we could not wander. I filled my canteen with ditch water and dosed it liberally with either chlorine tablets someone gave me or iodine. I've never understood why I didn't get dysentery or typhoid from this water—maybe I overdosed it with chlorine.

"We were put through our first shakedown, they were looking mainly for weapons. I retained my field bag and food, tin helmet and a book—*For Whom the Bell Tolls*. We were in this place the 10th, 11th, and 12th [of April]. Most of the 34th [Pursuit Squadron] searched each other out and gathered in one general area. We were all approached on turning in our chow to Mess Sergeant Hardy and having him make as many meals as he could. I recall we had something to eat every day. On April 12th, they threw us out on the main road and we started the march out of Bataan."

P-40 pilot Sam Grashio passed up two opportunities to escape by air when he saw his squadron commander Ed Dyess refused to flee. Dyess procured an automobile and a handful of companions sought to find the rest of the scattered outfit. Said Grashio, "Cold reality enveloped us within a few minutes. We met a Japanese tank and staff car. We stopped at once, threw up our hands and waved white handkerchiefs. A Japanese soldier standing in front of the tank motioned us to drive closer. We did and again alighted with our hands up. A Filipino interpreter with the soldier complained that we were violating surrender instructions because we still wore sidearms.

"The Japanese without a word proceeded to club Dyess mercilessly. For good measure, he then stole two rings of mine, a crash bracelet, and a pen and pencil set. Then he motioned for us to get back into the car and resume driving toward our outfit. As we proceeded, our captor pulled close to our vehicle, smiled inexplicably, and threw my jewelry back into our car. But as soon as we stopped, other Japanese lined us up in groups of 100, and stole my possessions all over again, save only my flying ring, which I managed to tie inside my underwear."

According to Alva Fitch, "About noon of the 11th a Jap force occupied the area of the creek from which we were getting our water. I went to pay a call on the commander thereof. He was quite civil and told me to send my Filipinos to Bagac and that he would give me a pass to take my Americans to Mariveles. I sent the Filipinos to Bagac at once and with one car and one truck we started for the Jap CP. We were no sooner on the road than trouble began. A party of Japs took our truck and car and began taking watches, money, etc.

"I walked the 300 yards to the CP and protested. The officer was 'so sorry' but 'you should bring all of your men to my CP.' After about two hours of argument and waiting, he gave me another car and a pass to Mariveles. He cautioned us not to drive after dark. We started for Mariveles, driving fast so as to get as far as possible before something happened. We went about five kilometers before we were stopped by a Jap whose car was broken down. After about an hour of arguing in a wide mixture of tongues, he took our car and told us to wait, that he would bring it back. It was just getting dark. We knew from experience that the road was no place to wait, so we crawled off into the jungle and holed up for the night.

"The next morning," Fitch remembered, "we split our last can of beans and started walking. It was a hot day, a dusty mountain road with considerable traffic. Everytime we encountered any Japs we were searched and robbed of a few more of our possessions. About 10:00 A.M. we arrived at a motor pool where we located the car taken from us the night before. We showed our pass and opened negotiations for the recovery of 'our' transportation. After thirty minutes we

got[an] answer: 'Very sorry but I have no car to give you.'
We resumed our walk.

"The west side of Bataan is quite devoid of rivers. The
few streams were so contaminated that we didn't dare drink
from them. We were unaccustomed to the sun, so it didn't
take long to become thirsty. Our loads were light. All they
had left me was one pair of extra socks and my empty canteen. In the early afternoon we were able to thumb a ride in
an empty truck and rode for about ten kilometers. We arrived in Mariveles about 3:00 P.M. and expected to find food
and transportation to wherever we were going. We found
nothing, except several hundred Americans, as bewildered,
hungry, and poverty-stricken as ourselves. We were herded
into what had been the public square and thoroughly
searched.

"After about an hour of milling around, a Jap climbed up
on a truck and made a speech. 'You take a little walk to
Balanga. Maybe you get food there.' Balanga was about
forty kilometers away. I didn't think we could make it but I
was no longer in a position to dispute with the Imperial
Japanese Armed Forces." As Fitch's report indicated, one
immediate policy of the Japanese was to separate the indigenous people from the U.S. soldiers.

What also soon became clear was that the occupiers of
the Philippines made no distinction between rank and file.
The diary of Clifford Bluemel indicated the attitude from the
first day of his incarceration: "9 April 1942 Captured in
company with Col. Lee Vance [CO 26th Cavalry] Col. Edmund J. Lilly [CO 57th Scouts] . . . Questioned by G-2 [In-
telligence], 21st Jap Division. Hit in head by Jap. Lt. Col.
believe name is Kusiamato. No food since breakfast. Slept
on ground, during night moved to tent [with others] that was

closed and the odor was terrible. I laid on the ground with my head near the door so I could get air.

"10 April 1942 Shortly after daylight I was again taken to Kusiamato who again questioned me. He gave me a handful of cold rice, some tea for breakfast. We marched toward Mariveles with the division. After about an hour a truck was obtained. Stopped in abandoned army camp. Here we were permitted to scavenge and I found a pair of trousers, three pair of socks, shaving brush, shirt, and mess kit. No dinner or supper. A Jap soldier gave us some sugar and water during the night. Slept on ground, no blankets.

"11 April 1942 Shredded coconut and sugar for breakfast. The five of us were put in a truck to go to Orani. Truck also contained Philippine Scouts and Philippine Army enlisted men. Truck reached Balanga, the five officers were put on a truck returning south from where we came. We were taken off about ten kilometers south of Cabcaben, turned over to a Jap detachment, told we would remain in zone of Corregidor shell fire until Corregidor fell. We were given some American canned food. Each of us was given a cot. We were permitted to go to a nearby stream and bathe."

On 13 April, a large body started toward Cabcaben. Riding in a former U.S. Army truck under guard, Bluemel and fifteen officers and enlisted men passed columns of Japanese troops. Shells whistled in from Corregidor and both the Nipponese and their prisoners scurried to cover. The truck brought them back to Balanga where Bluemel downed a plate of rice and endured another grilling about the fortifications on Corregidor. He convinced the interrogators he knew nothing of value. They lodged him in a guardhouse with Brig. Gen. Luther Stevens, an American officer with the constabulary, and Maj. William J. Priestly from the 57th Infantry. Released from the confines of the guardhouse on

15 April, Bluemel, along with Stevens and Priestly, joined an American column of fours, and started to walk toward Orani.

The terse diary entry for 16 April noted: "Left Orani a.m., no breakfast. Stevens hit by Jap on passing truck. Jap sentry made me leave him, threatened to shoot me if I did not move."

After the war, Bluemel amplified his description of the incident. "A Jap riding in a passing truck struck Stevens on the forehead with a bamboo pole. Stevens staggered and his glasses fell off. I held him with my right hand and caught his glasses with my left. We fell out of the column and sat down. He said, 'That was hard to take.' The column passed. At the end, a Jap with a rifle on his left shoulder and a .45 caliber revolver (U.S.) in his right hand, stopped, pointed the revolver at me, grunted, and motioned for me to get up. I tried to tell him in English that a general was hit and hurt. He pulled back the hammer and again grunted and motioned for me to get up. I did. He then pointed the revolver at Stevens and did the same. I helped Stevens up. I still tried to argue with the Jap. He motioned Stevens off the road and into the dry rice paddies. He went about fifteen yards. I thought the Jap was going to shoot Stevens. The Jap then pointed the revolver at me and motioned me up the road to join the column. He left Stevens in the rice paddies and then ran past me to the column. I rejoined the column."

On the road again, Bluemel heard firing to the rear. "Saw Filipinos who had been shot a few minutes before. A grueling march, no food, little water, many who fell out shot." The group stumbled into Lubao after dark and Bluemel, who managed to buy some rice and sugar enroute, gulped it down when they halted for the night. Bluemel met a Japanese officer who spoke English. "I told him I was a general and asked for a ride, as I understood all generals were given them. While talking with him, a squad of American officers marched in, halted and reported. [They were late, having fallen behind the main body of the column.] The Jap immediately accused them of trying to escape and said they would be shot. I told him if they planned to escape they would not have marched in a squad formation. It showed they had no intention of escaping. They had become tired and dropped behind. They had marched in the required formation to join the column. The Japanese officer sent them to the other prisoners near us. He gave me a meal at his mess."

Alva Fitch, having conceded he was no longer in a position to argue with the enemy, had started the forty-kilometer hike toward Balanga. Near little Baguio the prisoners managed to fill their canteens. Then the Japanese separated the Filipinos from the Americans, who spent a hungry night without bedding and hordes of insects. "A few men had some C rations," said Fitch. "That served to make the rest of us that much hungrier. At daylight we were awakened with the rumor that we were to have some breakfast. After two hours of milling around and counting and recounting, we started down the road again. This time we went about four kilometers and were taken off the road to wait for trucks or breakfast. Neither came. About noon we were back on the road. About 2:00 P.M. we arrived in Cabcaben and were herded into the schoolyard. We were very hot and thirsty. Stillman, Semmens, and I slipped away and filled our canteens at the barrio pump. We were slightly beaten for our pains, but the water was worth it.

"At dark we arrived at Limao [about ten miles from their starting point]. Most of us had a much-needed bath in the bay. We found an artesian well and drank all the water we wanted. We held a conference and decided we had enough of marching in the sunlight. We decided to get up about 2:00 A.M. and march to Balanga where we had been told we would be fed. Without taking the Japs into our confidence, we formed for the march on schedule and started. The guards came along without protest. We arrived in Orion about 8:00 A.M. and were marched into some rice paddies and ordered to sit. There we stayed until midafternoon in the heat of a bright day of the dry season. We were not allowed to get water or move around. About 4:00 P.M. we resumed our march to Balanga, arriving just before dark. [They had traveled about twelve miles.] We were placed in some open fields, already overcrowded with American and Filipino prisoners. We learned they had not been fed and insofar as they knew there were no provisions at Balanga."

Fitch continued. "I noticed an increase in the number of corpses along the road between Orion and Balanga. I noticed also that many of them had not been dead two days; they had been killed since the surrender. My friends at Balanga explained anyone who became exhausted and fell out of the march column was immediately shot or bayoneted by the guards. There were no sanitary facilities at Balanga. This did not concern most of us much as we had been three days without food and could never get enough water to spare for urine. There were two small spigots at Balanga and it was necessary to stand in line for several hours to get your canteen filled. We found there were a few small turnips in the ground. By digging for an hour with a sharp stick, I obtained one apiece for myself and my lieutenants. It is impossible to imagine how incomparably delicious they were.

"After not having any breakfast, we were formed in columns and put in open fields for another day of 'sun cure.' Late in the afternoon, we resumed our northward march. The marked increase in the number of dead along the road kept even the weakest in column. Sometime during the night we arrived at Orani. We were marched into a barbed wire enclosure so crowded that it was very difficult to sit down. The ground was well covered with the feces of the dysentery patients that had already been there. We had reached a point where little things like that didn't bother us very much. And if we couldn't sit down, we could sleep standing up.

"The next morning I found a blanket that someone had abandoned. That made me a member of the upper class, owning valuable property. In addition, I had slipped out of our cage during the night and filled my canteen. About 9:00 A.M. we started marching north again. The troops were tired and we were going at a very sharp pace. Even the Americans began breaking down and falling out along the road. I helped Chaplain Duffy along until he quit trying. I then commended him to his maker and left him to the gentle mercies of the Japanese. While we were crossing the bridge at Colis Junction, old man Uddenburg jumped off the bridge and was shot.

"I ran into a classmate of mine, Jimmy Vaughn, a signal corps major who was in poor shape. I helped him along and every now and then he'd stop and sit down, then we'd get him on his feet and move on. Finally, I couldn't get him up and a Jap came along and told me to move on. I tried to explain to him but he jabbed me in the butt with his bayonet. Then he shot Vaughn through the chest. I've been told that Filipinos took him to one of their houses where he died. I saw two American soldiers bayoneted for crawling into the shade alongside of the road. The number of Filipino bodies was shocking, even to us, who abhorred the sight of a Filipino soldier."

Although tens of thousands partook of the death march, the mass of humanity dispatched from Bataan was not one endless column. Instead, packs of 1,000 to 1,500 men formed groups overseen by parties of guards that seldom exceeded twenty-five. Without any schedule or routine, the only consistent aspect was movement as quick as possible and mercilessly urged on.

John Olson, who survived the trip, recalled, "Shuffling along through powder-thin dust that was often four to six inches deep, prisoners and guards soon had their sweat-soaked bodies covered with a thick coat of tan that gave a uniformity of appearance to both groups. Half strangled by the layers of dust that clogged their noses, the pitiful victims had trouble breathing. Some Japanese wore surgical-like face masks that strained out much of the air they breathed. The haze that hung over each group billowed up into the trees as the endless processions of Japanese trucks, tanks, and artillery pieces passed enroute to positions at the base of the peninsula.

"Sometimes, if a prisoner was indiscreet or careless enough to come close to one of the troop carriers, a few of the occupants thrust menacingly at him with their bayonets while emitting animal-like screams and jeers. Those who were targets of these attacks and did not move quickly enough to dodge were slashed or even severely wounded. These unfortunates were forced to tend to themselves as they continued to stagger forward.

"The Japanese guards would tolerate no stopping at any place other than the spots where they had been instructed to halt. Anyone who attempted to fall out of the march was quickly set upon with a club, rifle butt, or a bayonet. Pushed or kicked to his feet, the sufferer would be thrust back into the ranks. In the beginning, some men screamed at their tormentors that they were sick, wounded, or too exhausted to go on, and refused to move. The reaction was swift and decisive. A fierce jab with a bayonet into the chest or a bullet in the head was administered with dispatch and the body was pushed into a ditch or the bushes. This message quickly sank into the aching heads of the others. Keep going no matter how hard it is to put one foot in front of the other! He who cannot move will soon be unable to move forever more!"

Harold Johnson remembered self-protective measures and even a slightly more benign approach. "Everyone had a different pace he followed during the march because there were plenty of opportunities to hide out. You didn't know what the result would be if you got caught. Some people were bayoneted. Other people were helped into calasas, the little cart pulled by a pony and sent on. It depended on the whim or mood of the guard. Some days we covered eight to ten kilometers; others we spent the entire day in the broiling sun. Some days I just hid out, rested, and Scouts gave me a hand. There were stops at regular intervals where the Japanese tried to take care of us. There was always a water source, maybe one spigot with hundreds lined up.

"I had one advantage, the services of the Philippine Scouts. The Scouts were moving around, relatively freely. They would search for their officers and say, 'You come see me in an hour and I'll have some rice for you. You would find them an hour later with a gallon can, half filled with porridge, rice, and they would give you a section of sugarcane so you could suck it."

"I was dead tired," said Fitch of his arrival at Lubao. "I doubt if I could have gone another hour. I had been a prisoner five days, walked more than eighty-five miles, and eaten one raw turnip. My worldly wealth consisted of a blanket, a towel, a spare pair of socks, and a canteen, all except the canteen picked up along the road." Their first morning at Lubao, Fitch and his companions were tendered a half-cup of "very dirty unsalted rice porridge. We stayed at Lubao several days, continuing to receive the same luxurious rations. There was only one small water spigot for three or four thousand men. It was only with great difficulty that you could obtain one canteen of water a day. I saw one American soldier bayoneted to death for trying to buck the water line. They took another across the road and shot him. Many Americans and Filipinos died here. We had no tools for digging so the dead were simply stacked in one corner of the yard.

"One morning, two thousand were marched to San Fernando [about ten miles north]. I went along. We spent two days in San Fernando. Here again there were no sanitary facilities and only one small water spigot. The Japs gave us three meals of 'lugao' [rice porridge] a day and pointed out we should be very grateful as our own army had fed us only twice a day. Two days later we were taken by train to Capas, about twenty-five miles north, and we marched from there to the partially completed Philippine Army camp at O'Donnell. I was damn glad to arrive, little knowing that the name O'Donnell would make the Black Hole of Calcutta seem a Sunday school picnic."

The hapless prisoner drew little surcease during the short train trips to Capas. John Olson said, "These tiny boxcars were similar to the World War I French 'Forty and Eight' [forty men or eight horses]. But into each of them were forced one hundred, not forty men. Too crowded to sit, much less lie, they watched the doors slam shut. Then began three to four hours of excruciating sweltering in this fetid sweat box. Some collapsed, the weakest died. Even the Japanese guards suffered. A few disregarded their orders and cracked or even opened one of the doors while the train was in motion. In so doing, they undoubtedly saved a number of lives. Even so, when they finally stopped at the station in Capas, everyone was wobbly and totally exhausted."

According to Olson, when he stumbled from the boxcar, hordes of Filipinos materialized in the Capas train yards. While the Japanese rushed about shouting commands and perhaps counting—it was gibberish to the prisoners—the civilians eyed the gaunt, gasping, sweat-soaked human cargo. "A Filipino boy dashed over to one of the Americans and thrust a stalk of sugar cane into his hands and scuttled back behind his comrades. Others, encouraged by his success, emulated his action with bananas, sugarcane, rice wrapped in banana leaves, sugarcane candy, and cups of water. A Japanese, suddenly aware of what was going on, uttered a strident command. Instantly, the guards turned on the crowd and by jabbing, shoving, and shouting, forced them back. Sullenly, they withdrew but expressed their animosity by hurling the remains of the food over the heads of the guards to the expectant Americans."

The captives formed up for the last brutal leg of the Death March, the final six-kilometer hike under a broiling sun to O'Donnell. As Olson and his contingent of Americans, with a large number of Filipino prisoners, trudged toward their destination, the locals furtively flashed the "Vee for victory" with their fingers, tossed food, and even stashed cans of water along the way.

From the extremities of the Bataan peninsula, where most of the prisoners began, the Death March to O'Donnell stretched 105 killing kilometers, or about 65 miles, and lasted about two weeks. The bulk of those consigned to the camp reached it between 14 and 25 April. Exact numbers on deaths from disease, thirst, malnutrition, or at the hands of guards along the way do not exist. But hundreds of men un-

doubtedly perished. Even worse, the maltreatment of the
Death March coupled with the woeful diet and miserable
health conditions endured during the siege of Bataan weakened the prisoners to the point where massive losses followed at O'Donnell.

At the same time as they overran the Philippines, in addition to swallowing up the colonial island empires of the
West, the Japanese armies advanced in mainland Asia, knif-
ing deeper into China, snatching much of Burma, and ex-
tending control over bits of the former French possessions
such as Siam [Thailand]. Nipponese soldiers backed by a
formidable air arm obliged the Allied ground forces to either
surrender or retreat. The only major resistance to the Imperial forces lay in the Flying Tigers of Claire Chennault.

To maintain the esprit and retain the freedom to act as he
saw fit, Chennault, himself now on active duty as a brigadier
general, had delayed the induction of the AVG into the Army
Air Corps. Meanwhile, the Flying Tigers received some Kitty-
hawks, the newer versions of the P-40, ships with added
firepower, more speed, and better visibility. One thrust at
Japanese airfields in northern Thailand caught a large number of enemy planes packed onto the Chiengmai base and
burned or riddled an entire complement of Japanese planes.

General Joseph Stilwell, chief of staff for the forces under
Chiang Kai-shek and Chennault's boss, regarded the Flying
Tigers as of limited offensive value. He viewed their role as
one of observation, bomber escort, and as showpieces to
boost the morale of Chinese ground forces. All of these roles
demanded grueling long-distance flights that exposed the pilots to Japanese fighters. In mid-April, the fliers stationed at
the Loiwing base flat-out refused to perform what they believed was a poorly plotted raid by Blenheim bombers

against Chiengmai that would, unlike the previous successful strike, put them over the target in a vulnerable position.

Chennault met with the dissidents and flashes of temper ignited ugly talk. Although they had fought for months against superior forces with meager resources, some pilots thought he accused them of cowardice. George Paxton, who had absorbed five bullet wounds during an early encounter, wrote in his diary, "The pilots are bitter. They feel Chennault is bloodthirsty and will sacrifice the AVG to the last man."

When the discussion broke off, twenty-eight of the thirty-four pilots signed a petition that described the type of mission ordered as unreasonable and too perilous in light of the quality of the American planes and the strength of the enemy. Unless such operations were canceled, they would quit. Chennault faced a revolt that could spread to his base at Kunming. The AVG commander refused to accede. He declared he would not accept their resignations and any attempt to do so would be tantamount to desertion in the face of the enemy. Tex Hill was one of the few nonsigners. He argued, "Hell, we're not a bunch of mercenaries over here. Hell, since we've arrived here our country's involved in war and this is part of our war. It's not just like a coldblooded job. Whatever has to be done, we've got to do it. We've got a man who's our leader who says this is the way it should be done. We've got to advise him of all of the facts and our thinking on the thing, but if he makes up his mind and says it's still necessary, we've got to do it."

The issue turned moot as the British bombers scheduled for the affair were delayed and a few days later, the invading Japanese ground forces forced the Flying Tigers to hastily evacuate Loiwing. Some defections followed but apparently for other reasons than the aborted raid. Most notable was Greg "Pappy" Boyington. An accomplished pilot whose fondness for whiskey had made him a disruptive force, he left with a dishonorable discharge signed by Chennault. Later in the war, the Marines decorated Boyington for his exploits as a leatherneck fighter pilot.

Even as the Flying Tigers rebelled against their leader, they heard the astounding news that U.S. bombers had struck at the heart of Japan—Tokyo. Under the urging of Winston Churchill that the war against the Third Reich have priority, President Roosevelt had agreed to focus on the Western Hemisphere. Stung by the succession of defeats in the Far East, Roosevelt and his advisors cast about for some way to bring the war home to the Japanese. They sought a method that might give the enemy pause while uplifting the morale of Americans shaken by the losses in the Pacific and the impending conquest of the Philippines. While none of the Navy's carriers and their short-ranged aircraft could be risked in an operation against the Japanese home islands, staff members for Chief of Naval Operations Ernest J. King proposed that B-25 medium bombers might be launched from a carrier at a viable distance and then, after dropping their bombs, land safely in China. It would have been easier for the B-25s to find refuge in the Soviet Union but that country, still at peace with Japan and mindful of the dangers of a two-front war, was unwilling to risk offending the Japanese.

Chosen to lead the expedition was then-colonel James Doolittle, who began work on the project in February 1942. Jimmy Doolittle grew up in Alaska and earned his wings during World War I. He never reached France in time for aerial combat but, as an Army pilot between the wars, indulged a lust for risk-taking with acrobatics, air races, and cross-country jaunts in the primitive planes of the era. He backed up his feats with studies of engineering and then quit the service for commerce. Doolittle was horrified by the growth of the Nazi air arm and the belligerence of Adolf Hitler. He quit his job and returned to the Air Corps with an assignment from Hap Arnold to head up special projects. His knowledge of aeronautics, expertise in fuel, and his derring-do all recommended him for the mission.

Pilot Robert Emmens belonged to the 17th Bomb Group (Medium), which flew the twin-engine B-25 Mitchells from a base at Columbia, South Carolina. A drop-out from premed at the University of Oregon in 1937, Emmens had succumbed to an advertisement, COME TO THE WEST POINT OF THE AIR, RANDOLPH FIELD, AND LET THE ARMY TEACH YOU TO FLY AND PAY YOU AT THE SAME TIME. By the time of Pearl Harbor, however, he was preparing for operations overseas with some antisubmarine patrols. "Somewhere between the middle of February and the first of March word came that then–lieutenant colonel James Doolittle was looking for a group of crews for a volunteer flight, no word as to what it was to be. The Group commander called for a meeting of all members of all of the squadrons and announced there would be a picking of some twenty crews who were asked to volunteer for a very secret mission. He asked for a show of hands. The entire group stood up. Every man in every squadron volunteered for this mission.

"I had gotten my Regular Army commission and was one of the oldest men—by this time we were getting second lieutenants wet behind the ears. Some had been promoted to first already after about three or four months being on active duty. Here I was on duty since 1938, back to second lieutenant [RA status]. My squadron commander Jack Hilger looked at me and said, 'You have to stay behind—you are the oldest guy in the squadron now—and run the squadron.

I am going on this mission.' All my friends left. They were ordered to Eglin Field, Florida.

"News began coming back to the group. Word started that they were practicing these strange maximum takeoffs, that the B-25 had to get off in 400 feet. We couldn't imagine why such a crazy maneuver. The B-25 loaded normally took a 1,500-foot run. We heard they were out over the Gulf flying a long mission over water, and they were allowed to fly at only 50-foot altitudes and at very reduced throttle settings. Normally a B-25 cruised at 210 to 225 miles per hour. But these [training for the mission] couldn't cruise over about 165."

Under Doolittle's supervision, auxiliary gas tanks replaced the B-25 belly turrets. Additional fuel storage came from tanks in the bomb bays, with rubber bladders holding another 160 gallons in crawl spaces above the bomb bays. Twin .50-caliber machine guns in the top turret and a single .30 in the nose was all the firepower aboard. Wooden broom sticks, painted black to simulate gun barrels, poked out of the tails to discourage fighter approaches from the rear.

Emmens could only puzzle about the bizarre doings at Eglin until he received a telephone call from Ed "Ski" York [born Edward Cichowski], the only West Pointer attached to Doolittle's complement. His surname, taken from that of the World War I hero Sgt. Alvin C., had been adopted after graduation because Ski supposedly believed Cichowski would handicap his career. According to Emmens, York was not expected to make the mission. "He had been assigned to be the operations chief. He would schedule the flights only."

Manning the office at Columbia, Emmens answered when York rang up to explain they had just lost an airplane after an engine misfired during one of the maximum takeoffs. "York said, 'We need another airplane right away down here.' I said, 'Ski, I will see you at about 3:30 or 4:00.' I went to my tent, packed my footlocker, stenciled it to 1443 East Main, Medford, Oregon, which was my home. I packed 20 pounds; all the crews were allowed to take was 20 pounds of clothing—toilet article kits, socks, change of underclothes. I looked around and found a guy to be copilot and an airplane in commission sitting there."

To Emmens's astonishment, the field at Eglin was deserted, not an airplane in sight. After landing he found Ski York sweeping out the operations building. "There were two or three other guys there. I said, 'Where is everybody?' He said, 'They've all left for the west coast. Do you want to go on this thing?' I said, 'Ski, more than anything.' " According to Emmens, York said they could form a substitute crew. He told Emmens, "See that fellow playing solitaire? He is left over among the navigators. That guy sleeping in the corner is an engineer." Within a few minutes York and Emmens put together the full crew of five.

"We left that night about 6:00 or 6:30," said Emmens, "and never even sent a message back to Columbia. We landed at Sacramento [after refueling in Texas] about six o'clock in the morning. [York] introduced me [to Doolittle] and said, 'We would like to be the new crew to substitute.' Doolittle looked at me and we shook hands very cordially. He asked, 'How much time do you have in a B-25?' suspecting, I think, that I was brand new with my second lieutenant's bars on. I said, 'Sir, I have about 1,000 hours.' He said, 'Do you want to go on this thing?' I said, 'yes sir, I do.' 'All right, York [said Doolittle], you are the new crew.' It was that simple."

The fliers and sixteen B-25s loaded onto the carrier *Hornet*. Doolittle allowed them one all-night fling in San Francisco and then on 2 April, the carrier bore them off toward their still-undisclosed mission. Out beyond the Golden Gate and in the Pacific, the leader held a meeting at which time he announced the target was Tokyo. According to Emmens they had not guessed their destination and instead figured they were bound for Bataan. "Sixteen targets had been picked. As the pilot of each crew walked past a table, he was handed a target folder. No specific target was assigned to a specific crew. Then the pilot got his crew together and we spent the next two weeks studying that target folder. Our target was to be a steel factory on the north outskirts of Tokyo."

Bill Bower, whom Doolittle appointed engineering officer, recollected, "Doolittle was as close as he should be. Everything was on a first-name basis. But he had all of these things to consider. You didn't go putting your arm around him telling him your personal thoughts and he didn't tell you his. There wasn't time for horseplay; it was all business. After we passed Hawaii we picked up cruisers, destroyers, a tanker, and the carrier *Enterprise* as part of a task force under Adm. William Halsey. We [each] had two 500-pound general-purpose bombs and two canisters of incendiaries. On deck, there was a ceremony where they put on the bombs some medals given to people by the Japanese in the past.

"We were going to launch the planes 400 miles off the coast of Japan [on 18 April] in the afternoon, bomb Tokyo at night, and then arrive in China in the morning. We were discovered by a picket ship [the *Nitto Maru*] about eight o'clock in the morning on the 18th. It was promptly sunk when the *Enterprise* launched their aircraft and the cruisers shelled it. They called general quarters and announced we would launch immediately." Officially, at 8:00 A.M. as the Japanese picket boat succumbed to the American guns, Admiral Halsey sent a message, "Launch planes. To Colonel Doolittle and gallant command, good luck and God bless you."

According to Bower, "We were then eight hours at forced draft from our [planned] launching point which put us somewhere in the area of 640 statute miles from [that] site. [Other estimates make the distance 700 or even 800 miles.] "I stopped and bought a carton of Lucky Strikes and went up to the plane with my B-4 bag while they were refueling the planes, topping off the tanks. They brought these tin cans on; we each got five of them, which would amount to fifty gallons of gas. They were stowed aboard and we were told to uncover and start our engines."

Emmens reported that every morning they awakened at 5:30 A.M. for a battle station drill where the Army pilots ran to their planes while the carrier's gun crews manned their guns. As the sun rose, the all clear would come. On this day, however, he said, the instructions directed, "Army crews, man your airplanes. Prepare for takeoff. This is not a drill."

"I remember running to the room where I was staying. I picked up my small bit of belongings and beat it up on the deck. Every gun on every ship was going off. I have never seen such a display of firepower. The pom-pom guns off the *Hornet*, every gun off every cruiser and destroyer at this silhouette of a freighter, and here came the fighter planes off the [*Enterprise*]."

The efforts to destroy the enemy trawler hardly qualified as a textbook demonstration. The initial salvos from the cruiser *Nashville* splashed harmlessly in the ocean. A plane from the *Enterprise* strafed the vessel but its bomb missed by 100 feet. Halsey ordered the *Nashville* to point blank range. Not until a third salvo was the *Nitto Maru* fatally hit. The "engagement" with the hapless trawler lasted twenty-nine minutes, long enough for a radio message to Tokyo to advise of the presence of an American force. The Imperial

Navy mobilized ships to search for the flotilla that within minutes was steaming hastily back toward Hawaii.

Said Emmens, "I saw Doolittle take off, then number two, number three. . . . I looked at that deck and it looked a little bit like a postage stamp. On a wet deck the B-25 with its brakes locked and the power full on would tend to skid forward even with locked wheels. They had put two cork pads about three or four feet square with the wheelbase of the airplane. Each airplane had to taxi and put its front wheels on those cork pads because the procedure for takeoff was to sit with locked brakes, the power all the way on, clear up to the top, flaps all the way down that are normally used to slow an airplane down when it lands, but in this type of takeoff, it acts as a lift for a little bit. It helps to get the rise but you must get those flaps up immediately to reduce the resistance, and the stick all the way back.

"Full power it took both of us with our arms around the wheel to hold it in the full-back position, elevation position. We had absolutely no problem at all. We had at least fifty feet of deck ahead of us when we were airborne. Then immediately you let up on the stick to get your nose down where you are going to gain speed and start bringing those flaps up and your wheels up immediately. We slowly leveled out, gained speed. There was no formation flying; it was too costly [in fuel] because you juggled the throttle to get in formation. Each airplane had its target, knew where it was going, and each airplane flew individually. There was to be no talk, no intercourse between airplanes. Back down then to fifty feet and the reduced power setting."

Bower noted, "Because of the way the carrier was constructed, you couldn't take off until you passed the pivot point at the center of the island. Everybody therefore had the same takeoff distance. I had seen one of the planes in front of us take off with his flaps up so it was obvious that it was no problem. We maintained radio silence in a loose formation. I was with Ross Green and Ski York. We formed in threes for five flights." In the roughly four hours from the *Hornet* to landfall, the aircraft gradually separated until they saw little of one another. "We set up our own navigation. We found a ship near landfall and my gunner shot at it. The countryside had been described to us in great detail by Lieutenant Forrest [the Navy briefing officer]. It was amazing that he had such knowledge of it. We came ashore well north of Tokyo, somewhere around the 36th Parallel, maybe 100 miles north of Tokyo. Right on the deck, there was an opportunity to look at the countryside. I thought, my God, what peaceful, pretty countryside this is. Why on earth would they want war; it was a natural thought; all countryside looks pretty from the air.

"As we approached Tokyo Bay we went across an airfield where some of the aircraft were operating and flying around the field. We cut across the bay and climbed to 1,000 feet. There were some barrage balloons [apparently the Japanese had prepared for the possibility of an attack] which we went through. Although there was a haze we broke out as we came to the western shore and could identify our target. We bombed the target. I don't recall any aircraft but I saw some shooting. We returned to the bay and set course over the water on a southwesterly direction for China. We had been concerned that at nighttime how were we going to identify [landmarks] but it was daylight and we didn't have any difficulties. About an hour or so later we came upon a Japanese cruiser that launched an airplane, but fortunately it didn't catch us.

"We got down to the southern tip of Kyushu and set course across the East China Sea. We figured we'd make landfall after dark and wondered how we'd know when we reached the coast. At dusk we could see some shoals and shallow water so we felt we were near the coastline. The fuel supply held up; our consumption was normal. Obviously we were going to have to climb because of the weather. We were scheduled to land at an airfield 200 to 400 miles inland where there was to be fuel for us. There was to be a beacon on but only at our [scheduled] arrival time and then it would be turned off. Sometime around 11:30 P.M., fifteen hours after takeoff, the red light [indicating low fuel] came on and a few warning lights, so everybody got ready [to jump]. When Waldo Bither was trying to come up from the bombardier's compartment his parachute opened and he calmly repacked it. I said, 'Let's go' and I trimmed the airplane up and jumped after the rest. Our plan was that the last man out would turn around and walk in a northeasterly direction. First man would walk southwesterly.

"I landed on a pretty high hill. Immediately rolled up in the parachute and went to sleep, which I think was a logical reaction. It was just as well, because when dawn came I was right on the edge of a cliff." Bower hid his chute and hiked down the mountain to a road. He had retained a .45 automatic carried by his father in World War I. When he met some Chinese people he attempted to talk to them with the few phrases taught to the Doolittle raiders before their takeoff. The farmers did not understand him. On a piece of tissue paper, Bower drew pictures of an airplane, an American flag, and a train, but no one seemed to grasp the meaning. He walked farther in their company to a tiny village where, wet and tired, he was fed hot soup, peanuts, and rice. After dark, his copilot came in with men in black clothes. Two more of the crew showed up. The four Americans spent an uncomfortable night in a house infested with lice where the occupants relieved themselves in a bucket in the corner. But Bower said he was well treated.

Chinese guerrillas brought in the last of the five-man crew and the group started to walk in the direction of Chungking. "We had no idea whether they were guerrillas leading us to safety or taking us into a trap. But we had faith in these people. There wasn't much you could do. I don't know what would have happened if we had seen Japanese. We were taken care of pretty well. The word was out but anytime the Japs started toward us, we were under cover."

After an arduous trek they met a man who spoke some English and owned a 1940 Plymouth automobile. He drove them to a town where they remained for a week before continuing their journey by car, train, and bus. At one point they were forced to double back because of advancing enemy troops. Along the way the Americans met English-speaking missionaries who joined the party. At one site a province chief tossed a bash in their honor. Eventually, the group reached a point where a C-47 picked them up and flew them to the Chungking base, where they were housed in Generalissimo Chiang Kai-shek's compound until they departed for the States along with other survivors. Under orders not to disclose their identities, the Doolittle raiders reached Miami where customs officials regarded them with considerable suspicion. Eventually the saga ended with a reception in Washington, D.C., and a subsequent tour to sell war bonds and uplift American spirits.

Emmens related his experiences: "The last word we got on the *Hornet* was, 'Good luck, boys. I hope you make it. If you have any trouble, we will pray for you. But don't come back to the *Hornet*.' They turned around immediately after the sixteenth airplane took off and the whole business went back to Hawaii as fast as they could. There was nothing they could have done. We couldn't possibly land [a B-25] on the deck."

Ski York and Bob Emmens realized they were in difficulty even as their ship neared the Japanese coast. Their B-25 had never been adjusted to consume fuel with greater efficiency. "The first thing we saw at that low altitude was a little black blip on the horizon, which was Mount Fuji. As the coastline was coming into view, we measured [the gasoline] as carefully as we could and found there was simply no way in God's world we could fly back out to sea, down to the bottom of Japan, and all the way into the coast of China. There was a chance, if we turned slightly right over Tokyo—Russia was quite a little bit closer. Roosevelt had asked Stalin to please accept our sixteen airplanes, which would have assured the success and termination of the mission at least resulting in landings. Stalin refused flatly. We were told this in our briefings on the *Hornet*.

"There can be situations that arise that demand you do something that may not have fitted into the original schedule. The only dry land in sight was Japanese and that didn't seem to be too healthy a solution to our being short of gas. The alternative was square miles of blue ocean in enemy waters and that didn't seem very attractive for our dilemma. There was no objection on anybody's part when York [said], 'Let's go to Russia. We can make it, we think.'

"We bombed at approximately noon. We listened all the way in to a baseball game. There was no evidence that they knew we were coming. We dropped our bombs on the steel factory. Each airplane was equipped with a camera in the tail, mounted between the two broomsticks that had been painted black. The camera was set to trip to cover the trajectory drop of the bomb and its strike. Ours was the only one that was ever retrieved because all the rest of the airplanes crashed. We dropped our bombs. We felt the explosion of them even at 1,500 feet. One of them went right down the stack of the steel mill. After dropping our bombs we immediately dropped back down to the fifty-foot altitude. We had no opposition whatsoever."

Because the American bombers traveled singly and their navigation scattered their approaches, the Japanese when they finally realized an air raid was in progress, could not mount a coherent defense. The element of surprise enabled almost every plane to dump its ordnance before gunners on the ground could train their weapons or interceptors could find the attackers. Doolittle seems to have been most at risk. He spotted fighters in the sky as he neared Tokyo but managed to lose them. Over the target antiaircraft shells burst around his plane, spattering the fuselage with shrapnel, but caused no damage. The mission chief headed for China. Several others ran a mild gamut of antiaircraft fire or saw enemy planes but none incurred damage.

Emmens remarked that they carried only an outline map of the Soviet Union. Concerned that any drift to the left might bring them down in Korea, York corrected to the right and the navigator brought them over the Sea of Japan until they crossed the coast. They decided that Vladivistok might be heavily defended and it would be risky to approach the city at dusk. "As we hit landfall, we saw a great big field and as we flew over it, a big white circle in the middle indicated it was some sort of auxiliary field. About that time the engineer [Theodore H. LaBan] poked me. Here was a Soviet fighter airplane practically flying formation with us, a big red star on it, and wiggling his wings, the international signal, 'Land, or I will shoot you down.' We gave him the wiggled wings back, 'Don't bother to shoot us down; we intend to land.'

"He followed us all the way down to the ground. There was the barest chance, faintest possibility that it could be [the Japanese]. We decided we would leave the engines running until the first people came up around the airplane. We would look at them, and if they had slant eyes—even though we registered empty—we were going to take off, fly out to sea and due north toward Russia. But the guys who came up around the airplane didn't have slant eyes. They stood there grinning. They didn't know what we were. We shut the engines off, took our .45s and pistol belts off and were greeted immediately by a bunch of soldiers with at least five Tommy guns.

"We were conducted, marched, rather, across the field into this building with Tommy guns in our backs. It was about 6:30 in the evening. They put us at a table with these [four ranking] navy officers. We tried to speak to them and they tried to speak to us. We didn't know a word of Russian and they didn't know a word of English. Finally, by gesture alone, we were taken to a bathroom, a rather primitive outside trough, that slanted down and went into a hole in the ground. Also by gesture we were finally able to get over to them that we would like something to eat. We hadn't eaten since the morning on the *Hornet*, and nothing in the airplane all day long. They brought us some black bread and some soup

"I had studied German and I had studied French. I tried both of those, nothing. York was Polish and he tried to remember some Polish words but couldn't make a breakthrough. Finally, [from] one of the men came the word 'San Francisco.' So we said, 'San Francisco.' That was our first breakthrough. We shook hands all around." A man who spoke a bit of English appeared and so did a large map. York uttered "Alaska" and the interpreter nodded yes. Then York traced his finger from Alaska, through the Kuril Islands, down through Siberia to Vladivistok and said "Goodwill flight." No airplane in existence could have flown that enormous distance nonstop but for the moment their inquisitors accepted the explanation. However, a pilot appeared and when York demonstrated the route, he smiled and pointed to Tokyo.

After a dinner featuring vodka toasts, York advised a Soviet colonel of their role in the Tokyo raid. The following morning, the crew sat down to a breakfast banquet with about two dozen Red officers including several generals. The visitors swallowed numerous rounds of vodka that accompanied toasts from both sides; the Americans hailed Stalin, the Red Navy, the Red Army, and their hosts championed Roosevelt, the U.S. Navy, the respective Air Corps. Over a five-hour period they dined on a sumptuous repast. The fliers asked to be put in touch with the U.S. consul but the request was ignored. The era of good feeling disappeared after they were transported to another area and new, sterner inquisitors questioned them. Emmens and company learned they would be interned indefinitely.

At the controls of *Bat Out of Hell*, the sixteenth and last airplane to leave the *Hornet*, was Bill Farrow. The copilot, Bob Hite, actually was senior to Farrow but he and his crew had not been chosen to fly the mission. Farrow, unhappy with his deputy, asked Hite if he'd like to replace him. "I would have gone as bombardier, rear gunner, nose gunner; I would have gone in any position to be on that raid because I really felt it was going to be a great raid and I wanted to be on it. After I accepted to go with Bill, I had people offering me $500 for my place."

Bat Out of Hell, at the back of the pack, its tail hanging over the carrier's stern, nearly slid backward into the sea when the propwash of the plane immediately ahead lifted *Bat Out of Hell*'s nose. As the front end of it rose, sailors and bombardier Cpl. Jacob DeShazer struggled to restrain the bucking aircraft with ropes tied to hooks. The nose dropped just as a sailor slipped on the deck and a whirling propeller slashed his arm so severely it required amputation. According to one account, once aboard, DeShazer discovered that in its gyrations, *Bat Out of Hell* had slammed its plexiglass nose into the tail of the aircraft in front of it, gouging a jagged hole.

Farrow and Hite lifted off the damaged bomber and set a course for Japan. "We never saw one of our aircraft on the way in," said Hite. "We didn't see anyone into our target. We could have bombed Osaka or Nagoya and we chose Nagoya because we had homed in on Asahi Point. We had an aircraft factory and old storage tanks. As we approached the area we saw many Japanese fighter aircraft . . . [but] we climbed into the clouds, which were at about 7,000 feet. We stayed in the clouds to avoid detection and flew dead-reckoning courses to the area of Nagoya. Then we found a hole and let down through it. We had four incendiary clusters, 500-pounders. The aircraft factory was afire and the oil storage tank was afire when we departed the area to go across the China Sea. [The flak] was all over."

In spite of the damage to the plane and the drag from the opening in the bombardier's compartment, *Bat Out of Hell* stayed aloft for more than fourteen hours when the indicators reported empty tanks. All five men bailed out, with Hite the fourth and Farrow the last to exit the plane. "I landed in a rice paddy," recalled Hite, "and hit my right ankle on a rock. I hurt it pretty bad. I got my parachute off finally and I was right up to my waist, in the mud, slime, and so forth."

He climbed onto a dike in the paddy and began an aimless hike that took him into a cemetery where he jogged in place to keep his circulation flowing. In the morning, when the chickens crowed and daylight broke, Hite started to wander toward some houses. "The first two or three houses I tried, I backed off on account of the dogs. I found a house later on in the morning that sort of accepted me. There were no dogs. It was a man and his wife, and I think they had three or four children. They had cows and donkeys in the barn. I had a pocketful of Lucky Strike cigarettes and Mounds candy bars and about $5 in silver. I was prepared to offer anything that I had for help. I tried to explain that I wanted to go to Chungking. The family accepted me pretty good. They ate my candy. I didn't know the Chinese women would smoke but this Chinese lady was smoking those Lucky Strike cigarettes like they were going out of style.

"I kept insisting that I go find Chiang Kai-shek. They had taught us that 'wa-su-mei-ko-lin' was probably the way to say that 'I am an American' in Chinese. I repeated that several times. I thought they understood. The man put on a little shawl and a big flat hat and his little wooden shoes and motioned for me to follow him and I did. He led me through rice paddies and dikes for about thirty minutes to a house. In front, about twenty yards from the house, was a soldier walking. He was a Chinese soldier without saber or rifle, or any armament. He spoke English. I gave the Chinese coolie some more silver and thanked him and he went back toward his house and left me with the soldier. The soldier asked me who I was and I said that I was an American and that I was here to help Chiang Kai-shek. He was very friendly and said, 'Let's get something to eat.' We went toward this little cluster of houses. As we approached, about fifteen Japanese soldiers came running out with bayoneted rifles and surrounded me." Hite was the last of his five-man crew to be captured. All of them had dropped in an area occupied by the invading Japanese.

Chiang Kai-shek, whom Hite insisted he hoped to aid, opposed the operation at its inception. The Generalissimo asked for a delay until he could transport more troops to the landing fields expected to receive the B-25s after they struck Japan. Unfortunately, when Chiang finally acquiesced, there was confusion because of a misunderstanding of the date line. Worse, the American forces working with the Chinese could not confirm the storage of fuel, the signal systems, or the conditions at the outlying airfields designated for the Doolittle flyers. Four separate attempts to install American experts failed because of either bad weather or Japanese interception. The chances that the flares, beacons, or homing signals might guide the aircraft, feeling their way through the dark over unfamiliar territory, fell to zero. It was an appalling case of what can happen when the desire to put on a show overwhelms the necessity for careful planning and execution of all aspects of an operation.

An entire squadron of medium bombers was wiped out at a moment when the Allies could ill afford any losses. Not a single B-25 landed successfully in China. Four crash landed with two fatalities. Crews parachuted from eleven planes with one death. The only bomber that touched down intact belonged to York and Emmens. Eight Americans, including Farrow and Hite, became POWs. The Doolittle raid killed fifty people, wounded another 250, and damaged a number of buildings and installations. In terms of hurting production of war materials, the effects were minimal, but the attack did cause the Japanese to bring home some air units for protection against future raids, which would not come for another two years. To convince the people in the occupied territories not to assist Americans in such endeavors, the Japanese embarked on a furious campaign of reprisals that brought death to many Chinese.

10

Final Defeat in the Philippines

ALMOST IMMEDIATELY AFTER THE BATAAN GARRISON WAVED
the white flag, Japanese artillery had moved into positions
where it could rain explosives upon the fortified islands still
held by the defenders. The last bastion lay only three miles
from the enemy guns. Air raids increased in tempo but the
mounting fury of artillery exacted the greatest toll. Paul
Bunker on 13 April noted in his diary, "This was another day
of artillery activity. The Japs plastered us with shells from
morning to night." A few days later Bunker reported, "Six
heavy bombers attacked Fort Drum and dropped bombs, but
all were misses, for I distinctly felt them in our tunnel. This
evening a flash came in, saying that Tokyo this morning was
under a four-hour bombardment. It cheered us up to think
that maybe Nippon is at last getting a touch of her own medicine."

Albert Svihra, the Army legal officer who had been
among those transferred from Bataan to Corregidor, described a relatively secure existence that dissipated as the in

tensity of attacks built. "During March and April, although we were under intermittent artillery fire and bombardment from the air, we were able to take off a little time now and then to sit outside the east entrance of the tunnel [Malinta] under a tent fly with a number of wicker chairs to have a cigarette—no smoking being permitted inside the tunnel—and to discuss the news. At 12:30 P.M. each day our radio station, the Voice of Freedom, broadcast the news from the U.S.

"About the only other pleasures of the tunnel were reading and an occasional bridge game. We were on reduced ration as in Bataan. If anything, we were on about one-third, instead of one-half. Our meals, prepared by Chinese boys, formerly employees of the Officers' Club at Fort Mills, and served cafeteria fashion, consisted first [breakfast] of either a small portion of cooked raisins or cracked wheat, a piece of toast, two small pieces of bacon, and all the coffee you wanted without sugar. For lunch a cup of soup, and either a piece of whole wheat bread or a biscuit, or a small meat pie. Supper, the only decent meal, consisted of rice or a small canned potato; stewed corn beef or corn beef hash, or occasionally, fresh carabao or baked ham; one vegetable, corn, peas, or sauerkraut; a piece of bread; a small portion of dessert, usually a fruit cobbler, custard cake, or fruit; and a cup of coffee. Toward the end, the food particularly at luncheon increased somewhat but at no time did one leave the table satisfied. However little we got, still the meals were fairly well balanced and the deficiency diseases seldom appeared on Corregidor, although not uncommon at Bataan where food was more scarce and less varied."

Despite his protestations of meager fare, Svihra's description of meals tends to corroborate the image of life in the rear echelons held by the unfortunates fighting on Bataan. The presence of orderlies and mess boys rather than potential defenders on the Rock is also indicative of skewed priorities when choosing people for residence at the fortress. Conditions rapidly worsened, as Svihra observed. "Artillery fire and air bombing were increasing in intensity. Our outdoor toilets and shower baths, about one hundred feet [away] had been demolished. The shells and bombs shook the very tunnel itself, often landing just over or near the entrance, filling the tunnel with smoke, dust, and the acrid fumes of picric acid, and making it so dark inside that despite lights, one could scarcely see ten feet, and causing apprehension that the entrance had been blocked. The power plant was off for days, and the tunnel lighted by an auxiliary diesel engine that on occasions went out of commission, throwing everything into total darkness. Meals were often delayed and sleep often became impossible.

"One evening, there was quite a gathering of enlisted men at the west entrance to the tunnel, out to have a cigarette. It was a moonless but otherwise clear night. Suddenly there was heard the whining of a shell, then a burst, followed by a shower of stones from the top of Malinta Hill, just above the entrance. There was apparently a terrific rush for the entrance, in which several men were knocked down and trampled on. There followed another big shell that this time landed between the high, steep sides of the entrance, killing or injuring some fifty men. It was a grim sight to watch litter bearers carrying in armless, legless and even headless forms through the main tunnel to the hospital lateral."

To mark Emperor Hirohito's birthday, 29 April, and to celebrate it, the Japanese unleashed the heaviest bombardment yet seen. They continued to torment the occupants of Corregidor for the next six days. The puny remnants of the U.S. Pacific Fleet soon sank to the bottom of the bay as gunfire destroyed the minesweeper *Tanager*, gunboat *Min-*

danao, and tug *Pigeon*. Crews scuttled several other small vessels. The defenders sensed the imminence of the final act as Japanese planes and artillery shifted their aim from the gun emplacements and installations on Corregidor to its beaches. At around 9:30 P.M. on 5 May, searchlight units equipped with sound-detection systems reported the sound of landing barges warming their motors. About 2,000 Japanese soldiers loaded the small craft for the quick run to their assigned stretches of the coast.

Unfortunately, the preparations for the assault went largely for naught. The coxswains operating the launches could not make out the landmarks **by which** they planned to steer. Strong currents conspired to carry them 1,000 yards away from their planned touchdown points that would locate them close to Malinta Hill. When the first waves approached the shoreline, the 4th Marines were well dug in along with a bunch of GI **and Philippine** Army refugees from Bataan, coast artillery **Scouts, and** even some Filipino messboys. Machine guns, rifles, **and a few** pieces of artillery slaughtered the hapless enemy trapped in the flimsy barges.

Although the defenders staggered the invaders in this encounter, the Japanese troops established a beachhead. And once they penetrated the thin crust of resistance at the water's edge, the Nipponese pushed forward. In support, batteries on Bataan raked the island and kept Wainwright shifting units of his diminishing army. Japanese reinforcements numbering about 6,000 started to arrive, bringing with them light artillery and ultimately a handful of tanks. Untrained sailors and airmen equipped with rifles could not cope with the determined, well-schooled foe. Although the American-led forces fought hard for hours, even counterattacked, the defensive perimeter continued to shrink. By 10:00 A.M. on 6 May, the Japanese were closing in on the Malinta Tunnel. Already between six and eight hundred defenders were dead; the thousand jammed into Malinta Tunnel would be massacred if the fighting continued.

Through the siege of the Philippines, Washington had issued a series of messages that falsely raised hopes of succor and admonitions not to yield. At the time Wainwright had succeeded MacArthur, President Roosevelt directed him "to continue the fight as long as there remains any possibility of resistance." Wainwright recognized the situation as hopeless. He radioed President Roosevelt: "With broken heart and head bowed in sadness but not in shame I report . . . that today I must arrange for the surrender of the fortified islands of Manila Bay. . . ." A similar message went to MacArthur.

Madeline Ullom remembered the cease-fire: "A corpsman stopped to gravely inform us he saw the white flag at the tunnel entrance. We heard the time of a broadcast was set. We gathered around Major Richardson's radio in the dental clinic. A desolate, numb, unbelievable feeling engulfed one. We listened to the words we had pushed to the backs of our minds. Tears came to our eyes. No one spoke. We walked away as though we were in an unrealistic situation. Colonel Paul Bunker, Lt. Col. Dwight Edison, and a bugler marched to the Topside parade grounds. Taps were played while they stood at attention. The flag was lowered. A white sheet was run up. Many had tears running down their cheeks."

Giving up turned out to be considerably more complicated than running up a white flag or announcing a willingness to cease resistance. The Corregidor radio station, starting at 10:30 A.M. and twice more during the next hour and fifteen minutes, had broadcast a statement to the Japanese command that the defenders would end hostile action at noon on 6 May, lower the American flag, and hoist the white one. Upon complete cessation of Japanese shelling and air raids, Wainwright would dispatch a pair of staff officers to Bataan where they could meet the Japanese and arrange a formal surrender.

The attackers continued to bombard the beleaguered on the harbor forts and the ground forces pressed ever closer to the Malinta Tunnel. Wainwright sent off three messages just before noon. One went to Maj. Gen. William F. Sharp, head of the Corps that covered the Visayan-Mindanao troops, the southern island defenses. Wainwright advised Sharp he was relinquishing his command of those forces and Sharp now would report directly to MacArthur in Australia. By this means, Wainwright hoped to surrender only the men on the Manila Bay islands.

The brief statement to President Roosevelt summarized the hopeless military situation and defended his decision: "There is a limit of human endurance and that limit has long since been past. Without prospect of relief I feel it is my duty to my country and to my gallant troops to end this useless effusion of blood and human sacrifice."

MacArthur received a similar message, in which Wainwright noted, "We have done our full duty to you and for your country. We are sad but unashamed. . . . Goodbye, General, my regards to you and our comrades in Australia. May God strengthen your arm to insure ultimate success of the cause for which we have fought side by side."

A truce party chosen by Wainwright reached a Japanese officer, who demanded the general come to him. Having carefully taken his pistol from his holster and placed it on a desk, Wainwright, with four from his staff, drove in a Chevrolet sedan bearing a white flag to a rendezvous point. They were met first by a Lieutenant Uemura, who demanded that Wainwright surrender all the Fil-American forces in the

Philippines. The general, still hoping to salvage a resistance under Sharp in the southern part of the archipelago, was not about to discuss terms with a lieutenant. He demanded an audience with a higher authority. Colonel Motto Nakayama from General Homma's staff appeared and, when Wainwright claimed he held only authority over the harbor forts, the colonel angrily insisted in Japanese that any surrender would have to include all military units in the Philippines. After one of Nakayama's lieutenants translated the harangue, Wainwright countered, "I will deal only with General Homma and with no one of lesser rank."

Nakayama agreed to arrange a meeting with Homma on Bataan. Wainwright with one of his staff was led by Nakayama and his translator toward a dock. Enroute, a barrage of Japanese shells forced the group to halt. Wainwright yelled, "Why the hell don't you people stop shooting? I put up my white flag hours ago." Nakayama replied through his interpreter, "We have not accepted any surrender from you as yet." After some delay, an armored tank barge anchored offshore; Wainwright and the others boarded it by means of a rubber raft and set off to meet Homma. From the dock at Cabcaben the general and several of his officers were driven to a battered white house with a large porch. A second boat brought in more of Wainwright's staff. Sipping cold water, they waited for Homma. From where they sat the Americans could see explosions on Corregidor, a mix of enemy shells and demolition of supplies and weapons by their colleagues.

According to a Japanese correspondent on the scene, statements by Wainwright that he possessed only the power to surrender the forces on Corregidor and the other fortified islands in the bay produced an uproar as the Japanese commander conferred with his subordinates. Homma thumped his fist on the table. "At the time of General King's surrender on Bataan, I did not see him. Neither have I any reason to see you if you are only the commander of a unit of the American forces. I wish only to negotiate with my equal, the commander in chief of the American forces in the Philippines. I see no further necessity for my presence here."

The burly Homma, 5'10", 200 pounds, started to rise from his chair. Wainwright conferred with his chief of staff, and realized that his host would not accept further piecemeal surrenders. "I will assume command of the entire American forces in the Philippines, at the risk of serious reprimand by my government following the war," announced Wainwright.

But Homma's gorge seemed to overflow and he flatly rejected the change of heart. "You have denied your authority and your momentary decision may be regretted by you. I advise you to return to Corregidor and think this matter over. If you see fit to surrender, then surrender to the officer of the division on Corregidor. He in turn will bring you to me in Manila. I call this meeting over. Good day." The Japanese newsman said the Americans were "bewildered" by the abrupt departure of Homma. The Wainwright people had to be appalled. Assuming their war over, the garrison had already destroyed its weapons. The enemy could slaughter them with impunity.

The Americans debated alternatives until Wainwright offered to surrender the entire American forces in the Philippines to General Homma unconditionally. The Americans volunteered to send a representative to the other islands to arrange for their capitulation. On Corregidor, Al Svihra, aware of Wainwright's mission, prepared himself for the inevitable. He packed his musette bag with a first-aid kit and toilet articles, some personal papers, groups of pictures of his wife and daughters, and awaited his future in a tunnel lateral.

"Around 5:00 P.M., a Jap officer, accompanied by soldiers armed with Tommy guns and flamethrowers, entered the tunnel. Instructions were to stand by in headquarters lateral, to unload all arms and stack them, and have with us such articles of equipment and clothing as we could conveniently carry. We were ordered to move out of the lateral into the main tunnel which by that time was a mass of humanity, empty tin cans, discarded arms and equipment, filth, and trash. We tried in vain to make our way in a column of twos, through the mass of people to the west entrance. Even then we could hear enemy planes outside, bombing somewhere on the west side of the island. The enemy continued to shell this island with artillery fire."

Because of the danger outside, the Japanese permitted the inhabitants to remain inside the tunnel. When an officer started to inspect the area, he was followed by armed guards. "The latter stopped here and there along the way and plucked watches, rings, fountain pens from among the unfortunate lining the path through the tunnel."

By midnight of 6 May, the Japanese had completed a document of submission and Wainwright signed it. The provisions specified by Homma required the American general to surrender all forces in the Philippines, including those in other areas, within four days. All commanders were to assemble their troops and report to the local Japanese authorities. In the morning his captors pressed upon him the task of fulfillment of the terms. Wainwright had to rescind his directive to General Sharp and reassume command of the Visayan-Mindanao area. To ensure Sharp's compliance, Wainwright sent an emissary with a letter. Adding to Wainwright's humiliation, the victors ordered him to broadcast from Manila instructions to some smaller units still operating in northern Luzon. A pair of Americans also traveled to this area to personally contact the commanders. The bulk of these Luzon remnants refused to concede, however. They hid themselves in the mountains and became part of guerrilla movements.

The largest segment of Fil-American combat soldiers still under arms belonged to Sharp. While the enemy had wrested about half of Mindanao, most of Sharp's army remained intact. Even as Sharp had absorbed Wainwright's original message giving him independence of Corregidor, MacArthur, mindful of the imminent fall of the Rock, radioed Sharp, "communicate all matters direct to me," thereby assuming command of Sharp's Visayan-Mindinao force.

Upon hearing Wainwright's Manila broadcast in which he retrieved his authority over his Corps, Sharp relayed the gist of the statement to Melbourne and requested clarification. MacArthur quickly responded, "Orders emanating from General Wainwright have no validity. If possible separate your force into small elements and initiate guerrilla operations."

MacArthur advised George Marshall in Washington of the situation and stated, "I have informed him [Sharp] that Wainwright's orders since his surrender have no validity. . . . I believe Wainwright has temporarily become unbalanced and his condition renders him susceptible to enemy use." At his headquarters in Australia, MacArthur of course had not been privy to the details of the meeting between Homma and Wainwright. He could not have known that the Japanese held the entire 10,000 survivors on Corregidor as hostages against surrender in the southern islands. If Sharp failed to accede to Wainwright, the enemy might very well execute close to 10,000 soldiers, sailors, and airmen. While neither Homma nor any of his staff ever issued a threat of this nature, Wainwright and his staff feared that at the very least the Japanese would resume firing on the hapless residents of Corregidor.

Sharp reserved his decision until he met with the officer bearing a letter from Wainwright that set down reasons for him to capitulate. Once Sharp became convinced of the very real possibility that the enemy would resume its war against the defenseless garrison on the Rock he felt obliged to follow Wainwright's lead. He ordered weapons stacked, the white flag flown. Sharp issued orders to subordinates for submission on other southern islands but poor communications delayed receipt of the word. In some instances local commanders were unwilling to accept defeat. In a number of places units as large as battalions vanished into the interior for rebirth as guerrilla organizations. However, by 9 May the Japanese were satisfied that all organized outfits had yielded and told Wainwright, "Your high command ceases and you are now a prisoner of war."

Army nurse Madeline Ullom remembered scenes shortly after Wainwright acceded to Homma's demands. "Miss Davison [the chief nurse] told ten of us to report near the hospital tunnel to have our picture taken with Colonel [Wibb] Cooper [top-ranking medical officer]. The Japanese officer, who was in charge, told us he was a graduate of the University of Utah. He assured us in excellent English not to be afraid. He wanted a picture of us in a line with a Japanese armed guard at each end to show we were protected. The pictures would be forwarded to General MacArthur's headquarters.

"Retinues of high-ranking Japanese officers inspected Malinta Tunnel. The white sheet that covered the entrance to the nurse's lateral was once quickly jerked aside and the delegation of Japanese attempted to enter. The alert, stalwart

Miss Davison demanded a courageous, 'Halt!' They did immediately. She informed them they could not enter without previous arrangements. Heat and humidity of the lateral was intense. Many nurses were ill with malaria, dengue, and dysentery and skin conditions. Several nurses had elevated temperatures. Only a bottom sheet could be spared for the beds. Miss Davison strode to our commanding officer to report the incident. A brief time passed before a standard with a sign in Japanese was placed at the entrance. Thereafter, arrangements for inspections were made well in advance."

Al Svihra, during the first days in captivity on Corregidor, shared a large room with more than a dozen other officers. "Since we were given the freedom of the tunnel the first day, we were able to pick up a supply of canned goods cached in various parts of the tunnel. We had plenty of wet rations [cans of meat, vegetables, beans, hash], milk, coffee, some fruit, and a few odd cans of various other foods. Jap sentries guarding the tunnel came in frequently to use the toilet and bath. Although they had evidently been instructed not to molest us, some were bold enough to stop on the way out to see how they could despoil us."

According to Svihra, the Americans played bridge, read old magazines or books, did laundry, and prepared food. At the entrance to the tunnel lay the bodies of soldiers killed or who had died from wounds during the attack. As several days passed, bodies bloated, flies swarmed, and terrible odors mixed with the foul stench of a broken latrine. The Japanese refused permission for burial parties.

On 11 May, Svihra became one of the last to move to a beachfront installation of two balloon hangars and a work shed, the former home of the 92d Coast Artillery. "There were already jammed into the area about 10,000 to 12,000 officers and men. With the exception of a few hundred in each hangar, the men had hastily prepared shelters from the sun by spreading out shelter halves, blankets, pieces of canvas cloth, anything readily available, propping them up by means of poles. Most of the men were in dirty and tattered uniforms. It was no uncommon sight to see a soldier wearing an army cotton shirt, sailor trousers, marine shoes, and a Philippine Army fiber helmet.

"Sanitary conditions were deplorable. Men were using any place in the hills, forming a perimeter of the camp as a latrine. The Filipinos were even relieving themselves in the sea, the only place we had for bathing or washing our clothes. I was told that for the first two days or so, the Nips issued no food for the prisoners. Thereafter they issued limited supplies, not to exceed two meals a day and consisting mostly of rice, dry and wet rations, corn beef hash, flour, and shortening. The only source of water at first was a shallow well located near one of the hangars. Later a pipeline which had been put out of commission was repaired and from one spigot furnished an additional supply."

The captors organized the prisoners into groups of 1,000 with a pair of American officers assigned as leaders. A further subdivision created units of 100 with a captain and lieutenant in charge. The arrangement facilitated distribution of rations but without cooking utensils or organized messes, the inmates at the site ate poorly prepared meals on an irregular basis. Dysentery, diarrhea, and skin diseases inevitably spread. Svihra scrounged some sulfa tablets to cure his condition but with medical facilities limited, no general relief could be achieved until the tools to dig latrines, garbage, and trash pits became available. The increase in the water supply and proscription on use of the sea as a toilet improved health conditions.

Unpleasant and as hazardous to the health as circumstances were for the captured on Corregidor, the situation for the Bataan prisoners was far more deadly. Their life under the victors had begun with the Death March. Those who did not perish enroute had reached the destination of Camp O'Donnell, weakened by malnutrition, dehydration, and disease, battered by maltreatment from their guards. The horrors multiplied in the camp, a site without facilities for the more than 50,000 residents (8,675 Americans, roughly 42,000 Filipinos), with neither food, water, or, perhaps most important, the sanitation vital for preservation of already weakened bodies. O'Donnell was a sun-baked, almost shadeless, water-poor semidesert without mosquito control and rampant malaria.

"O'Donnell, drenched in the glaring, blazing heat of a tropical sun, was certainly no place to be with a shortage of water," said John Olson. "For some fifteen days we did not have a drop of water for washing teeth, face, hands, or mess kit. I licked my mess kit as clean as possible, wiped it with paper, and set it in the sun to sterilize." Ultimately Olson compared the place to the infamous Confederate stockade at Andersonville during the Civil War where thousands of Union soldiers died because of the conditions.

Of his arrival at O'Donnell, Tom Gage said, "I remember two things: Filipino soldiers digging graves, graves, graves, and Filipinos in the river, bathing, urinating, and drinking. They died like flies." Just about every prisoner still on his feet lurched and tottered onto the grassless parade ground in front of what was the Japanese headquarters. Soldiers, wearing fresh, clean, white shirts, khaki shorts or breeches, and armed with large sticks, pummeled the arrivals into a formation for the first indignity, a shakedown that took away blankets, pencils, pens, watches, lighters, cigarettes, shelter halves; in short, just about every personal item the men had managed to retain during the Death March.

Camp commandant Capt. Yoshio Tsuneyoshi, an overage caricature of a Japanese soldier, decked out in very baggy shorts, riding boots with spurs, and a white sport shirt, whose printable nicknames included "Baggy Pants," "Whistling Britches," "Little Napoleon," and "Little Hitler," then delivered what John Olson called his "goddamn you!" tirade in his native language. Through his interpreter he iterated that his sole interest was in dead Americans and those that died. They were not prisoners of war and the Japanese did not care whether they lived or died. Only the generosity of the Japanese spared their lives. The penalty for attempted escape was death.

The rationale that denied official prisoner-of-war status was that some USAFFE units had not surrendered and would not do so until August. In addition, the Imperial government had never signed the 1929 Geneva agreement regarding the humane treatment of prisoners, although the Japanese issued statements that so far as circumstances permitted they would act in accord with the Geneva provisions. In practice, however, the handling of prisoners throughout the war fell far short of the minimum requirements of the Geneva Convention.

Initially, the Japanese specified no distinction between officers and enlisted men. All would receive the same treatment and rank conferred no power. Tsuneyoshi refused to meet with General King, the senior American, or King's opposite number among the Filipinos. Instead he would see only their representatives, through whom he passed on his ukases and listened to requests and questions. Obdurate, harsh, and prone to tantrums even in these sessions, Tsuneyoshi blocked many of the simplest means to improve

A rescue launch plucked from the water a sailor who jumped overboard from the shattered battleship *West Virginia*. (National Archives)

During the infamous Death March after the fall of Bataan, captives improvised litters for those unable to complete the hike to a prison camp. (National Archives)

The U.S. carrier *Yorktown* listed badly after being hit during the Battle of Midway. (National Archives)

Battle-weary and malaria plagued, leathernecks from the 1st Marine Division relaxed behind the lines on Guadalcanal while fresh forces relieved them. (National Archives)

P-40s flew off the deck of a carrier to support the ground forces in North Africa. (National Archives)

Working with a Sherman tank, infantrymen expanded the beachhead on Bougainville in the South Pacific. (National Archives)

Shattered palms and flame-thrower smoke marked a marine assault upon a sand-banked blockhouse on Tarawa. (National Archives)

Torpedo bombers from U.S. carriers ranged the skies over a Japanese armada in the South Pacific. (National Archives)

Near Italy's Rapido River, an antitank squad defended against an enemy counterattack. (National Archives)

Crewmen aboard the U.S. Coast Guard cutter *Spencer* watch a depth charge explode during a successful attack upon a German submarine, the U-175, which menaced a North Atlantic convoy. (National Archives)

During the bomb run of B-17s from the 94th Bomb Group over Berlin in May 1944, *Miss Donna Mae* drifted beneath another Fort as it released its 500-pounders. The camera in the aircraft dropping the ordnance captured the images.

The doomed *Miss Donna Mae*, still level, has lost the elevator and the plane soon plunged to earth. There were no survivors. (Wilbur Richardson)

Half-drowned soldiers in the English Channel on D day were hauled on an inflatable raft to Omaha Beach. (National Archives)

In September 1944, U.S. infantrymen first broke through the formidable German defensive wall known as the Siegfried Line. (National Archives)

The aircraft carrier *Princeton* suffered a mortal blow from a suicide raider during the Battle of Leyte Gulf. (National Archives)

Boyd's Boids, a B-17, managed to stagger back to England before it crash landed and broke apart. (Dick Bowman)

Troops fought house to house to capture Cologne. (National Archives)

On Iwo Jima, marines crawled over the black volcanic ash deposited by Mt. Suribachi, whose summit overlooked them and provided a deadly observation post for the enemy. (National Archives)

The capture of the Remagen Bridge over the Rhine hastened the Allied advance into Germany. (National Archives)

Soldiers in an amphibious truck broached the last formidable natural defenses of Germany in March 1945 as they crossed the Rhine River. (National Archives)

Marine Corsair fighter planes operated from landing strips in the Philippines to provide ground support for army troops. (National Archives)

Flames threatened to explode a Navy Hellcat fighter aboard the carrier *Enterprise* after an errant antiaircraft shell aimed at a kamikaze sprayed the deck with hot shrapnel. (National Archives)

Struck by a kamikaze off Okinawa, the aircraft carrier *Bunker Hill* spewed fire and smoke as more than 350 men died and another 250 were injured. (National Archives)

conditions. The death toll climbed steeply after the first week of O'Donnell's operations.

Tsuneyoshi had warned that anyone who tried to escape would be killed, a violation of the Geneva rules and one largely observed by Japan's partners in Europe. At first glance conditions at O'Donnell seemed to invite breakout. Only a few strands of wire marked the boundaries and at night the thick grass could hide a figure from sentries posted on the handful of watchtowers. Beyond the enclosure lay a dense jungle, ideal for evading a search party. But the ordeal of Bataan, the Death March, and the first days at O'Donnell sapped the mental and physical strength of even the most resolute of men. Men who were barely able to totter to a latrine could hardly imagine themselves able to endure the effort required for flight.

Olson, who kept what records he could of life at O'Donnell and who interviewed many survivors, says there were no genuine attempts to escape. However, the Japanese executed at least a dozen prisoners, almost entirely those discovered in possession of items believed removed from the bodies of their own casualties on Bataan.

"Most days in camp were monotonously alike," said Sam Grashio. "We were awakened about 6:00 A.M. by the bugler, if we had not been already roused by the maniacal yelling of the Japanese taking early morning bayonet practice. Then we went to the mess hall for breakfast. This always consisted of about half a messkit of lugao, a soupy form of rice. Many men simply ate their meager breakfast, then lay down again and slept most of the day, a habit that became increasingly prevalent as we grew weaker from the lack of food. The main activity of everyone in camp who was not dead or wishing himself dead was trying to get more food. If someone was sick and about to die, others stayed close to him, less from compassion than from hope of getting his rice ration."

According to John Olson, many, many more of the incarcerated would have died of malnutrition or starvation but for truck drivers and work crews dispatched to chores outside the camp. Filipino civilians donated or sold food to the Americans on the work details. The transactions occurred when the attention of the guards was elsewhere or even with the knowledge of more humane merciful soldiers. In turn, the prisoners carried back items to the camp, ingeniously hiding the contraband during routine shakedowns. Some of the fortunate shared their treasures gratis while others sold or bartered for profit.

For more than 1,500 Americans and an estimated 20,000 Filipinos there was no help. They died, mainly during the first two months at O'Donnell. The numbers appalled the Japanese high command, if not Captain Tsuneyoshi. Starting in June, began an American exodus to a new, somewhat less malignant installation at Cabanatuan. Also, with hostilities in Bataan and Corregidor ended, the Japanese dismantled Hospital Number One and shipped the medical personnel with their equipment to O'Donnell. In addition, the cessation of fighting brought release of the surviving Filipino soldiers into the civilian population. Although the hellhole of O'Donnell did not discharge its last inmate until January 1943, it no longer figured as an element in the fate of the erstwhile defenders.

The first weeks of imprisonment for those held on Corregidor had differed significantly from that of the men on Bataan. There was no Death March for them, but the time came for them to join their colleagues in camps on Luzon. After almost two weeks, the incarcerated on Corregidor, bearing backpacks made soggy from a downpour, hiked to one of the island docks. Fishing launches ferried them out to a pair of freighters converted into troop transports. The Americans anxiously observed the ships' courses, concerned the direction might carry them to Formosa or Japan. To their relief the vessels veered toward Manila.

The landing craft at the city disgorged the men in relatively shallow water, from knee to armpit depth. "It must have been a rather amusing spectacle for the Japs to see us kerplunking into the green polluted water of the bay," remembered Svihra. "We waded some 100 yards into shore where we were promptly formed into groups of 100 willynilly and then marched up the Boulevard. Our shoes were soaking wet, making it extremely uncomfortable to walk with the water oozing out of them at each step. A few had taken off their shoes before debarking and carried them on their shoulders to keep them dry. When these reached shore, they attempted to change socks and put on their shoes. However, the Japs had other ideas. They compelled these people, with rifle butts as prods, to put on their shoes and without tying them to form with the nearest group.

"We marched up the Boulevard under supervision of mounted Jap guards, past the Polo Club and other familiar places. There were no cars on the Boulevard and no calesas and only an occasional Jap military lorry, some of which were evidently captured in Bataan. As we approached the residences on the Boulevard, we noticed a few people, Americans and Filipinos, gathered in groups. They were kept well back from the street by sentries and Manila police, evidently to prevent any communication with us. Occasionally, someone in these groups (when the guards' backs were turned) would wave to a friend, relative, or perhaps a wife waved to her husband, for there were many American Manilans who had enlisted or were commissioned in the Army at the outbreak of war. They all looked pretty sad and we observed many tearful eyes.

"We were halted for a few minutes to permit us to obtain water from some GI cans which were very conspicuously advertised as an act of charity by the Japanese Women's Club of Manila. We had hardly taken off our packs when we were ordered to form a column again. We continued our march. As we reached the high commissioner's residence we noticed the Rising Sun flying from it. The same was true of the Elks Club. This was practically an uninterrupted march of about seven to eight kilometers, on a hot, sultry May day. As a result many were forced to drop out. Most were made to rejoin their groups by thumpings with a rifle butt."

To Svihra's shock, their destination was Bilibid Prison, a massive pile of stone and dungeonlike buildings that ordinarily housed convicted Filipino criminals. The erstwhile legal officer was pleasantly surprised by the better sanitation in the new digs and the three meals a day, although the food was limited. Prisoners supplemented their diet through what Svihra labeled "Jap soldier-racketeer sentries," who acted as intermediaries between the inmates and Filipino peddlers outside Bilibid. The guards let down baskets from their posts atop the walls; the vendors put in bananas, mangoes, molasses, and the like. The prisoners passed up money, most of which went into the pockets of the troops before it got to the sellers.

The Japanese, who had signaled a sense of respect for the privacy of the Army nurses captured on Corregidor, continued to deal benignly with the women. Nurse Josephine Nesbit described the move from Corregidor to the mainland. "During the trip to Manila, the Jap officer in charge of the boat graciously offered tea and rice cookies to the officers and women. It was midafternoon by the time the boat docked and the passengers were unloaded. The officers and men were taken off first and most of them marched away. Incapacitated patients went in trucks. When the women assembled on the dock, the thirty-eight Filipinos were put in one group and the sixty-eight other women in a second group. All were counted several times before trucks arrived to take them away from the dock. The Filipinos went to Bilibid Military Prison.

"The American women were taken to Santo Tomas Internment Camp [a site of a local university known to inmates as STIC] where they were excitedly received by more than 3,000 internees. While baggage was searched and the women interviewed by the Japs, they were fed their evening meal. The most satisfying food they had in months. The fresh pineapple was the first fresh fruit they had eaten since the war began."

11

At Sea and in the Air

HISTORIANS HAVE QUESTIONED THE WISDOM OF GERMANY'S declaration of war against the United States, but American efforts prior to 7 December 1941 had already come close to open combat. Merchant ships ran a devastating gauntlet of German submarines from the moment they left ports in the United States until they docked in Great Britain or at Murmansk, the only port open in the Soviet Union. For a time, the British Navy, coordinating efforts with the Royal Air Force, had staved off the U-boat attacks upon convoys. But after the fall of France, subs operating from French ports relentlessly prowled the western Atlantic exacting a sharp increase in the toll on shipping.

To bolster the British resistance to what Roosevelt and his advisors perceived as an inevitable threat to their country, the United States in September 1940 swapped fifty aged destroyers that dated back to World War I for naval bases on colonial islands in western waters. While Hitler scrapped restrictions for hitting cargo ships, he cautioned against incidents that involved American warships. U-boats refrained from hunts in the waters off the American coasts.

When the United States, in January 1941, accepted the responsibility to protect freighter convoys sailing the North Atlantic, a confrontation with German subs became inevitable. The Roosevelt administration convinced Congress to pass the Lend-Lease Act on 11 March 1941. With a vague promise of repayment for goods provided, the United States now geared up with war materials for Britain. The Germans could hardly ignore the role being played by the officially uncommitted United States. Meanwhile, torpedoes blasted ships of various registries, bearing lend-lease goods. Admiral Harold Stark, chief of naval operations reported in early April 1941, "The situation is obviously critical in the Atlantic. In my opinion, it is hopeless except as we take strong measures to save it." However, not until June 1941 was the American Navy ready to begin this role, to which had been added responsibilities for guarding the Caribbean.

American escort vessels and U-boats sparred without either side landing a punch until October 1941, when a wolf pack ravaged a convoy 400 miles from Iceland. During the wild melee, the destroyer USS *Kearny* absorbed a hit but managed to steam into port. About three weeks later, a torpedo smashed into the destroyer *Reuben James* on picket duty 600 miles from Ireland. The magazine ignited a violent blast that tore the ship in half. As it slid below the surface, several of its depth charges detonated, killing some survivors floating in the sea. Only 45 crewmen of the 160 in the ship's company were rescued.

Only in November 1941 did Congress agree to lift restrictions on freighters sailing under the American flag and allow them to not only travel in the war zone but to arm themselves and fight when attacked. Following the official state of war against the European Axis partners, the struggle in the Atlantic fully involved the United States. The losses in ships and cargo during the first years staggered the Allies. At the height of the Battle of the Atlantic, German U-boats destroyed from 7,000 to 8,000 tons worth of vessels a month, a pace beyond the capacity of shipyards. Tens of thousands of seamen perished. Submarines stalked and attacked during daylight hours, even surfacing to finish off a vessel already crippled by a tin fish. The hard-pressed navies mustered huge 100-ship convoys but even with flocks of escorts ranging from destroyers up to battleships to shepherd them, the wolf packs savaged an average of 20 percent of each group.

Convoy PQ-17 epitomized the first year of the runs to the Soviet port of Murmansk, the most perilous voyage because the route not only carried the merchantmen into U-boat-invested waters and exposed them to heavyweight German surface warships, but also put them within range of the *Luftwaffe*. PQ-17 was organized at the Icelandic port of Reykjavik in late June 1942. The initial escort consisted of six destroyers, two flak ships, a pair of submarines, eleven corvettes [miniature destroyers], minesweepers, and armed trawlers. A task force of Allied cruisers, two battleships, a Royal Navy aircraft carrier, and another flotilla of destroyers joined the procession.

German undersea raiders and aircraft, initially frustrated by the protective screen and the weather, on 4 July scored with an airborne torpedo that reduced the Liberty ship *Christopher Newport* to a powerless hulk. It was sent to the ocean bottom by the guns of a warship. Having tasted blood, the *Luftwaffe* dispatched waves of Heinkels and Focke-Wulfs and although a number of planes were shot down, half a dozen vessels reeled from blows and several sank.

As a U.S. Navy captain, Dan Gallery commanded the patrol-plane unit stationed at Iceland. He recalled that PQ-17 only left port after a near mutiny by the crews of the merchant ships was quelled by the promise of the additional naval escort of the capital ships and heavy cruisers. "They were supposed to protect the convoy," said Gallery. "Actually they tagged along about 150 miles astern [when the attack began]. I was in the RAF headquarters and we were looking at the chart showing where the convoy was. It was up around the North Cape of Norway and it was having a bad time. We got a flash that the *Tirpitz* [one of the few German battleships] was coming out to attack the convoy. The air commander and I just rubbed our hands together and [I] said, 'Boy, this is it. The *Washington* and the *King George V* [the American and British dreadnoughts that outgunned the *Tirpitz*] will get the *Tirpitz* today.' He said, 'Boy this looks like it's going to be the best Fourth of July since you blokes declared your independence.'

"Then about an hour later, we got this message from London: 'All warships retired at high speed to the west, convoy scattered.' Everybody just slouched out of air force headquarters and went back to their huts and either cursed or wept or both. That convoy was slaughtered. The British Admiralty had withdrawn the big ships, unwilling to risk its prize assets in a showdown with the *Tirpitz*, its cruiser companions *Scheer, Hipper*, and accompanying destroyers."

Explained Gallery, "The reason behind that order from London was that our battleships had been catching hell along about that time. We had lost our whole fleet at Pearl Harbor. The *Prince of Wales* and the *Repulse* had been sunk at Singapore. All the shipyards were full of battleships that had been damaged by either torpedoes or aircraft. So the British were simply gun-shy and they weren't about to risk any more big ships within range of either torpedoes or aircraft."

When PQ-17 broke up, the freighters, like rabbits caught in an open field and beset by flocks of raptors, frantically fled for the safety of the Soviet shores, 450 miles away. Gun crews using .30- and .50-caliber machine guns futilely sought to fend off a series of assaults from the heavens. A few small but better-armed warships using 3-inch guns attempted to protect the merchantmen while the U-boats operated with impunity. Of the original thirty-three vessels carrying supplies to Murmansk, twenty-two, including fifteen under the American or Panamanian flag, went down. As a dispiriting footnote, the *Tirpitz* and its accompanying ships, misled by the information from the *Luftwaffe*, fumbled around the area without ever finding the convoy or the navy forces.

The fate of PQ-17 led to modifications and innovations that ranged from winter clothing to bigger guns and, most important, better air support. To buttress the work of the warships, aerial patrols from the States, bases in Greenland, Iceland, and Great Britain scoured the seas in search of submarines. Later, small aircraft carriers accompanied convoys, providing constant air cover against the roving marauders. Within a year the Allied forces could shift from a defensive posture to an offensive one and the balance in the Battle of the Atlantic tipped.

During this first year at war, the U.S. Navy, critically wounded at Pearl Harbor, and now engaged in a two-hemisphere conflict, faced a formidable challenge from the Japanese forces rampaging through Asia and the South and Southwestern Pacific islands. To satisfy the legitimate and political claims of the armed forces, the Joint Chiefs of Staff broke the Pacific theater into two separate fiefs. They named Douglas MacArthur supreme commander for the Southwest Pacific with responsibility for Australia, the Philippines, the Solomon Islands, New Guinea, the Bismarck Archipelago (between the Solomons and New Guinea), and part of the Netherlands Indies. His resources included soldiers, airmen, and some naval units.

Admiral Chester W. Nimitz had assumed the post of commander in chief, U.S. Pacific Fleet (CinCPAC), on 31 December 1941, the post formerly held by Admiral Kimmel. His territory stretched over the vast reaches of the Central Pacific, from the Aleutian Islands in the north, down through Midway, the last bastion before Hawaii and Fiji, and Samoa that lay along the route to Australia. To the west lay the Japanese strongholds dotting the ocean, islands grouped under headings as the Ryukus, Marianas, Carolines, Marshalls, and Gilberts.

A 1905 graduate of the Naval Academy, Nimitz had an excellent reputation among his peers, having served on a variety of ships from submarines through battleships and in staff jobs. Unlike MacArthur, Nimitz offered no showmanship; he was soft-spoken and patient. But beneath the placid exterior lay a determination that augured well for an aggressive approach. His subordinate, Adm. Raymond Spruance, complimenting Nimitz's personality, emphasized, "The one big thing about him was that he was always ready to fight. . . . And he wanted officers who would push the fight with the Japanese. If they would not do so, they were sent elsewhere."

Shortly after the new year began, the carrier *Saratoga* was plowing through the seas several hundred miles west of Oahu. Aboard was Lt. Comdr. John "Jimmy" Thach, a graduate of the Naval Academy and leader of a fighter squadron. Thach had already distinguished himself by his design of a

tactic that became known as the "Thachweave." Instead of
the conventional Vee formation, he designed a two-plane
arrangement of leader and wingman, a tactic that provided
mutual protection for the pair. From a survivor at Pearl Harbor, Thach had also learned about the capabilities of the
enemy. "He confirmed that a Zero could turn inside of anything we had. He said he had pulled up and was on this fellow's tail and was just about ready to shoot him and the Zero
just flipped right over his back and was on his tail and shot
him down." The Grumman Wildcat lacked the Zero's speed,
maneuverability, and rate of climb. Americans benefitted
from greater firepower, self-sealing fuel tanks, and armor
plate to shield the pilot and vital points.

As the *Saratoga* moved at a six-knot pace, a dental officer remarked on the slow speed. He said, "Gee, if there was
a Japanese submarine anywhere in this part of the ocean, it
would seem like it could catch us easily." Thach agreed,
adding, "It would take a long time to launch an airplane if
you had to get up to speed to do it." The skipper had been
ordered to travel slowly in order to conserve fuel.

"That evening," said Thach, "I was sitting in the wardroom eating when it sounded like the bottom of the ship
blew out, a whole big explosion—a huge, loud, ear-splitting
explosion. All the dishes went up in the air. I remember seeing my executive officer, who was sitting right by me, reach
up in the air and catch a roll that was coming down. Everybody went to 'general quarters' immediately. We got to the
ready room and word came from damage control that we'd
been hit by a very large torpedo, obviously from a submarine. It had knocked out two boilers.

"The *Saratoga* cranked on twenty-seven knots and moved
out with that big hole in the side. We had a hole big enough
to drive two trucks through, side by side, flood two boilers,

and still move at 27 knots." The torpedo actually blew up in a deserted spot on the ship, limiting the dead to a half dozen. The carrier sailed to a shipyard at Bremerton, Washington, for refurbishing.

Thach and his squadron transferred to the *Lexington*, which, a month later, plowed toward Rabaul on New Britain Island, a huge Japanese base. On the morning of 20 February, Thach remembered, "I was on combat air patrol with [Edward] Butch O'Hare leading another two-plane section and Bert Stanley leading a third. So, we had six planes on combat air patrol. [There] was real, honest-to-goodness, no-fooling radio silence. No one dared open up, because we figured if we did they might get a bearing on us. I almost jumped out of my seat when this loud voice of the *Lexington* fighter director came in giving me a vector and said there's apparently a snooper about thirty-five miles away. I started out after him and Butch O'Hare started to follow me. I turned around, looked at him and motioned him back. He didn't want to go back but inasmuch as I knew there couldn't be fighters in the area it could only be large aircraft. I figured that my wingman and I could take care of that. So I made him go back. I also calculated that if there's one snooper, there'd probably be another. It was important to get these planes and knock them out before they could report the locations of the *Lexington* task group."

The direction given Thach sent him into a heavy thunderstorm and when he queried his controller he was advised the interloper was also in the squall. "Once we were in the soup, we couldn't see very much. We came into a rift, an opening in the cloud for just a second, and right below me was this great huge Japanese insignia. I saw two engines on one wing and then just as quickly we were in the soup again. Here he was right below me, like about twenty or thirty feet. About that time the fighter director called and said, 'We have a merged plot' [radar showing both planes in the same space]. I called back, 'We sure do. If it had been any more merged, we would have crashed into him. I just sighted him.' "

The snooper disappeared, but circling about, the American caught a vague outline of the Japanese plane. Within seconds, both aircraft broke into the clear and Thach readied for an attack. He directed his wingman to move to the other side where the pair could bracket the target and guard against any turns. "I took what I figured was the proper lead on him and waited until I got close enough, coming in from the side, and opened up with all six of those guns. It was a really good blast of tracers. I took a good lead on him and on the engines on the right wing. Bullets would carry into the cockpit, through the engines, or round the engines into the cockpit. I looked back and nothing happened. No smoke, nothing! I thought, have I got blank ammunition?" His partner maneuvered for a run when the wing of the victim burst into flame.

"This was an Emily [a four-engine bomber]. We'd never seen one. We had no intelligence that they had that kind of an airplane. I knew it was huge and I could tell it had a cannon because when the cannon was shooting, it would make smoke rings. I really felt sorry for him because here he was doing his job and obviously had gotten off a message on the location of the *Lexington* task group and I hadn't hit him soon enough because I couldn't find him in the soup.

"We didn't have to make any more attacks, just watched him. He started burning and six huge long bombs dropped in the water. A few minutes later his nose went down and in he went with a splash. Made a big cloud of smoke they could see all the way to the *Lexington*. I felt sorry for the crew because some of them, maybe all, had convinced themselves they could defend with all those guns against a fighter-type aircraft. How else could they feel? It was the same sort of feeling when we were doing gunnery training and the same sort of propaganda that our big bombers were putting out to bolster their feeling of being able to survive against attack by fighters. I never believed it. We landed aboard and everybody wanted to know what it was like, what happened when we made the attacks, what kind of attacks, were they the same we did against the sleeve, and we said yes, the same thing you've been doing all the time. O'Hare was fit to be tied. He wanted to get in quick. This was the first enemy airplane any of us had seen."

O'Hare did not have to wait long before his opportunity for combat. Thach was studying charts and intelligence reports for information about the Emily when, he said, "The flight order sounded. 'Fighter pilots, man your planes.' I knew we had something coming and I figured it was an attack, or else another snooper." In fact, a large number of Japanese aircraft sallied forth from Rabaul intent upon destroying the task force. Other units preceded Thach and he sat for a time in his airplane watching. "It wasn't long before we could see from the flight deck, in the distance, some smoke and airplanes falling. I could see these bombers in close formation headed for us. The enemy was at about 8,000 feet. Later, I learned Noel Gayer [in command of a section] had called down, telling our own antiaircraft fire to please shorten their fuses to 8,000 feet because that was the altitude of the enemy bombers and he was being bothered by bursts of antiaircraft fire above them where he wanted to maneuver for attacks. We didn't have influence fuses [ones triggered by a target]. We had time-set fuses, so many seconds. This was the situation the first part of the war. We did half our fighting in the middle of our own AA fire and the other half in the middle of the enemy's."

The carrier dispatched Thach and Butch O'Hare with their wingmen. Said Thach, "I started climbing in the direction they were going so that if I ever did get to the altitude maybe I could get some of them, all the time watching these airplanes falling out of the air. Sometimes there were three or four falling at once, just coming down with dark red flame and brown smoke coming out. We didn't have a very high rate of climb, only 1,100 feet a minute when we were fully loaded with our 1,800 rounds of ammunition and full of gas. I managed to get up there and start working after I saw three of them still in some kind of formation. They split and were starting to run away individually. I made an attack on one from the low side because I didn't have enough altitude and it burst into flame and started down.

"About this time I saw one of my planes coming in dead astern [of another bomber] and a flash right on his windshield where, apparently, a cannon had hit him and he went into a spin right on in. He made a bad mistake by coming in on the tail of a bomber that had a cannon [there]. I was pretty mad at this character who had shot down one of my pilots and I wasn't going to let him get home free. I managed to get a little bit above his level before starting the approach. I was amazed; I was definitely out of his range but he was shooting all kinds of stuff at me. You couldn't see it, looking right at it. You had to look behind to see it. I put what I thought was a real good burst into his wing root and fuselage and nothing happened. I got out and made another run, pulled out, looked at him again and all of a sudden he disintegrated, just blew up.

"I didn't have my wingman with me. We were a little disorganized because we never had a chance to join up after taking off. It wasn't really necessary because against bombers you didn't have to defend yourself with maneuvers. It was all right to just go hell-bent for election and that airplane that can get there the first gets there. Then, over the radio I got the impression there was a second wave, another nine-plane group of Bettys [two-engine bombers]. We didn't know what they were because they were entirely different from anything in our intelligence manuals.

"Butch was vectored out after these people and intercepted when they were about six minutes away. We had a practice, charge all your guns and fire a short burst to be sure you've got 'em charged and your gun switches are all on. His wingman did this and nothing happened. He apparently had a short or some open circuit and couldn't get any gun to fire. Butch realized this and waved him back but he didn't want to go. Butch shook his fist at him but he came on and maneuvered to try to draw some attention to himself while Butch went in and made the attacks.

"They [the Japanese] stayed in rigid formation. That was the best thing for them to do. First they've got to have a bomb pattern if they want to hit the ship and [need] a whole proper formation for the right pattern. Furthermore, it gives all the guns from each airplane a chance to shoot to defend themselves. [O'Hare] got in, lined them up and apparently knocked down two in one pass. Then he went to the other side to work on that line back and forth. Inside of six minutes he had six down. At first he was given credit for only five. They thought antiaircraft had shot down one. Afterward one of them came down and approached like he was going to crash into the *Lexington*. We got photographs of that airplane and one engine had completely fallen out of the wing. Butch had shot that engine out. Of the twenty aircraft we met that day, nineteen were shot down." The Americans

counted one pilot killed, two aircraft lost. In their zeal to hit
the task force well out to sea from Rabaul, the Japanese
could not dispatch short-range fighters to cover their vulnerable bombers. While the *Lexington* celebrated its aerial
victories, the asset of surprise had also been a casualty and
the fleet aborted the proposed raid on Rabaul.

In early March word came of a Japanese expedition into
New Guinea at Salamaua and Lae, a pair of towns at either
end of a horseshoe-shaped harbor. The invaders met no opposition but intelligence reported a concentration of transports, cargo ships, and naval vessels. According to Jimmy
Thach, no one knew whether air cover protected the enemy
but the carriers *Yorktown* and *Lexington* received a mission
to disrupt the operation. The plan called for torpedo planes
to attack all the shipping in the harbors with the Wildcat
fighters along for protection.

The fleet hugged the south coast of New Guinea via the
Coral Sea and the Gulf of Papua with the idea that the
raiders would fly over the Owen Stanley mountain range to
surprise the targets. Lt. Comdr. Jimmy Brett led two torpedo
squadrons that included an ancient type known as a Devastator. "They were more devastating to the crews in them
than they were to the enemy. They were absolute firetraps,"
said Thach. "They were underpowered, and carrying a huge
torpedo and all the gasoline, they could just barely get off
the deck if they started right at the stern and the ship making 25 or 30 knots, they could barely stagger into the air."

The jagged ridges of the Owen Stanleys stuck up 10,000
feet. No one was certain whether Brett's ships could even
ascend above these. Thach watched the torpedo planes mill
about in search of more altitude or a passage. Brett started to
fly parallel to the lowest ridge and he noticed a sunny area
over some fields. Having trained as a glider pilot, he recog-

nized that that portended thermal updrafts. "Sure enough," said Thach, "he circled around, rising, finally got enough and just washed himself right over the ridge.

"We went into Salamau and Lae and there were the cruisers, getting underway, pulling up anchor chains. There were a lot of transports. Brett went in with his torpedo planes and I took my fighters in. I left Butch O'Hare upstairs. He didn't like that, either, but we didn't know whether we were going to run into some Zeros and we wanted to go down, strafe just ahead of the torpedo planes to give them a chance. I figured that no matter how many planes there were where we were coming in, Butch could give them a busy time before they got down to us.

"The torpedo attack was beautifully executed. You could see the streaks of torpedoes going right to the sides of these cruisers, and nothing happened. I saw one or two go right on underneath, come out the other side, go over and bury themselves in a bank on the shore. Some obviously hit the cruisers and didn't explode. We had bad fuses and very erratic depth control. I didn't see any torpedo explosions. What a heartbreaking thing after all of that effort, all of that training, the wonderful experience Jimmy Brett used to get there." It was one more instance where defective torpedoes thwarted American efforts. Only a single enemy aircraft, a float plane with a small-caliber gun, attempted to deflect the attack. It was quickly shot down. But except for some dive-bomber hits and the strafing, the ships in the harbor escaped serious damage.

Undeterred by such ineffective jabs, and on the verge of completing its conquest of the Philippines, the Japanese moved southeast to reinforce and extend Nipponese domination. The strategy, designed to isolate Australia, called for occupation of New Guinea, the Solomon Islands, and control of the surrounding waters. Intelligence reports received by MacArthur and Nimitz indicated a Japanese strike force bound for Port Moresby, New Guinea, separated from Australia's Queensland peninsula by the Coral Sea. To deny them a foothold at Port Moresby, the Americans plotted to hit the invaders at sea with land-based Allied aircraft from Australia and a naval force that would include the air groups aboard the carriers *Lexington* and *Yorktown*.

On 3 May an Air Corps reconnaissance mission spotted an invasion of Tulagi, one of the Solomon Islands. Hidden by rain squalls, a group that included the *Yorktown* approached within twenty miles of Tulagi. The carrier launched its torpedo planes, dive bombers, and fighters. The pilots and gunners scored some hits but, as so often happened, wildly overinflated the targets struck and damage inflicted. Had the tacticians acted upon this information the results would have been disastrous, for the bulk of the enemy navy had gone unscathed. Both sides then followed their own agendas for the next several days. The Japanese busily deposited ground troops at various sites while keeping an eye out for the Allied forces. A formation of four B-17s from Australia came upon an enemy carrier near Bougainville Island but none of their bombs dropped close to the ship. Throughout the war, high-altitude bombers recorded little damage to ships underway.

Dive bombers from the Japanese force aimed at the U.S. destroyer *Sims* and the oiler *Neosho*. The *Sims*, struck by a trio of 500-pounders from a fourth wave of attackers, exploded and sank with only sixteen survivors. The battered oiler remained adrift several days before the crew was rescued and the vessel scuttled. Faulty communications led to an all-out strike by planes from the *Yorktown* against what proved to be minor elements of the enemy, but before the

Japanese could exploit the mistake, ninety-three American aircraft pummeled the foe's light carrier *Shoho* and a flight leader radioed the *Lexington*, "Scratch one flattop!"

On 7 May, in the Coral Sea, Paul Stroop, a 1926 graduate of the Naval Academy, a member of the U.S. Olympic gymnastics team in 1928, and a former dive-bomber pilot, was aboard the *Lexington* as flag secretary. As the carrier recovered its aircraft, he recalled, "It was a very fine, successful day. We hadn't found the main body of the Japanese and up until that afternoon they hadn't found us. Our search planes had returned and we were running a cruising formation at dusk when we sighted some lights coming over the horizon. On the *Lexington*, we thought these were some of our own planes from the *Yorktown* returning. We were not sure that they had all their planes back. We knew that the *Lexington* planes were all aboard. These planes were in very good formation. I remember noticing the port running lights of the formation all in a beautiful echelon. One of the things that struck me as odd was that the red color of the port running light was different from the shade of running lights that we had on our own planes.

"About the time we sighted these lights, one of our screen destroyers began firing at the planes. I remember a voice message went out over the TBS [Talk Between Ships system] to the skipper of the destroyer, telling him to stop, that these were undoubtedly friendly planes coming in." The TBS instructions, said Stroop, probably came from the air officer of his ship. However, he recalled, "Chillingworth [the destroyer skipper] came right back on the TBS and said, 'I know Japanese planes when I see them.' I had subconsciously noted there was a difference [but] at the moment I didn't consider them enemy planes. Actually, these were Japanese planes that had mistaken the *Yorktown* and *Lexing-*

ton for their own ships. They came in with lights on and were ready to get into the landing formation. There was a lot of confusion, but after Chillingworth identified them as enemy planes, everybody began shooting. The Japanese broke up their formation, turned out their lights, and disappeared. I don't think we hit any that night."

American search planes glimpsed the main enemy strike force with its two big carriers, *Zuikaku* and *Shokaku.* Said Stroop, "Lieutenant Commander Bob Dixon, the commanding officer of the search squadron, stayed as long as he could in the vicinity of the Japanese carriers, giving us locations, speed, and direction of their movement. He did a classic job of shadowing these carriers, taking advantage of cloud cover when he could and reporting back to us."

From the *Yorktown,* coveys of dive bombers and torpedo planes, protected by fighters and led by Dixon, drew a bead on the *Shokaku.* According to Stroop, "The distance was a little greater than we wanted, maybe something over 200 miles, particularly the TBDs, torpedo planes that were carrying heavy torpedo loads and would not have too much range. An attack was scheduled to take place about 11:15 to 11:30 and the *Yorktown* and *Lexington* were in an area of good visibility, whereas the *Zuikaku* and the *Shokaku* still had the advantage of cloud cover. A good many of our attack planes could not ever make contact with the *Zuikaku* or the *Shokaku.* Those that did were quite effective. They damaged one carrier, the *Shokaku,* considerably, and the other a slight amount. However, the Japanese managed to control the damage and get away.

"About eleven o'clock we began getting indications on the radar of a large group of planes approaching us. We figured that the Japanese were doing the same thing we were. They had their attack planes coming down." On the bridge,

Stroop recorded entries in the war diary. At 11:20 he noted, "Under attack by enemy aircraft. . . . They came down in a very well-coordinated attack with torpedo planes and dive bombers. [At the moment] you're a little curious and you're a little scared. You wonder what the outcome is going to be. They were fixed-landing-gear dive bombers [known by the code name "Val"]. You were convinced that the pilot in the plane had the bridge of your ship right in his sight and this didn't look good. Fortunately they were not strafing because if they had been, I'm sure they would have made topside untenable.

"The minute he released his bomb you could see the bomb taking a different trajectory from the aircraft itself, generally falling short because their dive wasn't quite as steep as it should have been. The torpedo planes came in about the same time and launched at about 1,000 yards. They were down to flight-deck level. We got, I believe, four torpedo hits, although only two were officially recorded. I watched some of the torpedo planes passing from port to starboard [the hits were all on the port side]. It was pretty discouraging. They'd launch their torpedoes and then some of them would fly very close to the ship. They were curious and sort of thumbed their noses at us. We were shooting at them with our new 20 millimeters and not hitting them at all.

"We had fighters overhead and they were credited with knocking down some Japanese planes. We'd also taken some of the dive bombers and put them on close-in patrols against the torpedo planes, figuring they could overtake them possibly and disrupt the attack. They were not successful and the torpedo planes pretty much got through. The *Lexington* took, I think, three bomb hits. One of the most spectacular was on the port gun gallery. A bomb exploded and immediately killed and burned gun crews in that area.

The Marine gunners were burned right at their stations on the guns. That particular bomb started a fire down in the officers' country, the next deck below, and it killed a couple of stewards down in the pantry. We had another bomb in the after part of the [carrier's] island and another one pretty well aft.

"All of these bombs started fires which we figured we could control and put out. We learned a lot from this action—that ships of that kind had too much inflammable stuff aboard. The furniture in the admiral's cabin was wood and fabric and that burned. Paint all over the ship had an oil base and wherever we got a fire, the paint on the bulkhead burned. We learned that our fire-fighting equipment was not adequate, that we needed to redesign our hoses and hose nozzles."

In spite of its wounds from the three bombs and four torpedoes, the carrier achieved twenty-seven-knot speed. Through counterflooding, the ship returned to an even keel and like the *Yorktown* recovered its planes. The task force formed up, heading for Brisbane, Australia. "About 2:00 in the afternoon," recalled Stroop, "we heard a rather loud, submerged explosion. My first reaction was that a Japanese submarine had fired a torpedo with an influence fuse that had gone off under the hull. It seemed like that kind of explosion, deep down, probably beneath the ship. However, we found later it was not an enemy torpedo but leaking gasoline fuel, caused by the bomb hits, that had collected in the elevator well. Some spark set off the fumes. The immediate effects were quite disastrous. Communication between the bridge and central station was lost. [The damage-control officer and much of his staff in the central station were wiped out in the blast.] Fires throughout the ship accelerated. Fire developed underneath the number-two elevator.

"Word came almost immediately that the engineering spaces were untenable and had to be abandoned. The engineer crews on the afternoon watch shut down the main engines. Here was the ship, dead in the water and, worst of all, there was no fire-fighting capability. From then on it was hopeless. We had a destroyer come along to try and get hoses over but this was absolutely hopeless. The fires began increasing in size and by 3:00 or 3:30 the decision was made to get the wounded and the air-group personnel off. They brought destroyers alongside and got these people off." Because the carrier lay dead in the water, the planes could not be launched.

"We continued to try to fight the fires but it became increasingly evident that the ship not only couldn't be saved, but that it was very dangerous to stay aboard much longer. Fire had gotten increasingly violent on the hangar deck. We were beginning to get explosions, apparently torpedo heads going off from storage. Finally, Admiral [Aubrey W.] Fitch, to ease the captain's problems and ease him into making the proper decision, said, 'Well, Fred [Capt. Frederick Sherman], it's time to get the men off.' This was around 5:00 in the afternoon. The order was given to abandon ship. Everyone sensed this was the proper thing to do and they ought to do it in a hurry. We had lines over the side; the sea was calm; the water was warm; and it was still daylight. The men starting going down over the side of these lines and being picked up by boats from other ships. We didn't have any of our own boats in the water. We lost about 150 people in this total action, many of whom were killed in the initial attacks and then from the internal explosion. I remained on the bridge with Admiral Fitch, his orderly, his chief of staff, the communications officer, and the flag lieutenant. We were probably the last to abandon ship except for the captain."

The small party with Stroop selected the port side, forward, as the best place to go over the side. As they walked toward that area across the flight deck, Stroop said they felt the heat from fires that raged just beneath them. Stroop remembered that even in this moment, protocol continued. "The admiral's Marine orderly was still with him and he walked across the flight deck with the orderly in an absolutely correct position, one step to the left and one to the rear, carrying the admiral's coat over his arm. The admiral was the only officer who arrived on the rescue ship with a jacket, just because the orderly had taken it with him. The Marine orderly also had kept all of the dispatches that were handed to the admiral during the action. When the admiral would read a dispatch, he'd hand it to the orderly, who put them in his pocket. As flag secretary, my job had been, among other things, to keep the war diary that I wrote in longhand. Just before I left the bridge, I tore all the pertinent pages out of the diary, folded them up, and stuffed them in my pocket."

When they reached the rail, the sun was setting and all of the boats, heavily laden with survivors, had headed for the other ships. Stroop, who had not semaphored a message in fifteen years, wigwagged attention from a cruiser and requested a boat to pick up the admiral. "When the boat was quite close, we started getting ready to go down the lines. The admiral's orderly tried to insist that the admiral go first. He was still very proper and finally the admiral, a little annoyed, ordered the orderly to go. The admiral wanted to be the last to leave the flight deck."

The rescuers had hardly brought Fitch, Stroop, and company to the *Minneapolis* before an enormous explosion shattered the blazing hulk of the *Lexington*, sending tongues of flame the height of the mast. "We had probably fifty aircraft parked, tied down in the launching area of the flight deck. Many of these were loaded with ammunition in their fixed guns, and with fuel in their tanks they made a spectacular fire. The ammunition cooked off and the night sky was filled with tracers coming off the deck of the *Lexington* as well as the fire engulfing the entire bridge area."

The task force steamed away and a destroyer stayed behind to sink the flattop. The tally for the Battle of the Coral Sea indicated a win for the Nipponese. They lost fewer ships than the United States. But the invaders of Port Moresby backed off, reducing the menace to Australia. Encounters like these and other operations seriously attrited their experienced air crews.

Barely a month later, the two adversaries squared off for an even more critical bout, the Battle of Midway. The Americans possessed one striking advantage, intelligence on the enemy's movements. A team of expert cryptanalysts and radio operators working together not only broke the highly complicated Japanese naval codes but refined the work sufficiently to recognize the enemy ships from which messages emanated. (This was an entirely separate activity from cracking the Japanese diplomatic code known as "Purple.")

Eager to deliver a knockout blow before the Americans could recover, Adm. Isoroku Yamamoto, architect of the 7 December assault, had plotted an invasion of Midway that would allow the Imperial Navy to sweep the ocean clean of Allied vessels and might provide an opportunity to seize even Hawaii. The strategy envisioned landings upon the Aleutians, which pointed a protective arc toward Midway. The atoll had also provided a base for operations that ranged from the Doolittle raid to penetrations of U.S. ships into the Coral Sea. Some Japanese leaders considered the proposal too ambitious and preferred consolidation of earlier gains.

Yamamoto threatened to resign unless his plan was accepted and associates acquiesced.

A mighty fleet of warships and troop transports assembled and sailed toward the target, designated in coded messages as "AF." Again, the Japanese believed their destination would come as a surprise. Hypo, the U.S. code-breaking operation, divined the movement and the intelligence experts interpreted the purpose of the armada. To confirm the reading, U.S. intelligence expert Comdr. Joseph Rochefort manufactured a sting. He arranged for a message in the clear from Midway reporting that its water-distillation system had malfunctioned and a water shortage had developed. Within forty-eight hours, the Americans recorded a Japanese transcription advising that AF had water problems.

During the last week of May, Hypo produced another vital intercept, a precise account of the order of battle for the enemy fleet now bearing down on Midway. Marine ground and air units crowded onto the island to ward off landings. Army B-17s shared airstrips with Marine fighters and dive bombers. Barbed wire ringed every possible point of entry. But the principal first line of defense lay with the seagoing Navy.

Jimmy Thach and his fighter squadron landed aboard the patched-up *Yorktown* when it was 50 to 100 miles out of Pearl Harbor on its way to join the task groups that included the carriers *Enterprise* and *Hornet*. When he took off from Hawaii, Thach knew only of an impending big fight in the Pacific. Once aboard the *Yorktown*, he listened to a complete briefing on the opposition. Thach was reassured after a visit with his engineering chief who promised all planes would be ready. Leaders of the dive-bomber and torpedo squadrons, none more senior than a lieutenant, agreed with Thach that he could only send a portion of his fighters [the bulk would remain behind to protect the *Yorktown*] to escort the torpedo planes. He explained, "If you had enough, you would stack your fighters up to and including the dive bombers. The torpedo planes were old firetraps that were so slow and awkward and no self-sealing tanks. They needed protection more than anyone else, so that governed our decision in this case."

Thach faced high noon off Midway with considerable trepidation. "I was very concerned about whether the torpedo planes could get in or not. I knew that if the Japanese were together in one formation and had a combat air patrol of defending fighters from all the carriers we would be outnumbered. We were also quite concerned that the Zero could outperform us in every way. We had one advantage in that we thought we could shoot better and had better guns. But if you don't get a *chance* to shoot, better guns matter little." He was disturbed that only six fighters could make the mission, violating the principle of the weave which was predicated on sets of fours. Because the Americans divided their forces into two groups, Task Force 16 under Spruance, and Task Force 17 commanded by Adm. Frank Jack Fletcher, a gap of more than twenty-five miles separated the *Yorktown*, with TF 17, from the *Enterprise* and *Hornet*, with TF 16. The distance between the flattops reduced opportunities for a mutual-protection fighter shield.

On 3 June, the Japanese took the first step toward implementing their plan. The bombs fell not at Midway but at Dutch Harbor in the Aleutians. The purpose was to defang any American air power there and influence the U.S. to spread its resources even more thinly. Carrier-based bombers and fighters blasted several installations, destroyed a couple of Navy Catalina PBY patrol planes, and killed about twenty-five men. A scattering of soldiers then landed on the remote tundra of Kiska and Attu. Japanese intelligence vastly overestimated the U.S. military forces manning the inhospitable terrain. Kiska's "defenders" amounted to a handful of unarmed weather specialists and Attu had no military components. Strategically, the operation amounted to a waste of effort. The occupation posed no menace to Alaska nor did it divert American attention.

On that same day, the pilot of one of the PBYs that shared the long-range over-the-ocean searches with B-17s saw fly-specks on the horizon. It was the first sighting of the foe. At that distance, the only weapons immediately available to attack were the Flying Fortresses. They sallied forth. Nine B-17Es discovered a section of the enemy fleet. Armed with 600-pound bombs, the Americans dropped their ordnance from high altitude while antiaircraft gunners retaliated with great enthusiasm. Although the Air Corps announced a number of hits, it was a draw; neither side landed a punch. A slapdash scheme equipped some PBYs with torpedoes for a night run at transports. The untried, hastily improvised operation actually scored a hit on an oiler but the remarkable feat would be dwarfed by the immense scale of battle that began 4 June.

On that morning, from the main body of Yamamoto's force, a first wave of 108 bombers and fighters roared off the carriers to smash Midway. A far lesser number of Marine fighter pilots with inferior aircraft—Wildcats and Brewster Buffalos—hung about the ready shack prepared to intercept them while antiaircraft crews manned their guns and scanned the skies. Shortly before 6:00 A.M., the puny Marine outfit scrambled its obsolete interceptors against the oncoming flights. They were no match for the attackers. Of the twenty-six men who met the enemy, fourteen died and several others were wounded. In full view of the furious defenders, the foe machine-gunned to death a helpless American who had bailed out. However valiant the U.S. fliers, their achievements seemed modest. They and antiaircraft knocked down perhaps ten or twelve enemy planes and damaged more than thirty. However, the bombers inflicted only moderate damage, all of it repairable. The Japanese leader of the assault dispatched a message back to the commander of the air fleet that submission of Midway required another attack wave.

Having absorbed the opening blow, the Americans sought to counterpunch. The first effort involved flights from Midway by the latest version of a torpedo plane, the TBF Avenger, plus dive bombers and twin-engine medium-bomber B-26 Martin Marauders. None of these achieved any successes and most were shot down or badly mauled by Japanese fighters and antiaircraft. Almost as futile, B-17s struck at the fleet and missed.

Even as the vast array of Imperial Navy ships bobbed, weaved, and fended off the attacks while recovering their planes from the first Midway wave, the Japanese commanders suddenly became aware of American carriers within striking distance. They vacillated whether to prepare for another whack at the island or to take on the opposing fleet. They also had to factor in how much cover they would need for their own vessels. Protection for the Japanese flattops would lessen the escort for any assault upon Midway. And although the defenders of the atoll greatly overestimated their results against the first wave, they had significantly reduced the total resources available to the Nipponese.

Intercepts of transmissions between enemy planes and carriers indicated to the Midway eavesdroppers the course and rough location of the oncoming ships. At sea Task Force

16 had closed to within 100 miles. Admiral Spruance, not an aviation expert, after consultation with his chief of staff, an experienced airman, realized if he signaled his planes to attack at this point they had a magnificent opportunity to strike before the enemy could get his aircraft aloft. The catch was the Devastator torpedo bombers operated at a maximum combat range of 175 miles. They could not expect to make a round trip. Fully aware of the grim consequences, Spruance ordered a coordinated attack of the TBDs, dive bombers, and fighters. Just before 8:00 A.M. the catapults on the *Enterprise* and *Hornet* began to shoot their squadrons from the decks. A total of 116 aircraft set out for the quarry.

Glitches in communications of information from Midway-based scouting planes and an American submarine trailing the enemy force almost derailed the entire venture. Some twenty planes from the *Hornet* never located the target and could only return to the flattop. But one squadron, VT-8 from the *Hornet*, followed an unerring track right to the heart of the Japanese fleet with three carriers. At this early stage of the war many of those on the mission, like Ens. George H. Gay, while schooled in theory, had little practice or experience in their craft. When he took off that morning it was the first time he had ever borne a torpedo in his plane. Many of his companions were equally unversed, although their leader, Lt. Comdr. John C. Waldron, had done his best to school them through chalk talks and lectures. In the ready room as they were about to leave, Waldron, the only Annapolis graduate in the squadron, handed his men a mimeographed plan of attack to which he appended a brief message.

"Just a word to let you know that I feel we are all ready. We have had a very short time to train and we have worked under the most severe difficulties. But we have truly done the best humanly possible. I actually believe that under these conditions we are the best in the world. My greatest hope is that we encounter a favorable tactical situation, but if we don't and the worst comes to the worst, I want each of us to do his utmost to destroy our enemies. If there is only one plane left to make a final run-in, I want that man to go in and get a hit. May God be with us all. Good luck, happy landings, and give 'em hell."

Unfortunately for VT-8, the plan to catch the Japanese with their planes down failed. Aware of their approach, a flock of fighters lurked in the clouds. Gay thought at least thirty-five Zeros jumped the doomed squadron even before the antiaircraft guns opened up. The fighters slaughtered most of the Devastators before they could unleash their torpedoes. Two of the ships hit the water before Gay saw Waldon's plane flame up. Gay remembered seeing him stand up, trying to jump, but he crashed into the sea. Making a run toward a carrier, Gay glimpsed two others from his squadron but suddenly they, too, disappeared. Through his intercom he heard his radioman, Bob Huntington, murmur, "They got me." When Gay swiveled his head for a quick look back, he saw the radioman's head lifelessly lolling against the cockpit. Something stabbed the pilot's upper left arm. A hole appeared in his jacket sleeve. With his right hand he ripped the sleeve, removed a machine-gun bullet from the wound. Injured further by shrapnel, he guided his stricken plane by holding the stick between his knees.

Some 800 yards from the enemy carrier *Soryu* he discharged his torpedo. Gay thought an explosion followed but in fact the tin fish passed harmlessly by the carrier. Pulling up, Gay flew down the length of the ship, and performed a flip turn at the fantail as the *Soryu* abruptly reversed course.

Passing over the bridge, Gay said he "could see the little Jap captain up there jumping up and down, raising Hell." At this point a quintet of Zeros fell upon him, shooting out his controls and ailerons. The Devastator plowed into the ocean, a wing tore off, and the fuselage sank, but not before Gay clambered out with a rubber life raft and seat cushion.

In the water, Gay artfully tried to conceal himself from the Japanese sailors by ducking beneath his black rubber seat cushion. Several spotted him but they forgot his presence as another bunch of American torpedo planes now menaced their vessels. Again, the slow-moving TBDs succumbed to the Zeros and antiaircraft fire; only four of fourteen escaped the withering fire and returned to the *Enterprise*. The squadron failed to damage a single ship and the enemy fleet steamed on, intent upon destruction of the U.S. task forces.

The *Yorktown* dispatched its torpedo planes commanded by Lance "Lem" Massey, with six puny fighters under Jimmy Thach, about forty minutes after Task Force 16 commenced its operations. Thach recalled, "I told the people who were going on the attack that nobody was going to be a lone wolf, because lone wolves don't live very long. They had to stick together because that was the best way to survive and protect the torpedo planes. I reminded them of the tricks we heard played on some people. A Japanese fighter would pose in a position a little below where it looked like you could easily go out and shoot him, giving you this so-called advantage but his friends were waiting topside to come down and pick you off if you pulled out alone.

"It was a beautiful day. There were little puffy clouds up around 1,000 to 1,500 feet that sometimes would get a little thicker and other times they'd open up and be very scattered. I could see ships through the breaks in the little puffy clouds. We had just begun to approach about ten miles from the outer screen of this large force. Several colored antiaircraft bursts [exploded] in our direction, one red and another orange, and then no more. I wondered why they'd be shooting at us because we weren't nearly in range. We soon found out we'd been sighted from the surface screen and they were alerting the combat air patrol. A very short time after these bursts, before we got anywhere near antiaircraft range, these Zero fighters came down on us. We'd been trained to count things at a glance and I figured there were twenty.

"The first thing that happened was that [Ens. Ed] Basset's plane was burning. He was shot down right away. I was surprised they put so many Zeros on my six fighters. I had expected they would go for the torpedo planes first. But then I saw they had a second large group that were now streaming in right past us and into the poor torpedo planes. Several Zeros came in on a head-on attack on the torpedo planes and burned Lem Massey's plane right away. It just exploded in flames. Beautifully timed, another group came in on the side against the torpedo planes. I had to admire these people; they were plenty good. This was their first team and they were pros. It was the same team that hit Pearl Harbor. [Meanwhile] a number were coming down on our fighters, the air was just like a beehive. It didn't look like my weave was working, but then it began to. I got a good shot at two of them and burned them. One of them had made a pass at my wingman, pulled out and then came back. I got a head-on shot at him and just about the time I saw this guy coming, Ram Dibb, my wingman said, 'There's a Zero on my tail.' He was about forty-five degrees beginning to follow him around which gave me the head-on approach. I was really angry because this poor wingman who'd never been in combat before, very little gunnery training, the first time aboard a carrier and a Zero about to chew him to pieces. I probably should have ducked under this Zero but I lost my temper a little and decided to keep my fire going into him and he's going to pull out, which he did. He missed me by a few feet and I saw flames coming out of the bottom of his airplane. This is like playing 'chicken' with two automobiles on the highway headed for each other.

"They kept coming in and more torpedo planes were falling, but so were some Zeros, so we thought at least we're keeping a lot of them engaged. The torpedo planes had split for an 'Anvil Attack.' They'd break up and spread out on a line on each side of the target so that they could have torpedo planes coming in from various points. If the ship turns he's left a broadside shot for several torpedoes and he can only comb one [head directly for the missile and barely avoid it].

"I kept counting the number of airplanes that I knew I'd gotten in flames going down. You couldn't wait for them to splash but if it was real red flames, you knew he'd had it. I had this little knee pad and I would mark down every time I shot one that I knew was going. Then I realized this was sort of foolish. Why was I making marks on my knee pad when the knee pad wasn't coming back. I was utterly convinced that none of us were coming back because there were still so many of these Zeros and they'd already gotten one. I couldn't see Tom Cheek and Dan Sheedy anymore. There were just two others I could see of my own, Macomber, Ram Dibb, and me. Pure logic would convince anyone that with their superior performance, and the number of Zeros they were throwing into the fight, we could not possibly survive. It takes a second or two to look down to your knee pad and make this mark—a waste of time. I said, talking to myself, 'if they're going to get us all, we're going to take a lot of them with us.'

"We kept working this weave and it seemed to work better and better. I haven't the slightest idea how many Zeros I shot down. I just can't remember and I don't suppose it makes too much difference. It only shows that I was absolutely convinced that nobody could get out of there, that we weren't coming back and neither were any of the torpedo planes. Then the attacks began to slack off. Whether they were spreading out and working more on the torpedo planes that were unprotected, I don't know. I saw three or four of them that got in and made an attack. I believe at least one torpedo hit. All the records, the Japanese and [Naval historian] Sam Morison's book, said none hit. I'm not sure that people aboard a ship that is repeatedly hit about the same time by dive bombers really know whether they got hit by a torpedo or it was one of the bombs. I was aboard the *Saratoga* when she was torpedoed and the *Yorktown* when she was bombed and I couldn't tell the difference.

"I was looking at a Jap fighter when I saw this glint in the sun. It just looked like a beautiful silver waterfall, these dive bombers [American] coming down. I've never seen such superb dive-bombing. It looked to me like almost every bomb hit. Of course there were some very near misses. There weren't any wild ones. Explosions were occurring in the carriers and about that time the Zeros slacked off even more."

As the enemy fighter cover appeared to fade, Thach and his flight escorted several of the battered torpedo planes away from the combat zone. Then, upon conclusion of the dive-bomb attack, he hung around. "A single Zero appeared flying slowly below and to one side of us. I looked up toward the sun and sure enough there were his teammates poised like hawks waiting for one of us to take the bait! We didn't. I saw three carriers burning furiously before I left."

Of the forty-one Devastators that lumbered off the Americans carriers on 4 June, only four battered ones staggered back to their nests. George Gay, plucked from the sea several days later, was the only survivor from his entire VT-8 Squadron. "Those pilots were all my very close friends, especially Lem Massey," mourned Thach. "I felt pretty bad, just sort of hopeless. I felt like we hadn't done enough, that if they didn't get any hits, this whole business of torpedo planes going in at all was a mistake. But thinking about it since, you couldn't fail to send them since this was a classic, coordinated attack with torpedo planes going in low and the dive bombers coming in high, although it is usually better if the dive bombers hit first and the torpedo planes can get in better among the bombs bursting."

The SBD Dauntless dive bombers from the *Enterprise* and the *Lexington* fell upon the flattops at a most opportune time. Aboard the Japanese carriers crews were busily preparing planes for the second wave attack on Midway, while the air cover, still at low altitude because of engaging the torpedo bombers, were in no position to intercept. A 500-pounder struck the carrier *Kaga* squarely on the flight deck amidst the aircraft, loaded with fuel and ordnance. An instant inferno erupted with most of the sailors below trapped. Probably already fatally wounded, the *Kaga* rocked from three more hits of near-equal magnitude.

On the *Akagi* the first Zero bound for Midway barely lifted off the deck before the first of several 1,000-pounders whistled down from the plunging SBDs. As in the case of its sister ship, the flight deck of the *Akagi* was jammed with fully armed and fueled planes. A holocaust ignited among them and magnified several times over the destructive power of the American bombs. The explosions blew 200 men overboard as its crew scrambled for lifeboats.

A third Japanese carrier, *Soryu*, drew the attention of the *Yorktown*'s dive bombers. Lieutenant (jg) Paul Holmberg, first in line, dove into the maelstrom of antiaircraft fire to within 200 feet before he pulled up. His daring was rewarded as an explosion ripped up the deck, blasting an airplane in the midst of a takeoff into the sea. Five hits and three near misses transformed a puissant warship into a blazing wreck. Elated at their successes, the crews of the SBDs straggled back in search of their carriers. Aside from several that were shot down, a number of the Dauntlesses ran out of fuel and ditched. Other ships picked up most of the airmen.

Only one Japanese carrier, *Hiryu*, remained afloat. Aware of the destruction of its three sisters, *Hiryu* stolidly followed the orders, "Attack the enemy carriers." Because no torpedo planes were ready, only dive bombers and fighters could go. The *Yorktown* radar alerted the Americans to the oncoming enemy. A flight of twelve Grumman Wildcats tangled with the Japanese, scoring some knockdowns, but still the bombers continued their run.

More of the attackers splashed into the sea from aerial combat or antiaircraft shells but one released its explosive just before the American gunners smashed it into three pieces. The bomb struck on the flight deck, killing or wounding a number of men and curtailing antiaircraft. A pack of planes pursued the *Yorktown* until they scored two more hits. Immediate preventive measures were taken upon word of the imminent attack, and the well-trained damage-control parties enabled the *Yorktown* to resume a respectable speed and remain operational.

Undeterred by losses incurred, the Imperial Navy directed

a second strike from *Hiryu* at the American carriers. It seemed to have become as much a matter of pride as of strategy, for the successive engagements had sharply trimmed the quality available. Even planes already damaged had to be used while air crews were both weary and mentally stressed. Nevertheless, aware of the presence of the *Enterprise* and the *Hornet*, the Japanese commander instructed his air commanders to seek them out as well as the already-wounded *Yorktown*.

The hunters soon focused on their nearest target, the *Yorktown*. Again, radar, a device not possessed by the Japanese, signaled the approach of unwelcome visitors. On this occasion, the assault included ten torpedo planes accompanied by a half-dozen Zeros. A force of Wildcats that outnumbered the Japanese fighters shot down three of them and several torpedo planes. As the torpedo planes started their runs a few yards above the surface of the water, American cruisers trained their big guns on the sea ahead of the aircraft, hoping to create waterspouts that might knock them out. Still, five broke through the cordon and dropped their missiles. The *Yorktown* evaded a pair, but two smashed into her side. Water flooded portions of the ship, not only shutting down power but producing such a severe list that the flight deck canted down until one side almost touched the ocean. A protective screen of destroyers formed around the crippled ship. In a desperate effort to preserve the vessel a skeleton crew remained aboard.

Meanwhile, scouts advised the two task forces the location of the *Hiryu*. Just about everything that could fly took off. Not realizing they had hit the *Yorktown* on both attacks, instead of two separate carriers, the Japanese did not expect such a heavy assault. Dive bombers from the *Enterprise* demolished *Hiryu*, starting fires that raged from bow to stern.

In terms of carrier warfare, 4 June stood as a landmark U.S. victory. However, despite the loss of airpower, the enemy fleet still outnumbered and outgunned the Americans. The land-based defenses of Midway might well have folded under an invasion. During the night of 4–5 June, the fleets jockeyed for position. The weaker Americans strove to avoid any confrontation against the foe, who was not only stronger but also skillful at night operations. The Japanese sought to smoke out the Americans but Spruance and Fletcher refused to snap at any bait.

During the following few days, the loss by the Japanese of all their carriers enabled the Americans to pummel other vessels with aircraft from flattops, supplemented by the Army and Marine ground-based units on Midway. They victimized enemy destroyers and cruisers. However, a Japanese sub sneaked through the screen surrounding the barely moving *Yorktown*. One torpedo exploded the destroyer *Hammann* amidships while two others that slid beneath the *Hammann* found their mark on the *Yorktown*. The destroyer broke in half and quickly disappeared beneath the sea. Although sailors worked frantically to keep the shattered carrier afloat, the damage was too great. Some eighteen hours after the last injury it sank.

The Battle of Midway ended as the Japanese retreated towards the home island. Their official toll listed four carriers and a heavy cruiser sunk, heavy damage to another cruiser and a pair of destroyers. More than 332 aircraft were destroyed and the casualties in manpower, including many veteran proficient pilots, added up to 2,500. The U.S. losses were the *Yorktown* and *Hammann*, 147 planes, and 307 men. The enemy did extensive damage to Midway installations, and in the Alaskan waters lesser harm to Dutch Harbor, occupying Kiska and Attu, uncontested.

It was the first great victory for the Americans in the war. The Japanese would never again venture that far east. Beyond the deaths of comrades, the one sour note for the Navy lay in the unwarranted credit given to the Army Air Corps. In fact, although the bombers from Midway air strips tried on four separate occasions to strike the ships from various levels of altitude, and despite their claims to the contrary, the Army airmen scored only minor hits.

12

American Airpower Concepts

WITHIN TWENTY-FOUR HOURS AFTER THE FIRST BOMBS FROM carrier-based Japanese airplanes exploded at Pearl Harbor, the United States had entered a worldwide war in which the flying machine, largely a bit player previously, assumed an ever larger role. But, on 7 December 1941, what would become the single largest component of the American aerial arm, the Eighth Air Force, which carried the heaviest portion of war in the skies to Germany, did not even exist on paper. For that matter, the entire U.S. Air Force hardly deserved the name, so lacking was it in combat aircraft both in terms of numbers and performance capability against what the enemy mustered, as well as in qualified airmen.

The inadequacies of U.S. airpower at the start of the war were due to lack of imagination and money. As late as 1939, a Naval War College instruction to students dismissed "the idea that aviation alone can achieve decisive results against well-organized military or naval forces," a position refuted three years later at Midway. Because of poor intelligence and racial chauvinism, military leaders also could not believe that the Japanese might produce airplanes and pilots of quality. Few believed in the need to build better torpedo planes or bombers. At the same time, air power proponents who urged programs for research and development in the field encountered stiff budgetary restrictions.

Brigadier General Billy Mitchell, during the 1920s, was driven from the service because of his outspoken faith in the concept of strategic bombing as the key to modern war. But as time passed U.S. airmen accepted his ideas and those of others who believed airplanes could blast a foe's ability to manufacture war goods, destroy means to distribute the tools of combat, and cripple armies. That led them to put their appropriations into bombers that they believed could fly higher and faster than enemy interceptors. They were further inspired by the introduction of the Norden bombsight, a device that promised great accuracy for daylight raids. Accordingly, the Army downplayed the importance of what were known as pursuit planes, interceptors, or fighters because they seemed to lack offensive capability against the targets predicated in strategic bombing.

Only with the advent of war in Europe did the American hierarchy begin to revise its ideas. Missions to England convinced airmen that enemy interceptors could threaten their prime weapons, the four-engine bombers. The existing U.S. fighters could not compete with the best of Germany and Japan. Aircraft bombing from high altitudes posed minimal threat to moving targets like ships, a fact heavily underscored during the first year of war against the Japanese. Conditions mandated new machines, improvements on older ones, new weaponry, and new tactics.

With the British appealing for, if not demanding, American airpower to add to their efforts against the Axis powers, Lt. Gen. Henry (Hap) Arnold, as head of the Army Air Corps, secured approval from the War Department to activate an air force as part of the U.S. Air Force in the British Isles. He chose Maj. Gen. Carl Spaatz, a World War I combat pilot, respected tactician, strategist, and administrator, to head the outfit and nominated Brig. Gen. Ira Eaker, a Spaatz pal, to run the bomber command. Even before the Spaatz and Eaker team could begin to mobilize the airplanes to carry out the task, they encountered fierce opposition from the brass in charge of all U.S. Army efforts in England. The traditional resistance of ground commanders to grant any autonomy to the air forces succumbed only through the intervention of Chief of Staff George C. Marshall of the Army. The vehicle tapped for Spaatz and Eaker was the Eighth Air Force, activated in January 1942.

While the newly formed outfit initially consisted of a medium bombardment group, two pursuit groups (the designations of fighters or interceptors were not yet in vogue), and auxiliary units, other priorities reduced the Mighty Eighth to a bare skeletal form as the Japanese advanced in the Pacific. The original bomber group committed to the Eighth joined Lt. Col. James Doolittle to train for his mission against Tokyo. Other aircraft allotted the Eighth were siphoned away to participate in the critical antisubmarine warfare off the U.S. coast and for other responsibilities.

Ira Eaker took up station in England, in February 1942, as the head of the Eighth Bomber Command. But the parent organization, as such, was not in residence until 11 May 1942, when the first contingent of thirty-nine officers and 384 enlisted men set foot in the United Kingdom. Eaker, at the time all too aware of what little of material strength he brought with him, rose to speak to an assemblage of RAF guests at an early June ceremony at the newly opened High Wycombe headquarters. "We don't do much talking until we've done more fighting. We hope that when we leave you'll be glad we came. Thank you."

Eaker's twenty-three words could hardly offend the host country as they implicitly recognized that six months after the declaration of war, the American contribution to the air war effort in Europe had been only money and goods, while British fliers continued to pay a bloody price. But while the British approved the gracious note, furious discord marked the opinions and policies of the two allies even before they joined forces to fight.

A tour with the U.S. military mission during the Battle of Britain opened Carl Spaatz's eyes to some of the weaknesses of the Air Corps. He quickly realized that the effectiveness of the British radar system, crude as it was, detected aircraft long before they could be seen. He understood that the protection of invisibility through distance, darkness, or cloud cover no longer pertained. His talks with RAF pilots and commanders revealed that the weakness of the German bombers, which were restricted in distance, were too lightly armed to defend themselves, flew too low, and maintained level flight, created a recipe for disaster. Because enemy fighters appeared able to reach the altitude of the B-17 and B-24, the heavyweights needed rear firepower to ward off attacks from behind and armor plate to shield personnel and vital organs of the aircraft. He also accepted that escort fighters would be desirable, but the solution of how to load enough fuel on the smaller aircraft without destroying maneuverability and speed remained a problem. In contrast to earlier attitudes, the bomber specialists would welcome the P-47s and P-51s to the arsenal.

The Americans' approach met opposition from their allies. The RAF had seen their own fighters smash German bombers during daylight forays. They remembered, too, the loss of fifteen two-engine Vickers Wellingtons from a total of twenty-four during an early daytime raid against Germans; and noting a similar British attack on Augsburg, in which seven out of twelve Lancaster heavyweights went down, the Royal Air Force insisted that only under the shroud of darkness could strategic bombing successfully hammer the enemy. In the spring of 1941, having weathered the Battle of Britain, and now intent on carrying death and destruction to the enemy, the British tested about twenty Forts delivered under Lend-Lease to the RAF. After training and some modifications to incorporate the local control system, a trio of Forts headed for Wilhelmshaven on 8 July. The raid was a fiasco; the bombs, dropped from 30,000 feet, missed the target, and the machine guns froze up when German fighters attacked. Subsequent missions against shipping and other objectives produced dismal results, almost half the sorties aborted, only a couple of planes reached primary targets; eight of the twenty B-17s were lost or grounded for repairs. Not a single enemy fighter had been knocked down.

British enthusiasm for the B-17 and daylight operations vanished. The Americans noted that their allies insisted on operating at well over 30,000 feet, excessive even for the high-altitude bomber, leading to overloads on the oxygen systems, a freeze-up of weapons, and a reduction in air speed, thus lessening the ability to defend against enemy fighters. Finally, the RAF relied on the Sperry bombsight, considered quite inferior to the Norden. But, unconvinced by the arguments of the Americans, when B-24s were delivered, the RAF shunted them away from strategic-bombing operations and into antisubmarine patrols. Spaatz and his associates remained committed to their notion of daylight bombing from high altitudes. Only the U.S. possessed the Norden sight which the strategists believed guaranteed effective delivery.

The failure to convert the British to the potential of the heavy bombers for their designed purpose dogged Ira Eaker from the moment of his arrival to command U.S. forces. Not only did the ally clamor for immediate deeds by the Americans but it insisted that the proposed approach would be a disaster. Not too subtly the Brits suggested that all American aircraft come under RAF control. No one in America, certainly not Chief of Staff George C. Marshall, or Hap Arnold as boss of the Air Corps, could stomach that. Spaatz and Eaker would have to prove to the British that daylight, precision bombing could work.

The Allied commanders agreed, however, on the need for a strategic-bombing campaign. Aerial assaults on production and transportation centers, combined with a blockade, economic pressure upon neutrals, hit-and-run operations by commandos, sabotage by people in occupied lands, and the murderous war between the Soviets and Germans, could bleed the Axis powers. The strategy aimed to weaken the enemy and provide prime conditions for a frontal assault by ground troops in the West. The RAF publicly wondered if intensive bombing might obviate any need to invade the Continent.

The British policy makers, aware that night attacks sacrificed precision, introduced the notion of "area" bombing. Destruction in the vicinity of a strategic site, while perhaps not inflicting all the desired damage on the target, would destroy the surrounding neighborhood, which included workers. Psychological as well as physical injury would result; the ideas of Giulio Douhet, a 1920s advocate of total war, rendered real. The approach dictated the design of British aircraft; bombers with great range, oversize loads, and, because of the presumed protection by darkness against opposition, less armament and fewer crewmen. Because of their nocturnal rounds, the Lancasters and Stirlings sallied forth without fighter escort; indeed the British made no effort to extend the short range of the otherwise-superb Spitfire. At the end of May and the beginning of June 1942, just before the first Eighth Air Force elements arrived, the RAF scrounged aircraft from training and noncombat commands to mount Operation Millennium, the first thousand-plane saturation raid upon Cologne. More than two-thirds of the attackers consisted of two-engine planes with no margin for error if they were to return to base. The bombs killed 469, wounded more than 5,000, and destroyed 45,000 homes. Subsequently, similar assaults blasted Bremen and the Ruhr with widespread havoc but relatively little effect on the German war effort, other than to stimulate production of fighters. From a propaganda viewpoint, however, the attacks seriously wounded *Luftwaffe* chief Hermann Goering, who had boasted in 1939, "My name is not Goering if any enemy aircraft is ever seen over Germany, you can call me Meyer" [an antisemitic reference].

The U.S. airmen predicated their faith in the daylight approach on the ability of the Norden sight to pinpoint targets and on the ability of the Forts and Liberators to fly high enough and fast enough to defeat efforts to stop them. Their theorists denigrated area bombing as a wasteful dispersion of resources. The British convened the Butt Committee, charged with an investigation of the effectiveness of the RAF by the War Cabinet Secretariat. It statistically analyzed night bombing through the use of photography. The results were discouraging. The averages indicated only one of three attacking aircraft over Europe came within five miles of the target, with the best achievements registered for France but a severe drop to one in ten for areas like the German Ruhr. Some of the nighttime missions struck the wrong cities or dummy versions erected by the Germans in empty fields. To enhance accuracy British scientists developed a pair of radar-based systems: Gee, and then H2S, both of which aided navigators to locate targets. Gee was supposed to locate an airplane precisely enough to bomb within a tenth of a mile of the target. In practice it was less accurate; its range was limited, and over German territory the enemy successfully jammed it. H2S used its beams to indicate ground features, giving airmen a rough picture of the territory below with readings that distinguished water, open fields, and built-up areas. Both of these tools would be adopted by the U.S. airmen operating from the United Kingdom.

The Americans argued that precision bombing could take out key elements in the enemy war effort, rendering him weak if not helpless, more quickly than area bombing could. The Air Corps stance also reflected reluctance to the inevitable slaughter of noncombatants by area bombing. Even the Japanese at Pearl Harbor had concentrated on military targets. Earlier, however, Italian airmen bombed and strafed Ethiopian citizens in 1935, and the Germans struck at the town of Guernica in Spain while supporting the rebels under Gen. Francisco Franco. The *Luftwaffe* then hurled death and destruction upon Polish cities before finally striking at Coventry and London. The actions provoked outrage about such barbarism. As the RAF commenced its nighttime area bombing that wreaked havoc among civilians, the Allies muted the talk about victims, but initially, American officials could argue their approach as more humane. As World War II stretched over the years, daylight bombing eventually spared relatively few civilians in Europe, and when B-29s began massive raids on the Japanese home islands the net effect was the same as the area bombing practiced by the British.

Serious weaknesses afflicted the initial American plan. The exaggerated and legendary belief that the Norden bombsight was accurate enough to drop a bomb in a pickle barrel not only overstated the capacity of the instrument but it included no recognition of what happened under combat conditions with exploding antiaircraft shells and enemy fighters, guns and cannons blazing, careening through bomber formations. Furthermore, the Messerschmitts and Focke-Wulfs could reach altitudes above those favored by a B-17 or B-24, and flew hundreds of miles faster than any bomber. Spaatz, having witnessed the Battle of Britain, undoubtedly realized the potential for interception but he hoped that extra armor and greater firepower would rebalance the equation in favor of the Air Corps. He also counted on the newer American fighters that might provide more extended escort service than what previously existed.

Jim Goodson, Bill Dunn, and the other U.S. volunteers, as members of the RAF, did not qualify as Americans carrying the Stars and Stripes into the air war. British officialdom and the local press forcefully criticized both the absence of U.S. forces and the American ideas. Implicit in the ongoing controversy were questions of command and control. Spaatz, Eaker, and Arnold all feared that if they converted themselves into warriors of the night, they would become subservient to the RAF's bomber chief, Sir Arthur "Bomber" Harris, thus surrendering the limited independence wrested from the U.S. Army hierarchy. Furthermore, the B-17s and B-24s would require substantial changes to adapt for a different kind of work. The engine exhausts for the Forts, for example, spurted flames, making the aircraft obvious to any night marauders or even ack-ack gunners. Crews also would need considerable retraining.

The initial reticence displayed by Eaker at that first luncheon did not mollify a growing impatience with the pace of the American combat effort. Winston Churchill constantly nagged U.S. leaders to put their planes in the air, their bombs on targets. It was not simply an attempt to relieve his forces from carrying the weight of the war. The British Empire, already shrunken by the Japanese in the Far East, was losing more ground in North Africa to the German *Afrika Korps*. There was genuine worry that Germans would shortly overwhelm the Soviet Union unless the Allies applied pressure that diverted the enemy and strengthened Red Army resolution. There was even talk of an invasion late in 1942 or early 1943, preposterous and most certainly doomed to a devastating loss in light of the British Army still recovering from its mauling at Dunkirk and the lack of trained, properly equipped U.S. troops. The fortunes of the United States were near bottom, with the Japanese having swept over the Philippines, Wake, Guam, and lands formerly held by Allies.

The first units that would fly against the European enemies under U.S. insignia were echelons from the 97th Bombardment Group, a B-17 outfit, and the 1st and 31st Fighter Groups with P-38s and P-39s, respectively. They expected to sail from New York early in June, arriving a few days after the combat aircraft, with their crews and pilots, ferried themselves across the Atlantic.

Everything bound for Europe suddenly appeared in jeopardy with the discovery of the Japanese fleet bearing down on Midway. Both the 1st Fighter Group and the 97th Bomb Group reversed course and tracked toward the West Coast, prepared to reinforce the defenders of Midway. The 31st

Fighter Group, whose pilots were to have depended upon the 97th's B-17 navigators to lead them over the Atlantic, now boarded ships for England.

On the heels of the victory at Midway, the British, from Churchill on down, continued to press the Americans, including Maj. Gen. Dwight D. Eisenhower, who had assumed command of the European theater of operations, United States Army (ETOUSA), to do something. In North Africa, *Afrika Korps* commander Erwin Rommel threatened the Suez Canal, while across Egypt, the British and Australians barely hung on in front of Alexandria. On 2 July, the Nazi juggernaut smashed into Sevastopol, completing the conquest of the Crimea. German radio sneered at talk of an American airpower debut.

The Nazis seemed to have better intelligence than Washington. Hap Arnold, unfortunately, to placate the British Prime Minister, had told him on 30 May 1942, "We will be fighting with you on July 4th." At the moment he made his rash promise, Arnold believed the 97th would have trained for a month over England and be ready to commence operations. Eaker and Spaatz had precious little with which to work. When word reached Eaker, he reportedly remarked, "Someone must have confused the 4th of July with April Fools' Day."

To fulfill their boss's order, Spaatz and Eaker in desperation turned to the one unit actually on hand, the 15th Bombardment Squadron. It was not a heavy-bomber outfit. Far from it, the 15th, originally intended to employ night fighters, flew twin-engine Douglas A-20s, four-man light bombers that the British called Bostons. The aircraft used by the 15th actually belonged to the RAF and carried the British insignia. One crew from the unit, with Capt. Charles Kegelman as pilot, flying with the RAF 226 Squadron, had been, on 29 June, the first to bomb occupied Europe during a raid on a marshaling yard at Hazebrouck.

With the 15th was Bill Odell, a Chicago youth born in 1915, who entered the army under the Thomason Act, an officer program established at his college, Washington University in St. Louis. Odell and his fellow members of the 15th reached England in mid-May of 1942 and the crewmen were assigned to RAF outfits that flew Bostons. "These were front-line, operational units doing battle almost every day. Every day was packed with learning opportunities. Covered were the essentials to survival in combat; aircraft identification, communications procedures, ditching techniques, discussions of all phases of aircraft operation, and combat flying."

Another member of the 15th was Marshal Draper, a bombardier. "The spirit [of the first Americans in England] was willing but the supplies were meager. The German submarine campaign was in full swing and confusion reigned. I had an abbreviated course in the Royal Air Force navigation system and did a little practice bombing."

As 4 July approached, Odell kept his diary informed. On 2 July, while at Swanton, he went off on another preparatory exercise. "We're practicing for a 4th of July show somewhere over Germany [occupied Europe]. We expect to make an American low-level attack on fighter airdromes during daylight. General Spaatz and Eaker arrived and Keg talked to them. They wanted us to put on a 'circus' without fighter escort. Just shows how much our brass hats know or how they value the cost of mens' lives." The July 4th event brought out Spaatz, Eaker, and Eisenhower, who met the crews going on the sortie. They shook hands with everyone. "It was obvious they had been told it was not going to be a 'piece of cake.' Their faces were somber, if not grim. Then to dinner and the food did some good."

The planned U.S. Independence Day affair, endorsed by President Roosevelt as a highly appropriate date for actual entrance into the shooting war, met none of the concepts behind the Eighth Air Force. Instead of a huge armada of heavy bombers soaring far above the clouds, penetrating deep into enemy territory while relying on the precision of the Norden sight, a dozen Bostons, all of which belonged to the RAF, with six U.S. crews combined with an equal number of Britons, would raid four enemy airfields in Holland at low level. British bomber command had balked at a high-level excursion because the Spitfires ordinarily assigned to escort such raids were already committed to other operations. Civilian leaders may have relished the effort by the U.S. Air Corps, but the senior RAF people recognized the operation as more show biz than strategy.

Bombardier Draper recalled, "Our assigned target was De Kooy, a *Luftwaffe* base on the northern tip of Holland. The fight was led by an RAF pilot with Capt. Charles Kegelman and 2d Lt. F.A. Loehrle, both US pilots, flying the wings. I was the bombardier-navigator in Loehrle's plane. Just before takeoff, the RAF officer who normally flew in this plane handed me a one-foot by two-foot piece of armor plate and a steel infantryman's hat and said, 'Be sure you put the plate under your feet and wear the hat.' I have been told that this practice was vigorously discouraged later because of the added weight in heavy bombers with a larger crew. Nevertheless it probably saved my life since I was the point man of our plane.

"The flight took off, formed up, and we headed east at a height of about fifty feet above the water toward Holland. About ten miles from the target we passed a couple of small boats that appeared to be fishing craft but were picket boats, called 'squealers' by the RAF, and whose function was to alert the shore-based antiaircraft defenses, as we soon discovered.

"A few moments later, we were approaching a seawall on the shore when heavy flak opened up. Tracers were going by and above the plane and on both sides of my head like flaming grapefruit. This kind of situation, like hanging, concentrates the mind wonderfully, and everything went into slow motion. I could not see why we weren't getting hit but we cleared the seawall and I felt the plane lift as we let the bombs go. We immediately turned left and came face to face with a flak battery. [The German word for antiaircraft was *Fliegerabwehrkanone* which U.S. fliers shortened to flak. The British usually used 'ack-ack,' a World War I term.] The four wing guns were firing but we were so close the fire was converging beyond the battery. I glanced at the air-speed indicator, which registered 285 mph, and suddenly realized the battery gunner was shooting directly at me. We were getting ripped right up the middle as we passed over, about two feet above the gunner's head. We were fifteen feet off the ground at this point. That was my last memory of the attack."

In his diary for 4 July, Odell scribbled, "Up at 5:15 and had a cup of coffee in the mess hall. Then to the operations room and turned in papers and got packet for combat flight (concentrated food, water purifier, compass, and French, Dutch, and German money). Had no trouble but was a bit anxious on the takeoff. After getting in the air, we settled down and flew right on the trees to the coast. When we went down on the water, felt a bit uneasy because there was a cloudless sky but no fighters appeared. Found land ahead and could spot the landmark of the lighthouse a long way off."

In the diary, Odell reports, "Swung over the edge of the coast even lower than the leader and stayed right on the grass. I opened the bomb doors, yelled to [bombardier Leslie] Birleson and then it started. I fired all the guns for all I was worth and Birly dropped the bombs. I saw the hangar but that wasn't my dish. I saw Germans running all over the place but I put most of my shots over their heads." Two gunners on RAF Bostons manned single, flexible machine guns from rear upper and lower positions. Affixed to the fuselage also were two pairs of .303-caliber machine guns located on the lower port and starboard sides of the ship. A pilot like Odell could fire all four in unison by depressing a single trigger on his control column.

As the raiders zoomed over the airfield, dumping bombs and spraying machine-gun bullets, the defenders fired back. "Our bombs were okay," Odell noted, "but I thought we would crash any moment for I never flew so reckless in my life. The next moment we were flashing past the coast and out to sea—the water behind us boiling from the bullets dropping into it all around. I kicked and pulled and jerked from side to side. Didn't look at the air speed—was trying to miss the waves. Over the target we were doing 265 but shortly after I opened it up a bit.

" 'Digger' [another pilot] claims he shot his guns into a formation of groups lined up for inspection. His bombs hit well before they should have. 'Elkie' was a bit behind but he got rid of his load. He got a broken radio antenna and a mashed-in wing edge. I picked up a hole just above the pilot's step and a badly knocked-up bomb door. We zigged and zagged until three miles out, then closed up waiting for fighters. None came. We reached the coast and were the first home.

"All came back except Loehrle, Lynn, and a Britisher (Henning). Loehrle was hit by a heavy shell and hit the ground right in the middle of the airdrome. 'He flew into a million pieces,' one of the rear gunners said. And I owed him one pound ten shillings. I feel like a thief! Lynn was following before the flight hit the target but never came away from it. His wife is to have a baby in November. He really wasn't cut out for this game. At breakfast he was salting his food, trying to hold the salt spoon steady, yet throwing salt all over his shoulders. I hope he didn't crash. Henning was shot down by an ME 109 that took off just ahead of him. He tried to get it but it turned, got behind him and set one motor on fire. He crashed into the sea. Keg got his right prop and nose section shot off by heavy stuff right over the target. His wing dropped, hit the ground and he managed to right it and come home on one motor."

While a gunner said he saw Loehrle's bomber crash onto the tarmac, Draper, the bombardier on the fallen A-20, said, "I woke up lying on my back on the bottom of the North Sea in about twenty feet of water, very confused about where I was or what I was doing there. I thought I was dead and kept waiting in the gray gloom for something to happen. Then I sat up and saw my breath bubbling up through the water and finally realized I was submerged.

"When I surfaced I was opposite a small beach under the seawall and with the tail of the A-20 protruding from the water, which was all that was visible of the plane. Various subsequent reports had us crashing in flames, or disintegrating, but I saw no smoke or signs of fire associated with the plane and no debris. However, for me to be vectored nearly sideways to the plane, which appeared pointed to the west, I must have been subjected to very powerful force.

"I swam ashore, walked a few feet from the water's edge, and sat down, overcome suddenly with an enormous fatigue. Somehow I had been taken right out of my parachute harness and flotation vest and my uniform was ripped to shreds. Also, I was bleeding from an assortment of places. A path led up from the beach to the seawall and I could see several soldiers at the top of the path but they made no effort to come down. So I sat and rested for a time. After a while, my mental tiles had clattered back into place, somewhat, and it occurred to me that I might be better off starting up the path than sitting on the beach bleeding like a stabbed hog. I got to my feet with some difficulty, trudged across the little beach and started up the rather steep path. To my astonishment, the soldiers came rushing down the path and grabbed me by the arms. They were mumbling 'minen,' 'minen' as if to excuse some perceived lack of hospitality in not coming to my aid. The beach had been mined, presumably by the Dutch before the Germans got there.

"The next thing I remember I was lying on a table in what appeared to be a first-aid room. The cast had changed from the *Wehrmacht* to three *Luftwaffe* types, one of whom was holding my eyelid up and looking at my eye with a little flashlight. He straightened up, turned off the flashlight and announced to the room at large, 'Shock.' Then he asked me, 'Have you lost many blood?' I corrected him, 'That's much blood. You mean much blood. I don't know.'

"I was still functioning in an offset mode. I did notice that my clothes had been removed and I could see my shoes lying on another table. The rubber heels had been torn off—shoe heels were a common hiding place for escape materials. I thought that must have been a big disappointment. I was already acquiring a *Kriegsgefangener* [POW in German; shortened to "kriegie" by those who were incarcerated] mind-set." In fact, Draper qualified as the very first U.S. Air Corps prisoner in Europe.

The 4 July event was celebrated in newspapers and Kegelman received a Distinguished Flying Cross. But, overall, the affair was a fiasco. The tactics had no relation to the concept of strategic bombing. The three Bostons shot down represented a 25 percent loss; an insupportable rate of casualties. The bodies of the other three men with Draper were recovered. Furthermore, most of the aircraft that made their way home needed considerable repairs from the shot and shell inflicted by flak gunners and enemy fighters. One researcher, George Pames, claims that Eisenhower was so dismayed he "never again permitted men of his command to engage in needless combat to satisfy American pride or produce media events for propaganda purposes."

13

Opening Offensives

THE 15TH BOMB SQUADRON'S VALIANT BUT INSIGNIFICANT achievements only increased the pressure for the debut of the four-engine, heavyweight bombers upon which the entire daylight strategic-bombing program of the Eighth Air Force was predicated. Furthermore, the American commanders wanted control over the fighter escorts and while RAF efforts on their behalf would be welcome, Spaatz and Eaker always planned the Eighth would field its own.

By the second week in June, after the decisive defeat of the Japanese Navy, the 97th Bomb Group resumed its path toward England. It was too late for the fighters who had also been diverted. Their pilots were already on the high seas with their P-39s to follow. The trip by the 97th to the United Kingdom was almost akin to the earliest voyages against the uncharted Atlantic 450 years earlier, although Columbus sailed through the southern climes rather than the shorter and much less forgiving North Atlantic.

The 97th's itinerary began when the B-17s headed to

Presque Isle, Maine. After a pause in Goose Bay, Labrador, the flights scheduled stopovers at a pair of outposts in Greenland, then Reykjavik, Iceland, before touchdown on the United Kingdom soil at Prestwick, Scotland. Several from the group crash-landed in Greenland but heroic rescue efforts saved the crews. The first ship from the 97th cleared the Atlantic on 1 July. The remainder straggled in twenty-six days after the migration began. They had lost five aircraft but no personnel.

Among those who brought his bomber to Scotland was Walt Kelly, a twenty-three-year-old tavernkeeper's son from Norristown, Pennsylvania. "When we got to England, the facilities and conditions were A-OK but we did have problems keeping the planes flying. The RAF told us we would get our butts blown off if we persisted with daylight bombing. We were told that the *Luftwaffe* was highly skilled and that their 88s were very accurate, both of which were confirmed later. For our part we were ready for action and wanted to prove ourselves in combat. We were impatient for the big day to come. We didn't have to wait long. August 17th, 1942, turned out to be a beautiful sunlit day—one of a very few since our arrival in the United Kingdom. Our very first combat briefing was full of detail about the Messerschmitt 109 and the Focke-Wulf 190 fighters, our escort (RAF), and specifics about the marshalling yards at Rouen, France, our target.

"It was cause for celebration for finally we were gonna get it done or fail desperately in trying, as many, especially the RAF Bomber Command, predicted. We in the 342d Squadron of the 97th were confident. We just wanted to be let loose to punish Hitler and the *Luftwaffe*." On this uncharacteristically bright, clear day, the lead element of the twelve B-17s spotted Rouen ten minutes before turning into its bomb run. "I can see the target. I can see the target," exulted Lt. Frank R. Beadle, the bombardier in *Butcher Shop*, flown by Maj. Paul W. Tibbets, who just shy of three years later would pilot the *Enola Gay* over Hiroshima. Also on *Butcher Shop*, in the copilot seat, group commander Col. Frank Armstrong, hearing Beadle's cry, snapped over the intercom, "Yes, you damn fool, and the Germans can see you, too."

Temporarily chastened, Beadle switched open the bombbay doors and as he cut loose the ordnance, sang through the intercom, "I don't want to set the world on fire . . ." Walt Kelly in *Heidi Ho* described the experience: "It was a cakewalk. We saw little opposition and it seemed to me like a realistic practice mission, like one we had flown in recent days. We were cocky when we took off and more so when we landed. There was lots of hoopla and queries from the press. Several planes buzzed the runway before landing" [a stunt forbidden but often unchallenged].

From a ringside seat in the lead plane of the second flight, Ira Eaker observed what his tiny air force wrought. He was pleased enough to announce, "A great pall of smoke and sand was left over the railroad tracks." Armstrong chimed in, "We ruined Rouen," hardly descriptive of the actual minimal damage done. Rail traffic was disrupted only temporarily and no serious impact upon the German war effort occurred. Perhaps delighted at any addition to the efforts of his forces, Bomber Harris sent a message. "Congratulations from all ranks of Bomber Command on the highly successful completion of the first all-American raid by the big fellows on German-occupied territory in Europe. Yankee Doodle went to town and can stick yet another well-deserved feather in his cap."

The debut of the U.S. heavy bombers prompted an outpouring of self-congratulatory declarations. In Washington, Hap Arnold wrote a memorandum for the attention of Gen. George C. Marshall, and to the attention of Navy head Adm. Ernest J. King and Adm. William Leahy, an adviser to the president. "The attack on Rouen," claimed Arnold, "again verifies the soundness of our policy of the precision bombing of strategic objectives rather than the mass (blitz) bombing of large, city-size areas." In fact, the attack of 17 August proved little as the 97th encountered limited opposition, most of which was handled by the RAF Spitfires.

The euphoria dissipated rapidly. "We weren't wiped out as the British predicted," said Kelly. "But this to them was just a token raid in which the Germans were taken by surprise. Early claims of enemy fighters shot down dwindled to one as gunners were pressed for confirmation of kills. High altitude, precision, daylight bombing would have to be proven over deeper and more difficult missions. We still had to prove we could hold our own in aerial combat over continental Europe." Eaker, too, recognized deficiencies. He felt the crews lacked discipline and seemed nonchalant about combat. He voiced disapproval of loose rather than tight formation flying. He called for added drill in oxygen use, advocated lengthening the hoses to give men more freedom to move, and for improvements in the masks, which were clumsy and tended to freeze up.

In August 1942, a force of some 7,000 largely Canadian troops with a few American Rangers and some British commandos raided the channel port of Dieppe. The defenders inflicted heavy losses upon the Allied forces notwithstanding air support that included the 97th Bomb Group and the American 31st Fighter Group, the first unit from the States to meet the *Luftwaffe*. The 31st had expected to cross the Atlantic in their P-39 Airacobras chaperoned by the B-17s of the 97th that would provide navigation data. However, the flap over Midway that detoured the B-17s forced the 31st personnel to travel to England by ship. Once in the United Kingdom, their P-39s still on U.S. docks, the pilots of the outfit climbed into the cockpits of Spitfires.

Frank Hill, a New Jersey high school graduate in 1937, was initially assigned to P-40 Warhawks, then worked with the Airacobra. "The Spitfire was really a welcomed airplane," said Hill. "After only a few flights, we were unanimous in our praise for it and thankful not to have the P-39. The Spitfire was an easy plane to fly and to maneuver. Our mechanics were quick to adapt to the engine and armament. In less than thirty days, we were ready to go."

To ease the 31st into combat, it flew what Hill calls "indoctrination—sightseeing—missions along the coast of France." Mostly these were practice "rodeos," maneuvers designed to entice enemy aircraft to put in an appearance. On 26 July during a sweep that carried him over occupied France, Lt. Col. Albert Clark, an unlucky member of the 31st, bailed out after engine failure and became the first fighter-pilot prisoner from the Eighth Air Force.

Hill and the 31st participated in the 19 August action over Dieppe. "We had been over Dieppe only a few minutes when the RAF operations center that was controlling all the fighters [the Eighth Air Force relied on some British facilities, particularly during joint efforts] reported that a dozen or so enemy aircraft were approaching Dieppe from the direction of the big German airdrome at Abbeville. A few minutes later, a flight of aircraft arrived above us, at about 12,000 feet and immediately commenced an attack on my flight." Hill on this venture led four ships.

"I wanted to keep my flight together and avoid giving away the advantage. As the Germans attacked, their formation broke up into pairs. I turned up toward them and flew at them head-on as they came down. This made it hard for the German pilots to keep their sights on us, and it forced them to attack us head-on. One pair of FWs came in real close, and that gave us an opportunity to fire our guns directly into them. On this pass, my number-four airplane, piloted by Lt. D. K. Smith, received a burst of cannon fire through its left wing. It left an eight-inch hole on top and took out about two feet on the underside of the wing.

"After about three minutes of trying to keep my flight from being hit—by constantly breaking and turning into the Germans—I found myself in position to get a good shot at one of the Focke-Wulfs, so I fired all four .303-caliber Browning machine guns and both Hispano 20mm cannon at it. The German swung out to my left and I got in another good three-second burst of cannon and machine-gun fire. I fired into his left side at a forty-five-degree angle from about 300 yards down to about 200 feet. The Focke-Wulf started pouring black smoke. He rolled over and went straight down. I followed the smoking FW down to about 3,000 feet, but at that point I had to pull out because the ack-ack coming from the ground was really intense and I didn't want to lose any of my planes to ground fire. The last I saw of the Focke-Wulf it was about 1,000 feet over the Channel. It was still smoking and still in a steep dive.

"We climbed back to 8,000 feet. It was quiet for a few minutes, and then more Focke-Wulfs came down. We headed up and kept breaking into them. As my wingman and I turned into them, making it harder for them to track us in their sights and forcing them to come at us head-on, my second element was given an opportunity to fire on them. This was our first combat and we didn't know much else to do except turn into them and fire as best we could. We were fighting defensively, but we had a chance to hit them as they came down to hit us.

"It was constant look-see-turn for about thirty-five minutes. Then we started to get low on fuel. I had run out of cannon ammunition by then. I don't think I did much damage after I hit the first Focke-Wulf. I made one last attack on another Focke-Wulf from above and behind. I don't think I hit him. If I did, I didn't damage him very much. I was getting ready to turn for home when my element leader, Lt. Robert "Buck" Ingraham, called, 'Snackbar Blue-three going down.' I thought he was going down after something but then I saw him bail out at about 7,000 feet. As Buck approached the water, I saw two boats heading toward him. I thought he was going to be picked up okay. I later found out that these were German E-boats and he was a prisoner for the rest of the war.

"When we got back to Kenley [the 31st airfield] we refueled and had the airplanes ready to go in about ten minutes. We picked up another pilot to fill in for Buck Ingraham and D. K. Smith got another airplane. [All units ordinarily included extra pilots and crew as well as reserve aircraft.] I was wearing a leather jacket and when I landed after the first mission, I discovered that it was soaking wet from sweat. B flight flew four missions that day, and we had quite a time. I fired my machine guns and cannon on each mission. We learned a lot. Flying and firing on each mission was quite an indoctrination to fighting."

As Hill's account indicated, the short distance to the action permitted Spits to go to work, return, refuel, rearm, and sortie again. These conditions enabled the Spitfire to dominate the Battle of Britain. The same advantage, however, would accrue to German interceptors when the Eighth Air Force began to penetrate deep into the Continent. Because no one could confirm that the German fighter he last saw smoking in a steep dive actually crashed, Hill only received credit for a "probable." Lieutenant Samuel Junkin of the 31st was the first of the Air Corps in Europe to score a kill, although Junkin was severely wounded and shot down during the same action.

For the 97th Bomb Group, the price increased sharply on its fourth mission aimed at Rotterdam. Delayed by an abort and some mechanical failures, the Forts arrived sixteen minutes late for a rendezvous with fighters. In sight of the Dutch coast, the Spitfires reluctantly peeled away to go back to base. Almost instantly hordes of enemy fighters replaced them. Several Forts were shot up and crewmen killed or wounded. On 6 September the 97th lost its first airplane to enemy fire and the first operation for the 92d Bomb Group cost it a B-17. Enroute to hammer the Avions Potez aircraft factory at Meaulte close to the French coast, escorted by Eagle Squadron Spitfires—planes crewed by Americans who had volunteered for the RAF before Pearl Harbor and still controlled by the British—the B-17s barged into flocks of interceptors. The seemingly reticent enemy had only been analyzing the American bomber procedures and developing a tactical approach. Charles Travinek, a radio operator and waist gunner, said, "Midway over the water all hell broke loose. Goering's Abbeville Kids were waiting for us with 200-plus *Luftwaffe* fighter planes, ME 109s and FW 190s. They stayed with us, constantly firing away until our planes were crippled while fighting our way through direct hits over the target.

"Three of our engines were shot out as we dropped our bomb load over Meaulte. The fourth engine was feathered. Our vertical stabilizer was shot out as was the oxygen and intercom. Our plane began making spasmodic drops of 500 feet to 1,000 feet in altitude. We hit the ceiling with each sudden drop along with the unsecured equipment. Then we rapidly dropped with the flying objects to the plane's rubber walkway." In a crash landing, the right wing tore off and the ball turret smashed through the tail on impact. "Bill Warren, the ball-turret gunner," said Travinek, "was the only crew member not seriously hurt—just a gash on his head. He dragged Bill Peltier, tail gunner, away from the plane to safety but was unable to get [William] Dunbar, [Thomas] Matson [radio operator] and [me] out because we were wrapped up in the metal of the bomb bay tanks and the radio room.

"Warren then went to the nose of the plane looking for possibly injured officers. He found none. Warren realized they must have bailed out. Instead, he found Paul Drain, bombardier, trapped in the cockpit with a broken leg. He got Drain out and over by Peltier. Matson, Dunbar, and [I] managed to extricate ourselves from the twisted wreckage and crawl to safety."

According to tail gunner Peltier, "No bail-out alarm was sounded. Whether due to pilot failure, or the electrical system being damaged by shell fire is open to debate. Anyway, four of them jumped, pilot, copilot, navigator, and the engineer. Six of us were left behind, four gunners, bombardier, radio operator. The plane was in a steep glide, pretty close to the ground, when the bombardier [Drain] managed to straighten it out a little. We crash landed in a wheat field. I've never explained the miracle of how all six of us survived that crash."

A band of French Maquis, guerrilla fighters, reached the scene an hour or so after they came to earth. Recalled Travinek, "When they saw the shape we were in they explained that they couldn't take hospital cases which would have slowed them up in their work. Warren and the French officer destroyed the bombsight. Warren also gave him five submachine guns with about 5,000 rounds of ammunition and all Colt .45 automatics."

The French freedom fighters slipped away as German soldiers located the wreck and the survivors three hours later. The troops transported the wounded to hospitals for medical treatment before the entire bunch headed for the stalags. Officially, the reports on the first Fortress shot down listed nine men as MIA. But in fact there were ten. Staff Sergeant William Dunbar, an armament chief in the ground crew, wanted to get an idea of a combat mission. He had approached the crew led by pilot Lt. Clarence Lipsky and asked to go along. Qualified as a .50-caliber gunner, he was welcomed aboard and stationed at one of the waist positions. Under these circumstances, his presence went unrecorded and he may have been carried as AWOL for the three years he endured as a kriegie. Dunbar was by no means the last ground crewman to volunteer for combat missions although the regulations expressly forbade such guests.

The 15th Bomb Squadron had resumed its strikes on 5 September. Odell, with his bombardier off in London, stood by as a reserve. On the following day he joined a concerted effort after a briefing on the target, Abbeville. "I led the second box [a formation of aircraft]. Met the fighters, mostly American Spitfires [from the 31st], and cruised across the channel at sea level until I thought we were sure going in low level. The visibility was remarkable. We climbed and had a very peculiar bomb run. Brown told me to open the bomb doors and no sooner were they opened than Brown said the bombs were gone. We turned, diving away, and not until we were almost to the coast did any flak appear. It was way off and I saw only a few bursts at all. The trip home was uneventful except we were a bit off course."

On the following morning, Odell was summoned to appear at Wing headquarters with squadron commander Maj. John Griffith. "It seems we had missed the target—by about twenty miles! Thank goodness I couldn't be blamed. I gave my ideas about where we bombed and it turned out to be a dummy airdrome near Dieppe." Odell recalled the hearing before a board of five U.S. officers and an RAF wing commander, all of whom were senior to the squadron commander and Odell. "Griffith was grilled sharply. From the beginning, the tone of the questions made it apparent that no excuse would be accepted for his flying on a heading that would cause him to lead the twelve-plane formation to a dummy airdrome instead of Abbeville.

"When Griffith proposed the most likely fault was a miscalibrated compass, he was then blamed additionally for failing to oversee required instrument maintenance and compass checks in the squadron aircraft. I squirmed a lot, watching Griffith take the heat. The senior board member made it clear that the Eighth Air Force could not condone the failure of any aircraft to locate its assigned target. Such a gross error smacked of poor training, sloppy navigation, and inept squadron commanders unable to lead and accomplish a simple mission. That kind of conduct was not acceptable and contrary to the standards being set by what would be the mightiest air armada ever assembled [and] which boasted of unerring 'pickle barrel' bombing accuracy.

"When the ordeal seemed close to a conclusion, I was asked to describe the mission, and had to admit that about midway across the channel, Lt. Cecil Brown, my bombardier, advised me over the intercom that he thought we were off course. My cockpit compass reading did not correspond to the plotted course, but not all that much and Griffith may have deviated momentarily and would make a correction. I added that flying under fifty feet at midchannel, no land was in sight to check our position visually to verify we were off course.

"When I hesitated after being asked why I didn't advise Griffith of the situation, Maj. James Beckwith, supported by the RAF wing commander, came to my defense on that crucial question. They noted I had acted properly, having no other choice but to follow established operational procedure by maintaining radio silence. Not to do so would alert enemy defenses; the formation would come under attack and I, more than anyone present, knew the consequences."

Griffith was relieved of his command and Odell believed he got a raw deal. "He made an error but, as it turned out, making an example of him did nothing to prevent the same situation from occurring time and again. Postwar strategic bombing survey studies cite numerous instances, particularly after the Germans began emphasizing camouflage and dispersal of industrial facilities, of flawed Eighth Air Force bombing missions launched at or lured into attacking simulated targets." The review also revealed numerous samples of poor bombing accuracy.

"These errors were not made public by the Eighth Air Force during the war. Censorship was the shield, justifiable for intelligence and morale purposes. [Reading] the Strategic Bombing Surveys, I did not run across any case of disciplinary action meted out to squadron, group, or wing commanders to equal the brusque way Griffith was stripped of his command that curtailed his career opportunities from that time on." Actually, the unfortunate Griffith eventually earned the silver leaf of a lieutenant colonel in command of a B-29 squadron. He and his crew were lost during one of the firestorm raids upon Tokyo in 1945.

The role of lighter bombers as part of the Eighth Air Force began to phase out as new B-17 and B-24 units entered the war. Two Flying Fortress groups, the 92d and 301st, began operations against the enemy. The 97th with Walt Kelly continued its runs. "It did not take long before an opportunity to prove we could hold our own in aerial combat over continental Europe." According to Kelly, on 6 and 7 September, "We smashed our way through heavy *Luftwaffe* opposition to bomb targets in France and Holland, knocking off seventy-seven Nazi fighters in the two sweeps." Official totals for the three bomb groups were 16 kills, 29 probables, and 22 damaged.

Jim Goodson, the survivor of the *Athenia* sinking, had not immediately switched from the RAF after Pearl Harbor. But in the summer of 1942, he remembered, "I got a call from Charles O. Douglas of Fighter Command who said, 'Before, we invited you to join the Eagle Squadrons. Now I'm ordering you to report to the 133 Eagle Squadron of the RAF tomorrow morning. I turned up at Debdum [the airdrome], walked into the officers' barracks to find every room empty. There were half-finished letters, toothbrushes, shaving mugs, but no pilots. Every single one who had gone out with the 133 on a mission had been shot down. No planes returned. This brought the war home very sharply. We had the job of reforming the 133 Eagle Squadron virtually overnight, which was accomplished by bringing in pilots from RAF squadrons.

"The ground crew was all British and they were wonderful people with great dedication. I became close friends with my mechanic and I remember when I came back from a mission, he'd say, 'How did we go?' I would say, 'We got two' or 'We got one.' [Goodson became an ace.] It was always a team effort. We both had our names on the plane; it was our plane."

The operations of the Eighth Air Force during the summer of 1942 marked the first American offensive effort against European adversaries. Army chief of staff George Marshall and his planners had proposed Bolero, a quick build-up of men and supplies in England that would lead to Sledgehammer, a landing on continental Europe in 1942, followed by Round-up, a full-scale invasion for the spring of 1943. British leaders considered the scheme somewhere between unrealistic and preposterous. Prime Minister Winston Churchill anticipated another Dunkirk. He dissuaded Roosevelt and argued in favor of an approach through "the soft underbelly"—Italy via North Africa.

Meanwhile in the Pacific theater, the success at Midway emboldened the high command there to plot their own aggressive thrust. Driven away from the coast of Asia and out of the islands stretching to the south and southeast, the Allies clung to Australia none too firmly. The four best Australian infantry divisions were engaged thousands of miles away, three of them in North Africa and one retreating in Malaya. Still up for grabs lay 600-mile-long New Guinea, which hung over Australia. However, the Nipponese Imperial forces already held a strong position with conquests of adjacent New Britain and New Ireland. Furthermore, the Japanese had established footholds on New Guinea at Lae and Salamaua, preparatory for an advance upon Port Moresby, located on the other side and facing directly at Australia.

To complete their occupation, the Imperial Army placed 11,000 soldiers on the northeastern coast of the island in the vicinity of Gona and Buna, Papua New Guinea. In an astonishing military feat, a force of Japanese soldiers trekked up and into the rugged Owen Stanley Mountains, the same range that had almost thwarted the American naval flyers aiming at shipping in the Gulf of Papua. Australian units also in the Owen Stanleys at first refused to believe any army would attempt such a march along the Kokoda Trail, but once convinced they fought off the invaders in a series of jungle battles among desperately hungry and malaria-stricken soldiers.

To the east and southeast of New Guinea lay the Solomons, several hundred islands of volcanic origin, ranging in size from a few hundred square feet to substantial land masses that form a set resembling footprints. Bougainville anchored the northerly end while ninety-mile-long Guadalcanal stood at the other extremity. Douglas MacArthur sketched out a scenario in which he would direct a joint operation that employed amphibious troops, carrier- and land-based bombers against occupied Rabaul, on New Britain. The port had acted as a staging platform for future expansion into the South Pacific including the conquest of New Guinea at the peril of Australia itself. Eager to capitalize on the Midway victory, Army chief of staff George Marshall, his Air Corps chief, Hap Arnold, and Roosevelt himself were intrigued. But the Navy quickly pointed out that enemy air bases ringed the area and it opposed putting its carriers at risk and under the command of MacArthur. He, as Southwest Pacific theater commander, modified his proposal, drafting a scenario in which he would begin by capturing bases in the Solomons where Japanese had begun to appear, and evicting the foe from New Guniea before taking on Rabaul.

While the strategy struck everyone as feasible, the notion of control by MacArthur infuriated the Navy, and particularly Adm. Ernest J. King. A 1901 Naval Academy graduate,

King had worked on surface ships, submarines, and in his mid-forties qualified as a naval aviator in order to command a carrier. Extensively versed in technical knowledge to accompany his vast experience, King was caustic, and known for a vitriolic temper. He brooked little disagreement from subordinates and freely disputed his superiors. Like too many of his contemporaries he drank more than moderately. In line to become chief of naval operations, to his great disappointment the post went to Harold Stark. On the verge of retirement, King performed so well as the director of Atlantic operations during the period in which the U.S. acted as the arsenal for Great Britain in return for bases, King was named to the post of Commander in Chief, U.S. Fleet. In effect he became CNO while Stark dealt with the civilian policy makers.

Given King's personality and the traditional rivalry of the two services, MacArthur's grandiose drama with himself as central actor drew less than rave reviews. His proposed moves poached on territory designated for the realm of the Navy's Admiral Nimitz. Furthermore, RAdm. Richmond Kelly Turner, chief of the Navy's War Plans Division, advised King, "It is a far different matter attempting to establish advanced bases in the Solomons than in the islands heretofore occupied." King and Marshall fought out the issue in Washington. The admiral wrote his own script for dealing with the enemy outposts like Tulagi in the Solomons. He included dispositions of Army outfits and told Marshall that Navy and Marine units would proceed even without support of Army forces in the Southwest Pacific. Now MacArthur was outraged. He accused the Navy of seeking to reduce the Army to a subordinate status, which he divined had long been part of a sinister plan to gain control of the entire defense establishment.

King and Marshall worked out a compromise. The Navy would be responsible for the Tulagi area and in addition take on a slice of the Solomons, the island of Guadalcanal. In return the Army would get full cooperation from the Navy for a campaign against the enemy already on New Guinea, Rabaul, New Britain, and New Ireland. The Air Corps, broken into a pair of mobile units, would be available anywhere needed in the Pacific through the control of the Joint Chiefs.

The prize wrested by the Navy from MacArthur was a dubious one. Ancient volcanoes, superabundant rain, year-round humidity, and tropical heat had made Guadalcanal into a mountainous, thick jungle whose constantly rotting vegetation in the mucky soil acted as a giant petri dish for the cultivation of bacteria and bugs. But like the Americans, the Japanese had also recognized its strategic potential despite the inhospitable climate and terrain. A small Nipponese detachment set up shop on Guadalcanal's northern coast at Lunga Point, across from Tulagi, to construct an airfield.

Watchtower was a hastily mounted navy operation focused on putting more than 11,000 Marines ashore on Guadalcanal, with additional leathernecks to seize Tulagi and two smaller Japanese-occupied outposts, Gavutu and Tanambogo. From the start glitches in coordination hampered Watchtower. Command for various phases was split among VAdm. Robert Ghormley, designated as overall boss; RAdm. Frank Jack Fletcher, Expeditionary Force chief, who divided his fleet into two elements, adding more layers of command; and the leader of the 1st Marine Division, Gen. Alexander A. Vandegrift. The parties had their own notions of objectives and Ghormley viewed the project pessimistically. Indeed, most of the senior navy people thought it jeopardized the remnants of the Pacific fleet.

Nevertheless, almost 100 vessels, including carriers and a

small task force ordinarily under MacArthur's Southeast Asia command, sailed from New Zealand. Fortunately, Japanese patrol planes, frustrated by thick clouds and rain, never saw the fleet. On 7 August, following offshore bombardments, Marines of the 1st Division simultaneously waded onto the beaches of Guadalcanal and the three other objectives—the two-mile-long Tulagi, and smaller atolls, Gavutu and Tanambogo, that were connected by a 500-yard-long causeway.

The 1st Marine Raider Battalion waded through armpit-deep water over a coral reef onto the Tulagi beach at 0800. No hostile fire greeted them as the Japanese expected an invasion in a different sector. Raider exec officer Lt. Samuel Griffith, a 1929 Naval Academy graduate who had studied under the British Royal Marine Commandos, led the initial arrivals. But overall command of the battalion rested with hard-bitten career Marine, Merritt Edson. As a captain he had helped wield the big stick when the U.S. intervened in Nicaragua in the 1920s during what some referred to as a civil war and others a struggle between the government and bands of banditos. Reporter Richard Tregaskis described Edson: "He was a wiry man with a lean, hard face, partly covered by a sparse, spiky growth of grayish beard; his light blue eyes were tired and singularly red-rimmed in appearance for he was weary now from long days of fighting . . . his eyes were as cold as steel, and it was interesting to notice that even when he was being pleasant, they never smiled." On the eve of the invasion of Tulagi, the soft-spoken, red-haired Edson quoted to his troops a Japanese propaganda broadcast of the previous evening. "Where are the United States Marines hiding? The Marines are supposed to be the finest soldiers in the world, but no one has seen them yet [a regiment had been in the Philippines]." He drew a predictable response from his men.

For the first few sultry hours, the Raiders pushed into the dense bush without firing a shot. But the advance brought them within range of enemy positions embedded in a ridge and the Marines received an indoctrination in how the Japanese would fight the war. The 500-man garrison manned a series of well-constructed dugouts, caves, and tunnels, entrenched positions that required extreme measures to overcome. At this stage of the war, there were no flamethrowers—later the standard means for dealing with the concealed emplacements. On Tulagi, they improvised with pole charges shoved into the enemy positions under the cover of smoke and heavy small-arms fire. Bogged down before a hill, Edson called for help from the sea. The cruiser *San Juan* blanketed the site with 280 5-inch shells, enabling the Marines to advance until darkness arrived. Again, the Japanese showed one of their favorite tactics, the night charge. The invaders clung to their positions and the following day wiped out the enemy. Only three were taken alive.

The 1st Marine Parachute Battalion approached Gavutu by boat instead of from the air. As the first wave dashed across the sandy strand they came under light but deadly enough fire to kill the battalion intelligence officer. Considerably heavier resistance met the second wave. Fierce firefights enveloped the invaders and again the defenders burrowed into the hardened fastness of caves scooped out of the coral. Reinforcements from reserve elements and a few tanks weathered withering fire until both the defenders of Gavutu and neighboring Tanambogo were subdued.

In contrast, the first hours of the Guadalcanal invasion passed without opposition. The leathernecks swiftly moved inland a few miles before they encountered the thick jungle with its overarching canopy of huge trees. A cacophony of bird calls sounded from above the men, soon panting for breath in the sweltering humidity. Through the thick vegetation they glimpsed rats the size of rabbits, wild dogs, pigs, and lizards ranging up to crocodiles slithered in and out of the streams. Woefully poor intelligence misled the Americans about the roughness of the terrain—hills turned out to be mountains—and only with machetes could the troops slash trails through Kunai grass whose razor-sharp, man-size stalks concealed the foe and cut into exposed flesh.

In Rabaul, the Japanese forces received word of the Solomon operations and reacted. Coast watchers scattered through the islands alerted the Allied headquarters in Australia of bombers and fighters headed toward the invasion area. Wildcats from the carriers *Saratoga* and *Enterprise* dueled with the aerial armada. While the Japanese Zeros destroyed half of the U.S. fighters, the Americans disrupted the bombers enough to prevent serious damage to the fleet disgorging men and supplies on the Guadalcanal beach. A second raid later in the day was no more effective. The ability of the Japanese to mount these air attacks worried those in charge of the ships. Vandegrift received word the carriers would remain only two days, then depart, leaving his men short of food, ammunition, and weapons and naked to aerial assault. He pleaded for more time and grudgingly was granted one additional day of protection by the flattop planes.

By the end of the second day, the Marines had advanced far enough to capture the airfield site. Correspondent Tregaskis who accompanied the 1st Marines onto Guadalcanal noted considerable booty—trucks, food, clothing, tents, and even the newly built wooden barracks that had been expected to house Japanese soldiers. "When we entered the Japanese tent camp we knew why we had been able to sail into Tulagi Bay and under the Jap guns without being fired upon. The enemy had been caught completely unawares."

Shortly after midnight, on 9 August, Tregaskis and the Marines in the Japanese tent camp heard an airplane and saw greenish white flares floating in the sky. A few minutes later furious cannonades, salvos that flashed in the sky followed by the boom of explosions, rent the night heavens. "We knew that there was a sea fight going on. Possibly it was the battle for Guadalcanal. Possibly if our people out there lost the battle, the Japs would be ashore before morning, and we would have to fight for our lives. We knew the fate of all of us hung on that sea battle. In that moment I realized how much we must depend on ships even in our land operation."

What Tregaskis had seen was the first of the engagements in the Solomons between the Imperial Navy and the Allied seapower. Gaps in a surveillance net designed to detect the approach of Japanese warships, and a weather front that hampered reconnaissance, enabled a cluster of cruisers and destroyers to slip into the passageway between the double line formed by the Solomon Islands. The section of water became known as the Slot, with Savo Island marking the north end of the channel between Guadalcanal and Tulagi. Coast watchers who reported the flotilla could not track the vessels and pinpoint their target. Fletcher, apprehensive about the strength of the Japanese bomber and torpedo plane attacks, and having lost a fifth of his fighters, yanked out his carriers with their escorts. The cargo ships also fled, leaving the Marines severely short on food, ammunition, and other materials.

To forestall an attack on the Guadalcanal landing site, a

sizable Allied task force remained to prowl the Slot. However, it was broken into two, in order to cover both approaches around Savo. Again, faulty communications and poor intelligence led the commanders to believe no attack was imminent. Around 1:40 A.M., as the Australian cruiser *Canberra* meandered along with an American equivalent, the *Chicago*, plus some destroyers, the flares seen by Tregaskis silhouetted *Canberra* to the enemy force. Within five minutes, twenty-four shells from the Japanese blasted the cruiser into a pyre. Even as flames mushroomed from the *Canberra*, a torpedo smashed the bow of the *Chicago*. Guns from both sides erupted furiously before the Japanese broke off to seek the other Allied components.

Within a few minutes, four of the Japanese cruisers opened up on the American counterparts *Vincennes*, *Quincy*, and *Astoria*. The crews and captains of these ships had noted gunfire and explosions to their south but still were late to sound general quarters. Searchlight beams from the enemy fixed upon the trio of American cruisers, and expert Japanese gunners fired accurate salvos at the ships. Torpedoes and shells punished the *Quincy*. An officer sent to the bridge for instructions recounted, "When I reached the bridge level, I found it a shambles of dead bodies with only three or four people still standing. In the pilothouse itself the only person standing was the signalman at the wheel. . . . On questioning him I found out that the captain, who at that time was laying [*sic*] near the wheel, had instructed him to beach the ship and he was trying to head for Savo Island, some four miles distant on the port quarter. I stepped to the port side of the pilothouse and looked out to find the island and noted that the ship was heeling rapidly to port, sinking by the bow. At that instant the captain straightened up and fell back, apparently dead, without having uttered any sound other than a moan."

The *Vincennes*, like the *Quincy*, foundered during the battle. The *Canberra* and *Astoria* remained afloat a few hours, but the former was scuttled while the latter gave up the ghost on her own. Two destroyers and the *Chicago* survived although badly battered. An air attack sank the destroyer *Jarvis*. All 247 hands died. Aside from several hits on attackers, the Allies scored only one notable success when a submarine sent a cruiser to the bottom. More than 1,000 sailors died defending the Slot. In the months ahead, battles in the passageway bestrewed so many ship carcasses on the floor of the Slot that it became known as "Iron Bottom Sound."

Except for Pearl Harbor this was the Navy's worst hour of the war. Yet, the task force which could have ravished the Guadalcanal landing site unopposed retreated. Unaware that Fletcher had absconded with his carriers, the Japanese admiral in command feared his force vulnerable. Meanwhile, for the moment, the Marines were totally on their own, limited to half-rations for five weeks, short on ammunition, without artillery, and exposed to air attacks.

Walter Vogel, the sailor who had left the *Houston* for medical treatment of a head wound, had not returned to the ill-fated cruiser, and when he reached Australia was assigned to the destroyer *Blue*. It partook of the patrols in the Slot until late in August when, while escorting vessels, Vogel, who was on the bridge, recalled, "The sonarmen picked up the sound of high-speed propeller noises. Immediately two big torpedo wakes appeared. They were coming right at us. The skipper gave full-speed ahead and full right rudder. But we were struck on the starboard side aft. The explosion was tremendous. It shook the destroyer from bow to stern. Our screw shafts were damaged and also the steering room destroyed. We had temporary loss of power and electricity while our stern was almost blown off. We lost eight men killed, twenty-two wounded. We were flooding aft. I thought this is another ship I've lost."

Another destroyer attempted to tow the *Blue* but the lines parted. When a dispatch reported a large enemy naval force heading down the Slot, the crew received orders to scuttle the ship. After Vogel and his shipmates abandoned the *Blue*, the *Henley*, a companion vessel, fired a torpedo that missed and then sank it with a barrage of 5-inch shells.

Lacking reinforcements and bereft of support from the big guns of the Navy, the 1st Marine Division on Guadalcanal reverted to a defensive stance, protecting the beaches and still-under-construction Henderson airstrip. The one saving grace was the thinness of the enemy ranks on the island. The Japanese could not mount a strong attack without more troops. Nor could Rabaul dispatch air attacks until planes and crews arrived to replace those lost earlier.

Interrogators of several captured Japanese convinced the division intelligence officer, Lt. Col. Frank Goettge, that a substantial number of starving, disease-ridden troops and laborers wandering about the bush could be induced to surrender. Instead of a heavily armed combat patrol originally scheduled to sweep the area, Goettge took a smaller team with limited firepower. Led by one of the prisoners, the Marines traveled by boat and went ashore shortly before dusk. As Goettge gathered his officers to discuss their next move, an ambush slaughtered almost the entire patrol, including the leader. Before he died, a sergeant blew off the head of the Japanese guide. Only three of the twenty-four Marines escaped. One of the survivors witnessed knife- and sword-wielding Japanese savaging the members of the patrol.

The incident set a tone for dealing with the Japanese, one in which no quarter would be given. Subsequent experiences, like that of Marine Don Zobel, who came upon an American corpse with at least thirty bayonet wounds, provided more evidence. "His penis cut off and shoved into his mouth in the Japanese way of the ultimate insult," confirmed, to the Marines, the barbarity of the foe.

The inability of the enemy to evict the Marines enabled the 1st Engineer Battalion, improvising with abandoned Japanese equipment, to complete the rudiments of an airfield. On 20 August, a dive bomber and a fighter squadron, launched from the escort carrier *Long Island*, flew 190 miles to land at Henderson Field. General Vandegrift personally welcomed the Marine pilots to residence on Guadalcanal.

Unwilling to concede Guadalcanal, the Imperial Army, diverting some resources from the New Guinea campaign, started to ship fresh troops to the island. Misled by faulty intelligence on the American strength of nearly 8,000, a total force of 2,000 soldiers, commanded by Col. Kiyano Ichiki, boarded ships bound for Guadalcanal. A detachment of some 900 slipped ashore west of the Marine beachhead. They headed toward the perimeter set up along a tidal lagoon known as Alligator Creek to the leathernecks, but which in fact contained crocodiles. A large sandbar blocked outlet to the sea. Parallel to the stream ran the Ilu River, erroneously listed by the poor American maps as the Tenaru River.

On the night of 19–20 August, some sixty Marines patrolling the bush suddenly bumped into a Japanese unit. After a thirty-minute firefight, the Americans counted more than thirty enemy dead and among the corpses found map

cases, documents, and other paraphernalia that seemed out
of the ordinary. At headquarters, intelligence experts deciphered enough of the material to find these troops had only
been on the island a day and already seemed well versed in
the defenses around Alligator Creek. The Marines hastily
added some artillery, dug in deeper, and settled in behind
barbed wire to await hostile visitors.

The enemy attacked the well-entrenched U.S. forces and
after initially being repulsed, regrouped in a stand of coconut trees. Dick Tregaskis made his way to the front. "Out
in the glassy blue water I saw globs of water jump up where
the bullet struck. 'They've got a Jap out there,' said my
friend. 'He's trying to swim around and get in behind us.
We've killed a lot of 'em that way.' " Three more leatherneck rifle companies led by Col. L. B. Creswell arrived to
surround the Japanese.

"The volleys of machine gun and rifle fire," reported Tregaskis, "from the depths of the grove across the river, grew
louder. Colonel Creswell's people were rolling the Japs toward us. Suddenly I saw the dark figures of men running on
the strip of beach that bordered the palm grove. The figures
were far off, probably a half mile down the light ribbon of
sand, but I could see from their squatness that they were
Japs. There was no time for any other impression. In a few
seconds the black, violently moving blobs were squashed
down on the sand and we heard a fusillade of rifle fire. The
Japs did not get up again.

"A rumbling of powerful motors came from behind us.
We turned to find a group of four tanks moving down the
trail through the coconut palms. . . . We watched those awful
machines as they plunged across the spit and into the edge
of the grove. It was fascinating to see them bustling amongst
the trees, pivoting, turning, spitting sheets of yellow flame.

It was like a comedy of toys, something unbelievable to see them knocking over palm trees which fell slowly, flushing the running figures of men from underneath their treads, following and firing at the fugitive. It was unbelievable to see men falling and being killed so close, to see the explosions of Jap grenades and mortars, black fountains and showers of dirt near the tanks and see the flashes of explosions under their very treads. We had not realized there were so many Japs in the grove. Group after group was flushed out and shot down by the tanks' canister shells."

To add to the carnage, fighter planes from Henderson had strafed the coconut grove. The engagement lasted until about five in the afternoon before the Battle of Tenaru River ended with wary Marines, rifles in hand, heads swiveling constantly, cautiously moving among the shattered land and the bodies. Colonel Ichiki committed suicide rather than be taken captive. Wrote Tregaskis, "Japanese dead are dangerous, for there are usually some among them alive enough to wait until you pass, then stab or shoot you. Our marines had by this time learned to take no chances. The dead were shot again, with rifles and pistols, to make sure."

The next round involved naval vessels and aircraft. Hoping to inveigle the Americans into exposing their carriers while simultaneously ousting them from the island with a much larger landing party, the Japanese sent a convoy of transports accompanied by major naval units, including a trio of carriers—*Ryujo*, *Shokaku*, and *Zuikaku*. When coast watchers notified the Americans of the advancing ships, swarms of dive bombers, torpedo planes, and fighters from the *Saratoga* rose to the bait. Unfortunately they could not locate the target because the Japanese had slyly retreated.

In a counterstrike, Betty bombers from Rabaul combined with airplanes from the flattop *Ryujo*. The operation proved a bust; Marine fighters from Henderson Field destroyed sixteen Zeros and Bettys at a cost of three Wildcats. Far worse for the attackers, in the exchanges between carriers, while *Enterprise* quit the scene with moderate damage, *Ryujo* added her hulk to the growing junkyard at the bottom of the sea. The Japanese Navy prudently withdrew the *Shokaku* and *Zuikaku* rather than risk further carrier losses, leaving the transports and their destroyer escorts open to air attacks.

The Cactus Air Force—Cactus was the code name for Guadalcanal—dive-bombed the oncoming warships and transports on 25 August and blasted the largest vessel, the cruiser *Jintsu*, forcing it to retire to the base at Truk. Hits on a transport, the *Kinryu Maru*, by the Marine flyers caused a destroyer to come alongside for rescue. A flight of Army B-17s dumped its load close enough to the ship to sink it. Rabaul recalled the Japanese expeditionary force, affording the Marines on Guadalcanal a brief respite.

During the interlude, Seabees carved out a second strip but amenities for the airmen remained scarce. Correspondent Robert Sherrod wrote, "Living conditions were appalling. Pilots had to fight and fly all day on a diet of dehydrated potatoes, Spam, or cold hash—and sometimes Japanese rice. . . . Sleeping in a mud-floored tent was constantly interrupted by Japanese planes ('Louie the Louse' or 'Washing Machine Charlie') that flew around murdering sleep and dropping occasional bombs, or by destroyers or submarines that stood offshore and lobbed shells at Henderson Field. When a man could get away for a bath in the Lunga River, the only time he could take his clothes off, he frequently found there wasn't any soap. If he didn't catch malaria from the anopheles mosquitoes that swarmed into his foxhole, he was almost certain to get dysentery that tormented his bowels."

Marine units on Tulagi and Gavatu, including Edson's Raiders and the Parachute Battalion, added their weight to the embattled leathernecks on Guadalcanal. They arrived none too soon because the enemy demonstrated renewed vigor in his effort to end the American presence. Actually, the commander for the task forces in the area, Admiral Ghormley, had notified General Vandegrift he deemed his resources insufficient to support the Guadalcanal operation. Ghormley believed a massive ground, sea, and air attack organized from Rabaul and Truk would overwhelm the American fleet and the Marines. Admiral Richmond Kelly Turner, Ghormley's subordinate in charge of the amphibious forces and nominally Vandegrift's immediate superior, in his typical fashion, over a bottle of whiskey, told the Marine general that he believed he could deliver reinforcements in the form of the 7th Marine Regiment. Vandegrift cringed as Turner then counseled a strategy to sprinkle the fresh troops around the island where they could repel each attempt to land. With the Japanese already in strength on Guadalcanal, the recipe spelled disaster for such small, separated units. Vandegrift sidestepped the bizarre proposal, and continued to plump for a landing at the established beachhead by the 7th Marines.

Japanese ships bombarded the Raiders by night and planes raided the area during the daylight hours. The fighting intensified; the Americans now went on the defensive. Tregaskis, back at a command post, observed, ". . . this morning the din of firing grew so tremendous that there was no longer any hope of sleeping. Our batteries were banging incessantly, the rifle and machine-gun fire from the direction of the Raider lines had swelled into a cascade of sound. Louie the Louse was flying about and flares were dropping north, south, east, and west.

"We were drawing up a strong skirmish line on the ridge-top. Reinforcements were on the way up. We knew that the Raiders . . . out on the ridge had their hands full. We knew then that a major Japanese effort to break through our lines and seize the airport had begun." The original aim of Edson's mission had been to seize a supply area and eliminate the garrison there. But now the Japanese had brought in thousands of well-armed troops whose positions lay less than 2,000 yards from the vital U.S. asset, Henderson Field and General Vandegrift's command post.

"Snipers were moving in on us," said Tregaskis. "They had filtered along the flanks of the ridge and taken up positions all around our CP. Now they began to fire. It was easy to distinguish the sound of their rifles. There were light machine guns, too, of the same caliber. Ricocheting bullets skidded amongst the trees. We plastered ourselves flat on the ground."

Subsequently, he reported, "As the first light of dawn came, the general was sitting on the side of the ridge, talking to some of his aides. A Jap machine gun opened up, and they high-tailed for the top of the ridge with me right behind. We were heading for a tent, where we would at least have psychological shelter. Just as we reached the tent, a bullet clanged against a steel plate only two or three feet from us. It was amusing to see the rear ends of the dignified gentlemen disappearing under the edge of the tent. I made an equally undignified entrance."

The standoff reached a climax on 14 September as waves of Japanese soldiers rushed the Marines dug in on "Edson's Ridge." Officers flourishing swords led their warriors who shouted Banzai and sought to challenge within bayonet range. Some did engage the Marines in close combat but the leathernecks held their ground or relinquished only a few yards at a steep price in enemy lives. Tregaskis noticed that

Edson, who had spent the night at the lead edge of his people, had a bullet hole in his collar and at the waist of his blouse. "Along the flank of the hill, where a path led," said Tregaskis, "we passed strewn bodies of marines and Japs, sometimes tangled as they had fallen in a death struggle. At the top of the knoll, the dead marines lay close together. Here they had been most exposed to Jap rifle and machine-gun fire, and grenades.

"At the crest of the knoll we looked down the steep south slope . . . there were about 200 Jap bodies, many of them torn and shattered by grenades or artillery bursts, some ripped, a marine told us, by the strafing planes which we had seen this morning. It was up this slope that the Japs had sent their heaviest assaults many times during the night and each time they tried they had been repulsed." Sporadic attacks occurred in the next several days but the fury of the assaults diminished and then the Japanese retreated deep into the bush.

On the water, however, American fortunes nosedived. A task force that included the carriers *Hornet* and *Wasp*, supplemented by the fire power of the powerful new battleship, *North Carolina*, steamed northwest from the island base at Espíritu Santo to bring fresh troops and supplies. On 15 September, the flight decks teemed with fully gassed and armed planes, prepared to ward off any aerial assaults. Everyone remained at the ready, scanning the skies, but from beneath the sea, a submarine fired a spread of four torpedoes at the *Wasp*. Two struck home with tremendous explosions, reducing the aircraft to fiery wrecks while below deck, water mains ruptured, fuel in the pumping system fed the fires, and seawater poured into the hold. Another undersea boat loosed its tin fish and one gouged a huge hole in the hull. More explosions from its ammunition and ordnance stores created an inferno. Recognizing his vessel was dying, the skipper gave the order to abandon ship. An escorting destroyer delivered the final blows with torpedoes. Nevertheless, the convoy sailed on.

On 18 September, Tregaskis strolled down to the beach where cargo vessels, warships, and transports hove in sight. Thousands of reinforcements in clean fatigues marched inland to relieve the embattled Marines of Edson's Ridge. The fight for Guadalcanal was a long way from over but the U.S. forces were there to stay.

14

Paratroopers, Raiders, Rangers, Marauders, Alamo Scouts

UNTIL THE INDUSTRIAL REVOLUTION, FIGHTING MEN CAME IN two simple models, on horseback or on foot. Over time the mounted knight exchanged his lance or sword for a cavalryman's Mauser; the yeoman swapped his bow or pike for a rifle with bayonet. The age of science, invention, and machines created refinements in explosives, innovations in weapons, massive firepower. In addition, the new techniques of manufacturing introduced specialization, a concept naturally manifested in modern warfare.

Beyond the obvious tasks associated with artillery, armor, and electronics—gunner, loader, tank-driver, wireman, the literally hundreds of military occupational specialties—also was born the notion of the singular unit. Designed to carry out unique missions, they received special instruction, weapons, and gear tailored for an individual purpose. With one exception, these were all relatively small outfits. Separated from the general run of the military, they accrued a sense of élan which members and their superiors exploited.

Of all of the World War II special units, the largest by far was the airborne. Men who served in the armies of America during World War II may recall the nearly ineffable aura that enveloped the label of "Airborne." Paratroopers received extra instruction in infantry tactics, use of explosives, and survival behind enemy lines. They had a reputation for toughness, for daring as well as for brawling with non-jumpers or "straight legs." To be sure there were some tangible trappings to envy or relish, the highly burnished boots and the silver badge marked a "trooper"—even that name distinguished him from the common "soldier." Many GIs with long military experience as well as raw draftees, perceived them as harboring a death wish. Sensible people would hesitate to hurl themselves from an altitude of several thousand feet, dependent only upon yards of silk or nylon to prevent a fatal plunge. They drifted helplessly toward the ground, unable to unlimber their weapons, while the enemy could slaughter them in their descent.

Still, the army never lacked recruits. Mel Trenary, a member of the 517th Parachute Regimental Combat Team, was one. "I volunteered for the paratroopers because I wanted to prove to myself that I had the ability to build my body into something worthwhile and at the same time I could do something that the average person wouldn't want to do. My first jump was a surprise. We put on our chutes, sat on benches until finally we walked to the plane. The harness was so tight I could hardly stand upright. As the last person on board, I sat right next to the door, looking out. This was my first time in an airplane and I was fascinated. It was hard to believe, at that time, that a heavy machine like this could go up into the air. I had of course seen planes but it was different being inside one as it went up.

"They had trained me right. It was all automatic. When the red light went on, I got up and stood at the door. I didn't look down, but I could see the horizon anyway because of the plane's movements. When the green light came on, I felt a tap on my leg and I jumped out, just like they had taught me. I had my eyes closed, but I could feel my body going upside down. When the chute opened, it flipped me right side up and I knew everything was working right. I opened my eyes and watched others come out of the plane. I was the first one out of the plane and I had felt that if I didn't go then some of the others might chicken out. Later, one of the guys told me that as he saw me get ready by the door, he thought, 'if Trenary can do it, so can I.' "

Even before Pearl Harbor, while the notion of such airborne units barely existed beyond the paper stage, U.S. paratroopers already bore the status and the stigma almost inevitably stamped on an elite outfit. James M. Gavin, an orphan, enlisted man, then graduate of West Point, who led four combat jumps in Europe and finished the war as commanding general of the 82d Airborne Division, was part of the tiny group that created the paratrooper role. "We had an idea. We wanted to tell these guys that they were the most capable guys on earth. And when they land, it doesn't matter who they meet; they can really lick them under any circumstances. And any parachute squad is worth a platoon of anybody else. We want these guys to find out that there's nothing too good for them; no bed too soft, no food too good, no conditions too good for them to live. But, by God, when combat comes, then there's not too much to ask from them. We really expected to ask anything of them and we expected them to come through.

"We tried to give a whole dimension of how to train human beings and how to get them committed and dedicated and believing in what they were doing and how to make them very combat effective, consistent with trying to find the kind of leadership that could lead these guys. You had to be as good at anything as they were, and oftentimes better and be quite willing to do anything you asked them to do."

The parachute itself wasn't that new: Leonardo da Vinci, along with his designs for manned flight, in his fifteenth-century *Codex Atlanticus* noted the possibility for safe passage from the skies. "If a man have a tent of linen of which the apertures have all been stopped up . . . he will be able to throw himself down from any great height without sustaining any injury." Da Vinci sketched four triangular panels jointed at the top from which a human figure dangled.

During World War I, only the Germans, in the waning days of the fighting, equipped some of their pilots with parachutes, although both sides outfitted balloonborne observers with chutes. However, in October 1918, Col. Billy Mitchell, chief of the American Expeditionary Force airmen, approached Gen. John "Black Jack" Pershing, who commanded all U.S. forces in France, with a daring plan: ". . . he should assign one of the infantry divisions permanently to the Air Service . . . we should arm the men with a great number of machine guns and train them to go over the front in our large airplanes which would carry ten or fifteen of these soldiers. We would equip each man with a parachute, so that when we desired to make a rear attack on the enemy, we could carry these men over the lines and drop them off in parachutes behind the German position." The November armistice quashed further consideration. Still, under Mitchell's prodding, a standard, practical parachute was developed for use at least by pilots.

During the 1930s, Soviet, French, and Italian forces embarked on parachute programs in varying degrees. Nazi Germany, forbidden to rearm by the Treaty of Versailles, sponsored glider clubs whose craft showed an obvious potential in warfare and secretly started to build a paratroop corps. The notion of airborne fighting men, "a sword of silk" in the rhetoric of one advocate, languished in the U.S. But in 1939, George Marshall, as Army chief of staff, enlightened by intelligence reports of the European interest in airborne and parachute soldiers, ordered a feasibility study. The hasty research study, while it supported an experimental program to develop infantry traveling by air, remarked that combat groups dropped behind enemy lines could well be on suicide missions.

William Yarborough, USMA 1936, was among the pioneers of American parachute troops. "Some of the best training material in the early days on parachute techniques was Russian," said Yarborough, "and it was translated by my father, a Russian linguist and intelligence officer who served with the 31st Infantry in Siberia during World War I. As a kid I saw a picture of Russians lying on the wing of an airplane, jump at the command 'Turn loose.' I remember thinking, of all the stupid ways to make a living, or the most tenuous ways to go into combat."

Not until fighting broke out in Europe was there an American effort to create paratroop units. The entire project received a boost with the news of the German successes, using parachutists, to overwhelm the Netherlands and Belgium on the way to overrunning France in the spring of 1940. On 25 June of that year, the very day the French admitted their defeat to Adolf Hitler in the same railroad car that witnessed the German surrender in 1918, an order to the commandant at Fort Benning, Georgia, called for a platoon of recruits for parachute training.

In 1940, jumping out of an airplane, in spite of Leonardo da Vinci's theoretical assurance that given enough canopy one could throw himself down from a great height without fear of injury, seemed a highly dangerous business. The offhand suggestion by those who first investigated the use of such troops that their roles could become kamikaze-style missions added to the sense of risk. Sensitive perhaps to excessive demands upon men while the country was not yet at war, the brass decided that no one should be forced to be a paratrooper. Those first candidates for the new type of soldier, like the Commandos, Rangers, and other elites, were thus asked to break the First Commandment of the soldiers, "Never volunteer!"

Those in charge of those first volunteers screened for both attitude and athletic ability. A recruiter might perform a series of tumbles and then ask the potential trooper if he could manage a similar stunt. That provided insight into physical agility but according to Gavin, the gymnastics were really designed to show off the trooper. "It impressed young kids, who thought if a guy can do that and with that sharp look, it must be a pretty good outfit." Once in training, the regimen required intensive conditioning. The original platoon exercised, marched, and ran beyond the norm. In the absence of towers* to learn how to cushion the impact with the ground,

---

*Major William Lee, who commanded this first detachment, discovered that the makers of the grand parachute tower installed at the New York World's Fair in 1939 had a pair of towers in Hightstown, New Jersey. He arranged for his unit to spend ten days at nearby Fort Dix and train on the two high platforms. Eventually, similar but higher towers were erected at the major paratroop training sites, Fort Benning and Camp Mackall, North Carolina, with a minisize one at Toccoa.

would-be troopers jumped off the backs of trucks and for advanced practice leaped from moving vehicles.

The art of tumbling to avoid injury seemed critical. Anyone who failed to roll in the prescribed manner immediately received a critique that ended with a command of "Gimme ten!" on the basis that extra pushups cured carelessness. Well before behavioral scientists publicly proclaimed the virtues of "aversive training," those running the infant paratroop program thus employed punishment as a way to instill an instinctive resort to the right techniques.

Even the tumbling evolved through painful experimentation. That same sort of trial and error marked landing techniques for actual jumps. Originally, the experts instructed recruits to strike the ground with feet spread to the width of the hips. Only after countless sprains, cartilage damage, and broken bones did anyone realize that touching down with feet close together better distributed the shock and reduced injuries.

Those first volunteers spent hours learning how to pack their silk. Not until well into World War II did the art of parachute rigging become a responsibility of specialists while the troopers themselves concentrated on their roles as airborne fighters. The gear issued to the would-be paratroopers consisted mostly of hand-me-downs. Each volunteer for that first platoon received two pairs of Air Corps mechanics' coveralls, a leather flying cap like those sported by World War I aces, and a pair of boots with a strap across the instep designed to give support to ankles stressed by that first contact with the earth. One genuine innovation made at the very start of the program was the reserve chute carried on a man's chest. Throughout World War II, American troopers were the only ones afforded a second chance if the main chute failed to deploy.

The instructions placed great stress upon the way in which a man exited the airplane door over the drop zone. Charles La Chaussee, who served with the 517th, described the method as calling for "a quarter-turn in space toward the tail of the plane, head bowed, knees slightly bent, and with both hands on the reserve parachute. Correctly executed, the good body position eased the opening shock and lessened the chances of the parachute snagging on equipment as it opened." However, as La Chaussee noted, in a mass jump, only the first man had an opportunity to follow the manual. The rest were lucky if they went out feet first, many wound up diving head down. Any delays, counted even in seconds, meant that even if the pilot throttled down properly, the stick of twelve to fifteen troopers would be strung out over a great distance, seriously reducing effectiveness.

Following the first successful jumps of the test platoon, the brass scheduled a mass demonstration to indicate the tactical potential of airborne. Several members of the platoon on their way to the barracks after watching a Western film at the Fort Benning post theater discussed the added dangers of such an untried maneuver. One man teased Pvt. Aubrey Eberhardt that he would be so scared he wouldn't remember his own name. Eberhardt, in a sudden inspiration, said he would shout the name of the Indian warrior bedeviled by the U.S. cavalry in the movie. True to his word, Eberhardt, as he exited the door of the C-47 the next day, yelled, "Geronimo!"

Although celebrated in the popular media, the invocation of Geronimo was a short-lived tradition. Experts in the field soon taught men to forget about the chief and count, "One thousand, two thousand, three thousand . . ." and if the main chute had failed to open, it was time to yank the ripcord of the reserve. Furthermore, succeeding classes of paratroopers considered the cry juvenile. Russel Brami, a member of the 517th and who made a career of being a paratrooper, says, "I never heard anyone yell 'Geronimo!' We used to claim the translation of Geronimo was, 'Who pushed me?' The usual comment, if any, when a guy jumped was, 'Oh, shit.' "

The tangible morale builders for paratroopers followed soon after the graduation of these initial recruits. In January 1941, the men received authorization to wear their boots with trouser legs tucked into the tops while in dress uniforms. The patch with the white parachute against a blue background for the soft overseas cap followed. Airborne artillery used a red backdrop. The silvery badge with the wings curving up from the base of a chute to meet the canopy added an adornment. Bill Yarborough developed the design of a two-piece jumpsuit with plenty of pockets that replaced the mechanics' coveralls. Redesign of the boot improved its function and style, the leather's potential for burnishing gave new meaning to spit-and-polish.

Airborne training stressed hand-to-hand combat and demolition. Yarborough explained, "The philosophy we built into those outfits was that wherever you land, you are liable to land in the wrong place. It's a coin flip. You are to do the kind of damage to the enemy that you are trained to do and don't let it worry you that you may end up in twos or threes, or a half a dozen. That's part of the racket."

Along with chutists, soldiers ferried to the battle scene in gliders came under the rubric of airborne. Unlike troopers, glidermen were not volunteers, although their exposure was arguably as dangerous. Moreover, not until well into World War II did they gain the right to wear their own winged insignia.

Even as the American and the British enthusiasm for airborne units swelled, the German version staggered from a near-fatal blow. The Nazi war machine, rushing to the rescue of its ally, Benito Mussolini's Italian army floundering in its invasion of Greece, drove the British to a last-ditch defense on Crete, the largest island of the Mediterranean Sea and a strategic block to the Aegean Sea. Among other things, Crete offered an airbase for Royal Air Force planes to bomb the Romanian oilfields, so essential to Hitler's panzers. General Kurt Student, the German airborne commander, convinced Hitler he could conquer the British forces—mainly New Zealanders—with his glider soldiers and paratroopers descending on Crete's three major airfields. The battle demonstrated the vulnerability of such units. The first error lay in sending gliders that were not preceded by paratroopers. As the first fragile sailplanes swooped to the tarmac, the heavily entrenched defenders slaughtered the occupants almost before they could tumble from their bullet-riddled craft. When the paratroopers arrived at the airdromes the British wreaked heavy casualties while many invaders still hung in their harnesses. However, a handful of the airborne gained a toehold. A withdrawal by the New Zealanders due to poor communications allowed the Germans to bring up massive reinforcements. The battle tide ebbed for the British, who performed a mini-Dunkirk to rescue many of their forces.

The victory notwithstanding, Hitler lost faith in airborne assaults. Of the 13,000 jumpers and gliderborne, 5,140 had been killed or wounded. The losses to the *Luftwaffe* in planes was also enormous, 350 aircraft were destroyed, including many transports that would be desperately missed when the Nazi armies headed east into the Soviet Union.

While the Germans all but abandoned the use of airborne, the British and the Americans, however, continued to have faith in the concept. From the Crete defeat they learned that a heavily defended position fell against a determined airborne operation that numbered less than half its foe. Furthermore, strategists perceived the importance of the tactical mistakes of the Crete paratroopers and glider forces that landed directly on well-entrenched opposition rather than to their relatively weaker rear.

The decision to build up U.S. airborne outfits received a final boost with the raid on Pearl Harbor. By the summer of 1942, airborne outfits had grown from the original platoon-size unit up to 3,000-man regiments. The powers at the top decided operations of full divisions were feasible and chose the 82d and 101st Infantry Divisions to be the forerunners of the new breed.

The granddaddy for World War II glamour was of course the British Commando. The phenomenon sprang from the fertile brain of Prime Minister Winston Churchill in 1940, after the fall of France and with the British troops thrown back to England. Immediately after the completion of the Dunkirk evacuation, Churchill told the House of Commons, "We shall not be content with a defensive war." He told his War Cabinet, "We should immediately set to work to organize self-contained, thoroughly equipped raiding units. Enterprises must be prepared with specially trained troops of the hunter class who can develop a reign of terror down the enemy coasts."

Because missions would require participation of air, naval, and ground forces, the British created the organization known as Combined Operations, headed by Lord Louis Mountbatten. Within a relatively short time, Commandos stung the enemy with hit-and-run raids that, while of very limited strategic value, at least buoyed morale.

In the United States, these exploits inspired some adventurous and highly aggressive souls. The Marine Raider Battalion that stormed Tulagi was one such copy, although the results were not always what was expected. Merritt Edson's battalion resembled an assault force rather than a commando-style group. The members had all received extra training in close combat and physical conditioning. They also organized their platoons differently with extra firepower. There was a premium upon strong leadership, as exemplified by Edson, whom correspondent Robert Sherrod described. "He hated the Japs, as only men who have met them in combat hate them. Whenever, during his hour-long lecture to correspondents the day before we left Base X [this account was written during the war], he used the phrase 'killing Japs' or 'knocking off Nips' his eyes seemed to light up, and he smiled faintly."

Harry Manion of the 4th Marine Raider Battalion had volunteered for the duty. "The Marine Raiders were formed with ten men to a squad, a squad leader and three fire teams. The teams could have two submachine guns and one M1 rifle, a Browning automatic rifle and two M1s, or two BARs and one rifle. BAR men also carried a .45-caliber pistol and two magazines. "I was a BAR man and in the Raiders you always had a buddy. We did almost everything together. You must protect and help your buddy at all times. We became almost as one. Sometimes a nod of a head would suffice for many words. This could mean the difference.

"War in the Pacific seemed to have a time schedule. Fight in the daylight and dig in at night. The Raiders went around the clock. Whenever the enemy was most relaxed, we liked to hit him. On patrol we could lie within a foot or so of the enemy and breathe normally. Weapons ready if needed. Knives, rifles, etc., but never used unless absolutely necessary. This 'trick' is not easy to learn." Manion commented on a common aspect for all elite outfits. "Many senior officers were totally opposed to the concept of Raiders. We knew we were a breed apart from other Marines. They had artillery, naval gun-fire support, air support, heavy mortars, and good resupply, or at least better than ours. Their medical support was much greater. Most of our beans, bullets, and bandages were personal items."

Another well-publicized Raider leader was Evans F. Carlson. A marine officer whose career included a stint at the Roosevelt White House as an attaché, who retired from the Corps and then, as a member of the diplomatic service, spent some time with the Chinese Communist Army, he exploited his acquaintance with the president to organize the 2d Marine Raider Battalion in his own unorthodox style. Carlson stressed the Chinese Red attitude, "gung-ho," pulling together with much less attention to the usual hierarchical structure of the military. The romantic sense of the adventure, and his father's favor, apparently inspired James Roosevelt to sign on with Carlson's Raiders as executive officer. In a high-risk venture while the struggle for Guadalcanal was still in doubt, 222 men under Carlson and Roosevelt traveled by submarine to Makin Island in the Gilberts, a thousand miles northeast of Guadalcanal. Although the Japanese garrison numbered only eighty-three soldiers, a shot accidentally fired during the landing aroused the defenders. In a muddled battle, the Raiders erased the smaller force. But upon returning through a ferocious surf to their submarines, confusion led to nine Marines being left behind. When the Japanese reoccupied Makin they discovered the nine and beheaded them.

The U.S. Army equivalent of the Commandos began with the agreement of Chief of Staff Marshall and Lord Mountbatten for the training of Americans to replicate the British version. A veteran of World War I, Lucian K. Truscott, a colonel in April 1942, after having spent nineteen years at the company-grade level, joined Mountbatten's staff. General Russell P. Hartle, commander of the first American soldiers stationed in the United Kingdom—the 34th Infantry Division and the 1st Armored Division—nominated his aide, an ambitious 1929 West Point graduate, Capt. William O. Darby, to run the new outfit. "He was the right man in the right place at the right time," said Warren "Bing" Evans, a member of the 1st Ranger Battalion and sergeant major for Darby. "He was a helluva combat soldier, a good leader who didn't hesitate to break the rules if he thought it would help him."

Darby quickly selected several officers as his cadre and began to interview volunteers. The first recruits underwent a rigorous physical examination and an interview to ascertain whether they seemed mentally and emotionally suited. Evans, big and agile, in 1938 had graduated from South Dakota State, which he attended on basketball and football scholarships. "We were all a bunch of egotists, volunteers, good physical specimens, and intensely patriotic," recalled Evans. "We'd all heard of the Commandos and that's what initially inspired us. Most of us were farm boys from the Midwest and the Commandos thought we were soft. They underestimated us because we broke every record that had been set during training."

The 1st Ranger Battalion consisted of fewer than 400 soldiers, less than half the size of a normal infantry battalion, divided into six companies. They learned their craft at Achnacarry, a castle in Scotland and a Commando depot. Physical conditioning through arduous marches, climbing exercises, and stream crossings built strength and endurance. Intensive work with weapons that ranged from .45-caliber pistols, rifles, BARs, sub and fixed machine guns, through light mortars enabled the Rangers to deliver maximum firepower. They studied map reading, demolition, fire and maneuver, amphibious landings, and hand-to-hand combat. Ordinary infantrymen might be lightly schooled in several kinds of ordnance and activities, but the focus of the Rangers was much more thorough.

James Altieri, an original member of the 1st Battalion, remembered, "Every morning was spent on a long speed march or mountain climb. We were driven relentlessly until it seemed our aching bodies could take no more. The sight of men dropping out on the marches, broken and beaten, was disheartening. Each day the distance of our march would be lengthened until we were doing twelve miles in two hours, which included a five-minute break. At the breaks men would drop like sacks of beans, tired and exhausted. Each day I thought would surely be the last for me."

Along with the physically grueling regimen, the Commandos directed live fire during exercises. "When Company F made the practice landings," said Altieri, "machine-gun bullets, fired from shore positions manned by Commando marksmen, would splatter rowing paddles to splinters in the hands of men that held them as our collapsible boats neared shore for landings. As we hit the beach, charges of dynamite exploded almost in our faces as we dashed madly for cover to evade the snapping Bren-gun bullets that kicked up dirt between our strides."

Allen E. Merrill, as an eighteen-year-old growing up in Buffalo, New York, in the first surge of patriotic fervor that enveloped young men of his age, attempted to enlist in the Marine Corps on 7 December 1941. Rejected because of color blindness, he applied to the Navy with the same result. "Spring came and I tried the Army. They welcomed me with open arms. Merrill's path to the Rangers included qualification as a paratrooper and flunking out of OCS, an opportunity that he said he never wanted. Neither commissioned nor a member of an airborne outfit, he sailed to England for duty with the 34th Infantry Division and engaged in amphibious training. While stationed in northern Ireland, Merrill saw a notice on the bulletin board about a new Commando-style unit being formed. Two officers would interview volunteers.

"What the hell, I decided to give it a try. What could I lose? I joined to fight a war and was just taking up space here, and Americans were fighting and dying out in the Pacific. They asked me things about my past life. Like, did I have many fights as a boy. Did I have a temper. Did I see anyone die or get killed. How did I feel about blood, my own or someone else's. They asked if I ever killed anyone. The answers were what I assumed most everyone would say. I had a few fights, won some and lost some. Then the tall lieutenant asked me if I could ever kill anyone, either with a weapon at close range or with my bare hands. I replied that if it came down to it, I could kill an enemy who was out to get me or to save another buddy's life. They asked if my being part German would affect me in fighting Germans. I said I would be able to kill them as a duty of a good soldier in wartime. I was not sickened at the sight of blood. They asked if my Catholic religion would stand in the way of my doing my duty as a combat soldier. I said, 'No, sir, it would not. That's what they had confession for.' " Merrill explained that his brief, involuntary OCS tour had kept him from remaining a paratrooper although he had attempted several times to return to the airborne ranks.

Accepted and transported to the Achnacarry site, Merrill noted, "Whoever had set up this operation had a devious one-track mind. All the important functions of living were strategically placed on separate hills. We were billeted on a good-size hill. The orderly room was located on another; the latrine on yet another, and the mess tents a fourth hill. You had to negotiate each hill during your 'off' hours when not on duty. Even being in good physical shape I found myself panting and breathless once we got to the 20/30-mile speed marches and the constant double-time in which we performed our tasks. Pushups were as common as eating and sleeping. Early morning PT wasn't ordinary PT as I'd had back at Fort Bragg. Innovations were added. We lifted tree trunks, ten men to a log, by the numbers, in rhythm and co-ordination. If any man goofed off, the rest knew it at once and that man was called to task then and there. We learned to work together from day one and if you couldn't, you were sent packing. There were grueling hours on obstacle courses designed for mountain goats, cliff scaling, hand-to-hand un-armed combat, day and night exercises under live ammuni-tion and in the harshest of weather. After the first week or so, many men fell by the way. They were returned to their units and replacements joined our ranks for their shot at this program. The officers got no special favors. Our leaders went through exactly the same rigorous training we did." There were casualties; one man fell to his death from a cliff; another died when struck by a bullet during a live-fire exercise.

After six weeks as a Ranger, Merrill developed pneumo-nia. While he convalesced in a hospital the 1st Ranger Bat-talion departed Achnacarry. He wound up in an engineer battalion. His new outfit refused to aid him in his quest to re-join the Rangers, and on more than one occasion his pleas infuriated his CO, whose ire infected the first sergeant as well, all to Merrill's detriment. All the Ranger hopeful could do was await an opportunity to rejoin the outfit.

Dwight David Eisenhower, the rapidly rising star of the

Army, in his capacity as chief of the War Department's Operations Division had counseled Truscott, "I hope that you will find some other name than 'commandos'; the glamor of that name will always remain—and properly so—British." A number of individuals would claim they suggested the name for the American facsimile of the Commandos and Truscott noted in his memoirs, "Many names were recommended. I selected Rangers." (The term dated back to the French and Indian Wars prior to the American Revolution and had been popularized in a best-selling novel by Kenneth Roberts, *Northwest Passage*.)

Early in the summer of 1942, the Allied High Command in London drew up Jubilee, a plan for a large-scale raid at Dieppe on the occupied French coast. The purpose was to test equipment and techniques for a full-scale invasion, evaluate the response of the enemy, and put on a show that might drain some German forces from the Russian front, or at least indicate to the Soviets good-faith intentions. To carry out Jubilee a combined force of some 5,000 Canadians, 1,000 British Commandos, and 50 Rangers [the official count, although Evans believes one more man was involved] boarded ships and boats for the cross-channel excursion.

The 262 vessels started across the channel the night of 18–19 August, nearly two weeks after Edson's Raiders struck Tulagi. Although enemy trawlers blundered upon the Allied convoy in the dark hours of the morning and opened fire, doing some damage, a number of Commando units came ashore and neutralized the Josef Goebbels Coast Artillery Battery (named for Hitler's minister of propaganda). But that was among the few triumphs. Shore gunners shot out boats from underneath Commandos and some Americans attached to Number 3 Commando had to swim for shore. They advanced a few hundred yards inland and

Ranger Lt. Edward Loustalot charged an enemy emplacement. A machine gun cut him down.

Wehrmacht soldiers rallied and inexorably shrank the beachhead. Only about a dozen of the Rangers ever got to the beach. Lieutenant Joseph H. Randall, working with a Canadian regiment, died from enemy fire right at the water's edge. He and Loustalot were apparently the first two Americans to be killed in ground action in Europe. Within a few hours, the Dieppe raid developed into a catastrophic event for the invaders. More than two-thirds of those in the operation became casualties, with nearly 500 dead, 800 listed as missing, and 1,800 taken prisoners. There were no boats to extract the surviving Commandos with their Ranger associates. The Rangers counted two KIA and another man succumbed to his wounds in England. Taken prisoner, most of the first Rangers to enter combat began almost three years of stalag life.

The 1st Ranger Battalion briefly renewed its training with the Commandos and then in September began to work independently toward a new mission. According to Evans, the experience at Dieppe only confirmed the necessity for the kind of intensive preparation common to Rangers and Commandos. With the German *Afrika Korps* punishing the British Eighth Army in North Africa, the Rangers prepared for the first major Allied campaign against the Axis powers of Germany and Italy, an invasion of North Africa under the code name Torch. For this operation they became attached to the 1st Infantry Division and responsible for providing a secure beachhead area.

Elite units also participated in the Asian war. In order to keep the Chinese forces viable, the Americans and British created a military supply lifeline that extended from India through Burma to the forces of Chiang Kai-shek. While the

American-trained and -equipped Chinese troops were directed by American general Joseph Stillwell, a force of 20,000 elite soldiers, skilled in guerrilla warfare, embarked from India to be inserted into the wilderness behind the Japanese lines where they would clear a path through Burma. More than three-quarters of them were Britons or men from the empire, and in command was Orde Charles Wingate, a nonconformist general. In parallel with Wingate's "Chindits," the Americans fielded a much smaller, 3,000-strong brigade, known officially as the 5307 Composite Unit. Stillwell's headquarters knew them under the code name Galahad and reporter Jim Shepley of *Time-Life* pasted on the label of Merrill's Marauders, in honor of their leader, Frank Merrill.

The men were all volunteers but apparently not screened for any particular skills or virtues. They were drawn from the professional army ranks as well as the citizen-soldiers who trained for jungle warfare after being stationed in India. They benefitted from two highly qualified leaders, Col. Charles Hunter, a 1929 West Point graduate who schooled them in the most useful infantry skills, and his classmate Frank D. Merrill, a former cavalryman with the insight to recognize the superior military ability of his deputy, Hunter.

During the China-Burma campaign, instead of hit-and-run units deposited by boats upon coasts, then extracted within a matter of hours, the Chindit-style operations kept the fighters in place until they used up their supplies. Then, they melted back to bases where they restocked weapons, and replaced casualties before returning to the jungle.

In the South Pacific, the Army would form a temporary special group known as the Alamo Scouts. They were not established until 1943 when Gen. Walter Krueger, commander of the Sixth Army, became concerned about the lack of intelligence on enemy soldiers occupying the islands destined for invasion. He proposed to form a small group who would surreptitiously insinuate themselves into enemy-controlled islands and bring back vital information on the disposition of troops, the fortifications, and conditions facing invaders.

Colonel Frederick W. Bradshaw, a former lawyer, and Krueger designed the program to manufacture the scouts. Bradshaw said, "We picked out a training center, a little paradise called Ferguson Island. Then we began selecting men. First we called upon the 158th Infantry—justly famous as jungle fighters—the Bushmasters of Panama. We asked for volunteers with qualifications beyond their prowess as foot soldiers. We wanted men of individual initiative and competitive spirit. They had to be men attracted by a game of great risks. They had to be crack marksmen, experts with the grenade, the knife, the Tommy gun and carbine, and also able to kill with their hands if necessary. All our men had to be steeped in woodlore and the techniques of individual camping, in signaling by numerous devices, in map reading and drawing maps."

The candidates underwent a rigorous six-week course that Bradshaw candidly admitted could not hope to instill all of the knowledge and skills required but would provide the basic qualities for their missions. As with the Rangers and Marine Raiders, survival of the rugged competition for membership generated an esprit de corps.

15

Torch

PERSUADED THAT A SMALL-SCALE INVASION OF CONTINENTAL Europe in 1942 was beyond their means, the Americans had agreed with the British to mount Torch, in which Allied forces would relieve the British Eighth Army sorely beset by the German *Afrika Korps* and Italian troops. In the Pacific, those desperately fighting to hold Guadalcanal bitterly resented the operation because it denied arms, ships, planes, and men for the war with Japan. Many American leaders believed the British had manipulated the United States into a policy designed to preserve their empire at the cost of American resources. General Joseph Stilwell, among those attempting to develop a strategy for the War Department, referring to the objectives of Torch, groused, "[Roosevelt] had been completely hypnotized by the British who have sold him a bill of goods. . . . The Limeys have his ear, while we have the hind tit. Events are crowding us into ill-advised and ill-considered projects. The Limeys want us in with both feet. So the answer is, we must do something now, with our hastily made plans and our half-trained and half-equipped troops." Stilwell's superior, George Marshall, also doubted the wisdom of the strategy and when the British surrendered at Tobruk in Libya, giving up 33,000 soldiers, the effectiveness of an invasion seemed questionable. At a dinner in London, Churchill explained to Eisenhower, "When Stalin asked me about crossing the Channel I told him, 'Why stick your head in the alligator's head at Brest when you can go to the Mediterranean and rip his soft underbelly.' " Using this argument Churchill had wooed and won the support of Roosevelt for Torch.

Torch presented the first major test for the newly named commander of American forces in Europe, Dwight D. Eisenhower. Unlike MacArthur, Eisenhower, a 1915 West Point graduate, remained stateside during World War I and never exercised a field command. During the 1920s and 1930s he held a series of staff positions, where he distinguished himself with his diligence, good humor, and appreciation of the chain of command. Undoubtedly his most taxing job was as assistant to Chief of Staff MacArthur from 1930 to 1934 in Washington, and as chief of staff for MacArthur after he assumed the post of field marshal responsible for building the newly created Commonwealth of the Philippines. Eisenhower neither privately nor publicly criticized the crucial decisions that revised War Plan Orange and reduced the ability to resist the Japanese.

While in Washington during the 1930s, Eisenhower came to appreciate certain qualities exhibited by MacArthur. He described him as a "rewarding man to work for, who never concerned himself with how many hours one put in so long as the task was accomplished." Indeed, many who knew Eisenhower saw much of the same in him. But the two were totally dissimilar in their relations to other human beings.

Aloof, humorless, enormously impressed with himself and his positions, MacArthur never had any confidants save perhaps his mother and then his wife. Eisenhower, on the other hand, was more often one of the boys; he laughed easily, enjoyed poker or bridge with colleagues, and seemed unconcerned with the niceties of rank.

Drawn to Washington at the birth of World War II by General Marshall, another man whom MacArthur had alienated, Eisenhower's skills quickly became apparent to the Army chief of staff. In those first weeks after the war broke out, Washington, and the various military arms, was, in the words of one historian, a "tower of Babel." The public and the press expected quick action and revenge. Powerful men rushed about, holding secret meetings that fomented wildly improbable schemes. Eisenhower at the War Plans Division maintained his equilibrium and displayed a keen insight into practical possibilities while tactfully dealing with influential if wrong-headed individuals. When the moment arrived to name the top American for European operations, there was no hesitation about the choice of Eisenhower. When he arrived in London in June 1942, he believed, along with Marshall and Secretary of War Henry L. Stimson, that he was there to run Operation Sledgehammer, a limited invasion of Europe to be followed by an all-out assault—Operation Round-up. Eisenhower was shaken by Roosevelt's agreement to substitute Torch for Sledgehammer; he had to proceed in haste.

"The decision to invade North Africa," wrote Eisenhower, "necessitated a complete reversal in our thinking and drastic revision in our planning and preparation. Where we had been counting on many months of orderly build-up, we now had only weeks. Instead of a massed attack across narrow waters, the proposed expedition would require movement across open ocean areas where enemy submarines would constitute a real menace. Our target was no longer a restricted front where we knew accurately terrain, facilities, and people as they affected military operations, but the rim of a continent where no major military campaign had been conducted for centuries. We were not to have the air power we had planned to use against Europe and what we did have would be largely concentrated at a single highly vulnerable base—Gibraltar—and immediate substantial success would have to be achieved in the first engagements. A beachhead could be held in Normandy and expanded, however slowly; a beachhead on the African coast might be impossible even to maintain."

Although Eisenhower later agreed that those opposed to Sledgehammer were correct in their argument that such an operation in 1942 was not feasible, his insistence that Torch presented more problems than a cross-channel beachhead is hard to understand. On D day, 1944, in spite of the enormous build-up of Allied forces, the German losses on the Eastern Front, the huge investment of Nazi troops in Italy, and the devastation from two years of strategic bombing, the Normandy venture faced far more powerful resistance.

North Africa in 1942 was a complicated mix of warring armies, intensive espionage, and a strange diplomatic protocol that portended the political independence and neutrality of the Vichy government in France. The Axis permitted Vichy to run French Morocco, Algeria, and Tunisia through its colonial appointees, backed by the French military, so long as the puppet leaders remained neutral if not hostile to attempts by the Allies to invade. German and Italian intelligence and the Gestapo supervised the Vichy-backed officials. Still, the situation enabled American consular and embassy people in North Africa to move about rather freely.

They accumulated intelligence about beaches, tides, bridges, railways, troop deployment, and coastal defenses,

A critical issue lay in the reaction of the local armed forces to an invasion. After France collapsed in 1940, the British, fearful the warships might become part of the Axis booty, attacked a portion of the fleet in the North African port of Mers el-Kébir. One battleship was destroyed, two other heavyweights disabled, and as many as 1,200 French sailors were killed. In ports controlled by the Royal Navy, ships flying the Vichy flag were seized and the crews interned. The Vichy government was enraged and the French Navy grew extremely hostile to the British.

A combined operation of Free French troops, under Charles de Gaulle, and British ships had sought to seize the West African seaport of Dakar, only 1,600 air miles from Brazil. Control of the port could shorten distances for the flights from the U.S. to the European theater. The colonial authorities arrested emissaries of de Gaulle when they came ashore and the coastal batteries fired on the British, who retaliated. The enmity of Vichy toward the British and de Gaulle increased.

These unhappy events occurred almost two years before Eisenhower assumed his command in London, but the antipathy toward major elements of the Allies remained. The American precursor to the Central Intelligence Agency, the Office of Strategic Services (OSS), advised the British and Free French to remain in the background to avoid offending the colonial forces. With 125,000 men stationed in North Africa and 500 aircraft available for their support, the Vichy French potentially posed a formidable obstacle to Torch. The American diplomat Robert Murphy, chargé d'affaires at Vichy, and associates delicately felt out high-ranking representatives of the French government in North Africa in an effort to ascertain their reactions to a U.S.-led invasion. The French colonies seethed with internecine intrigue and conflict and, although Murphy developed promising leads, the Allied command wanted to nail down commitments from military leaders and top officials that either they would join the invaders or at least not resist.

Mark Wayne Clark, a boisterous, outspoken West Point graduate of the Class of April 1917, had been named second in command. According to Clark, Roosevelt urged the planners for Torch that a senior officer be dispatched to North Africa to negotiate with the various parties. Murphy, through his contacts in Algeria, contacted the representatives of the French. Clark was the obvious candidate for the meeting. To accompany him he chose Col. Julian Holmes, a former diplomat fluent in French; Brig. Gen. Lyman Lemnitzer; Capt. Jerauld Wright from the U.S. Navy; and Col. Archelaus Hamblin, responsible for the operations supply and shipping.

"The first thing we had to do was get a submarine," reminisced Clark. "We met with Prime Minister Churchill and told him what we had in mind. He had Mountbatten, all of his chief cabinet officers there. When Ike revealed to him I had been selected to go, someone brought up the question of a British representative. I said the British will be represented by the submarine and any Commandos that will help us. He turned to me and said, 'What do you want? The whole resources of the British Empire are at your disposal.' He loved it, just loved things like that. I said I need a British submarine of sufficient size that will pick us up at Gibraltar, put us ashore, and get us out. We'll need all the paraphernalia to get ashore, kayaks, and Commandos."

Headquarters for Torch staff had been established in the tunnels of Gibraltar and Clark informed Churchill that a pair of B-17s would bear them there. The journey required a protective escort but at the same time had to be handled discreetly to avoid German surveillance. When the bombers touched down, cars picked up the passengers right at the ramp where they could not be seen by German agents lurking at the Spanish border only 300 yards off.

Said Clark, "I wanted some gold pieces, about $10,000 worth, in case we needed to bribe someone. [Jerauld Wright reported they each carried about $300 worth of gold Canadian coins.] We had passports in case we needed them to get out. I wanted civilian clothes cached someplace where we could get them." At Gibraltar, Clark met the British admiral of the fleet, whose attitude changed abruptly when informed Churchill enthusiastically supported the mission.

The admiral introduced Lt. Norman Jewell, commander of the submarine *Seraph*. "He was a magnificent fellow," said Clark. "Just radiated confidence. I talked with him about the mission. I asked if he knew what it was all about. He answered, 'No, sir. May I be frank? All we have been told is that we are going to take a bunch of screwy Americans who are to be landed on the coast of North Africa.' I said, 'is that all you've been told?' He said, 'Yes, sir.' I said what about getting us out? He said, 'Oh, yes, that's just as important, too.' He had a keen sense of humor."

It had been arranged for them to arrive at midnight when a light from a house on a cliff overlooking the sea would signal it was safe to come ashore. But because the flight to Gibraltar had been delayed by inclement weather, they did not reach the site until dawn was breaking. Rather than risk detection, the submarine remained underwater throughout the day. That evening it surfaced but no signal showed and the group had already retired when around midnight Clark was awakened and told the welcome bulb was lit.

"We went in sort of a diamond formation," recalled Clark. "One kayak got smashed against the waves, busted up. Only four of us could go in; one had to come back [to the sub]. We guided on the light in the house and had no problem. We picked up our kayaks and ran across the beach. We learned that [the people they were supposed to meet] had gone when we didn't show up [the night before]. They were risking their lives; they would be called traitors and would only come when we were there. They had arranged to get word to these fellows after daylight and they soon showed up." On hand, too, was Robert Murphy. The host, a man named Henri Tessier, had sent off all of his Arab servants to eliminate any gossip about his guests. Clark recalled, "There was a four-star general named [Charles] Mast. There was an admiral also; all the services were represented. There were five or six Frenchmen and we sat around a table. Everything had to be interpreted. I couldn't tell them we were coming in but I said eventually my country and the British hoped to come to North Africa and if we did we wanted to get their ideas on how we should do it." Actually, as Murphy and Clark knew, the first convoys sailing directly from the United States to participate in Torch were already at sea.

The French participants, said Clark, provided excellent intelligence. "They were prepared to give us everything. They had maps and all the information I needed, location of all the airfields, what harbors were mined, what beaches were mined, which commanders were more friendly than others." Clark lacked the knowledge or temperament to delve into the schisms among the French leaders. Murphy's responsibility was to sort out the most promising candidates for Allied support.

"I wanted to get out of there that night because the longer we stayed the more trouble we could expect," reported

Clark. "About three o'clock in the afternoon I recall looking out the window—they had put me in a French officer's blouse in case anybody happened to see me from the beach. The waves were coming up and there was a storm. It looked bad. The windmill was going a hundred miles an hour. I saw there wasn't much chance of getting out [to the *Seraph*]. So we went back and talked some more. The phone rang and a lookout in town informed Tessier that something was cooking in the police station. They were suspicious of the house because some Arab had gone down to the beach and observed footprints in the sand coming in from the sea. They had reported it and the police were on their way. We hid in the wine cellar. I sent one of the Commandos down to the beach and with the walkie-talkie to radio the submarine."

As the other Americans concealed themselves, Murphy said, "I posed as a somewhat inebriated member of a raucous social gathering. Fortunately, the police were not looking for military conspirators but for smugglers."

"The police came but they didn't find us," recalled Clark. "I decided we'd get out of the house, get into the woods and then down on the beach. We tried to get out when our boats sank and we lost everything. I had stripped down to nothing except the gold in a belt. [Clark felt he could swim better pantless.] We spent most of the night there in a little perimeter defense."

The police returned, inspected the house, and even looked over the beach, but did not see Clark's group and departed. "I went to the house; I had no shoes and my feet were cut from jumping on some sharp rocks," said Clark. "I got [Tessier] to turn his lights on. We got down on the beach. [Jerauld Wright] said there was a stretch where it wasn't as rough. I said we'll try it. Jerry and I went stripped down. The rest of them pushed us through the waves, big ones. Finally, we paddled out. We knew the submarine would be standing by because we had a message, a flash, one word, one letter that they'd be standing by. After about an hour, all of a sudden—there were no lights—they appeared and they grabbed us. One by one [the others] came out until the last one which smashed into the submarine and the boat sank. The fellows could swim and they had life jackets. I had a lot of stuff, maps and things strapped to me, but the kayak that went down carried weapons, infra reds, walkie-talkies, and papers with information about French officials. I was afraid it would be washed up on the beach.

"Ike met me when we got to England and he wanted to take me right away [to see Churchill] but I said God almighty let me have a little rest. They let me take a short nap and then we met with the prime minister. God, he loved it, just loved it. The king wanted to see me and he loved it. . . . I told how the police had raided the house while we hid in the empty wine cellar and the king said wasn't it too bad it was empty." Clark said he had been told that the best choice to command friendly French forces was Gen. Henri Giraud.

"Giraud wouldn't ride in a British submarine so we put Jerry Wright in charge of a British sub and picked up Giraud off southern France and brought him to Gibraltar." Clark's mention of Giraud as "the man we wanted" far oversimplified the situation. In the delicate interchanges with the French, the absence of specific information about the coming invasion prevented a commitment to any individual, such as Giraud. The French general, senior in standing to de Gaulle, had avoided disgrace during his nation's defeat, escaped from a German prison camp, and had never publicly supported the Vichy government. He seemed to have the proper credentials for what the Allies had in mind. However, he proved to have as grand a sense of himself as did the nettlesome de Gaulle. With the landings only ten days off, Giraud demanded he be named commander in chief for the campaign. At the same time, General Mast, when notified of the imminent arrival of Allied forces on the Algerian shores, expressed anxiety and displeasure. Looming over all was the question of how Adm. Jean Francois Darlan, commander in chief of all French military forces and the executive in charge of the North African territory, would behave. Darlan was a bitter foe of the British, receptive to the Nazi philosophy concerning Jews and a willing collaborator with the Germans. No one knew how much authority or influence Giraud, Mast, or Darlan could exercise over subordinates in the resident French armed forces.

From the United States, soldiers in the 3d and 9th Infantry Divisions and units from the 2d Armored Division boarded ships bound for North Africa. From England, the 1st and 34th Infantry Divisions plus the 1st Armored Division loaded onto transports. Attached to the 1st Infantry Division was the 1st Battalion of Rangers. Other vessels carried British fighting men. The Allied navies gathered round to ward off submarines and to add their punch with offshore bombardment. At a British airdrome, the 504th Parachute Regiment readied itself for Torch.

For the most part, the GIs going off to battle had spent at least a year in uniform and many came from the regular army. But their combat readiness was another matter. For example, Capt. G. V. Nicholls, a British veteran of tank warfare against the Germans, spent three weeks with the 2d Armored Division in February 1942, and noted, "The outstanding impression I had . . . was the supreme overconfidence of all ranks. From General [George S.] Patton downward, they seemed confident in beating any enemy with whom they were confronted and were fully prepared to begin operations at once." Nicholls quoted junior officers and enlisted men: "I would like to see German Panzers stop us"; "Give me a Light Tank and nothing will be able to stop us"; "These 75mm guns will smash anything the Germans have." Commented Nicholls, "This attitude is encouraged by General Patton's constant allusions to that imminent departure for the theater of operations. The junior officers thought the six-months continuous maneuvers in 1941 had fitted them for active service, and were satisfied that their individual training was well up to the standards of the British and Germans. In this opinion they were entirely wrong."

The British officer blamed Americans' assumptions on superior equipment and "better education and living conditions [which were] more than a match for the Japanese and the tired and unfit Germans. Any attempt to point out the German aptitude for mechanized warfare and the British experience during the past two years was discounted by most of the junior officers."

Hamilton Howze, a 1930 graduate of the USMA, had become a staff officer for the 1st Armored Division. Much of the North African campaign would be waged in desert country but Howze noted, "We did not have the privilege of desert training. We did not anticipate that there is no cover, or practically none in the desert against aircraft. The aircraft can easily spot you and knock the hell out of you. We suffered badly from German air attacks. Any vehicle running across the desert leaves a plume of dust behind which can go 300 feet high. We had bad training, unusual visibility, [were ignorant of] the ranges in which tanks could engage each other. These things came as a surprise. Going to Africa, we were thinking about Europe. The morale was very high. Everyone was excited and full of beans and anxious to go to war. The equipment we had wasn't as good as we thought it was, simply because we hadn't run up against the superior equipment of the Germans. But at the time we thought it was great stuff."

The 1st Infantry Division, a regular army outfit, was among the best-trained American organizations in the early days of World War II. Many of the soldiers were career military men. George Zenie, a Long Island, New York, native, unable to find a job, joined the outfit in 1940. "When I enlisted, my original company officers and indeed the officers of the 1st Infantry Division, were, for the most, West Point graduates. They ran their outfits by the book, but we expected that and we respected them. Our division commander, Maj. Gen. Terry Allen, and Brig. Gen. Teddy Roosevelt Jr., the assistant division commander, were revered. Our noncoms were also old army. They drilled us and worked us very hard. Later, in North Africa, Sicily, France, and Germany I thanked God they had pushed us." Zenie noted that the huge expansion of the army required the 1st Division to ship many of its better officers and noncoms to recently activated units. The replacements received by the 1st Division were "a mixed bag."

The 3d Infantry Division included Lt. William B. Rosson, a 1940 ROTC graduate of the University of Oregon, who chose to enter the service as a regular. He recalled training as "rather rudimentary. It was a peacetime oriented affair with more emphasis on spit and polish, cleanliness of barracks and what not, rather than combat readiness. We had no information on the German forces before embarkation. They kept us in complete secrecy of the destination and didn't know where we were going when we boarded the ships. We had 37mm guns [for antipersonnel and antitank purposes]. On the ship was the first time we saw and fired the bazooka.

The CO wore an asbestos firefighter's uniform for the first demonstration."

Amphibious landings, practiced by the GIs in England and the United States, only marginally resembled what lay ahead on Mediterranean beaches. Leisurely picking a route through rocks would not be an option when under enemy artillery and small-arms fire. A shortage of experienced crews to operate the landing craft further troubled those in command.

Operation Torch also offered the American airborne its first opportunity for combat. Chief of Staff Marshall had picked William Yarborough to become a member of the London Planning Group as the authority on airborne operations. "I suppose," said Yarborough, "because I was extremely enthusiastic about airborne operations and maybe having been one of the early, early officers in the activity. I went to England in July 1942 with more enthusiasm than real background knowledge, intelligence, and strategy. We didn't really know what the airborne goal or objective was." At the same time he became increasingly aware of problems with the Air Corps, which was supposed to transport the troopers. "They resented being taken off the kinds of jobs that provided support to air or army units. The installation of navigational gear to keep in formation had been delayed [because of lack of interest in hauling airborne]. The troopers themselves were superbly trained. The air group was gallant, fine, young, tremendous people but certainly had not had the kinds of training that the Germans had to go into Crete or someplace else."

Imbued with pride, the neophytes and uncertainly prepared combat troops headed for North Africa. Meanwhile, it was up to Eisenhower to pick which French steed to back. At one point, dispirited by his talks with Giraud, Eisenhower unleashed Clark upon the prickly Gaul. Clark informed the French general that he could either accept the limited role proffered or sit the entire affair out. When Giraud haughtily declared he would return to France, Clark claimed he said, "Oh, no, you won't. That's a one-way submarine. You're not going back to France on it," and left it to the interpreter to tell Giraud, "From now on your ass is out in the snow."

"Finally," said Clark, "we got him to come 'round. I would take him with me as soon as the Algiers airfield was captured and I would set up the command there as Ike's deputy. Giraud would be the supreme French commander for political, military, and everything else. That evening, Ike and I went back to our room where we got undressed and in our pajamas. Ike said, 'Let's have a drink before we go to bed.' He said, 'I wish I could go in with you but I can't.' I said, 'Of course you can't. You've got to stay at your headquarters.' "

As head of the American ground forces, Eisenhower had chosen Gen. George S. Patton Jr. A veteran of the expedition that hunted Pancho Villa in Mexico and the American forces in France for World War I, Patton had a well-established reputation for emotional outbursts and fractious conflicts. He quarreled with most of his contemporaries, regarded few if any his equal at strategy, and rarely tempered his criticisms of others with praise. Nevertheless, he gained the confidence of even those offended by his conduct, perhaps because of the strength of his belief in himself. His units were regarded as the most disciplined and well trained.

Still, fearful the personnel were insufficiently schooled and the plans equally inadequate, with typical bombast, Patton boasted he would "leave the beaches either a conqueror or a corpse." To a British admiral he sneered, "Never in history had the Navy landed an Army at the planned time and place. If you land us anywhere within fifty miles of Fedala [a site near Casablanca] and within one week of D day, I'll go ahead and win." He covered his reputation, however, by sponsoring a statement that warned, "This [the invasion of Morocco] cannot be considered a militarily sound operation of war."

Considered critical to the success of the strike into Algeria was the capture of the Tafaraoui and La Senia airfields near Oran. Shortly before midnight on 7 November, thirty-nine C-47s bearing paratroopers from the 2d Battalion of the 503d Parachute Infantry Regiment rose from the British base for a long night flight to the drop zones of the airports. Lieutenant Colonel Edson D. Raff commanded the battalion and Bill Yarborough, as the chief planner for the mission, accompanied the outfit. For guidance to the target the operation relied on the Rebecca-Eureka navigation system. In practice, the Eureka component on the ground transmitted a signal to the Rebecca aboard aircraft, enabling the planes to home in on the sites. Whether the C-47s landed at the airdromes or the troopers jumped depended upon whether the local military would fight or welcome the Americans. While still in the air, intelligence sources advised headquarters the French troops would be hostile. Unfortunately, efforts to relay the vital information to the planes were never received. The airborne had no clue whether to land or leap.

"Some of the pilots only arrived at the airdrome the night before they were supposed to take off," recalled Yarborough. Without the equipment to help maintain formation and without running lights because of the need to avoid observation, the untutored aerial chauffeurs lost contact with one another. Instead of an organized group, the flight broke down into small units of from one to six aircraft. On the

ground, Lt. Howard Hapgood, disguised in an Arab
burnoose, waited near Tafaraoui with his Eureka. He had
been given civilian status as a member of the diplomatic service and had smuggled the navigation aid into the country.
But when the time for the arrival of the airplanes passed
without any sight of them, Hapgood, "wisely," said Yarborough, "blew the thing up and vanished. He had been sitting
there for several hours operating this device. His chances of
survival would have been pretty low."

At dawn Yarborough looked out and saw only one other
airplane on his flank and no others on the horizon. "I stood
in back of Col. William C. Schofield, the Air Corps commander, and tried from my knowledge of the terrain models
and the maps to figure out with him where we were. We saw
lots of mountains but it wasn't until we saw a particular section of the coast of North Africa that we realized we were
well south . . . and west of where we should be. We decided
to turn toward our objective. We flew over Spanish Morocco
and saw two of our airplanes down. One with what appeared
to be spahis—troops on horseback rounding up the guys
who had gotten out of the airplanes. We knew that was not
the place."

Another group of C-47s headed toward the objective of
La Senia. Any notions of a friendly reception evaporated
when French antiaircraft guns started to bark. The flight set
down at Sebkra d'Oran, a dry salt lake west of Oran. The
crews of six more planes, including one with Raff, observed
a column of tanks approaching the aircraft on the ground.
Raff ordered his troopers to jump. Only after they landed did
they recognize the armor as American.

At this point the three planes with Yarborough spotted the
Sebkra d'Oran aggregation and they joined the people on
the dry salt lake. Raff, although injured when he crashed

into rocks after his jump, along with Yarborough organized an overland attack on Tafaraoui. They were twenty-five miles from the airdrome when word came by radio that other U.S. units had already seized the field. The armor commander asked if troopers could be flown in to relieve his tankers for pursuit of the enemy. Yarborough agreed to return to the planes and find some with enough fuel to make the trip. "It was unbelievable, the mud of Sebkra d'Oran," said Yarborough. "You couldn't move, you couldn't drive. It was like walking in flypaper." Nevertheless, they made their way to the C-47s, jammed seventy or eighty troopers into three with enough gas and flew toward Tafaraoui. As they approached at low altitude, three French fighters zeroed in on them. "We didn't have far to go and hit the ground. But it was enough to wash out the landing gear on the airplane I was in. We were hit broadside by the first pair of the Vichy fighters. They made two passes while we were in the air and they hit something every time. Then when we hit the ground, they flew over us one final time and peppered us as we lay there. The airplanes were a complete loss." They were still fifteen miles from the objective but after an all-night march, the men took over Tafaraoui.

In terms of the objectives of the mission, the first airborne effort was a flop. Not a single trooper had parachuted into combat. Only about a third of the airplanes remained operational. Yarborough commented, "The Rebecca-Eureka supposed [to bring us in on target] was put out of action because of the complexity of the plan. It is something that soldiers will never learn; that if a plan is simple, it's liable to work. If it's complex, its chances of working go down astronomically." Still, he noted, "We confounded the criticism of some experts. We were in North Africa with thirty-six or thirty-seven airplanes and almost a whole parachute battalion.

There weren't all that many casualties. We got our parachutes together, and five or six days later made another drop."

The first of those to come ashore near the city of Algiers were men from a British infantry brigade. They encountered no resistance and the French troops, in accord with word from General Mast, did not fire. More than 4,300 GIs with 1,000 Commandos struck three other sites near Algiers. For the most part the uniformed inhabitants responded passively with General Mast personally welcoming Commandos to Fort de Sidi-Ferruch. One garrison refused to put down its weapons but submitted after intervention by British planes from a carrier.

For the U.S. 1st Division, however, mistakes by those steering the assault boats created serious difficulties. The overloaded soldiers set down in deep water waded or even floated ashore. If opposition had been on the scene the situation could have been deadly. A third group, its numbers reduced when a submarine torpedo damaged a troop ship, also reached its destination in some disarray. Fortunately, their initial landings did not meet serious resistance.

Terry de la Mesa Allen, in command of these 1st Division troops, was a dropout from West Point in his final year before he earned a degree at Catholic University in 1912. Allen's background, his intense solicitude for his troops, and his less-than-abstemious enjoyments in off hours, set him apart from his contemporaries. He cheerfully admitted to a lack of interest in the academic end of a military education. When he attended the Fort Leavenworth Command and General School in the same class as Eisenhower, Allen graduated 221st while Eisenhower came out first among the 241 students.

Reporting for the *New Yorker* during the North African

campaign, A. J. Liebling said that in the eyes of superiors, Allen had come across as "slapdash and reckless" during peacetime. However, one of his staff officers, a USMA graduate himself, noted, "There are some generals that if they find the enemy in strong positions, they will go ahead and get you killed [a frequent critique of Patton]. But old Terry will find the way around and kill them all."

Ernie Pyle, the reporter for the Scripps-Howard newspaper chain, who ordinarily preferred the company of the lower echelons, said, "Major General Terry Allen was one of my favorite people. Partly because he didn't give a damn for hell or high water; partly because he was more colorful than most; and partly because he was the only general outside the Air Forces I could call by his first name. If there was one thing in the world Allen lived and breathed for, it was to fight. He had been all shot up in the last war and he seemed not the least averse to getting shot up again. This was no intellectual war with him. He hated Germans and Italians like vermin, and his pattern for victory was simple; just wade in and murder the hell out of the low-down, good-for-nothing so-and-sos. Allen's speech was picturesque. No writer could fully capture him on paper, because his talk was so wonderfully profane it couldn't be put down in black and white.

"Allen was shot through the jaw in the last war. That wound causes him to make an odd hissing noise when he is intense. He breathes by sucking the air in between his teeth, and it sounds like a leak in a tire. . . . As far as I know, Terry Allen was the only general in Tunisia who slept on the ground. All the others carried folding cots. General Allen wouldn't allow any of his staff to sleep on a cot. He said if everybody in his headquarters had a cot it would take several trucks to carry them and he could use the trucks to better purpose."

At Saint-Cloud on 9 November, French artillery wrought so many casualties on the 1st Division's 18th Regimental Combat Team, that Col. Frank Grier pulled back his three battalions to regroup while American artillery prepared to blast the town. Terry Allen, hearing of what had happened, tore out of his command post at Renan, a few miles off, sped to the regimental forward headquarters for a thorough examination of the entire situation. It was his first big decision. "No," said Allen, "We're going to bypass the town. We're not going to bombard it. I don't want to kill civilians. There are four thousand of them in there. Regardless of sentiment it would make a bad political impression. Third, if we bombard it and yet failed to take it by attack that would be disastrous. Fourth, it would [expend] too much ammunition. Fifth, it isn't necessary since we can reach our objective Oran without it." It is difficult to believe that in the same situation Patton would have hesitated to use the artillery. However, to some high-level critics, Allen's decisions smacked of pampering his men rather than strategic moves.

The first serious resistance on opening day had erupted in the Algiers harbor, where two British destroyers flying U.S. flags, bearing troops from both nations, all of whom wore American uniforms, raced toward the docks to seize the anchorage and prevent any French warships from being scuttled. Commandos assigned to knock out coastal batteries that protected the port were unsuccessful. A fusillade hammered both ships, forcing one to retreat. The other, having cleaved a boom blocking the entrance, raced to a berth where the infantrymen could debark and capture the major installations.

GIs of the 2d Armored Division assaulted Safi, a Moroccan town about 100 miles from Casablanca. Ernest Harmon, USMA Class of April 1917, in command, said, "Upon arrival at the beach we found about 200 men lying there with water lapping against the soles of their feet. There was a little sniper fire coming toward us and bullets were striking the sand here and there. I asked the captain of the troops on the ground what they were lying there for and he stated they were being fired at. I said, 'Yes, I realize you are, but how many people are firing at you?' He replied, 'About six.' I directed him to attack the house where the fire was coming from with a squad of twelve men and to get going with the remainder of the company on their objective as planned. The men were just having initial stage fright that all men have the first time they come under fire."

The opening phase of Operation Torch dismayed Patton, who stepped ashore shortly after noon at Safi. Bullets from stubborn French holdouts still smacked the surf as the general made his way onto the shore. He harshly criticized the actions of the soldiers. "The beach was a mess and the officers were doing nothing. I cursed and at last got a launch off to catch the boats [with reinforcements] and show them into the harbor. Had [General Jonathan] Anderson showed the proper push, this would have been done earlier. Just as I got the launch out, a boat turned end-for-end and drowned sixteen men. We only found three—they were a nasty blue color.

"The French bombed the beach and later strafed it. One soldier who was pushing a boat and got scared, ran onto the beach, assumed the fetal position and jibbered. I kicked him in the arse with all my might and he jumped right up and went to work. As a whole the men were poor, the officers worse. It is very sad. I saw one lieutenant let his men hesitate to jump into the water. I gave him hell. I hit another man who was too lazy to push a boat. We also kicked a lot of Arabs."

Tanks from the 2d Armored rolled ashore and with infantry drove some six miles inland. This would put the Allied ships in the harbor beyond artillery range while leaving behind scattered resistance within Safi to be mopped up later. When word reached Harmon of French reinforcements heading for the town from Marrakech, sixty miles off, he called for an air strike that destroyed the column.

Even as the first soldiers climbed onto the Algerian shores, Robert Murphy brought news of the assault to Admiral Darlan. Furious that he had not been consulted and brought into the drama earlier—although whether he would have gone along or alerted the Germans is not clear—Darlan accused the Americans of being as stupid as the British. About the same time, French Army headquarters, now fully aware of the invasion, staved off an uprising intended to aid the Allies. The accommodating General Mast was relieved of his command. A detachment loyal to Darlan overwhelmed rebels who had grabbed Admiral Darlan and Robert Murphy. The small force of Allied troops in Algiers harbor withdrew as the French Army counterattacked. Nevertheless, the expeditionary force had effectively isolated the city.

Some 200 miles west, an invasion enveloped the smaller city of Oran. The 1st Ranger Battalion, led by Darby, assaulted the harbor fort and a pair of French coastal batteries that guarded the port of Arzew. Manned by naval personnel, presumably with a grudge against the British for their bombardment of French ships, the battery had to be regarded as hostile. Darby split his unit with Herman Dammer, his executive officer, who led the 1:00 A.M. charge of Companies A and B against the bastion at sea level. The defenders offered little fight although snipers killed one Ranger and wounded another.

Darby himself landed half an hour later with the remainder of the Rangers silently working their way up the hill in the darkness. "I was with Darby," said Bing Evans. "He went about a quarter-mile past our marker and I told him we've gone too far. He didn't want to believe me but then he talked to Roy Murray and Max Schneider [the COs of E and F Companies]. They verified what I said. We got our bearings and went to the right place."

While James Altieri and his fellow Rangers fixed bayonets preparatory to an assault on the French positions, the 81mm mortar teams set up some 500 yards behind them. Two men with wire cutters crept forward in the darkness to open a path through the barbed-wire fences. Altieri noted, "They were gone only a minute when the darkness crisscrossed with orange-and-green tracer fire. The crisscross was joined by two more angles of machine-gun fire. Dirt was splattering all around us from the impact of the bullets." The defenders had been alerted by the fire down in the harbor where other Rangers under Herman Dammer engaged in a skirmish.

Altieri remarked, "Strangely, I wasn't scared. It was just like the Commando training. Close-landing bullets by now were a familiar experience. Also the drama of the battle was so completely absorbing, that there was no time to be concerned about personal fears."

Darby took charge, calling for a mortar barrage. Recalled Altieri, "In an instant the air overhead was filled with loud swishing, fluttering mortar shells speeding earthward on their mission of destruction. The entire hillside shuddered as the shells came crashing down, their flaming bursts illuminating the area in eerie shadows. For two minutes the mortar bombardment continued, then the order was passed down, 'Prepare to assault.' "

The Rangers rushed through the openings in the barbed wire and in the dugouts discovered French soldiers dazed by the explosions. Swiftly, they bagged some 150 captives including the commandant of the still-untouched Fort du Nord. Darby demanded the colonel surrender the bastion but was momentarily nonplussed when his prisoner said the French could not yield until they displayed valor. Darby then proposed token resistance. The troops in the fort could fire their rifles in the air once before coming out. On that note resistance at Fort du Nord ended. By noon Arzew was officially secure. Terry Allen, as commander of the 1st Infantry Division, to which the Rangers were attached, commented, "Their initial mission was accomplished with great dash and vigor."

Bill Behlmer, as an antitank crewman with the 1st Division, said, "We were briefed that we'd land at a seaside resort, Arzew, and our objective was the railroad station in Oran. The English crews dropped some of the trucks and guns in deep water and it was a mess, but we made it to the beach. This was the real thing, artillery shells, machine guns, mortars, small arms. We had our first taste of the gnawing feeling in the pit of the stomach. Fear! We secured the beach, but that first night was terrible. Everybody had an itchy trigger finger and fired at anything that moved, shot up half of the grapevines in North Africa. The corporal of the guard shot one of our sentries in the stomach."

Harold J. Taylor, a pre–Pearl Harbor draftee and communications technician with headquarters of the 3d Division's 15th Regiment, heavily burdened with a rifle, combat pack, ammunition, and half of a two-man, two-piece radio set, scrambled down the side of a cargo net into the landing boat in the darkness off the port of Fedala. "Beads of sweat covered my forehead while many things were racing through my mind—might I be killed!!! I also realized that I wasn't alone in this ordeal; there were many others with me and they too were experiencing similar feelings. Together we were supportive of each other. The knowledge that we would be together added comfort and a sense of security.

"As we approached French Morocco in the dark it became apparent that trouble was ahead. We were not approaching land in the designated area . . . large protruding rocks became visible in front of us. It looked like sure death as our landing craft was buffeted by the large waves that kept rolling off the rocks. The craft rolled back and forth on its sides, throwing men and equipment about. Had it turned over all aboard would surely have been killed.

"How the Navy man was able to stay at the control and move us out of the area and back to our convoy, I will never know. We picked ourselves up off the floor of the craft and retrieved our belongings. No one was seriously injured." Daybreak revealed that other landing craft also had problems. The beach, littered with debris as far as one could see, had the appearance of a major disaster. But in fact, Taylor and his unit quickly set out toward Casablanca.

Ships bearing men from the 7th Regiment of the 3d Division, also destined to go ashore at Fedala, rendezvoused at sea. William Rosson, assigned as assistant regimental S-3 [plans and operations], recalled, "A certain amount of fire from ashore and Casablanca began. It was quite exciting and a bit unnerving to see the tracers heading into the ship areas. Operations began at night for a dawn assault. There was no problem boarding the landing craft, but we spent what seemed an eternity circling about. I had the uneasy feeling we were off course going in as the naval gunfire began . . . as dawn broke. I could see explosions and some return fire from the French positions. As we approached the beach we came under scattered machine-gun fire from the Fedala strong point. The surf was fairly turbulent and quite a large number of craft had broached. I was amazed to see how many boats had ended up on the beach sideways."

Support for the amphibious assault at Fedala came in the form of airplanes catapulted off the decks of three escort flattops and the bigger carrier *Ranger.* Among the smaller carriers was the USS *Suwannee.* Torpedo bombers and fighters from the Suwannee accompanied by air groups from sister ships hammered submarine pens and targeted the Port Lyautey airfield. Rumors that French pilots would refuse to fight Americans proved false. Four U.S. planes were lost in dogfights that also brought down eight French aircraft. Two Wildcats off the *Suwannee* blasted a twin-engine bomber out of the sky only to learn they had knocked off a British Hudson.

David Jones, the pilot with the Doolittle Raiders who reached safety after parachuting from his B-25 over China, had returned to the States where he received command of a B-26 squadron in the 319th Bomb Group. In its early versions the twin-engine bomber known as the Marauder earned the nickname of "the widow maker." Said Jones, "We were in Baton Rouge about a month, and in that month the group lost seven airplanes, none out of my squadron. Guys flying into trees, the blind leading the blind."

The Martin Company produced a modified version, and equipped with new Marauders, the 319th headed for England via Presque Isle, Maine; Greenland; and Iceland. A series of crashes convinced the authorities the two-engine aircraft could not manage the long journey with normal gear and crew. "We had a crew of six on the B-26 with guns, armor plate, and the whole bit. [The order came] unload all your guns and you are going to take your armor plate out.

Three of the crew, the pilot, copilot, and crew chief were all we had." While Jones was marooned for eighteen days in Greenland because of bad flying weather, the experts decided weight was not the problem. "Four C-47s came in to give us all the equipment we had taken out of the airplanes. We took the armor plate, the guns, and we threw them all in the bomb bay, wired them down, and waited for the weather to change. We finally made it to Iceland and were there about ten days waiting for weather and then went to England."

Because the fighters were ill equipped to navigate the long trip from Land's End on the southwestern coast to North Africa, Jones, in his B-26, led a dozen P-38s to an air base in Algiers. "Christ, there were bomb craters and it was a mess, a big mess. We landed in all directions and straddling bomb holes and God knows what all. We must have ended up with almost two or three hundred airplanes on the field. No organization, no nothing. We just lived by our airplanes. In the morning you'd see hundreds of little fires. Everybody was cooking, even the fliers beside their own airplanes. We were loading 250-pound bombs when we could because we could muscle those in."

One of the first raids struck an enemy base at Sfax. "We went across the field with nine airplanes. We were on the deck and I missed the airfield. I could see it on the left so I made a 180 and by this time everybody was waiting for us. They shot everything at us. My left wingman fell off. We got home but we had lost this airplane and I felt pretty bad. The next morning, here this crew walks in. I had P-38s escorting us. They had seen and followed this airplane when it landed in the desert. The crew stayed with it. The P-38s then went home where the A-20s squadron with Charles Kegelman [a participant in the 4 July 1942 inaugural raid of the Eighth

Air Force] was and they got to talking, yakking. They fired up an A-20 and one guy went out and the guys were still at their airplane. The A-20 picked up seven people and took them home."

Flying into the Blida airport near Algiers on D plus one, Mark Clark nervously watched as German bombers attacked the installations now controlled by the Allies. No sooner did his B-17 touch down before another wave of enemy planes sent everyone scrambling. The French in the captured city ignored, if not insulted, Giraud. "We found that the Arabs would shoot Giraud on sight. He wasn't the right guy at all," said Clark. "Darlan was." As Eisenhower's deputy indicated, a cease-fire from the French forces required the cooperation of the admiral, who detested the British and who had easily fitted into the collaboration with the Axis countries.

"I had to meet with Darlan who was in full command," said Clark, "while we had to hide Giraud. We kept him hidden for weeks. I had to get Darlan to issue two orders; one to bring the French fleet out of Toulon [a seaport in southeastern France] and the second to stop the fighting." The British worried that the French warships might become Nazi property and then ravage Allied shipping in the Mediterranean. "Before he [Darlan] would stop the fighting between French and Americans he wanted certain guarantees. After four hours with him I sent a message home, using for the first time YBSOB [Yellow-bellied son-of-a-bitch, the code for Darlan]. I met him some more and finally got to the point where he wouldn't cooperate at all and I got tough. I had [Maj. Gen. Charles] Doc Ryder there with his 34th Division. We took a company of infantry and surrounded the place. I told him he'd be under arrest until he came around. He did come around. He issued orders and it stopped, although for about 48 hours there was still some going on."

Darlan, technically still subject to the government of Petain in Vichy, nevertheless instructed the French vessels in Toulon to prepare to sail in the event the Germans over-ran unoccupied France. When the Nazi leaders learned of Darlan's surrender they immediately threatened Petain, who relieved Darlan and cancelled his orders. The admiral vacil-lated, talked of revoking the commitment made to Clark, who informed Darlan that that was not possible.

To his chief of staff Gen. Walter Bedell Smith, Eisen-hower, confronted by the rivalry of Darlan and Giraud, wrote, "I've promised Giraud to make him the big shot, while I've got to use every kind of cajolery, bribe, threat, and all else to get Darlan's active cooperation. All of these Frogs have a single thought—'Me.' It isn't all this operation that's wearing me down—it's the petty intrigue and the ne-cessity of dealing with little selfish, conceited worms that call themselves men." To a friend he confided, "I am a cross between a one-time soldier, a pseudo statesman, a jack-legged politician, and a crooked diplomat. I walk a soapy tightrope in a rainstorm with a blazing furnace on one side and a pack of ravenous tigers on the other."

While Eisenhower found it difficult to comprehend the at-titudes of people whom his armies had come to liberate from the Nazi jackboot, Giraud understandably was miffed be-cause he had been deceived by Americans like Murphy on his status. De Gaulle was equally furious because he had neither been involved nor informed about Operation Torch. When he heard the news, he huffed, "I hope the Vichy peo-ple will fling them into the seas! You don't get France by burglary." It required Churchill to stroke de Gaulle until he converted into a supporter of Torch.

All of the dissembling, the "acting" he studied under a prima donna like MacArthur, taxed Eisenhower, but the experience probably helped him later in the war when he dealt with conflicting personalities and hard-held positions. But the stakes were huge; men's lives and the success of the venture depended upon how the North African French acted. The advance word was that those defending the various areas would meet invasion forces with all the firepower available.

Fortunately, although Vichy had fired Darlan, the French of North Africa decided to take their cue from him. As a prisoner of the Allies, the admiral had little choice but to call upon those within his former jurisdiction to cease fire and, on 11 November, the French military did lay down their arms. Unwilling to trust even the Vichy French, the Nazi armies then fully occupied the former satrapy with help from Il Duce [Benito Mussolini], who sent his legions into southern France and Corsica. Crews aboard the French ships in Toulon, unwilling to fight for either side, scuttled their vessels. With the capitulation of the French and Rommel in retreat, Churchill crowed, "We have a victory—a remarkable and definite victory." The triumph was short-lived.

While *Wehrmacht* strategists considered an Allied invasion of North Africa high on the list of probabilities, *der Führer*, who believed himself the best judge of military actions, had not taken the notion seriously. In fact, in the weeks before the opening salvos of Torch, the reinforced British Eighth Army under Bernard Montgomery opened an offensive against El Alamein with a 1,000-gun barrage. Spearheaded by 1,000 tanks compared to the 240 available to the Germans and 280 obsolete Italian ones, the British also mustered 1,500 planes against the 350 of the *Luftwaffe*. Hitler refused to permit an evacuation to Europe but allowed the embattled Rommel to retreat from Egypt to Libya. Without authorization from Hitler, Field Marshal [Alfred] Kesselring in Italy amassed troops and aircraft, and within thirty-six hours of the invasion the first of them debarked at an airfield in Tunisia. French soldiers on the scene might have repelled them but Vichy instructed its underlings in Tunis not to resist. Subsequently, Hitler ratified Kesselring's decision with orders to drive the Allies out of Algeria.

16

Grim Glimmers

WITH TORCH DRAWING SO HEAVILY ON U.S. RESOURCES, THE campaign in the South Pacific dragged on, short in manpower, rations, ammunition, and firepower. Admiral King, as the boss of all naval operations, and Admiral Nimitz, commander of the Pacific fleet, unhappy with the timorous approach of Adm. Robert Ghormley, replaced him with Adm. William "Bull" Halsey. A member of the USNA Class of 1904, Halsey, an indifferent student who almost flunked out in his third year, shone on the football field and in social situations. During World War I he commanded a destroyer in the war against German U-boats. Like a number of others of senior rank he learned to fly while in his forties in order to earn command of an aircraft carrier. Although he needed spectacles, Halsey nevertheless passed the eye exam, the beneficiary of some finagling with the medical records.

Unlike Nimitz, his junior by a year, Halsey, while well versed in technology and tactics, was an impulsive, hunch-driven commander with a penchant for blurting out his opinions, a characteristic one reporter called "an affinity between his foot and his mouth." But what recommended him for the job was the same sort of aggressive approach to war. Speaking to midshipmen and officers in 1942 during a brief stop at the Naval Academy, he glossed over tactics in favor of blunt bellicosity, snarling about "yellow-bellied sons-of-bitches." His election to command was welcomed by the Marine commanders. General Vandegrift described the admiral's visit to Guadalcanal as being "like a wonderful breath of fresh air."

The Japanese again determined to evict the enemy from Guadalcanal. Fortunately for Halsey and the defenders, the code breakers intercepted intelligence detailing the order of battle plotted by the Nipponese. Immediately, the Americans beefed up the forces in residence through the Americal Division, the only large-scale Army organization activated overseas. These GIs, graduates of former National Guard outfits, began to join the Marines on the island during the first week of November. More Air Corps bombers and crews took up station on Espíritu Santo from where they could batter enemy positions.

Convoy and task-force vessels steamed toward Guadalcanal from both directions. The two sides traded punches in the air as American fighter planes tangled with torpedo-laden Bettys bound for transports carrying more Americal infantrymen. The Grumman Wildcats and the antiaircraft fire knocked down almost all of the bombers and some of their Zero escorts. That band of attackers inflicted little damage. Pouring into the Slot, however, was a formidable flotilla of Imperial Navy warships, including a carrier, two battleships, cruisers, and destroyers. They considerably outgunned and outnumbered the opposing U.S. vessels, a force without a functioning carrier or battleship to block a bombardment of Henderson Field and its environs.

During the night of Friday, 12–13 November, General Vandegrift said, "For nearly an hour, we watched naval guns belch orange death with such rapid vehemence that the island seemed to shake beneath us." The two groups of warships apparently stumbled into one another while darkness covered Ironbottom Sound, the nickname for the water bed strewn with sunken ships. The Americans operated without the most modern radar aboard the vessels at the head of their column. In the confusion, the gunners exchanged huge shells—14-inchers from the Japanese battlewagon *Hiei*, 8-inchers from the biggest U.S. cruisers—torpedoes, and 20mm cannon with foes. In a number of instances, ships flying the same flag opened up on one another. Charging about in the black of night and rain squalls, they passed within point-blank range, enabling machine gunners to rake decks and superstructures. "It was like a barroom brawl after the lights had been shot out," said one survivor.

Shattering news filtered into Halsey. First, the cruiser *Portland* reported her steering room flooded, her rudder jammed by a torpedo blast. Then the cruiser *Atlanta* sounded a cry for help. The cruiser *Helena* announced itself the command ship of the task force, indicating terrible injury to the anointed flagship the cruiser *San Francisco*, and advised that "All ships are damaged." Before the action ended four American destroyers and two cruisers added their carcasses to the collection in Ironbottom Sound. Several other vessels absorbed such extreme hurt they were dubious candidates for repair. When dawn broke, small boats from Guadalcanal picked up hundreds of Japanese and Americans, many burned or wounded, floating offshore. More than 1,400 American sailors were killed, including the five

Sullivan brothers who went down with the light cruiser *Juneau*. That loss caused orders to be promulgated against allowing siblings to serve in the same unit. In terms of tonnage, ships, and lives the Japanese appeared victorious, but they were prevented from hitting the objective, Henderson Field.

Still intent upon a naval strike at Guadalcanal, Adm. Isoroku Yamamoto mobilized another fleet to sweep the Slot clean, annihilate positions around Henderson Field, and bring fresh troops into the fray. Halsey now relied on his partially repaired carrier *Enterprise*, a pair of battleships, *Washington* and *South Dakota*, and the airmen at Espíritu Santo and Henderson for the main defense of the sea lane and the turf. Cruisers, the first elements in the Japanese armada, approached close enough to Guadalcanal to lob nearly 1,000 shells at Henderson with no significant results. For their pains, they drew the attention of aircraft from the island and the *Enterprise* that scored major hits and sank a cruiser. Even more important, they ravaged the group of transports. The Nipponese regrouped, and upon the arrival of a battleship plus other ships the fleet aimed another blow at Guadalcanal. While the Japanese outnumbered the Americans by four to one in destroyers, the two U.S. battleships, armed with 16-inch guns, packed the most power.

Once again, it was nighttime in the Slot, just below Savo Island, when the opponents squared off. Although the longer-range weapons of the *South Dakota* and *Washington* commenced firing before the enemy could close near enough to retaliate against them, the American destroyers in the van quickly succumbed to the avalanche of torpedoes and shells. Two slid beneath the surface almost immediately after being hit and the surviving pair limped away seeking to stay afloat in spite of their wounds. One of them began to break up and subsequently was sunk by its sister ship.

Japanese cruisers and destroyers approached the *South Dakota*, hampered by mechanical failures that blacked out its radar functioning. Shells and torpedoes crashed into the battleship but its thick armor plate limited the damage. However, explosions in the superstructure killed, wounded, and destroyed systems required for gun control. More than twenty fires burned aboard the *South Dakota*. Unable to fight effectively, it withdrew, leaving the still-untouched *Washington* to cope with the entire Japanese force. It had already battered a destroyer and now took under fire the overmatched heavyweight cruiser *Kirishima*, which subsequently rolled over and sank. The aroused Japanese destroyers, like a pack of wolves after a particularly meaty specimen, unsuccessfully pursued the *Washington*, now retiring from the scene.

The naval battle of Guadalcanal was over. Overall, the Japanese lost more at sea than the Americans. But it was in terms of ground forces that the victory truly counted. Only about 2,000 soldiers of the Imperial Army, short on food and ammunition, were deposited on the contested island. During the same period almost three times as many American fighting men joined their comrades. Halsey, unlike his predecessor, risked major assets on the gamble that he could stop the enemy, and he won. Instead of another Bataan this was the first success in the island-hopping strategy. The Japanese high command wrote off Guadalcanal, but to their troops on the island their duty to fight remained constant and the agonizing struggle continued.

Robert Muehrcke, a corporal with the Americal Division, remembered conditions that would persist for another six months. "After the sun set, there was no smoking, no talking, and most of all, no above-ground movement. No one left the foxhole to defecate. Only one's eyes were above the foxhole edge. Firing at a Japanese ruse gave away one's position. One prevented this at all costs. The Guadalcanal full moon was a blessing. The light was bright enough to distinguish movement. Any unusual movement seen in the bright moonlight had a grenade thrown at it.

"Facing the enemy from a foxhole night after night, across a small strip of jungle measuring fifteen to twenty yards, was a true test of the emotional makeup of any fighting man. His prior combat experience, his military training, his emotional stability, as well as his preparation for each specific encounter, all influenced his reactions. At night, odors filtered down the defense line. One became especially aware of one's own body odor as well as that of his 'buddy.' It was distinguishable from the enemy's odor, so entirely different from the living Americans. The body odors of the living were mixed with the stench of the decaying dead, both Japanese and American—an odor never to be forgotten."

The losses at sea and on Guadalcanal enabled the Allies to focus on New Guinea. MacArthur had committed the newly arrived American 32d Infantry Division to fight alongside the Australian 7th Division. Fred Johnson served as a medic with the 128th Infantry Regiment [32d Division]. The outfit reached Adelaide, Australia, in May 1942. "Around September, we flew to Port Moresby and they sent us to the Goldie River near the foot of the Kokoda Trail. We ran patrols, looking for Japanese stragglers but never encountered anyone. The climate was extremely hot and humid with a lot of rain."

As the Japanese fortunes on Guadalcanal declined, they abandoned their quest for Port Moresby and dug in on the northeast coast. MacArthur sought to eliminate them. "In November 1942 we flew to a field on the north coast," recalled Johnson, "a short runway strip usable during the dry season. We marched along the beach toward Buna. Everyone felt real confident this would be a real short victory. We were led to believe it would be lightly defended by a lot of sick, starving Japanese. But they brought in a lot of men from Rabaul and it was heavily fortified, lot of bunkers, tremendous amount of machine guns. They didn't have artillery or big mortars so we didn't get a lot of wounds that caused amputations. That would come later in the Philippines.

"We could see the airfield they held and U.S. bombers hit the place. One came flaming down, crashed, and exploded. It was a sobering sight. The rainy season set in; rain kept pouring down. We didn't have shelter halves or raincoats. We were constantly wet. As medics when we first went into New Guinea we wore the brassards [Red Cross insignia], but they were removed quickly because we lost half of our medics who were killed in line companies around Buna and you didn't know whether the brassards made a good target or what. Almost all of us also carried weapons, Tommy guns or M1s, the whole war.

"I didn't see a lot of hatred toward the Japanese, not by the wounded or anyone else. The boys just felt they had a job to do. Everyone developed a lot of respect for them as infantry fighters who were extremely adept, courageous. We didn't know of any atrocities. There weren't a lot of prisoners taken. Most of them fought to the very end. The aid station was just set up alongside the road. Any wounded brought in would just wait there in the rain. There isn't a lot you can do at a battalion aid station under the conditions where often you are, at most, 300 yards or so behind the front lines."

Embattled Americans in the Pacific—from foxhole soldier to MacArthur speaking for his fief, and almost the entire naval command beginning with Admiral King down through the likes of Nimitz, Halsey, and Vandegrift—bemoaned the focus on Europe to the detriment of their concerns. But within the Western Hemisphere Torch also drained direct operations by the Eighth Air Force in England against the European enemy. The escort service provided by the first American squadrons, the 31st Fighter Group in Spitfires, was bolstered temporarily by the 1st Fighter Group manning P-38 Lightnings. These U.S.-built, twin-engine, double-boomed aircraft were blessed with speed and great range. As the first fighter unit to cross the Atlantic under its own power, the 1st Fighter Group, like its bomber predecessors, encountered serious problems. In mid-July six P-38s, confounded by the weather and misled by directional broadcasts from German radio, had no recourse but to land on the icecap of eastern Greenland. The Lightnings' wreckage couldn't be salvaged but the fliers all survived. Over time the accident rate during passage to England via the North Atlantic route would fall drastically and by January 1943, 920 planes had attempted the crossing with a loss rate of 5.2 percent, below the anticipated 10 percent.

However, the 1st Fighter Group, which went operational at the end of August and started full-scale sweeps in mid-September, left Europe for North Africa in November. In preparation for this departure and its P-38s, the Eighth Air Force in late September incorporated the American pilots of the Eagle Squadron into the just-activated 4th Fighter Group. Spitfires continued to be their aircraft. On 9 October, the Eighth Air Force mounted its most impressive show yet.

"Against Lille and other objectives," said Walt Kelly, "we sent 110 of our own bombers, 27 of which were B-24s. We downed 56 enemy fighters with 26 more probables. Our escort was credited with only five. Four bombers failed to return to the U.K., three B-17s, and one B-24 with one crew picked up in the channel. We had now provided ample evidence of who was to be boss of daytime air over Western Europe. This action was against some of Goering's most experienced pilots—some German aces had more than 300 kills [three years of war including duty on the Soviet front]. Our squadron morale was very high. We considered our flying and bombing skills to be the very best and were particularly proud of our tight formation flying."

Kelly's declaration of victory may have been premature but the thrust at Lille presaged the style that would become a hallmark of the Eighth Air Force. Eaker put up 108 bombers, the first occasion in which a raid exceeded the century mark, but unfortunately a total of 29 B-17s and B-24s turned back.

For their inauguration into combat that 9 October, twenty-four brand-new B-17Fs, designated as the 306th Bomb Group, warmed up their engines at Thurleigh Field for the trip to Lille and their first mission. In the command seat of one of the 368th Squadron's planes was a twenty-two-year-old native of Boise, Idaho, Lt. John Regan.

Regan flew one of the first of the 306th's Forts from Wendover to Maine, then to Gander, Newfoundland, before the final leg to Prestwick and the hop to the base at Thurleigh. "We had not been told about flak and German fighters because the people with us hadn't any experience in combat. The first mission of our group was against a factory in the city of Lille, not a very deep penetration but one that required us to be in formation. I had been a football player in high school and college and my feeling was like that. I was really excited. This was what I trained for. I was over here to fly combat. Boy, I was young, eager, ready to go.

"When we crossed the coast, we didn't have fighter escort. We climbed to altitude, went toward our target and we started getting attacked by fighters and the ground antiaircraft was shooting as us. I thought, 'My God! Those people are serious.' From that point on, combat was never thrilling to me. It was a job that had to be done and a job that turned out to be extremely tough. I imagine the rest of my crew felt very much like I did. Nobody was unsatisfactory and nobody did anything particularly outstanding.

"After we departed the target, I lost my number-two engine, which suffered some minor damage from flak. We had to drop back from the formation and were attacked by about 20–25 yellow-nosed ME 109s, Goering's own airplanes. Fortunately for me at the time, the Germans didn't know how to attack the B-17, still an airplane with which they were not familiar. They stood out, forming an echelon on my left side and they would peel off and try to attack us from that side. They just were not successful. When they did this, I would pull up so I would get the prop wash from the airplanes that were much farther ahead of me and these people would have to fly through it. I would then go from one side to another to keep them from attacking us as well."

Another first for Lille was the B-24s mentioned by Kelly. They came from the 93d Bomb Group. Among the new crews was Luther Cox, the twenty-four-year-old son of a Baltimore executive. Lu Cox was a navigator for the Liberator *Shoot Luke* in the 93d Bomb Group. Cox said the crews received limited preparation for combat. "The main emphasis was on formation flying. No aerial-gunner work. No instructions on strategic or tactical bombing. We had absolutely no idea how much weather flying we could get involved in when we were sent over to England." The name of the plane derived from the oft-heard cry in innumerable barracks crap games, "Shoot, Luke, you're faded." On the nose of *Shoot Luke* a painter depicted a hillbilly leaning against a tree while holding a long rifle.

Cox recalls the morning of his and *Shoot Luke*'s first mission, the raid on Lille. "After breakfast we all went into the briefing room, which was dimly lighted. The hustle and bustle of crewmen entering and finding their seats together was overpowered by the undertone of conversation that hung above the flyers. The lights on the stage in front of us came on and flooded the walls upon which hung some air-navigation charts. The fact that it was ice cold in the room didn't seem to be recognized, so intent was everybody to hear what the target would be. Throughout every mission ever flown, I am certain that the most important words offered from the briefing stage were, 'Gentlemen, the target for today is . . .' In that tense atmosphere we could clearly see our target and the course we were to take in and coming out. It was very important to be aware in great detail of your position at all times while over enemy territory for although you might not be the lead aircraft, all that had to happen was for you to have to drop out of the formation and then you would hear the voice of the pilot asking for a heading back to England and our base.

"As all the planes warmed up their engines it seemed as though the entire base had turned out to watch this great moment in the history of the 93d Bomb Group. We were lined up in snake fashion waiting for the signal from the control tower. At ten o'clock sharp, KK [Maj. Kenneth Compton, operations officer] pointed his Very pistol skyward and fired a flare, signaling number-one aircraft, the lead ship, to take off. One after another they staggered down the runway that seemed so short and finally lifted off the ground, each just barely clearing the perimeter fence.

"Finally it became our turn to line up and take off. Earlier, back when we were in our parking space, Murph [pilot John Murphy] had run each engine up to its fullest rpm, checking the array of instruments before him very carefully. Our faithful ground-crew chief stood by each engine in turn with a fire extinguisher, as Murph cranked up each one, waiting for the right speed of prop rotation and compression before he would energize the starter. Starting these huge engines could be anxious moments as each engine seemed to stubbornly defy being kicked in. They seemed to come to life with a grunt, a puff of smoke, and then that roar as she caught. The aircraft shuddered each time this happened.

"Now, at the beginning of the runway and with a crew at a peak of anticipation and excitement, Murph locked all four throttles and gradually moved them forward, as those four mighty engines began to come to life and roar, both Murph and [Frank] Lown [copilot] pushed as hard as they could on the brakes trying to hold *Shoot Luke* down. Finally, with the airframe of the plane fairly jumping up and down, they released the brakes and she seemed to leap forth as she charged down the runway. Carrying twelve 500-pound demolition bombs and 2,500 gallons of fuel, the gross weight of the aircraft was more than 70,000 pounds. Murph held her on the runway as long as he could in order to get her moving faster and faster until at almost the last moment he eased back on the wheel and she staggered off into the sky. He quickly called for wheels-up and Lown flicked the switch to bring them up. This greatly reduced drag and *Shoot Luke* took to the air like a huge bird."

For Cox's flight to Lille, operations decreed a bombing

altitude of 22,000 feet. As soon as he saw the coast of France, Cox alerted all gunners to watch for enemy planes. "Our lead navigator brought us in too close to Dunkerque and they threw everything at us but the kitchen sink. One of the very first planes to cross the coast of France received a direct hit in its bomb bay. Their plane seemed to disintegrate in midair. It was not until months later that I discovered that Captain Simpson and Lt. Nick Cox were the only two members of the crew to survive such a mighty explosion. One can only surmise that the force of the blast blew their aircraft apart and they fell free. The same concussion evidently opened their parachute packs. They survived practically unscathed."

Even as he witnessed his group's first loss in combat, Cox himself nearly became a casualty. As the plane approached the target, enemy fighters started to appear, and with bombardier Ed Janic, he manned a machine gun in the B-24 nose. Suddenly he fell unconscious on the floor of the nose. Janic saw what happened and immediately secured a walkabout bottle of oxygen to Cox's face. According to Murphy, "The bombardier called to say the navigator was sick and that it was suicide to go into combat with him in that condition. We had a hurried talk over the interphone and then saw there was nothing to do but turn *Luke* around and go home. It almost broke the hearts of the crew when they headed back for England [the bombs were dumped] and saw the rest of the group continuing into enemy territory. When the other ships and crews returned they told of flak like huge clouds and fighters in swarms, some of the ships had been shot to hell, but *Luke* was so far a virgin."

Ramsay Potts, a former college instructor in economics, commissioned and awarded his wings four days after Pearl Harbor, piloted one of the B-24s that continued on to Lille.

"I was flying element lead, a twenty-four-plane formation," said Potts. "It seemed to me that we had no sooner formed up and turned toward France than we were over there. This was due to a 100-knot tailwind at 23,000 feet. We were supposed to have fighter escort but we never saw them. Very shortly after we penetrated the coast of France, we ran into some FW 190s and they attacked from different directions. It seemed to me most of the attacks were coming in from the rear. I had a tail gunner who was a pretty good man but shortly after the first attack, I couldn't contact him on the intercom radio. I thought perhaps he had been hit. I sent the engineer back to find out. He reported the man was in a state of shock, not from being hit, just from fright and he had frozen up. He wasn't firing his guns; he wasn't talking to anybody on the intercom.

"Then my left wingman got hit and his airplane caught on fire. I got a report nine chutes were seen. This coming on the heels of the problem with the tail gunner was another sort of psychological shock, because Simpson, the man flying the plane on my left, was my closest friend in the squadron. We overshot the Initial Point to turn into the bomb run because of the very high wind at our altitude. As a consequence we actually made a very poor bomb run. We were subjected to severe fighter attacks during that time. We dropped our bombs and later learned we had not hit the target.

"We turned and now were going back against that wind. Until this time it seemed as if we had been flying for a very short time. Now I kept looking down at the French landscape and it seemed to me we were hardly moving at all. Minutes after minutes rolled by and it was an interminable amount of time throughout which we were catching sporadic fighter attacks. There had been flak over the target, which, since this was our first time, was a little nerve wracking.

"Finally we got home and we had two airplanes make crash landings on the field and they tore off their landing gears and one lost its wings. Then we got news that another one had crash-landed on the beach. Altogether I felt it was a pretty tough operation.

"I went back to my quarters after the interrogation and was trying to light the small pot-bellied stove we had with some sort of cinders that passed as a form of charcoal. I was so cold. I think it was not only because it was damp and chilly, but also I suppose I was experiencing a kind of shock reaction from this mission plus evidence of fear. I don't remember throughout the whole rest of the war ever again feeling as fearful about going on missions as I did right after this first one. I couldn't get warm. I put on all kinds of sweaters and heavy jackets and even wrapped a big tartan blanket around myself while I tried to get the fire going.

"It was a typical early mission and later there were ones that were really tougher. But I never felt as badly afterwards as this time. My friend Simpson and the copilot and about five other members of the crew were captured by the Germans. Two of the members of the crew were killed and one was unaccounted for, a tech sergeant named Cox." The latter succeeded in evading capture. He worked his way to Spain before returning to the United Kingdom more than a year after his plane was shot down.

W. J. "Red" Komarek, after a radio flash about the attack on Pearl Harbor, left his home in the Yorkville section of New York City to enlist. Komarek first sought the Navy but when he couldn't pass their eye exam walked a half block to the Army recruiting station and signed up for the Air Corps. Initially, Komarek signed up for a radio operator's course but when too many applied, he gladly dropped out in favor of gunnery school. Conditions at the gunnery instruction field were less than ideal. "The pilots were staff sergeants who thought they were going to gunnery school, not to ferry aerial gunners," recalled Komarek. "We had no helmets and no intercom with the pilots and flew in AT-6s and O-47s. You sat with your back physically separated from the pilot and your .30-caliber machine gun was stowed in front of you on a tracking swivel. The instructions amounted to the pilot telling you to fire when in position with the tow target, that is, when he waggled his wings, and to stop firing when he waggled his wings again. He said at no time should you release your seat belt. On the first flight you learned you can't substitute a handkerchief tied on your head for a helmet, you can't reach a stowed machine gun without releasing your seat belt to get the gun to the quarter position against the wind, you had to struggle like hell against the slipstream to clamp the gun down for firing at the tow target."

Komarek was assigned to the 93d Bomb Group equipped with B-24s and became a tail gunner for a Liberator named *Globe Trotter*. After four months of antisubmarine patrol over the Gulf of Mexico, Komarek, along with other airmen, sailed to England on a troopship. The B-24s practiced for their encounters with the enemy in mock combat with RAF Spitfires. "The Spits barreled in and we tracked in our sights and pretended leading and firing. Although the turret was equipped and fitted for gun cameras, they were not available to us. We had no way to evaluate our effectiveness." Nor did he relish the high-altitude flights. "I was cold and my seat seemed tiny and we appeared to go slow. I had to get used to adjusting oxygen for altitude and the heat suit. The door of the turret was a real obstacle. I never seemed to get enough heat in the suit and the electric gloves were worth-less. I was getting the impression that we should know these things by osmosis. If it weren't for the bull sessions with other combat men, we would have had a helluva time."

On the 93d's maiden mission to Lille, Komarek said, "Seeing my first flak burst I called the Skipper. Imitating John Wayne, I said, 'It looks like they're shooting at us, but the bursts are low and behind.' No sooner said and big black bursts with a whoosh and pebbles hitting the window sounds seemed to be all around us. I quickly forgot John Wayne. They found us and I had better imitate a tail gunner. I didn't see any fighter escort but a fighter was diving down on us. I watched fascinated as he dove below and disappeared. I didn't fire! Why? Buck fever? Then there was another. I tracked him firing short bursts. I wasn't leading him enough. My tracers were arching away from his tail. I led the next, firing short bursts when suddenly my sight was filled with a B-24, our left wing ship. I stopped firing momentarily. Did I stop in time or did I put a couple of fifties in its nose? I strained to see if there was any damage.

"I kept squeezing the green balloon on my oxygen mask. We were told to do this to prevent your saliva from freezing the vent, since this was a constant-flow system, the green bag would burst with the vent clogged. My green balloon was growing larger. What the hell am I doing here, anyway? I should be back in high school."

The tail gunner on *Globe Trotter* gaped at the sights and coped with his own problems. "God Almighty, what is that! A 24 trailing smoke . . . going down. I see chutes, one . . . two . . . three . . . watch for fighters . . . short bursts. The bal-loon on my mask is now twice as large. Pull the feed line off the intake and stick the hose in your mouth. I don't feel so good. Then it had to happen, biting down on a hose with pressure building, the hose spewed out of my mouth. Where did it go? Grab it from the turret valve and trace it down to the end. Am I seeing purple dots? Put the hose back in your mouth . . . don't bite down on it. Look for fighters. . . . There they are, twin booms, they're P-38s and Spits, just like the cavalry. What a sight! I had a seat on the fifty-yard line watching our fighters roaring in to attack. A fighter was going down . . . for every German there was a Spit or 38 on its tail. . . . An intercom check from the pilot . . . all okay, thank God, nobody got hit. I got through the mission, oxygen trouble and all."

Almost two weeks later, the 97th Bomb Group, on its final assignment for the Eighth Air Force before transferring to the North Africa–based Twelfth, reeled from punishment meted out over the Lorient U-boat bases. The tally showed 3 aircraft shot down, with 30 airmen missing, 6 planes damaged, 5 crewmen wounded. Worse, even direct hits with five one-ton bombs made no dent in the submarine pens. A navigator who saw the explosives fall dead on target reported, "They bounced off those massive concrete U-boat shelters like Ping-Pong balls."

Walt Kelly survived the Lorient debacle but the new place of business challenged even the most optimistic. "We were to be led to North Africa to participate in Torch by Jimmy Doolittle, the newly designated commander of the Twelfth. After several days [in transit] we flew on to Africa where the ground forces were still in the midst of skirmishes with the Vichy French who were supporting the Germans.

"Amid sniper fire and bare base conditions, we struggled to load bombs and refuel the planes from five-gallon cans. Some were hopelessly bogged down in the mud at Tafaraoui and couldn't operate. The turf field was a soggy mess. We offloaded the bombs and managed to fly out to Biskra, an oasis resort on the edge of the Sahara. We went from mud to sand. Every takeoff left a sandstorm behind. Some air crews, mine included, were lucky enough to have rooms at the Palace and other hotels in town." For the others, living standards dropped far below what they experienced in England. The flak and enemy fighters remained as dangerous as ever.

The 97th was not the only outfit lost to strategic bombing by the Eighth Air Force during this period. Ramsay Potts took a squadron from the 93d to a southern RAF base to perform sweeps and searches into the Atlantic, antisubmarine patrols as part of the preparation for Torch. The British had long advocated use of the B-24s with their extended range for combating U-boats.

"We didn't know anything about any invasion of North Africa," said Potts. "We were trying to locate submarines and use our depth charges to kill them. On a very long patrol down into the Bay of Biscay, we were returning. I'd gotten up out of my seat and looked over the ocean to the left and for just a moment I mistook what I saw for a flight of birds, way off, close to the water. This flock of birds turned out to be twin-engine German ME 210s. There were five of them. I jumped back into the pilot's seat and noticed a split in the flight. I was getting reports from the rear gunner and it quickly became apparent that two of them were trying to move ahead of us and two were turning in toward us. One had moved to get into position for an attack at the tail.

"As they started climbing, so did I because we had been below a ragged cloudbed that was maybe 2,500 to 3,000 feet above us. The first airplane came in toward us and as he approached, I turned sharply toward him. He then came right across the top of our airplane. It seemed I could practically reach up and touch him. Our top gunner just split him open and he burst into flames practically atop our airplane. At the same time the waist gunner was claiming that he was firing at another plane making an attack and the tail gunner was firing on a third. The waist gunner claimed he'd shot down his man and so did the tail gunner. Nobody saw the plane coming toward the tail go down except the gunner but one other crewman saw the plane shot down by the man at the waist.

"By the time I completed the maneuvers, I had done about a 270-degree shift, a part circle climbing and getting up and approaching the cloud cover overhead. When I ducked into the clouds we didn't have any attacks from the two ME 210s that had streaked out in front to intercept us. I stayed in the cloud cover, set a course that finally brought us to Land's End where we landed in high spirits because we knew we had shot down two airplanes and were claiming three. A message had gone on ahead of us. They knew we had been under attack and that we'd had an engagement. All of our squadron was out there and the RAF permanent party when we landed. They counted 156 .30-caliber holes in the airplane. No vital part had been hit and we felt pretty good. I had not been flying precisely as our operations procedure indicated. I should have been closer to the clouds but the deck had been lifting and I'd been careless and hadn't changed my procedure.

"Instead of congratulating me, the squadron commander said, 'What the hell were you doing, flying so far below the cloud cover?' He was not happy. Instead of being gratified that we had shot down two or three German aircraft, he was angry that I had exposed the plane. The RAF interrogated the intelligence people. They were skeptical. They did not believe one bomber could have an engagement with five fighter aircraft and survive. They questioned my crew for a very long time. Finally, they seemed to get a story that satisfied them. So they gave us two probably destroyed and one possible. Later, through communications intercepts, the coastal command established that we shot down three planes and the RAF considered it quite a feat.

"That evening I was sitting in the mess when an RAF corporal came in with a message for Captain Potts. It was a teletype from Air Chief Marshal Joubert who was head of coastal command. It congratulated me and my crew for a fine performance. He commended us so naturally I took it to the squadron commander and said, 'Look at this message from Joubert. Perhaps this will cause you to change your mind a little bit about what happened today.'

"He looked at it and said, 'You know what this proves?' 'No,' I said. 'What does it prove?' He said, 'It proves Air Chief Marshal Joubert doesn't know his ass from third base.' "

The use of B-24s as part of the antisubmarine campaign actually preceded the assignment of Potts and his unit by several months. Bill Topping, a native of a small town near Roanoke, Virginia, piloted during a tour with the 19th Anti-Submarine Squadron that patrolled the waters around Gander protecting convoys and searching for submarine wolfpacks. "I never saw a German sub but we did see what happened to ships getting torpedoed while in convoys."

When the U.S. Navy assumed responsibility for that sector of the Atlantic, Topping flew to England to perform anti-sub work in a B-24 off the southeast coast. Attached to the RAF, Topping and the officers lived comfortably in a hotel. "We had tea servings. I had a batman who took care of my clothes and shined my shoes. Next door lived a group of Land Army girls. The missions and techniques were the same as those of the RAF. Stay in cloud cover as much as possible, use radar to indicate someone was out there. We had depth charges and in an attack were to dive down to about fifty feet, and as bombardier I was to string out five depth charges. It was hours and hours of boredom, flying the Bay of Biscay, sometimes going to Gibraltar to refuel. I belonged to the whale and ale club, getting a couple of whales we dove on. The British were quite concerned about whales in the Bay of Biscay, always asking how many we saw and in what direction they were headed. But one day, it all came together.

"I spotted the subs, there were three, followed by four, all on the surface going toward France, probably for supplies including torpedoes. We broke radio silence and the navigator gave our position. Then we attacked. We dove on them and I tried to string out the depth charges. As we pulled out and swung away from them, we were taking a lot of hits from the subs. We had attacked the first three subs and were getting ready for another depth charge run when the tail gunner said, 'Nothing came out, no depth charges.'

"I rushed back to the bomb bays and I found out what had happened. We were helpless. We had been shot up so bad on the left side of the bomb bay that the main wiring system along the top left was shredded. There was nothing we could do and we had to stay out of range of shells from the subs, which could throw up a lot of lead.

"We waited until other planes came in, the first a British Sunderland. I said, 'Bring me some ammunition from the back.' I had a .50-caliber nose gun and I figured I can at least fire if we attack. We dove and I was shooting at the Germans on the subs who were firing at us and trying to get the Sunderland behind us. I don't know how many I hit; they looked like ten pins in a bowling alley, just being knocked off the sub. The Sunderland dropped some depth charges and the tail gunner told us he had dropped them and was still with us. Six or seven other planes came in and we proceeded to lead, telling them to follow us. They started hitting the other subs. One of the Wellingtons went into the water, losing all but one of the crew. Some Royal Navy sloops showed up. They fanned out, went through throwing their depth charges and firing off their decks. It was a long battle, lasted six hours, but it seemed like all day."

The British Air Ministry announced the engagement sank three U-boats but Topping upset his commanding officer. "Back at the base, my CO wanted to know why I didn't drop any depth charges. He was a West Pointer and we did not get along too well. I made the snotty remark, 'I just missed getting the Congressional Medal of Honor.' He asked, 'How come?' I said, 'I should have gone back into the bomb bay, grabbed one of the depth charges and dove out, giving my life.' That comment gave me a lot of trouble. I deserved it; I was always causing him a lot of headaches." Topping saw no more subs while posted to southeastern England.

Absorbing painful lessons on the job, group and squadron leaders realized their aircraft lacked protection for the crews. Enterprising engineering officers of one B-24 squadron arranged for a local contractor to pave the nose compartment floor with boiler plate, not only adding protection to the navigator and bombardier but apparently also providing better balance to the aircraft. All planes began to receive similar modifications. Sheet-steel plates added to the side of the ships shielded the pilots. In fact, engineers, maintenance workers, and factories responding to the complaints, critiques, and requests of air crews, constantly tinkered or changed in varying degrees all of the planes flown by the Eighth Air Force throughout the course of the war.

Ground crews improvised. Whit Hill, a mechanic with the 91st Bomb Group, recalled, "When we first arrived on the scene, our equipment was limited by a 'table of authorization' that was inadequate to say the least. We had no aluminum sheets to use for patches, rivet guns, or even hand-rivet sets, to rivet on patches. In Hangar #1, however, there was an RAF maintenance shop whose friendly personnel were more than ready to assist us all they could. We 'borrowed' sheets of aluminum and used their machine shop to make hand-rivet sets and other repair equipment.

"One day I was ordered to attend an airframe school at the Eighth Air Force's Burtonwood supply depot. While there, Captain Larson, our engineering officer, appeared, and together we reviewed the depot's supply bins. While he distracted the depot guide, I was busy loading up Captain Larson's staff car with much-needed but unauthorized equipment such as straight and offset electrical drills, rivet guns, rivet sets, bucking bars, etc. On return we were ready to meet the action. Meanwhile, the group sheet-metal crews had obtained surplus bomb-loading carts and modified them into portable sheet-metal workbenches that included electric and air compressors, a floodlight, workbench with vise, storage for sheet metal and parts, and room for eight toolboxes used by the sheet-metal crew, all towed by a Jeep assigned to the crew chief.

"At the end of each mission the battle and mechanical damage of each returning aircraft was assessed and time to make necessary repairs was estimated. The planes requiring the least amount of work were the first to be repaired. When there were many shot-up aircraft, the sheet-metal crews would help each out. There were times when the sheet-metal crews did not get to bed for seventy-two hours. None of the men from the ground crew—mechanics, electricians, prop specialists, bomb loaders, sheet-metal repairmen—had any set daily working hours. Everyday was Monday; it was 'work until you drop' and the password was 'how soon?' "

Frequent thick fogs, towering mountains of clouds, capricious winds, and sudden shifts from crystal-clear skies to ground-obscuring murk frustrated all Eighth Air Force pilots and navigators. Routine practice flights or trips to other bases could be as dangerous as a mission. The conditions forced innumerable unplanned landings, led to crashes, lost planes, and killed crewmen. For bombers shot up during missions, with hydraulic and electrical systems out of whack, and desperately wounded men aboard, the weather extended the nightmare beyond the zone of combat.

The efforts of the first heavyweight bombers, the airmen, and their ground support did not impress Winston Churchill, still unconvinced of either the quality of U.S. bombers or the daylight, precision-bombing campaign. In a letter to Air Chief Marshal Sir Charles Portal on 2 November, Churchill complained, "The number of American Air Force personnel [in England] has risen to about 55,000. . . . So far the results have been pitifully small. . . . Far from dropping bombs on Germany, the daylight bombers have not ventured beyond Lille." [RAF Lancasters had already paid their disrespects to Berlin and Cologne among other German targets.] The British prime minister expressed frustration with the political currents that defeated what he considered the Allies' best interests. "Considering the American professional interests and high reputation which are engaged in this scheme, and the shock it would be to the American people and to the Administration if the policy proved a glaring failure, we must expect most obstinate perseverance in this method." He gloomily concluded, "for many months ahead large numbers of American air personnel will be here playing very little part in the war."

Oddly enough, Eaker's opposite number in the RAF, Air Marshal Arthur Harris, the bomber chief, was one of the few Britons who approved of the U.S. theory and practice. He wrote to a subordinate commander, "I have never been apprehensive about the ability of the heavy bomber to look after itself in daylight vis-à-vis the fighter. There is not the least doubt in my mind that if we and all the available Americans started daylight attacks against the less-heavily defended targets in Germany by big formations of heavy bombers now, we should knock the German fighter force out of the sky in two or three months, by the simple process of shooting them down. . . . It has all along been our experience that whenever the rear gunner, even at night, sees the enemy fighter first, he either destroys it or the fighter refuses to come in and attack."

At the time Harris made these comments, December 1942, the U.S. Army Air Corps, for all of its 55,000 people in the United Kingdom, could never mobilize much more than seventy-five effective bombers for a mission, in contrast to the several hundred from the RAF. Harris, a man with a reputation for deviousness that masked his own implacable ideas, never showed any real willingness to switch his forces from night to day. Furthermore, as he should have known then and certainly was shown shortly, the contest between bombers and fighters was anything but weighted in favor of the heavyweights.

If anything, the situation for American airmen in North Africa was even more tenuous. Early in December 1942, David Jones, temporarily leading the 319th Bomb Group after its official commander was shot down and killed, received orders to hammer Bizerte. A newly designated group commander, Walter Agee, arrived, and to familiarize him with operations, Jones put him in his copilot's seat. "We were bombing at about 1,200 feet because we didn't have any bombsights. I get out to the airfield and whappo, they knocked out my left engine, and the trim and engine instruments, the bloody works are gone. I am cranking all the rudder and all the wheel I can get into it and it didn't have any air speed. I couldn't advance the throttle. I headed north to the coast, afraid the thing would snap on me.

"The terrain is like it is around El Paso, just a bunch of little nobs, sand hills. I went down in a kind of clear area and between two little sand mounds, sort of took the wings and then slid forward. The poor guy in the nose was thrown forward and out and then we ran over him. Agee was knocked out in the copilot seat. When we finally came to a halt I shook him a little bit, got him awake and out the top. Everybody got out and we went back, picked up the guy who was still on the ground. We took a piece of flap, put him on it as a stretcher, and headed north for the coast.

"We hadn't walked 200 yards and looked up and here is a whole line of skirmishers, German. I had a pistol in my pocket. I pointed at the pistol. [The soldier] took it out. Sam [Agee] was hurting a bit and kept saying, 'Don't let them give me any sulfa because I am allergic.' We got that point across. I think my nose was broken, my back was hurting. They took me and one other guy to Bizerte to the fighter headquarters and Sam and the other guys to a field hospital."

Fed cheese and wine, set in a deck chair, Jones went through a cursory interrogation that in his memory mainly consisted of questions about why the U.S. had allied itself with the "Russians" and a request not to run off. He was expected to leave for a European prison lager [camp] aboard Junker-52 transports the following day. But just as he walked toward his plane with a guard, "Here the sirens go and I looked up and saw the goddamn B-26s right at the bomb-release line. Everybody started running. I was hobbling like hell. There was a little depression and I fell in this damn ditch. The airplane I was supposed to get in had received a direct hit. There was nothing left but a hole."

Loaded aboard another ship, Jones flew to Italy where he rode a train bound for Germany. "We had lots of room in our compartment, while people outside were standing in the aisles. We stopped someplace and the Red Cross girls were just like everywhere. They were running around and giving out doughnuts and coffee. We were still pretty much gentlemen; we were combatants and they treated you that way." Later on in the war prisoners endured much harsher handling from civilian and military personnel.

17

Defeat

DESPITE DARLAN'S AGREEMENT TO A CEASE-FIRE FOR FRENCH military on 11 November, uncertainties remained about the reactions of military outposts. Anxious to secure forward footholds at airfields that could intercept enemy planes before they reached the jammed harbors at Casablanca and Oran, the 509th Parachute Regiment boarded C-47s to drop on Youks-les-Bains, close to the Algeria-Tunisia border. "We had two or three Spitfires escorting us," said William Yarborough. "It was real hostile territory. A German airfield was not far away. We could see on the ground fortifications that the French had thrown up and we felt these guys were the same caliber as those that had shot us down [near Tafaraoui] and didn't really like Americans. We felt we'd have to fight and they had all the advantages. They had the high ground overlooking the drop zone. It was a very tense moment after we hit the ground and marched up the hill toward these French fortifications, weapons in hand.

"Finally, Colonel Berges, got out of his foxhole, came

down to meet Ed Raff, stuck out his hand and embraced Ed. Then the troops came out of their holes and it was that way all down the line. They took the Zouave badge—they were the Zouave regiment—and pinned it on us. We joined together in picking up the parachutes and all signs we were there. There was a new spirit in the French. It was the first time they could turn and fight the Krauts. When a German JU 88 came the next day, expecting to land, he was shot down by French antiaircraft."

Amid the self-congratulations and puffery of the first successes against the Vichy French and some Italian troops in North Africa, some foresaw a much tougher war ahead. Lieutenant Colonel John Waters, a son-in-law of Patton, cautioned his exuberant 1st Armored Division tankers, "We did very well against the scrub team. Next week [figuratively] we hit the Germans. Do not slack off in anything. When we make a showing against *them*, you may congratulate yourselves."

By 24 November, Eisenhower had established his headquarters in Algiers and the augmented forces in North Africa began a campaign to push the enemy out of Tunisia. He delegated British lieutenant general Kenneth Anderson to lead an offensive of combined troops from his own country with the American 1st Infantry Division. As Waters had warned, the foe showed considerably more strength and counterattacks stalled advances. Increasingly, the weaknesses of the U.S. troops surfaced. They were not scrupulous enough in maintaining blackouts; they did not dig adequate foxholes; camouflage was perfunctory; reconnaissance was weak; communications broke down; vehicles in convoys followed too closely, offering prime targets for German planes. But in December, weather stopped the drive on Tunisia. Rain pelted down in torrents that mired tanks and wheeled vehicles. When Eisenhower, already troubled by a stretched-out battle line and supply shortages, watched four soldiers struggle fruitlessly to extricate a single motorcycle from the muck beside a road, he called off the offensive for two months.

On 24 December, an assassin fired a fatal bullet into Darlan. The vacuum in leadership enabled the Allies to broker an arrangement between Giraud and de Gaulle. The former would soon fade into the background while the leader of the Free French gradually strode to center stage.

The 44th and 97th Bomb Groups, with Lu Cox and Walt Kelly, in Liberators and Fortresses, as well as the 15th Bomb Group of Bill O'Dell flying lighter bombers, attacked enemy shipping and airdromes. The air war increasingly pitted fighter planes against one another or deployed fighters for tactical ground support. But the downpours transformed grass airstrips into little more than swamps, curtailing operations. The Germans enjoyed hard-surfaced fields.

Among those involved early in the game was the 33d Fighter Group, commanded by Lt. Col. Philip Cochran. An Erie, Pennsylvania, product, Cochran in 1935 enlisted in the Army Air Corps. With his experience Cochran earned command of the 33d. "I left the United States about October 28th," recalled Cochran. "I was on the British carrier *Archer*, a slingshot [catapult] job. I had thirty-five P-40s and I was in charge of the advance element of the 33d Group. These boys were very inexperienced and knew nothing about what we were heading into. The catapulting of the P-40s was very successful. Out of 103 we catapulted, we lost four.

"We landed on an airdrome where there were still snipers, but the armistice had been signed and we had no fighting to do. Our boys were in a state of what, for want of a better name, is called war hysteria. Why it occurs I don't know.

Everybody seemed calm enough—but we wrecked airplanes on the landing at Port Lyautey. We lost nine airplanes from our own action. Boys who had never shown any tendency to be nervous or do erratic things, suddenly, through some peculiar human reaction, did unlooked-for things—in landing the airplanes, mostly.

"We found we were terrifically in need of training. We trained very diligently for about three weeks on what we had heard from the front, mostly on formations. Then suddenly we were sent forward to the Thelepte area [just over the Tunisian border]. Our move forward was very, very confused. We ended up with two halves of two squadrons and, having brought seven people forward, I was the ranking person. We first lived in a French house and the first night we had the thirty-five pilots all sleeping in this house to get out of the cold. While lying there shaking with cold, I thought I would be the horrible example of the man who put all his pilots in one house and one bomb got every one of them. The next night we slept in the ground and I don't mean *on* the ground. At Thelepte there is a large ravine and our enlisted men went back to the primitive cave man method—they actually dug into the sides of the ravine and lived that way. Officers themselves dug—anybody who wanted to live there dug himself a hole—and, if he could get two fellows he liked and wanted to be that close to, those two helped him dig a larger hole. It was hard digging, too. Some of our little abodes went eight-feet deep. If you left the place where you lived, there was no way you could orient yourself in the dark and get back. Nobody moved after five-thirty or six o'clock in the evening. We spent all the hours of darkness in the holes and all the hours of daylight either jumping into other holes, or being on mission.

"We found right off the bat," confessed Cochran, "that the

Germans knew an awful lot more than we did and all we had
was our eagerness. We started out with very, very poor formations. We built formations tactically based on the defense
you have in the P-40. We learned the P-40 was quick in a
turn and you couldn't find a guy on the field who wasn't
ready to send a testimonial to the people of Curtiss Wright
because the quick turn of the P-40 saved every one of their
necks every time they turned around. I think I can count ten
times when, if the P-40 wouldn't turn, I would have been
gone long ago." Like Jimmy Thach, Cochran opted for a
two-plane unit.

Lacking radar, the airmen relied on an early-warning
system that resembled what Chennault employed. French
gendarmes stationed in towns between the lines would telephone the airdrome, advising the approach, direction, and
the number of aircraft. Unfortunately, Cochran noted, "Any
airplane was enemy to them. They were hard for them to
distinguish. They had us running like mad—chasing our
own planes some of the time." Still, the P-40 pilots frequently intercepted the JU 88s as they began their run from
11,000 feet down to 4,000. At first the Americans discouraged the raids by knocking down a substantial number forty
or fifty miles from their target. But then the enemy started
an escort service and the air war escalated.

While the Allied drive into Tunisia halted in December
1942, the Eighth Air Force resumed its buildup of men and
planes. To buttress Torch, the British-American high command had dispatched the 93d, 97th, and 301st Bomb Groups
along with the 1st, 31st, and 82d Fighter Groups to Doolittle's
command in Tunisia. With the 92d Bomb Group committed
to training, the transfers depleted the thin ranks of warriors
and machines available to Eaker. As winter approached he
could muster only recent arrivals from the 44th, 303d, 305th,

and 306th Bomb Groups and the only American-flown escorts, Spitfires of the 4th Fighter Group.

Captain Billy Southworth Jr. commanded one of the 303d's B-17Fs. Southworth, whose father led the St. Louis Cardinals in 1942 to a World Series championship, had himself shown promise as an outfielder and played for a high minor-league team before enlisting in the Air Corps nearly a year before the Japanese attack. After a training flight in which he deftly handled his plane with only three functioning engines, he noted in his diary, "Sergeant Means who has been with me for about two and a half months, said, 'You are good, aren't you, sir?' Hell yes, Means. They have confidence in me. Schueler, my navigator, nervous type, but a solid guy, wasn't at all bothered."

In addition to comments about the poor condition of the aircraft, the journal frequently notes the efforts of the Cardinals in the pennant race, the failings of superior officers, and romantic entanglements of himself and his associates. Southworth courted and broke an engagement before pursuing numerous "swell gals." He remarked on navigator Jon Scheuler taking "the fatal step" proposing by telephone, and later bombardier Milt Conver also married.

In Michigan, Southworth picked up a B-17 that would carry him to England. During a layover, he noted, "Had a party last night. We're all confined to the post so the girls came to see us. 'Spook' Hargrove threw a bottle through a window at the end of a BOQ. Lieutenant Mitchell put his hand through another and cut it badly. The boys were high. Colonel Hughes wanted to know who was baying at the moon at 2:20 A.M. Stockton was out with [name deleted by author] who likes to spread her affections about. Seems that all of the girls did.

"I'll never marry Helene hard as she's trying. Babs proposed persistently to me last night, second date. She's very pretty but wouldn't have her on a silver platter. There's Ann, wealthy in looks but lacks something. Ruth had everything but was too fond of herself. Betty a swell gal but too set in ways and lacks oomph. Cliffy might be a possibility, haven't known her long enough. I'd like to get into this damn war and return so I can settle down."

On the final day of October, Southworth could scribble notes about the last legs from Newfoundland to a field near Liverpool. "Got off on instruments and was in the soup three-quarters of the trip. It took us ten and a half hours. Dillinger, my copilot, slept most of the way. Means, the sergeant engineer, did likewise, while Doughty, Radio, and Schueler, Navigator, did a bang-up job. Jon missed his ETA by one minute. Land was sighted, all men were alert at their stations ready to fire (save Means, asleep). We were impressed by the jagged shores [Ireland], green hills, hedge fences, beautiful estates, picturesque, with ancient moats of King Arthur's time surrounding them. Airports then littered the way to Prestwick."

The 303d made Molesworth its home and Southworth said early in November, "Rained every day since we've been here. These muddy days, a foot deep in places I'll never forget. Cold, wet, and black nights, cold wind stinging your face while your feet just get used to that dead cold feeling. The British are a fine people. Take the bitter with the sweet, defeat and victory without feeling—they hang on, just keep hanging on. They aren't deceiving, love their country, and are proud of it. We'll win this war but it will take a long time."

Southworth expressed unhappiness with his superiors. "Lieutenant Joe Haas got Dumbbell [award for a blunder] after Captain Blythe and Maj. Calloway snafued a situation worse than Joe. Told Col. Wallace [group commander] of a desirable landing procedure, also the desirable way to fly a formation. It wasn't appreciated nor listened to, but I'll wager that they'll adopt it as their own idea. . . . God damn!! Flew with Maj. Calloway's outfit and he snafu as usual. He led a very poor formation and was lost nearly all the time. . . . Flew No. 2 with Maj. Sheridan. Dillinger is the poorest excuse for a copilot that I've ever seen. He went to sleep three times this morning on our flight." The Southworth crew named its B-17 *Bad Check* in the obvious hope that it, too, would always bounce back. Throughout the war, however, crews often flew different aircraft, sharing them with others and switching because of malfunctions or combat damage.

The winds of war blew together an unlikely companion for Southworth in the person of Jon Schueler, the navigator for Southworth's plane, son of a businessman who struggled through the Depression. Astigmatism in one eye eliminated pilot training and Schueler graduated flight training as a navigator. Like Southworth and the other young males in uniform, Schueler, too, partied enthusiastically when not carrying out his flight duties. "All of us knew we were flirting with death from the moment we saw the planes. It was like the feeling at the beginning of a love affair, when all of the enticement is joy, yet one senses also the excitement of unknown possibilities, sadness, treachery, death. Larry [another bombardier in training] and I had seen the two planes crash on that first day and the image didn't leave our minds."

A third member of the crew was Milt Conver, a native of Columbus, Ohio. A graduate of Staunton Military Academy in Virginia, he was an excellent boxer, swimmer, and college football player. After washing out as a pilot, Conver elected to become a bombardier.

Neither as opinionated as Southworth, nor as eloquent as Schueler, Conver filled his diary with matter-of-fact accounts of his days, noting whom he saw, problems in getting paid, festivities at the officers' club, and classes connected with his craft. In his accounts, on 22 August 1942, he noted Schueler's marriage. "Jean and I stood up for them. Gene Rochester took my hat by mistake." His entry for the following day reports the death of several friends, killed in a crash. "Bodies were so messed up they were hard to identify. My hat was found and they thought that I was on the ship." The source of the error lay in the cap taken by the unfortunate Gene Rochester at Schueler's wedding. On 24 August he announced his wedding to Jean. "I suppose both our families will be sorry and I know they'll say we're crazy." In fact, neither set of parents greeted the news with enthusiasm.

A soldier formed from still another mold, SSgt. Bill Fleming, a Jenkins, Kentucky, coal miner's son, one of eight children, born in 1924, operated machine guns from the waist of the Southworth plane during its first missions. "We got along pretty well. Billy Southworth was a very good pilot but he did not associate with his crew very much. He gave you the feeling that socially he was above you. In October 1942, at Battle Creek, Michigan, we received our new planes from the factory and flew them to Bangor, then to Gander and, finally, to Prestwick. Molesworth became our base of operation until the end of the war. None of the crew, myself included, at this time had ever fired a .50-caliber machine gun from a B-17. Most of our training was on .30-calibers out of small planes. We were due for some on-the-job training. At Molesworth we had a few practice missions. We were so young we didn't realize what we were getting into. Orders came for us to go 17 November on our first mission, Saint-Nazaire."

Bombardier Conver described the facilities at Molesworth. "There is a great deal of mud. The rooms are large enough, but the heating system—one small coal stove—isn't good at all. Being in a combat area, the Group is scattered all over the four parts of the field, as are the airplanes. The weather is as expected, rain and cold. I can't see how we can operate around here in B-17s and I wouldn't be surprised if we moved out of England in the near future."

On the eve of the first mission an exuberant Southworth declared, "On the morrow, pilots and crews will spring into action, all looking forward to a day of 'Success!' We bomb Saint-Nazaire submarine base, a heavily protected area. It will be our first combat experience. We expect to find opposition without looking too hard. It's not like patrol. Last raid on Saint-Nazaire, three Forts were lost."

According to Fleming, however, "Success!" was denied because, "Somewhere in the lead plane, the navigator got off course and we missed the entire target. We didn't come close and had to return to base with all of the bombs on board. We weren't allowed to drop them over occupied France. It was a big disappointment. There was no antiaircraft fire or enemy airplanes. Germans flew around us a couple of times wondering who we were. I guess they were as curious about us as we were about them."

On the morning of 18 November, Southworth awakened at 5:30 A.M. In his diary, he wrote, "Seemed as if I were going on a hunting trip back home. Carefully selected clothes, papers, pencil, oxygen equipment, pistol, etc. Off to eat a quick breakfast, then to the briefing room where we get the dope. The target La Pallice, French seaport, sub base, workshops, factories. Secondary is Lorient. I missed my place in the taxi procession as the wind and takeoff position had changed. All seemed to be taken care of before turning 'em over. Jenkins, a damn good man, to be my waist gunner, bombs loaded, crew intact. Twenty minutes before takeoff time I am told the primer is broken. I did all in my power to start them. It worked. Then due to some poor headwork on Lt. Robey's part, I lost my spot taxiing. I was mad, damn mad.

"We took off at 10:00. I quickly got into formation and stuck tight—no help from Dillinger [the copilot]. I did all the work that day. We were over an overcast, then there was the French coast. Peaceful, pretty country but we had been warned what would come. Approaching Nantes we were hopped by German pursuit and heavy flak. One of the boys said on interphone, 'Here they come, 6 UP.' Guns started to chatter, formation tightened. Bursts of flak came close. We began our evasive action. My arms began to ache, steam and sweat rolled off me. Dillinger sat there, looking out of his window, either scared to death or bored with it all. Flak would bounce our ship now and then. I just bore down harder, just flew tight automatically.

"We began to circle as though we were lost. Jon called up and said we were over Saint-Nazaire, a big Nazi sub base—good target. An FW dived at the 306 [Bomb Group] formation, then made a feint at us. We were being attacked from the rear. Our outfit downed three ME 109s of six attacking planes. Fleming and [Waldo] Brandt [tail gunner] sighted thirty FW 190s keeping out of range. We kept on circling. Flak made large bursts above, below, to the side, just a few feet from us. We flew through their smoke. Bomb doors finally opened, we were on our run. Flak bursts were intense—Bombs away.

"We started ours after the colonel had let his go. They were excellent hits. Ten 500-pounders in each ship, twenty-one of them after Roby turned back. They sure looked good. We then headed out to sea and home. I let Dilly handle the throttles to give one arm a rest. Soon enough he was asleep and we all but passed the colonel up. I was damn mad, hit his heavy flying suit with the back of my hand. The colonel landed at Chelveston, me and Goetz behind. It was the wrong target but a good one. Won't be much good for several months to come."

Conver reported, "About 12:10 P.M., we arrived at what the lead ship thought was La Rochelle. Both myself and Jon [Schueler] knew it wasn't. The antiaircraft batteries had opened up by this time but they hadn't gotten our range yet. We flew around and around waiting for the lead ship to do something. During this time, Jon and I figured out that we were at Saint-Nazaire. . . . The lead ship opened their bomb bay doors and the rest of us did likewise. We started on a bombing run but turned off due to the fact the sun was in our eyes, so they told us later. We then made a large circle and started another run. By this time the flak was getting very heavy and very close. We finally let our bombs go and I'm sure they hit the target even if we didn't get a picture of them. We returned by the way of water. My ears hurt; I was very tired and hungry."

The postmortem criticized the 303d for having struck at Saint-Nazaire instead of the briefed objective, La Pallice, 100 miles away. Furthermore, the 500-pounders could barely have scratched the concrete walls of the enemy sub base. At that the crews were fortunate the enemy was still apparently not well organized or proficient with its anti-aircraft.

Along with the 303d Bomb Group, the 305th, led by Curtis LeMay, had added its weight to the still-slender resources of the Eighth, making its first strike on 23 November. While junior officers like Southworth expressed satisfaction with their results, senior officers like LeMay, braced with the data provided by photo reconnaissance and other sources of intelligence, were aware that the strategic-bombing campaign was not inflicting serious damage. Furthermore, the enemy, having studied the tactics of the U.S. raiders, was raising the price of each foray.

LeMay decided that better results could only be achieved if the bombers maintained altitude and flew a straight course in the final moments before the drop. Evasive actions in the face of flak, implied in Southworth's descriptions of his first missions, defeated the work of the Norden bombsight and the concept of precision bombing. LeMay subsequently explained that he calculated, using an old artillery manual and compensating for the improvements of the German 88, that flak gunners would need to fire 372 rounds in order to guarantee a single hit on a B-17 in level flight. Whether his arithmetic was correct or not, LeMay believed the figures enough to like the odds. On the very first mission of the 305th LeMay announced to his dubious pilots they could take "no evasive action" over the target. He sought to allay their fears by announcing he would fly the lead aircraft. To be sure, the first ship over had a much better chance for survival than the tail-end Charlie when gunners had time to adjust for range and speed. Still, willingness to do what he asked of his subordinates gave him some credence.

American bombers, previously, also broke away from the bombing path when enemy fighters charged. LeMay directed his subordinates not to deviate from course because of the *Luftwaffe*. His luck and theory stood up in that initial raid; the Eighth Air Force intelligence photos showed that the 305th laid down twice as many bombs on target as any other group and lost no planes. It would take several months before the principles established by LeMay for his group, buttressed by the insights of other commanders, would become gospel.

Overall, however, the bombing continued to be erratic, with most of the ordnance missing the aiming point. LeMay also blamed inadequate training of navigators and bombardiers and the difficulty of concentrating upon the target while beset by the enemy fighters. He advised his superiors of the need for intensive instruction in navigation and target recognition under poor visibility or to pierce the veil of camouflage. He wrote to his mentor, Gen. Robert S. Olds, "There is a lot of difference between bombing an undefended target and running through a barrage of six-inch shellfire while a swarm of pursuits are working on you. . . . On our arrival here our gunners were very poorly trained. Most of them had not received enough shooting, especially at altitude, to even familiarize themselves with their equipment . . . due to weather and missions, the only practice we have had so far is shooting at FW 190s and ME 109s."

While the on-the-job education indicated improving marksmanship, LeMay searched for a way to circle the wagons when facing an attack by fighters. He theorized that the best means for bombers to protect themselves against interceptors lay in a modified staggered formation with the aircraft tightly packed. The arrangement pointed the maximum number of machine guns at would-be marauders. The combat box, for a bomb group based upon three squadrons, placed six to nine aircraft in the lead with a similar number as a second echelon 1,000 feet higher and to one side while the third squadron flew 1,000 feet below the leaders and on the opposite flank. When in proper array, a group could bear as many as 200 .50-caliber machine guns on any interlopers while a wing composed of several group boxes could respond to attack with between 500 and 600 machine guns.

The key for both bombing accuracy and for protection through tight formation flying was discipline, maintaining position no matter what the opposition did nor how difficult climatic conditions were. Gunners also needed to control themselves; indiscriminate shooting amid the tightly packed formations could and did result in deadly friendly fire. Other aerial warfare thinkers concocted similar schemes, but LeMay put his theories into practice. He personally supervised training runs from the top turret of a B-17. His insistence upon practice while other bomb-group crews enjoyed a respite from flight duty generated resentment. But the results achieved as a result of LeMay's demands impressed even those who scorned him as "Iron Ass."

Many months later, with all planes expected to follow the leaders and further ensure accuracy, the theorists developed the notions of lead navigators and lead bombardiers, with deputies in a position to take over should the guide abort or be knocked down. Unfortunately, at the time LeMay began to implement his ideas, there were so few units and crews in England, that opportunities to practice innovations were limited. The close-in formations, as Southworth experienced, demanded skill, knowledge, and concentration. Buffeted by winds, the turbulence of prop washes, and the jolts of ack-ack, it was inevitable that the huge aircraft, laden with heavy explosives, sluggish to respond at upper altitudes, would, even in the hands of the most capable pilots, collide as the margin of distance between them shortened. With just five full groups on hand, the numbers for mounting a wing-size box in the grand scheme projected by LeMay simply did not exist in the winter of 1942–43 and the early months of spring.

On 6 December, Milt Conver went on his second raid after having been unable to fly because of a head cold. He reported, "Someone saw an FW at 12 o'clock and at our same level. I scraped what ice I could from my window and got ready for him to come in. He dived a little to our right, then came directly at our ship from one o'clock. When he got in range I started to fire. I could see my tracers going into him, but he kept coming in at terrific speed until he was not more than seventy-five yards away. All this time Belk and Means were also pouring lead into him. Billy Southworth, who was sitting in the copilot's seat, said the Hun's prop started to stop. Fleming said the tail fell off, also part of the right wing, then the FW burst into flames. I must have fired more than 100 rounds without stopping and fear that I might have ruined my gun. We were all afraid we were going to be rammed. As Billy said, 'I could see his gold teeth.' Well, the fellow's a good German now. The thing that impressed me most was seeing the fire coming from his guns and the fact he only hit us twice."

The ebullience drained from Southworth as the missions continued. His diary refers to drunken brawls among the squadron officers and his frustration as the 303d's superiors refused to accept his recommendations for better tactics. Regular crewmen became unfit for duty. He noted his bombardier Milt Conver left *Bad Check* because of chronic ear infections. Respiratory problems felled navigator Jon Schueler. Flight surgeons scrubbed two of the regular gunners for what Southworth listed as "a dose," the GI slang for gonorrhea. The pilot himself sought treatment for a cold and sore throat, a threat to his own readiness.

Nevertheless Southworth was at the controls on 12 De-

cember for the run at Rouen/Sotteville, the same marshaling
yards stung by the first Eighth Air Force heavy bomber attack in August. "Twenty-one planes were scheduled for
takeoff, twenty took to the air. Two were knocked down before reaching target, nine turned back, and twelve dropped
their bombs, mind you," groused Southworth, "only twelve.
Smells like fish. Two minutes over the French coast here
come the Jerries, attacking in pairs and large numbers. Six
of our ships took positions on our right and an even level
(piss poor). Another bunch [was] on our left and level—
stinks. The Huns bore in. Here come four at me, firing
across my nose from one and two o'clock. Our guns, top turret and more guns blasted a steady stream. My window, already cracked, became streaked with cracks, at which I
became furious at Sgt. Means [top turret] for disobeying orders, firing forward as his zone was rear. The ball turret reported out of order.

"Flickenger received the shots meant for my ship. One
engine smoking, he disappeared behind me. Another moved
up into his place. Frequent attacks came from the rear. The
Spitfires had left us to return home. Continual attacks were
made by the yellow-nose FW 190s, often from the nose."
Southworth had observed the latest wrinkle in enemy tactics. The Germans had become aware that the front end of
the B-17F was highly vulnerable if one attacked from that
direction and at a slightly elevated angle. Only the top turret
then had a clear line of sight. The .30-caliber machine guns
used by a bombardier could not focus on hostile aircraft directly ahead.

Southworth's complaint about his bomb group maintaining the same altitude was justified. He remarked, "Our Forts
were so close and on the same level that [they] seemed to
lose effectiveness as the gunners couldn't fire and few tur-

rets could be brought into play. We made a turn for evasive purposes and *L*—— slid over, into me, missing by inches. I tried to get Dilly to watch him but he didn't and then again this numbskull slid fifty yards out of his formation and into ours. I skidded out of danger, extremely lucky to avoid a terrible crash. He hit our horizontal stabilizers, putting a damn good dent in it. I'll take a bow for being on the alert and saving our necks there."

Bad Check managed to dump its cargo in the vicinity of a railroad complex and fought off enemy fighters until Spitfires met the returning bombers. Although they had lost two aircraft with their crews, the surviving pilots buzzed the airdrome before settling in. "There was Schueler to meet us," wrote Southworth. "He's my boy." He proudly contrasted the 303d with that of the 91st assigned to the same target. Only six of its twenty-one aircraft crossed the Channel.

On 3 January, as dawn neared, an exultant Southworth scribbled in his diary, "Will be copilot with Col. Wallace [group CO]. We will lead five groups, 21 planes each. General [Haywood] Hansell, two-star boy will fly with us." Hansell served as head of Eighth Air Force planning. Southworth blithely remarked on the briefing data, "Smile lady luck. Over flak area of 56 heavy guns plus mobile installations of guns. Loads of fighters and loads of fun. Submarine installations and torpedo docks will be 'leveled.' What a red-letter day."

Indeed it was a momentous occasion. Acting as copilot while Wallace sat in the left seat, Southworth maneuvered a different plane than *Bad Check* to the French coast. In an elliptical and disjointed account he reported, "It seemed to be deadly peaceful. There was no escort. The general seemed to be a good stick. We got on a four-minute bombing run. The colonel thought he heard someone say, 'Bombs away' and he turned off the run a couple of seconds early. He had a fit but cooled down. All going too perfect, then here they came. Four FW 190s from the front. [They] shot two down. Of our first nine ships over the target, four were shot down; they got seven in all. We've lost nine crews and ships in combat on eight missions.

"The general served sandwiches on the way home. The general said that we had some good Indians on our ship. 'For plain unadulterated guts,' he said, 'you boys have it.' Schueler did a fine job. Was pleased until I found out our losses. Sheridan and Goetz gone. Sure will miss Goetz, one of my best friends. We were all at the club after dinner. Bought Schueler a drink. Then a bunch of us began to flip coins. Loud singing began. More liquor was ordered. At 10:00 we left for Diddington and the nurses. I was drunk for the first time. Don't remember a thing. Guess we tore things up, running in and out of huts while girls screamed. One walked me around while I staggered. Wow! Got home—said 'Do I live here?' Froze at night, had a cramp."

According to Fleming, the facts of war came stunningly home to him on this, his third mission, after he missed several with the *Bad Check* crew because of illness, including one sudden onset of severe pains enroute which earlier had forced Southworth to abort a mission. "By this time we had experienced some antiaircraft fire, but not enough to make you think somebody was trying to kill you. It wasn't that bad. The third mission [for Fleming] to Saint-Nazaire was the shocker for all of us. Over the target the antiaircraft fire was very heavy and it was hitting the planes, we started to realize somebody was really shooting at us. All of a sudden the plane on our wing, the squadron leader, Major Sheridan's took a direct hit and completely blew up. Pieces of it flew all over our plane, knocked holes in the wings and the stabilizer. It was a terrible shock to see. None of us could believe what had happened. But by the time we got off that target we knew Germany was no playground anymore. When we got back to our field, the ten empty beds from the lost crew made everybody realize what could happen."

Navigator Schueler described the routine of these first forays and his reactions. "We'd be awakened at 2:30 A.M. and we'd dress in the cold of the room and slog outside into the rain and muck and we'd have our breakfast and then we'd go to the briefing room. 'Attention!' We'd pop to and the colonel would stride down the aisle and mount the platform and announce the target. 'Saint-Nazaire' and we'd groan and laugh at the same time. From then on it was business. We'd be told the time of takeoff, the time and place of rendezvous, the point of crossing the channel, the initial point, the target, the procedure, and route back. Then we'd go to individual briefings, navigators' briefings, gunners' briefings, pilots' briefings, bombardiers' briefings. All night long the bombs were being loaded and the ground crew was working on the planes. We could hear the engines being revved up.

"As long as the momentum of activity was going, everything would be OK. I felt the excitement, the blood coursed through my veins. I felt the intensity of it. We would start the engines revving and I'd lay out my charts and have everything ready, oxygen mask, parachute. Check all the dials. Computer, pencils, Weems plotter [a navigational tool]. Milt Conver would be making wisecracks. We could feel the plane being readied, we could feel the vibration of readiness of men moving back and forth at their dials, controls, and guns. Everything was OK. We were a team and we knew each other and loved each other. The men were truly noble. The planes were noble.

"The B-17s are scattered around the field and it is seven in the morning, the first dim light of day. The first dim, gray silver light, mists rising from the fields. And then you hear engines starting here and there, some close, a roar, and then rrrrrrrmmmmmm, ready on one, ready on two, contact, ready on three, ready on four. And the four engines of the B-17 slowly throbbing, vibrations increasing, a spitting and grumbling, a lust for the morning air, a waking from the dead, a waking from the night, a waking to life, the life of the new day, of the throb, the heart throb of the plane, four engines beating, four propellers whirling, engines revving, echoing each other.

"The olive-drab B-17s would slowly move, brakes screeching, the ground crew watching, one of them helping to guide the plane around the circle onto the tarmac path to the perimeter track. One after another, lumbering out onto the track and then all of them, single file on each side of the field, two files moving, lumbering slowly toward the takeoff point at the end of the runway. All of them, engines growling and propellers twirling. The nose of the B-17 in the air, the body sloping down to the rear tail wheel, already in an attitude of urgency, of wanting to rise into the gray morning sky. Because of the morning light, because of the vast, flat stretch of the field, the planes looked larger and more powerful than they actually were.

"Men. Each an individual who lived and suffered, who had a woman or women, who sweated, crapped, lusted, who drank and got cold in the damp billets, who tried to light the stoves, who sat around and talked into the night, talking about the raids, and latterly, about the chances for survival. It really was beautiful, beautiful in many, many ways."

In a more prosaic tone, Bill Fleming reminisced, "Some of our equipment bothered us as much as the Germans. Our planes were open [at the waist positions for the machine guns] so the temperatures at 30,000 to 32,000 feet were forty to seventy degrees below zero. We had to dress very heavily. I wore long underwear, and a uniform shirt and pants, an electric suit over that, plus a fur-lined flying suit on top of it. On my feet I wore silk stockings, wool stockings, electric shoes, and fur-lined flying boots. My hands had silk gloves, wool gloves, electric gloves, and then the fur-lined flying mitts. You could barely move a finger and you always left one free to work the trigger of the machine gun. We didn't dare unplug the electric suits which were connected to the battery system. Without heat you would freeze to death in a matter of minutes. It was funny to look at the man next to you and see his eyebrows white with frost. There were several severe cases of frostbite. You did not dare fly while you had a cold because if you did, your oxygen mask, which was the old bag type, would freeze with ice and cut off your oxygen. We lost two gunners out of our squadron that way. One a ball turret and the other a tail gunner.

"We had to clean our guns after every mission using the solvent carbon tetrachloride. That kept the guns dry because any kind of moisture on them and they would freeze up. Later, of course, in the U.S. factories carbon tetrachloride was banned as a deadly poison. I wonder how many of our guys got sick from it. I remember over Halle, Germany, when it was so cold that our guns wouldn't fire. Fortunately for us, the Germans couldn't fire theirs either."

The astute if acerbic Southworth expressed his continuing exasperation with his superiors for their refusal to consider more effective formations. "What a bunch of little tin gods. I like the colonel but there sure are a lot of deadbeats running this outfit." He shifted his attention to the other major weakness. "Went down to see how progress, if any, was

being made on the new nose gun mount. We can't get that
too soon. It's a sheer waste of men and airplanes to attack
without nose guns. Just sit and wait to get shot down."
Eighth Air Force tacticians had realized the enemy's approach and they asked for modifications to protect the
planes. Subsequently, B-17Gs would come to Europe with a
chin turret whose pair of .50-caliber guns significantly improved a Fort's ability to defend itself against those who attacked at twelve o'clock high.

Whatever the formation, maintaining position demanded
strenuous effort at the controls. Southworth, an exception-
ally skilled pilot, speaking of an excursion to Lille, said, "I
fought and fought prop wash. As we neared the French
coast, it was so bad that when I turned one way, with all my
strength applied, the ship was going the other way toward
Buck [Glenn Hagenbuch] who was also flying formation
prop wash. I managed to push my nose down in time to
break out of it. I was 200 to 300 yards out of formation and
then had to battle my way back in there. This went on for an
hour or two, a battle all the way. We'd get out of formation
and nearly dive into other ships. The FW 190s didn't bother
me. It was the 17's prop wash. The plane felt loggy and flew
like a truck. We saw two B-17Fs ahead of us crash in midair.
The tail section came off one, broke in two and damaged the
wing of another so that it too spun in."

Subsequently, Bomber Command dispatched the 303d
with the Southworth crew to Lorient and Brest and their
severest test yet. "Little happened until we reached the target," said the pilot, "where huge puffs of heavy flak broke
in close proximity. It sounded like rain blowing on a tin roof,
or a limb cracking, a bolt of lightning. We had passed
through a solid bank of haze at 25,000 feet and then it was
clear as I have ever seen it over the target. There were about

fifty to one hundred fighters in the area. We watched groups of 190s at 30,000 feet. They would peel off, leaving beautiful vapor trails but soon to spell the end for some of my buddies.

"We dropped our bombs and turned off when the fighters attacked. Hagenbuch's engine failed and Colonel Robinson pulled off with another group, Cole and Reber with him. Both squadrons on our side left us, the three of us alone. We were sitting targets when the attacks came. Over the interphone a constant position report came through. 'Nine o'clock, lower six, upper five, two, low five, up three, eleven, low ten, twelve o'clock.' There was continuous shooting. An FW gained position eight to ten miles forward and started a long head-on attack. Upper-turret firing felt like someone pounding on my head, a loud noise with heavy vibration. My glass cracked in front of me. I bent my head slightly in case she let go. Our .30-caliber from the nose sounded like a toy or an electric sewing machine. The FW firing lit up like an electric sign. Robey, to my left was being hit in the fuselage and vertical stabilizer. Looked as if we would crash head on, so I raised my nose to allow my lower turret to fire back but instead pulled up violently, throwing everyone on the floor as the enemy grazed below me. At that moment, Dillinger pushed my controls forward trying to talk through his oxygen mask and the drone of the engines. I put the ship under control. Robey missed our tail by inches as he peeled off into a dive straight down, many thousands of feet, his tail gunner hanging on, firing both of his weapons.

"Attack positions kept coming in, and brief reports of an FW shot down and its clock position were briefly sounded off. We were headed toward Brest, heaviest flak-defended area in that section. We took slight evasive action. Our interphone went out and only the roar of the engines and the bark of the .50s could be heard. FWs were attacking furiously.

"Two miles to our left the 305th Group was moving up. We came within 200 yards of the 305th as flak pounded up in large black puffs. I covered Buck taking more violent evasive action as the 305th bombs fell. They pulled away from us like [Ernie] Lombardi and [Terry] Moore in a foot race." The former was a Cincinnati Reds catcher known for slow speed afoot and the latter an extremely fleet St. Louis Cardinals outfielder. Unable to gather with the B-17s of the 305th, Southworth and the remnants of the 303d huddled together hoping to mutually fend off further assaults.

"There were only a few attackers left. We had little ammunition. One waist gunner was out of the same as was the lower turret and the .30 in the nose. Low on gas and with an unpredictable radio, we landed at Exeter. Fleming had shot down two planes and Kirkpatrick shot down one from the ball turret. Upon our arrival at Molesworth, we learned of Reber's tough luck and the others' fate. Hate to lose the lot of them." [The 303d listed a staggering five aircraft shot down, with fifty airmen MIA. And those B-17s that reached the United Kingdom bore one dead and nineteen wounded.]

Conver noted the furious exchanges with enemy fighters. "Our gunners shot down three FWs. Fleming got two and Kirkpatrick got the other. We had three head-on attacks; one would have rammed us but Billy Southworth jumped our ship right over him. I thought sure I was a goner or else I was going to have a Jerry in my lap."

Captain John Regan of the 306th Bomb Group was awakened at 3:00 A.M. on 27 January and advised breakfast would be served an hour later, with the briefing at 5:00 for a mission against a German target. "This was somewhat routine," recalls Regan. "We had already bombed German targets in occupied Europe—routine, that is, if one could adjust to the tremendous pressures of combat and the all too often loss of close friends. Frankly, I knew of no one who could truthfully say that any combat mission was just routine.

"I wish it were possible to accurately describe the tension, the emotion that was evident in our thirty-five-man crew huts on those mornings when we were awakened for combat missions. One would have to be present to feel the electricity that filled the air. Some men shouted to relieve tension, others laughed out loud when nothing was really funny, and others were silent with their thoughts, probably fixed on coming events, or on loved ones. I even knew some who would silently slip outside in the darkness to become ill— they didn't want their buddies to see them. Everyone wanted to appear strong and tough—it is normal, we were all so young—but we had learned that war is hell and that the only romance or glamour associated with it is fiction.

"All was as usual until the 5:00 A.M. briefing. This took place in our combat-operations hut that had become very familiar to all of us. We sat together as combat crews and exchanged small talk while we waited anxious to find out what our target for the day was to be.

"A large map of England and Europe that took up most of the front of the briefing room was covered as usual with a blue cloth so that crews would only find out what the mission of the day would be after the briefing had started. At 5:00 A.M., our commanding officer and the operations briefing officer entered the hut. We came to attention and then sat down. After a few short, opening comments, our commander paused, then said, dramatically, 'Gentlemen, this is it.' and with that drew back the blue cloth covering the map, so we could see it and the telltale ribbon that would show our course to fly and the target for the day.

"Initially, there was a stunned silence and then the room erupted with shouts of exultation and wonderment, as the significance of the mission sunk in. Yes, we actually were going to hit the enemy near his heart. The excitement was intense. For a moment, even the fear of combat was forgotten, as exultation reigned. The historic meaning of this event sank in even further when we were told that our group had been selected to lead the mission. I was doubly thrilled as my squadron was to lead the total American bombing effort."

The mission that so galvanized Regan was the Eighth Air Force's first assault upon German turf in the form of the shipyards at Vegasack outside the city of Bremen. The 1st Bomb Wing, composed of the 91st, 303d, 305th, and 306th, contributed fifty-five B-17s. The planners had expected the B-24s of the 2d Bomb Wing—the 44th and 93d Bomb Groups—to participate, but all twenty-seven Liberators returned to base, defeated by the weather and an inability to navigate to the target. But despite the failure to unload their ordnance, the B-24s would endure a terrible pounding from enemy fighters.

Regan remembers, "The rest of the briefing was anticlimactic, as were the preparation of aircraft, the takeoff, the rendezvous with other aircraft, and the initial flight to target. As the bombers crossed the coast of Germany and headed for the primary target at Vegasack, it became apparent that the complex to be attacked was covered by low clouds, which made bombing impossible.

"What a dilemma! Over Germany for the first time, all aircraft with a full load of bombs and the ground at the target hidden by low clouds. To return to home bases without bombing would have turned this momentous event into a failed sortie. A choice of action had to be made. The air commander, Col. Frank A. Armstrong Jr., weighed the alternatives and elected to try to bomb the secondary target, the shipyards and docks at Wilhelmshaven.

"As this secondary target was approached there fortunately was a break in the low clouds that allowed the bombardiers to see the target and successfully drop their bombs. Although the size of the bombing effort that day was relatively small, it was a great morale booster for the young Eighth Air Force and all Americans. The Germans had been taken by surprise. They had not anticipated this attack and had probably felt that bombers would not dare penetrate the airspace over their homeland in daylight. There was some antiaircraft fire over the target, but it was not accurate, and a small number of fighters attacked our bombers, which attested to the success of the surprise aspect of the mission."

The critique of the mission, organized by Southworth's former passenger and sandwich purveyor General Hansell, sounded some ominous themes. "The Combat Wings on this mission did not keep close enough together to give shielding protection, one to the other. Fifty-five aircraft in a formation are not enough aircraft to be able to defend themselves. It is felt that most of our losses were the result of poor formation flying which resulted in aircraft becoming separated and an easy prey to fighters. Gunnery must be stressed . . . even when a formation brought all its guns to bear on some of the attackers during this mission, the enemy continued to come in firing. Poor visibility at the target made the bombing very difficult . . . a target as small as this one should only be assigned when the weather is very clear and visibility is good." For all of the theories of LeMay and the high command that agreed with his precepts, the air crews of the Eighth obviously required continued training and a more focused effort.

As January drew to a close, Southworth recorded a dismal inventory. "We arrived as a complete group on October 31. In three short (or long) months the group has completed some eleven raids and lost over 50 percent of the [organization]. We average about fifteen planes per raid, which means that we have lost about 120 percent of our combat equipment and are operating [by using] reserve. We still lack nose guns. Eighty to 90 percent of our losses have been from nose attacks on our squadron. Nine pilots were lost. L——— doesn't count as he has been on no missions. A white feather might be in order."

A bout of the flu mandated a hospital stay for Southworth. In his absence, Jon Schueler volunteered to fill in with another crew out to slam Saint-Nazaire once again. The experience shattered Schueler. Years later, he wrote a surrealist account of an extended nightmare. "Billy had been sick and was off flying. I had a cold, too, and was off flying but I wasn't in the hospital. We were called upon for a raid and we could only get a few ships out of the group in the air— because of lost ships, because of badly shot up ships, because of shortage of personnel. Either shot down or sick. Two minutes before Saint-Nazaire, the squadron is seven ships. At Saint-Nazaire it is two. This was the raid in which we headed into a steep descent down to the deck from 20,000 feet after dropping our bombs and pain shot through my head like I had never before imagined."

Savage as the reception at Saint-Nazaire was another calamity that struck on the voyage home—a headwind of 120 miles per hour. The hapless bombers, reduced to the pace of a tortoise, crawled toward sanctuary while predators stalked them. "I see the clouds, the clouds building up so that we couldn't see the ground, we had no sign of movement, the B-17s standing still and the Focke-Wulfs and

Messerschmitts coming in to meet them, coming in to knock us out of the sky.

"For a moment, for a long moment, I was not navigating, I was watching the planes falling, the head-on crash of a fighter into a B-17, the exploding, burning, war-torn falling planes, all too often no chutes in sight, the lonely men held to their seats, to the walls, to the roof of the plane as it twisted and fell, sometimes with machine guns blazing, and a spume of smoke for a long moment. It seemed endless. It seemed as though we would never get home. I was looking out of the window at the endless blue sky and white cloud beneath us. We waited for the Focke-Wulfs and the Messerschmitts and we watched the Fortresses fall. Falling Forts. I wanted to hold them. I wanted to go down with them. I wanted to go home. I prayed. I prayed, please God, I'm bored, please don't make this go on and on and on, it's boring, it's ennui. I can't stand this boring repetition, please God, get us out of here and get this over with. I was probably frightened, too, although I was seldom scared while actually flying.

"Had I been able to feel the fear, call it that name, I might have been able to feel the rage. Had I been able to feel the rage, I could have poured out the machine-gun fire. I could have slammed bullets into the sky, into the waiting Focke-Wulf. In combat, I could not feel the fear or the rage and therefore the love, and excitement of what I was doing. I was quite cool in combat. I'd always be so goddamned busy with charts, mental averages, counting, and noting falling ships. I was a cool cookie. And I lost everything in my cool. I drowned myself in it. I lost my way."

Upon his return from Saint-Nazaire, inner demons overwhelmed Schueler. "I started to feel guilty, responsible for every death. I was afraid, not sleeping, that I'd make errors and cause the death of many. It could happen—navigation errors, pilot errors. Ending in death. Planes falling, planes shot down. So many were dying and I felt responsible. But I felt more responsible for those who might die. The flight surgeon gave me sleeping pills and talked to the group commander about taking me off combat for a while to rest up. I had lost twenty pounds or more and was skinny as a rail. They needed an operations navigation officer and I was made that.

"We sent out as many planes as we could muster on a mission and instead of being on it myself I was left on the base. At the end of the day I was on the tower, looking to the sky, watching for the returning planes, counting when they appeared. One, two, three, four . . . nine, ten, eleven, twelve . . . twelve . . . twelve . . . there are no others. We look anxiously, scanning the sky. Then the planes are flying in low over the field. Then there is a flare from one and he's moving right down the runway without permission. He's floating down, landing, another flare denoting wounded on board and the ambulance is rushing toward the plane even as it rolls to a stop. . . . The group is badly shot up. One plane is missing."

Transferred to the VIII Bomber Command in High Wycombe, Schueler became increasingly uncomfortable in the almost luxurious surroundings: a private room, "superb food," and an office in an air-conditioned hillside burrow. The meetings and briefings took on the atmosphere of theater. "It was as though I was moving onto a stage, parts to be played until no one could clearly remember the reality. The reality of fight and fear and death, but also the reality of comradeship and effort, and aliveness, and meaning, and strength. I felt dead amongst the living. I felt weak, washed out, through." Schueler contracted mumps and collapsed into a depression complicated by a second childhood ailment, chicken pox. He entered a hospital.

Conver's diary noted a depressing discussion. "Diff and Barker are now having a heated argument on whether to spend all our money or save it. Diff says spend it, 'cause it won't be long until we're knocked off and our wives will marry again and some other guy will [get the money]. Barker says to send it home and save it 'cause even if we are knocked off, he knows where his is going and his wife will see that his family will get what they need. I'm inclined to agree with Barker. I'll send what money I can to Jean and I know she'll help my folks, if they need help."

Fleming commented on the status of the outfit. "In March of 1943, Lt. Schueler and Lt. Conver had left our crew. It was nothing against Schueler that he was grounded. All of our nerves were affected. We were now down to only three of the original nine crews in our squadron. No replacements. It wasn't anything to see some guy break down and cry. I felt like doing it myself many, many times." Conver underwent batteries of medical examinations until the doctors declared him unfit for high-altitude flight. He was sent back to the States. Schueler also went home and after hospitalization received a medical discharge.

Subsequently, the waist gunner himself began to fall apart. "Things were not looking good," says Fleming. "I was having blackout spells, running a high temperature. They put me in a hospital. They couldn't find out what it was. After six weeks, a young doctor discovered I had an infection of my inner ear that upset my sense of balance. They treated me and released me. By that time I had completed fourteen missions."

The brutal first months in the Solomons, the frustrations of strategic bombing, the disappointments in North Africa could all be marked up to necessary learning experiences. The Aleutians campaigns, conducted in the cruel Arctic climate, a frigid version of hell, off the southern tip of Alaska, offered nothing in the way of genuine rewards and seemed to have more to do with bragging rights than any contribution to winning the war. The Japanese, perhaps with an inflated view of their power because of victories in 1942, occupied Attu and Kiska, a pair of islands of no strategic importance to either side. Unwilling to allow this incursion into the Western Hemisphere to pass, the Americans responded with a buildup of forces in the area.

Air Corps pilot Stanley Long said, "I think the Aleutian Islands were perhaps the worst place in the world to live because of the high winds, fog, and rain. You lived in a sea of mud all of the time. We lived in pyramidal tents without a floor. The floor was wet all the time and would sometimes be ice it was so cold. If you stood, your head was practically in a steam bath."

Charles Pinney flew B-25s from another base where the crews lived in Quonset huts. He added, "We had our little outhouse that was a tent but it wouldn't stay up very long because we'd have winds that would get up to ninety miles an hour. Having a three-holer out in the tundra got to be a chore. Our mess hall at Cold Bay was a quarter to half a mile from the Quonset hut. It got to be too much of a drudge to even fight the weather to go there to eat. You didn't need an awful lot of food and the food was horrible. A lot of times we'd stay in our [hut] and eat crackers and some fruit juices. [When] things got better we had Vienna sausage and Spam."

Everytime the pilots took off they were at considerable risk of being lost. "We had no navigational aids at all in the Aleutians," said Long. "We were just green pilots out of flight school. I had no instrument training except for maybe four or five hours in Link trainer during flight school. Some of the charts were made from very early Russian surveys. And the Rand-McNally maps weren't accurate at all. I know of one instance where a big mountain showed up fifty miles away from where it was indicated on the map. We lost a lot of our boys over there—flying into situations like that. I know in our squadron we had twenty-five P-38 pilots come up and out of the twenty-five only nine lived to return to the States. [The main cause] was weather. A lot of times [after] we'd get a briefing, by the time we walked down to our airplanes, got in and started the engines, and started to taxi off, the field was socked in again and we couldn't go. We cancelled more missions than we actually flew. [In several instances] where we were able to find the field, the B-17 or B-24 went up, picked us up, and took us down through the overcast." According to Pinney, perhaps four times a year was there CAVU—clear air, visibility unlimited. Along with some B-25s the P-38s struck at the major Japanese installation on Kiska. "We did a lot of the dive-bombing and skip-bombing there," said Long. [They] were trying to build a runway near the camp area and we'd let 'em go for a couple of days and then we'd come over and drop a couple of 500-pound bombs on it and they'd have to start from scratch again, just manual labor. They didn't have big equipment." Against this backdrop, Long, in 1942, and a companion became the first P-38 pilots in the theater to shoot down the enemy when they downed a pair of flying boats.

The following spring, the 7th Infantry Division, although trained in the Nevada desert for use in North Africa, abruptly embarked on ships for an assault on the Japanese ensconced in the hilly frozen wasteland of Attu Island. At that time of the year, daylight stretches toward twenty-four hours. Ed Smith, a 1939 graduate of the USMA, led a battalion across the small sandy beaches. "We had trained for the desert and had no experience in north climates or living. The equipment was unsuitable, particularly bad for the feet. I had close to 1,000 people in the battalion when we started the assault. At the end of a week we were down to the size of a company, little more than 200 men. Men kept being taken out because of their feet, from trying to live on Attu and from being shot by the Japanese. They were always above us. Wherever the fogline was, we knew the Japanese were behind it. It was foggy most of the time. It got dark at about 2:00 A.M. and cleared by 5:00 A.M. We knew they could see us to fire but we could not see them to fire back."

Against the well-dug-in defenders, the GIs advanced very slowly. The foe took full advantage of steep ridges and sharp ravines to shield themselves against the offshore salvos of the American Navy. Unhappy with the progress of the campaign, RAdm. Thomas Kinkaid, commander of the North Pacific Fleet, fearful of an attack by a Japanese fleet, replaced the 7th Division commander. The decision typified the concerns of naval strategists versus those of Army commanders intent on overcoming the enemy with minimum expenditure of men and equipment. Placing the prerogative to judge ground-combat leadership in the hands of an admiral was as absurd as if the division chief had been handed control over the fleet. Ed Smith, more than fifty years later, criticized the relief of a man he considers "an outstanding commander."

The change had little to do with the final outcome. The fewer than 3,000 defenders could expect neither reinforcements nor evacuation. Squeezed into an ever-smaller piece of turf, about a thousand of those Japanese still on their feet erupted into one of the biggest banzai charges of World War II. Eyewitnesses swore the suicidal soldiers screamed such imprecations as "Japanese drink blood like wine!" The on-slaught surprised several units and overran some American positions.

Bob MacArthur was with the division's 13th Engineer Combat Battalion. "It must have been about 4:00 A.M., and we were in our tents playing poker, having a great time when suddenly these guys come streaming back, yelling, 'The Japs are coming.' The battalion commander, Lt. Col. James Green, a West Pointer, drew his pistol and said [to the fleeing GIs], 'This is as far as you go.' Grenades were being thrown back and forth, a lot of rifle, carbine, and pistols firing."

MacArthur improvised a firing line that drove off the first wave before organizing a withdrawal to a sounder location. His immediate superior, Capt. George Cookson, whose feet were in such wretched condition he merited evacuation, played a major role in mounting the defense. "It went on for most of the next day," recalled MacArthur. "They penetrated as far as the tents for the medics and field artillery." MacArthur then saw the remnants of the enemy kill themselves. "It was the damndest thing. I watched them up on a ridge, taking their grenades—they had a button that detonated them—bang them on their helmets and hold them to their chest while they went off. I couldn't fathom it. I heard they had been told that if they surrendered, we'd run them over with bulldozers." Only twenty-eight enemy soldiers were taken prisoner.

About three months later, the 7th Division GIs hit the beaches at Kiska. But to their astonishment no resistance greeted them. They fanned out in search of the enemy but found only deserted emplacements and booby traps. A flotilla of destroyers and cruisers, under the cover of a thick fog, had slipped into the harbor and the well-disciplined sailors and soldiers evacuated a garrison of 5,000. The Japanese presence in the Aleutians had ended with considerable cost to both sides and at a profit to neither.

18

Tunisia

ON 14 JANUARY 1943, PRESIDENT ROOSEVELT AND PRIME MIN-
ister Churchill met with Eisenhower at Casablanca where
the political leaders formulated "unconditional surrender" as
the only terms under which the Allies would cease fire. The
conferees still talked in terms of a cross-channel attack later
in the year. However, Churchill, to Marshall's concern, appeared to have talked the American president into a strategy
that would send Allied troops to Italy before France. Of
more immediate consequence was a strategy that placed the
British Eighth Army, pressuring Rommel from Tripoli,
under the overall command of Eisenhower in the campaign
for Tunisia that would begin as soon as the weather became
more friendly for armored vehicles and aircraft.

Promoted with a fourth star, yet still only a lieutenant
colonel in the permanent ranks, Eisenhower was dismayed
to discover that his II Corps commander, Gen. Lloyd Fredendall, had established his headquarters a full sixty miles
behind the front. He was further distressed to observe the

Corps of Engineers there engaged in a mammoth tunneling project. "It was the only time during the war, that I ever saw a divisional or higher headquarters so concerned over its own safety that it dug itself underground shelters." With his forces spread thinly Eisenhower would have preferred the engineers to be engaged in building front-line defenses. However, he did not instruct Fredendall to shift his attention and his resources closer to the foe. Nor was he happy with the attitudes of those nearest the enemy and who exhibited "a certain complacency." Discerning an overall slackness, Eisenhower ordered tightened training and battle discipline: "Every infraction, from a mere failure to salute, a coat unbuttoned, to more serious offenses, must be dealt with; or disciplinary action taken against the officer who condones the offense."

Symptomatic of the haphazard operations in the early weeks of Torch, Phil Cochran recalled a small group of paratroopers who suddenly arrived at his base. They told him of a plan sketched out in Algiers to disrupt German supply lines by blowing up a railroad bridge at El Djem. Because Cochran had flown over the area on several occasions they queried him on the bridge structure and the ground at the drop zone. Their transport pilots inquired about landmarks and how difficult it would be to find the bridge at night. It did not occur to the planners in Algiers that the excellent German radar would track the transports and that when no bombs fell the enemy would realize what was happening.

Cochran volunteered to fly over El Djem at dusk, pick out check points and compass courses. "I found the bridge," he said, "protected by only four men with two machine guns. They lived in holes conveniently located so the paratroopers could give them the hands-on-the-shoulders and knees-in-the-back business. I found the spot where they intended to drop and there were ravines as deep as a building. It would have broken every kid's legs on landing." Cochran asked the troopers how they intended to get back. "They answered, they would simply walk west. I know my mother could know this was wrong because they hadn't planned it at all."

Cochran informed Edson Raff, who requested headquarters in Algiers to cancel the operation, but the rear-echelon strategists insisted on proceeding. Cochran stuck his neck out by going along as copilot on one of the C-47s. For a few moments he confessed he was lost but then he saw a lake he recognized and headed for the drop zone. El Djem contained the ruins of an ancient Roman coliseum and when Cochran spotted the crumbling remains he directed the planes north to a point on the left side of the railroad before announcing, "Let them go. Then they rang the god-awful fire bell and the kids, one after another, counting to themselves, jumped. They were wonderful guys. One right after the other. You could feel the airplane lurch after each one. As soon as the last one went out my pilot jammed the throttle forward and said in the most awful voice—like he didn't want to think about it, 'Let's get the hell out of here.' "

The next day, Cochran flew over El Djem and glumly noticed the bridge still intact. "We figured we must have dropped them into enemy hands. Out of the thirty-five, only five came back. Instead of dropping them going north, I had dropped them going south. When they got to the railroad, they turned the wrong way and walked into town, four miles away. They blew up the railroad tracks in a few places and then most were captured sleeping in a haystack the next morning. It was complete stupidness throughout the whole thing."

For roughly six weeks the Allied foot soldiers manned static positions. When weather permitted, the small band of

P-40s at Thelepte, led by Cochran, harassed the enemy troops in Tunisia. "Our action started out trying to force an air war," said Cochran. "They wouldn't do it. We could go right over Gabès [site of an enemy air base] and they would watch you, say, 'go ahead.' " The *Luftwaffe* remained intent upon its objective of supporting the soldiers on the ground and attacking bombers aimed at Axis ships and installations.

"Then we started strafing. We made it our point to burn anything we saw in the way of equipment, including trains, trucks, locomotives. We had complete air superiority except around [the coastal area north of Gabès]. We were successful enough at this to have the Germans stop any movement on these highways at all in the daytime. We actually got so we could hunt the whole area and not even find a motorcycle rider. One day we caught a hundred Italian trucks who attempted to hide in an olive grove. Out of a hundred we burned, in five missions, eighty-seven of them, and lost one pilot. They didn't move any more in the daytime so we started going out at night."

Beginning in January, the enemy struck hard. A quick blow into the Ousseltia Valley was followed by a two-pronged thrust that overran the American positions through Faïd Pass and Gafsa before smashing Allied positions near Kasserine. The advance threatened to swallow up a large number of Allied soldiers, eliminate air fields like the one Cochran used at Thelepte, and capture a major supply base at Tébessa. The *Afrika Korps* under Rommel and another army led by Gen. Jürgen von Arnim initially routed the Allied soldiers. "We were told," said antitank crewman Bill Behlmer of the 1st Infantry Division, "we were to stop Rommel and his *Afrika Korps* from breaking out. We dug in our guns all night long. Other guys dug in their machine guns, mortars, etc. At dawn we decided to light up a cigarette. A few minutes later, a mortar shell hit behind us. Then another in front of us. We dove for cover, because we knew where the next would land. All hell broke loose, and we didn't stand a chance. The Germans had gotten there first and were dug in on the slope ahead of us. The out-of-action signal came and we took off, leaving everything behind."

John Waters, Patton's son-in-law, who had warned his men that they would be up against much stronger adversaries, was well aware of the inadequacies of U.S. tanks such as the M3, eighteen- to twenty-ton light model known as a "Honey." Their 37mm cannons had a range of only 1,800 yards while the 88s mounted on German tanks could blast away from twice that distance. Toward the end of November Waters and his battalion fought the much heavier Panzers and escaped only because the Germans failed to press their attack. At Kasserine Pass, however, the German armor destroyed two battalions from the 1st Armored Division and bagged Waters as a prisoner.

Sergeant Clarence W. Coley, radio operator for Col. Louis Hightower, a battalion commander of Combat Command A of the 1st Armored Division, recalled that 14 February began "just like any of those beautiful African days we had been having there in the 'cactus patch' near Sidi-Bou-Zid for the past week or so. We had been taking it easy, knowing the enemy was over there, somewhere the other side of Faïd Pass. We had all been instructed to dig holes, deep holes to sleep in because of reports of big guns moving into position to shell us. I, like the rest, slept as well as ever because everything was quiet that night."

In the morning at daybreak, the troopers performed their customary "stand-to," checking radios, engines, and guns. Coley climbed into an M4 Sherman named "Texas," and when the colonel arrived, the tanks moved out. They were patiently awaiting further instructions near the CCA's headquarters when Coley learned from the radio that the Germans had attacked Company G near a place known as the "oasis." Hightower returned from headquarters and with two companies of tanks the armor cranked up toward the oasis.

"We hadn't gone very far when we ran into blistering fire from many guns, including a lot of 88s," said Coley. "I didn't know much about what was going on but I did see many of our tanks get hit. Sometimes two or three men got out. Sometimes no one got out. Most of the tanks burned when hit [the Germans referred to Shermans as 'Ronsons' because of their high flammability when struck in certain areas]. The artillery got so hot and heavy and we were losing so many tanks due to being outranged, that the colonel decided to withdraw. We started backing out, keeping our thickest armor toward the enemy. The colonel told the driver to zigzag, and when we reached a suitable place, to turn fast and get going. I remember two men got on our tanks to ride out of the battle area—but I guess we were moving too slow for them because pretty soon they jumped to the ground and took off on foot.

"We moved on back toward Sidi-Bou-Zid and learned by radio that the Germans had put up a roadblock there. We were expecting to have to fight our way through it. I loaded my .30-cal. machine gun and was ready to fire at anything that looked suspicious but the roadblock did not materialize. Back in Sidi-Bou-Zid we pulled in beside a building and the colonel left us on foot to check the situation. As we had started before breakfast that morning, Clark, Bayer, Agee and I warmed up some C rations and had us a feast. It was around noon.

"We mounted up and moved out toward the desert. I don't

know in what direction but away from the enemy, which had all but wiped us out. The *Luftwaffe* paid us many visits that day. They seemed to have a twenty-minute schedule, just time enough to go back and load up again. It was getting up into the afternoon now, and was pretty hot and smoky in this whole area. As we were moving along we could see many other vehicles moving in the same general direction across the desert, half-tracks, peeps [the nomenclature for Jeeps in armored units], motorcycles, and trucks. About five tanks of Company H had moved on out ahead of us. As far as we knew, we were the only tank back there and the colonel seemed to want to bring up the rear, keeping between the enemy and our withdrawing forces.

"I suddenly got a call on my SCR-245 [radio] set. [The] message was that a bunch of German tanks were shooting up the column, knocking out trucks and half-tracks one after another. I passed the message up into the turret to Colonel Hightower who immediately tried to contact the tanks of H Company. But no luck. The colonel then said we would just have to take them on by ourselves. He immediately rotated the turret until the 75mm was pointed over the left rear fender at the German tanks . . . there were seven of them. Corporal Bayer, the gunner, started firing at them. I could hear [Hightower] complimenting Bayer on getting hits. Clark, the driver, was craning his neck trying to see the action. Agee, the loader, was busy keeping the 75 loaded. All the time we were firing at the Supermen, they were not wasting any time. We were getting it hot and heavy. I did not keep count but we received many hits on our tank. I could feel the shock and hear the loud noise as those projectiles bounced off.

"The rounds were running out in the turret racks but we had a few left in the racks underneath the turret. I took off my headphones, laid them up on the receiver, took the back of the assistant driver's seat out, very deliberately. It is when you have nothing to do that you are afraid. Sitting backwards on my seat, with my feet on the escape hatch, I began pulling the rounds from the racks underneath the turret and passing them up to Agee. I remember other times when I had needed to take rounds from those racks, it was very hard for me to get them out, because I was afraid of hurting my fingers, but this time those rounds came out easy. I didn't worry about my fingers. In fact, I wouldn't have given two cents for our chances to get out of that mess alive. I kept passing the ammo. Agee kept loading and Bayer kept firing that 75. Every once in a while I could hear the colonel tell Bayer that he had hit another.

"Our luck finally ran out. A round got stuck in the gun, wouldn't go in or come out. The colonel told Clark to move on out, and about the same time, one of the enemy guns got a penetration in our tank. The projectile came in the left side, passing through the gas tank, ricocheting around and winding up on the escape hatch just behind my seat. Thirty seconds earlier I was bent over in that space pulling ammo from the racks. I remember sitting there, watching that bit of hell standing on end, spinning like a top, with fire flying out of the upper part of it like it was a tracer. Our tank was on fire inside.

"I heard the colonel say, 'Let's get the hell out of here.' We started bailing out. I remember trying three times to raise my hatch but it wouldn't go up but about four inches. The colonel, Clark, Bayer, and Agee were all out of the tank while I'm trying to get my hatch open. I finally gave up trying and got across the transmission like a snake and up through the driver's hatch, diving headfirst out of that burning vehicle. Hitting the ground on my shoulders, I rolled over and before I got to my feet, I noticed the tracks were burning also. I took off after the rest of the crew who were not letting any grass grow under their feet. When I was between twenty-five and fifty yards away I heard an explosion. Looking back I could see fire shooting skyward from old 'Texas,' ammo or gas blowing up."

The crew hiked through the desert, "sweating out small arms fire from the German tanks." But the smoke and dust hid them. They reached a half-track with other refugees from the battlefield and made good their escape. "Texas" was credited with having knocked out four enemy tanks and distracted the enemy sufficiently for much of Combat Command A to evade capture.

The fighter planes and the ground personnel at Thelepte hastily abandoned their strip for an airdrome safely behind the fluid lines. Cochran and his associates flew off unharmed, leaving behind only some supplies. Then–Maj. Gen. Omar Bradley, as deputy commander to Fredendall, remarked, "There were pockets of gallantry, but for the most part our soldiers abandoned their weapons, including tanks and fled to the rear." General Ernest Harmon, head of the 2d Armored Division, ordered by Eisenhower to evaluate the ineffectiveness of the 1st Armored Division, recalled, "It was the first—and only—time I ever saw an American army in a rout."

Upon hearing of the calamitous events, Eisenhower issued orders for Harmon, already on the scene, to act as his deputy at the front. Harmon recalled, "The only thing I could think of was that when troops were running away, the first thing to do was to stop them, have somebody in authority tell them to stop and turn around. And the next thing was to try to win back the ground they had lost. My motto all day long was, 'We're going to hold today and counter-attack tomorrow. No one goes back from here.'

"I told [this to]all detachments that I met on the road. On the way to Thala where the British were located I ran across a colonel of the 26th Infantry of the 1st Infantry Division. He had about a battalion plus around him and he was gathering up more people. I told him to stay right where he was, that we were going to hold today and counterattack sometime tomorrow. He assured me he would hold, and I could depend on it. I put his unit down on my operations map.

"We finally arrived at Thala; the Germans were shelling the town. We had some difficulty getting in among the alleys and between the houses to the British Command Post, and for the first time I ran into the British. I was unshaven and dirty from my long trip all night long, no sleep, no breakfast and finally found my way into the command post of Brigadier Nicholson of the 6th British Armored Division. The British general as was usual was shaven, clean and spick and span. He looked me up and down and I'm sure I didn't make a very favorable impression on him. I showed him my orders and told him that I was in command of the front and asked him what his situation was.

"He replied, 'We gave them a bloody nose yesterday when they attacked and we are damned ready to give them another bloody nose this morning.' This seemed like very good news to me. Here was a man that had no idea of going away. I said, 'All right. Improve your position today; we are going to hold on all the front today and counterattack tomorrow. I have a battalion of tanks that are coming from Tèbassa and I am going to put them right behind you here on this hillside with orders not to move under any circumstances. They are to support you. They will be here almost momentarily, under Colonel Hightower.

"About this time there was a commotion and a brigadier general of the American Army, General [Stafford LeRoy] Irwin, who commanded an artillery brigade [from the 9th Infantry Division], came in. I had known Irwin at West Point, and he said, 'I have just got an order from General [Kenneth] Anderson the British commander to the north ordering me to pull out of here with my artillery brigade.' Nicholson spoke up: 'Oh, my God. You can't do that. If my men see your artillery brigade pulling out of here it will be bad on their morale.' I said, 'Indeed, it will. Irwin, you stay right here,' and I countercommanded the order. I figured if I won the battle I would be forgiven and if I lost the battle, the hell with it. Irwin smiled and said, 'That's just what I wanted to hear.' I was greatly heartened by the fact that nobody wanted to run, everybody wanted to stay and fight. All they needed was somebody to give them some positive direction."

Harmon checked in with II Corps boss Fredendall to report that the front appeared secure and he intended to counterattack in the morning and take back the Kasserine Pass. "He looked at me rather strangely," said Harmon, "but made no further remark." Harmon resumed his travels, with just his executive officer, a communications officer, his aide, and a driver. "Sometimes I think it is just as well to have a small staff. I think we have so many people on our staffs sometimes that they become cumbersome. It was sort of enjoyable to work with just a couple of people and we ran the battle just as well as if we had had a big headquarters of fifty—probably better."

The enemy opened up with what Harmon described as a rather weak artillery barrage. He sensed there would be no all-out drive at the Allied defenses. Several months later, intelligence studies of German documents found that Rommel had previously decided that if he could not reach Tèbassa

within two or three days he would have to withdraw in order
to meet Montgomery's Eighth Army advancing from Cairo
through Libya.

Returning to Thala, Harmon met Hightower and his battalion of tanks. "Colonel Hightower complained that his
people had never fired the tanks, had never even bore-
sighted the guns. Harmon ordered the armor onto a hillside
and climbed atop one vehicle with the colonel, and said, 'I
want you to stay right here. You can bore-sight to beat hell,
there is nothing in front of you but the Germans to shoot at.'

Harmon then conferred with 1st Armored Division commander Maj. Gen. Orlando Ward and other high-ranking
officers to draft a script for driving the enemy out of Kasserine. "One time in Morocco, Uncle George Patton and I had
a little talk on what to do in case we wanted to capture a
pass, and both decided the thing to do was to get at least one,
and if possible two promontories overlooking the pass. So
we staged a counterattack that was to start at midnight that
night, two columns with a double pincer movement. On the
right the 1st Armored Infantry Regiment and the 26th Infantry Regiment would attack for the high ground to get the
promontory on the right. The British had the Coldstream
Guards and the Hampshire Infantry Regiment and were
going to do the same thing on the left. We would pound the
plain, the center, and, when our infantry got to the heights
overlooking the Pass, we would move forward with the
tanks and drive the Germans through the plain. It was rather
simple but a very effective plan.

"The Germans had already started vacating the area during the night and by morning most of them had gotten out of
the Pass and were in full retreat. We organized a pursuit as
early as we could but they had mined the roads and mined
the Pass. We had to lift all these mines before we could pro-

ceed so they made a getaway. We have been criticized for not [moving faster] but I took command of troops that were running in the opposite direction and within twenty-four hours we turned them around to attack."

"We went back to General Fredendall's headquarters and gave him the news that the Germans were on their way out. He was in bed at the time and feeling no pain after a few drinks he was having in celebration of the occasion as word had already gotten to him. He called the British commander, General Anderson, and said a few unsavory things." Fredendall got on poorly with many people and perhaps worst of all with his British opposite number.

Having snapped at Anderson, Fredendall then encouraged Harmon to recommend relief of Orlando Ward, an obvious scapegoat for the Kasserine debacle. Harmon declined, defending Ward, and obliquely suggested that if Fredendall would allow Ward to operate his division on his own the results would be satisfactory. Amid the jubilant atmosphere at Torch headquarters, Harmon noted, "General Ike asked me if I was to go to relieve General Ward and I told him no. I thought [he] was doing very well but had been very badly handled by General Fredendall. General Ike then asked, 'What do you think of Fredendall?' I said, 'He is no damned good, you ought to get rid of him.' " According to Harmon, Eisenhower invited him to take over II Corps but Harmon believed it would be unethical since he was the one who advised, "my superior was no damned good and it would look like I sold him down the river." Instead, Harmon recommended Patton and subsequently Patton replaced Fredendall, with whom, perhaps not incidentally, he had a long and frequently testy relationship. Fredendall, curiously passive as a combat commander, went home with a medal and a promotion.

In four short days, the Axis forces had lost the power to mount a sustained offensive. However, by the time Rommel broke off the engagement, the U.S. II Corps counted 6,000 casualties, including 3,000 men captured and 200 destroyed tanks. It was such a sudden reversal of fortunes that although the Allied forces had engaged in a pell-mell retreat, the enemy could not remain long enough to exploit the booty. "A few days later," said Behlmer, "we returned and recovered our guns and equipment intact. We were losers again at Kasserine Pass, but we were getting smarter. 'Old Blood and Guts' General Patton took command of the II Corps, and we knew he was there to win even if he had us all killed doing it."

Hamilton Howze commented, "Patton quite wisely elected to make his presence felt as dramatically as he could . . . the whole Corps needed the impact of a new and vibrant personality . . . a new broom that was going to sweep hard and vigorously. He initiated some fines that probably would have had a tough time standing up in a court of law. He said that anybody who was caught standing outside a building without a helmet on would be subject to a $25 or $50 fine."

The installation of Patton as II Corps boss elevated the matter of form to its zenith. Omar Bradley, who disliked Patton for his profanity and bravado, nevertheless approved of the measures he took to build discipline. "Each time a soldier knotted his necktie, threaded his leggings, and buckled on his heavy steel helmet he was forcibly reminded that Patton had come to command the II Corps, that the pre-Kasserine days had ended, and a tough new era had begun." Patton even insisted his officers wear their insignia of rank upon their helmets although that certainly helped to make attractive targets of them for the enemy.

As part of the new attitude, Patton generally disdained actions that smacked of a defensive posture. Carlo D'Este in *Patton: A Genius for War* reported that he "shamelessly humiliated his friend Terry Allen during a visit to the 1st Division. . . . When he discovered a series of slit trenches around the perimeter of the command post, Patton demanded: 'What the hell are those for?' Terry Allen replied that they were for protection against air attack by the *Luftwaffe*. 'Which one is yours?' When Allen pointed it out to him, Patton walked over, unzipped his fly and urinated into it. 'There,' he said, 'Now try to use it.' "

According to D'Este, the bodyguards for Allen and his deputy, Gen. Theodore Roosevelt Jr., snapped the safeties off their submachine guns, ready to gun down Patton on a word from either of the two 1st Division generals. Patton quickly departed.

Patton's impetuous nature frequently carried him right to the brink of disaster. Hamilton Howze led the II Corps commander on a tour of the forward area. "He was in a command car behind us," said Howze, "and we came to a place with some U.S. Army engineers and some light tanks parked off to one side of the road. The engineers were probing with their bayonets and sweeping mine detectors back and forth across the road. They had already dug out some Teller mines, a terribly effective German antitank mine. I stopped my Jeep short of where the engineers were. I told General Patton, 'Sir, the road is mined. We can't go any farther.' He characteristically said, 'Damn the mines! Go on.' Hesitantly, I got in my Jeep, went past the engineers thinking that any moment might be my last. His command car followed me. His driver made sure that one of his sets of wheels was in the track of my Jeep; the others were [on the road] where no one had been. It was a foolhardy thing to do. Then a few hundred yards, actually much less than that, behind us a light tank hit a mine and blew up. At which time General Patton changed his mind and we very gingerly came about and back down the road. I am a great admirer of Patton. He had to exhibit a certain amount of flamboyance. He had to make a determined effort to make his personal presence felt. If this involved a certain amount of theatricality, so be it."

The changing of the guard also caused Maj. Gen. John Lucas to replace Bradley as Eisenhower's "eyes and ears." Almost immediately, Lucas and Eisenhower focused on the 1st Infantry Division for alleged deficiencies. In his diary Lucas noted, "He [Eisenhower] is not satisfied with the 1st but neither am I. The division has been babied too much. They have been told so often that they are the best in the world, that, as far as real discipline is concerned they have become one of the poorest. They look dirty and they never salute an officer if they can help it. They should be worked over by II Corps."

Lucas noted that he personally "drove out and told Terry to get after the saluting in his division." Lucas explained, "The military salute is the sign of fraternity and is important because it indicates the pride the individual takes in being a soldier and wearing the uniform of the great Republic. It has always seemed significant to me and I know this from my own experience that military courtesy—saluting, proper reporting, etc. improves as one approaches the front.

"Terry was rather on the spot because of the discourtesy of his men when the commander in chief drove through his area. It was hard to understand how a car with four stars on it could fail to be noticed. . . . It was reasonable to suppose that if General Eisenhower were treated in that fashion, one of lesser rank would hardly be treated any better."

With everyone unhappy about the slow progress in North

Africa, even before Eisenhower sacked Fredendall, Gen. Sir Harold Alexander, of the British Army, took over command of all land-based forces. Respected for his military expertise even by Patton, Alexander was dubious about the U.S. forces, whom he regarded as ill-trained, poorly disciplined, and weakly motivated. While still coping with North Africa, Operation Husky, the invasion of Sicily, was already starting to take shape on the Allied drawing boards, but there still remained the conquest of the *Afrika Korps*.

The stage was set for a decisive advance toward the coastline via Gafsa and El Guettar, towns on the Eastern Dorsal, the final mountain range before the sea. Hell bent on confounding Alexander's low opinion of the American forces, Patton directed an ambitious and successful campaign that routed the Germans and Italians from the objectives and beyond. Patton, dissatisfied with the 1st Armored Division's performance, had sent Orlando Ward packing and, with the 2d Armored Division training for Sicily, brought in its commander, Ernest Harmon, to take charge.

Harmon's description of his meeting with Patton on this occasion is indicative of a kind of manic-depressive quality about Patton. "I was shown to Patton's rooms," said Harmon, "where he apparently had lain down to sleep in the middle of the day. It was terribly hot and there wasn't a breath of air. Upon opening the door, General Patton was just sitting on the edge of his bed, putting on his boots. His dog Jimmy, with one black patch over his eye, was in the room and the whole room smelled fetid with dog smell and hot air. Patton wasn't in a very good mood, having just woke up from sleep. I reported to him and he grunted that he was glad to see me. He told me to get on out to Maknassy, some 40 miles to the east, and relieve General Ward.

"I asked him what I was to do, attack or defend, and with

this he flew into a kind of rage and said, 'What have you come here for, asking me a lot of Goddamned stupid questions!' I said I didn't think it was stupid. I simply asked two very fundamental questions, whether I was to attack or defend. He said, 'Get the hell out of here and get on with what I told you to do or I will send you back to Morocco.' "

Harmon then visited with Patton's chief of staff, who attributed Patton's behavior to his disgust with Ward and a reaction to being aroused from a nap. Ward apparently had backed and filled over a critical mountain pass for a period of time and Patton worried that the enemy might slip behind the Americans. Patton's deputy told Harmon his mission would be to retain the pass.

When Harmon arrived at his command, Hamilton Howze, the American operations officer, quickly apprised him of the situation. The new 1st Division CG directed his forces, including infantrymen from the 9th Division, to attack, with an objective of gaining several miles each day. "Patton called me up and said, 'What in hell are you doing out there?' I said, 'Nothing. We are just attacking here.' He said, 'I told you to stay on defense.' I said, 'You didn't tell me a damned thing. You just told me to get the hell out. We are just making limited-objective attacks to keep the Germans off balance and we are going to hold here, as [your chief of staff] said that's what you wanted.' He then replied, 'That is fine, okay, Harmon.' "

The new leader of the 1st Armored was hardly less quick-tempered than Patton. He angered many in his organization with a talk to his staff that implied the division had been less than exemplary. He instituted fines for any officer late for one of his meetings. He had very harsh words for a British unit that blocked his progress when it took time out for afternoon tea. He only barely contained himself when General

Anderson, the Briton in command of the army that included the 1st Armored, made some slighting remarks.

Later, members of an advance guard discovered a cellar full of wine and nearly drank themselves into a state of stupor. "That made me very mad," said Harmon, "so I told Colonel [Lawrence] Dewey, my operations officer, to get the names of the men who were drunk and have them shot right away. Colonel Dewey was a fine officer and with me pretty much during all of the war. He often softened the blow and he knew when I was mad and he knew what to do about it. I asked him about sundown if the men had been shot and he said, 'I think we ought to let the men live until sunrise, as it is usually customary to allow them to live until sunrise to say their prayers and what not.' I said, 'All right, but have them shot at sunrise for abandoning their mission in the face of the enemy.'

"At sunrise the next day I asked if they had been shot, and by this time I had cooled off a bit and when he said, they hadn't, I said to hell with it and that ended the matter. I don't blame the men so much, but at the time it seemed a very poor moment for anyone to incapacitate himself, especially when he was covering the movement of the column."

In mid-April, Patton passed the baton for II Corps to Omar Bradley and busied himself in preparations for Husky at Seventh Army headquarters. The combined drive by the Allied forces squeezed the enemy into an ever-shrinking area. The British Eighth Army under Montgomery advanced from the south and east, while that country's First Army operated north and west. In the center, the II Corps, including Harmon, pressed forward.

Bill Kunz was an enlisted man in headquarters battery of the 39th Field Artillery, part of the 3d Infantry Division, as it closed in on the enemy. "We were in a column with some infantry which did encounter scattered resistance. This was nothing more than machine-gun fire at some little crossroads. At the time, being relatively 'new' at the game [although involved in the original landing, his assignments had restricted his exposure to hostile action], the engagement seemed significant. A little later, we met some Australian troops. We were a source of amusement to them as we were towing 37mm antitank guns—small-caliber equipment. 'Where are you Yanks going with the popguns?' "

The final offensive, begun early in May, brought the 1st Armored Division to the outskirts of Bizerte. Harmon recalled coming up on the crest of a hill overlooking the city. He watched his tanks clamber into position for the final assault. "My aide and I got into a Jeep and drove to the edge of the plain where I saw some tanks firing but none moving to the front. I got ahold of the commander. He said they were under heavy machine-gun fire. I said, 'Follow me in the Jeep,' and that sort of shamed him. We all went forward and after I had gotten the tanks started, I moved off to see what my right tank force was doing. As we pitched over the brow of a small rise I ran into a whole company of German soldiers who were hugging the side of a cut to keep from getting slaughtered by our artillery. We had one of our artillery liaison planes hovering overhead directing fire into them. Captain Moody [his aide] and I dove off the Jeep and landed right among the German soldiers. They hugged the ground and alongside of them was ourselves. I said to myself, 'I've really stepped into it. I've gotten myself, a division commander, captured. I yelled to the German captain, 'Hauptmann, I've got to go back and have this artillery fire raised and arrange for your surrender. You come with me.' We got in the Jeep, turned around, went down the road about a mile where we ran into the forward observer for our artillery and arranged for some of our own infantry to go up and take the Germans prisoners.

"I sensed something drastic was about to happen. I rushed back to my command post, just in time. Colonel [Maurice] Rose, my chief of staff, told me we had three German officers who had just come in under a flag of truce and wanted to know what the terms of surrender were. The only thing I could think of was 'unconditional surrender. We propose to move immediately upon your works,' as my great Civil War hero, General Grant, said in front of Fort Donaldson. I told the Germans there weren't any terms except unconditional surrender. It was 9 o'clock. I would give them until 10 o'clock to make up their minds. If they hadn't surrendered by 11, I would move the attack forward and drive them into the sea. If anybody blew up any of the equipment or tried to escape we'd shoot 'em down. The senior German asked if I'd send one of my staff officers along with him so he could tell the German commander my terms. I said, 'All right, you go with them, Colonel Rose.' I don't think Colonel Rose cared too much for this but Colonel Rose's command car, with a flag of truce with three German officers blindfolded, rolled off toward the German lines. I telephoned General Bradley. He said, "Your terms are all right, Ernie. Have you any idea how many of them there are?' and I said, 'No, probably three or four thousand.'

"Pretty soon, Colonel Rose's voice came over the radio, 'The Germans accept your offer and wish to have you cease firing at once.' I said, 'How about those bastards on the left?' The first request had come from the Germans on my right flank. I hadn't heard from the commander on my left flank. My reference to the Germans as bastards coming in over the clear sort of nettled Rose, who had accepted an offer of a drink of champagne with the Germans. Soon Rose's voice came in, saying the left-flank commander accepted. I issued orders all along the line: cease firing, everybody hold his place, no forward movement. This ended the battle.

"Next thing was to collect the prisoners, and I was able to tell Bradley that a conservative estimate indicated we had at least 20,000 prisoners. I kept calling him and finally we had nearly 42,000 Germans, including nine general officers. It was a mighty big haul. We had all the roads blocked by tanks. We had the German people handle themselves. We told them to go into camps, stack their arms, bring their own rolling kitchens up, feed their men and stay in these temporary camps until we could evacuate them to the rear. They couldn't go anywhere. There was sea on three sides of the peninsula and we had tanks covering the other side. We shipped in truckloads of rations when they were needed. They were very orderly and well disciplined. I think most of them were glad the war was over. They were part of Rommel's *Afrika Korps*, Panzer troops, the elite of the German army. They were the best soldiers I've ever seen in appearance and behavior."

It was the first significant victory for an Allied campaign in the West and a prerequisite for the strategy aimed at the so-called soft underbelly.

Roll Call

Adair, Marion. The 4th Infantry Division battalion surgeon resumed his medical practice in Georgia until retirement in 1990.

Alison, John. Air Corps lend-lease consultant, fighter pilot with the Fourteenth Air Force in the China-Burma Theater, an ace, he retired as a major general.

Allen, Brooke. Commander of the 5th Bomb Group at Hickam Field, Hawaii, on 7 December 1941, he supervised training of B-29 crews and retired in 1965 as a major general.

Allen, Terry. Commanding general of the 1st and 104th Infantry Divisions, he is deceased. His only son, who graduated from the U.S. Military Academy, was killed in Vietnam.

Altieri, James. An original Ranger, he has been active in the Rangers Association as well as the World War II Remembrance Society and makes his home in Corona Del Mar, California.

Andrusko, Ed. After thirty-three months of service, earning three Purple Hearts with the 1st Marine Division, he expressed no regrets for his experiences. "I saw our countrymen united against our enemies in a worldwide war. The men in my company were my family and friends, our senior NCOs were our parents. Item Company was my home on land or sea. We protected each other and fought for each other. After the war, I felt I could handle anything in the civilian world and took on all challenges, started college a day after my discharge. We returning veterans had pride in our accomplishments, love for our families, and ambition for our future. We assimilated into the civilian world with ease." After a career in electronics, he lives in Colorado.

Ashe, Walter. The pre-war-Navy sailor sailed on a number of ships in the Pacific theater, was aboard the first vessel to dock in Korea after the fighting began there, and in 1966 retired after thirty years of service. He lives in Asheville, North Carolina.

Ashworth, Frederick. "There's only two guys in the world who have had the experience of essentially being in tactical command of the delivery of an atom bomb in wartime, and I am one of them. You're supposed to get very emotional about it. How did it feel? I didn't feel anything in particular. I guess it is just like so many other experiences. While they are going on, you don't really feel much of anything except that this is a job that has to be done. When you get shot at, you're not scared right then. You are too busy doing what has to be done. You do get scared after it's all over." He retired as a vice admiral and lives in New Mexico.

Austin, Gordon. An Air Corps fighter pilot, hunting deer in the Hawaiian Islands at the time of the Japanese attack, he had graduated from West Point in 1936—"I don't remember choosing anything. My father [an architect and veteran of the Spanish-American War] sent me." He retired as a major general.

Austin, Paul. Following his stint as a company commander and battalion staff officer with the 24th Infantry Division, he worked for a telephone company until retirement. "I was sick to my stomach, of all those who'd been killed or got wounded. But that's the infantry story. You take the mud, the pain, do without food, do without water, and you keep fighting." He lives in Fort Worth.

Barron, Frank Jr. Following his role as a platoon leader and company commander with the 77th Division, he became an executive in the textile industry. He makes his home in Columbia, South Carolina.

Baum, Abe. The leader of the ill-fated task force that bore his name went into the garment industry after the war. He retired to southern California.

Behlmer, Bill. The antitank crewman with the 1st Division received a prosthesis for his amputated right leg and worked in the aircraft industry.

Bernheim, Eli. After combat in the Philippines with the 11th Airborne Division, he worked in the family business before re-entering the service to participate in the Korean War. He retired after more than twenty years to enter business and now lives in Florida.

Biddle, Melvin. The Medal of Honor awardee from the 517th Parachute Regimental Combat Team spent nearly thirty years as an employee of the Veterans Administration in his home state of Indiana.

Bluemel, Clifford. The commander of the 31st Philippine Division in 1941 survived captivity and retired as a major general. He is deceased.

Bolt, Jones E. A P-47 pilot, he recalled the depths of the Great Depression when a man with rags on his feet for shoes asked for a job and his father, a textile manufacturer, had none to offer. "Everybody elected the ROTC [at Clemson University] because we got something like twenty-five cents a day." As a prisoner of war he struggled through the infamous march from StalagLuft III to Moosburg and said, "We found out that Hitler had ordered all of us shot. Goering [Hermann, the Nazi *Luftwaffe* chief] refused to carry out the order." He retired as a major general.

Bouck, Lyle. He became a chiropractor in St. Louis.

Bower, William. The Doolittle Raid pilot who reached China and escaped capture remained in the Air Force until he retired as a colonel.

Boyle, Bill. Commander of the 1st Battalion of the 517th Parachute Regimental Combat Team, he recovered from his wounds in the Ardennes, and served in Korea before retirement. After a few years in security he went back to school, and opened a business in accountancy. "My first company commander after I graduated from West Point told me, 'You take care of the men and they will take care of you.'" He lives in Saratoga Springs, New York.

Buckley, Pete. A glider pilot for D day in Normandy, Market Garden in Holland, and Varsity across the Rhine, he studied commercial photography under the GI Bill. "I came home ten years older than I should have been and I had enough of flying." His home is in Connecticut.

Bulkeley, John D. The 1930 United States Naval Academy graduate awarded a Medal of Honor after he helped MacArthur leave the Philippines aboard a PT boat, later commanded torpedo boats during the Normandy invasion, and then finished the war aboard the cruiser *Houston*, reborn after the original ship was sunk by the Japanese. He died a vice admiral in 1998 after sixty-four years of active duty.

Burchinal, David. A B-29 test pilot and participant in

raids on Japan, he had worked in a factory and been a union leader after graduation from Brown University before the war. He remained in the Air Force, helping develop the Air University curriculum; held staff posts at upper echelons and retired as a general.

Caron, George. The tail gunner on the *Enola Gay* is deceased.

Carlton, Paul. After flying a number of B-29 missions against Japan from China and mining the Singapore Harbor as well as the enemy-controlled portions of the Yangtze River, Carlton piloted pathfinder planes from the Marianas. "We would fly upwind over the target precisely dropping our bombs. Then the follow-on force would come in and bomb on our fire, downwind. The survival rate upwind was kind of atrocious." On one such occasion, the headwind reduced the pathfinder's speed to only eighty knots; ten out of the twelve in the operation went down. The upwind approach was abandoned. He retired as a general after running the Military Airlift Command.

Carmichael, Richard. He was a 1936 graduate of the U.S. Military Academy, after joining the Texas National Guard at age fifteen. Interviewed in 1942 about a number of subjects including morale, he remarked, "The two main topics, except at the dinner table, were bombing and women. I personally believe that if there were some form of controlled prostitution around an Army camp, it would be the best solution . . . it would control the venereal rate and keep the combat crews a hell of a lot happier." He noted that as a prisoner it struck him that the Japanese "were going to fight to the bitter end . . . the military . . . and the populace went along with whatever the military decided. They put us to work digging tunnels, caves actually, inside of hills not far from where our gardens were. We presumed that this was part of their last-ditch defense system." He left the service as a major general.

Carpenter, John. As a 1939 graduate of the USMA, he transferred from the field artillery to USAF, which brought him to the 19th Bomb Group in the Philippines in 1941. After he reached Australia, Carpenter flew missions in the Pacific, and following V-J Day held various staff posts before retiring as a lieutenant general. He lives in North Carolina.

Carter, Norval. The 29th Infantry Division battalion surgeon KIA in Normandy left a widow and two sons. Upon the death of Emma Ferne Lowry Carter in 1995, their son Walter discovered several caches of correspondence between her and his father. Walter Carter researched the experiences of his father and discovered in my book *June 6, 1944: The Voices of D-Day* an excerpt from Frank Wawrynovic's account that mentioned the circumstances of his father's death. Walter Carter wrote to me and very kindly allowed me to make use of portions of the collected letters of Norval Carter.

Chism, John. The medic with the 517th Parachute Regimental Combat Team left the service to attend college, where he earned a reserve commission and went on active duty as a field artillery commander during the Korean War. He remained in the Army until retirement as a colonel.

Cochran, Philip. After he completed his tour as joint leader of the 1st Air Commando unit in the Far East, he trained pilots until the war's end. Physical disabilities forced him to retire in 1947 with the rank of colonel. He provided technical expertise to Hollywood filmmakers before entering business in Pennsylvania. He died in 1979.

Conver, Milt. The bombardier with the 303d Bomb Group coped with respiratory infections that limited his missions with the Eighth Air Force. After V-E Day he left the service, entered business in Ohio. He is deceased.

Creel, Buckner. A platoon leader with the 77th Division on Guam and in the Philippines, he commanded a company on Okinawa. He fought in Korea, where he was wounded, and then in Vietnam before retirement. He lives in Arlington, Virginia.

Cutter, Slade. The former submariner and 1935 USNA graduate retired as a captain and lives in Annapolis.

Darby, William O. After the disaster at Cisterna that destroyed three of his battalions, the founder of the Rangers, who previously refused offers to lead regiments, took over the 179th Regiment of the 45th Division at Anzio. Subsequently named assistant commander of the 10th Mountain Division, he was killed by German artillery fire, two days before the enemy forces in Italy surrendered.

Davison, Michael. A USMC graduate, the former staff officer and battalion commander with the 45th Division earned a graduate degree at Harvard, commanded troops in Vietnam, and headed the army units in Europe before retirement as a general. He lives in Virginia.

Dawson, Frank (Buck). The 5th Ranger Battalion lieutenant who led pinned-down troops off Omaha Beach on D day entered the reserves following V-E Day, but when recalled for the Korean War elected the service as a career, which culminated in 1968 after a tour in Vietnam. He is deceased.

DeHaven, Robert. The USAF ace with fourteen victories retired as a colonel and lives in southern California.

DeLoach, James. The 32d Division company officer chose to enter local government after the war and lives in Columbia, South Carolina.

Duckworth, George. The 2d Infantry Division officer

stayed in uniform, retiring as a colonel, and lives in New Mexico.

Dunfee, Bill. The 82d Airborne trooper worked for a lumber business in Columbus, Ohio, and became a top executive with the organization.

Dunn, Bill. The Air Force fighter pilot began his World War II experience as an infantryman with the Canadian Seaforth Highlanders. After V-J Day he advised in China, Iran, and South America during the 1950s before he put in his papers.

Edlin, Bob. The 2d Ranger Battalion platoon leader in Normandy, the Cotentin Peninsula, and in the grim winter on the German border held the job of a police chief in Indiana before moving to Corpus Christi, Texas, where he operates an antique auction house.

Eller, Ernest. A USNA 1925 graduate and a gunnery officer aboard the *Lexington* at the Battle of Midway, he retired as a captain. He is deceased.

Ellis, Richard. A B-25 pilot in the South Pacific who had been drafted in 1940 before enrolling in flight training, he completed 200 missions. He left the service to practice law, but when called up for Korea he stayed on until retirement as a general.

Emmens, Robert. After the war, the Doolittle Raid pilot who spent two years as a "guest of the Kremlin" served as a military attaché and in intelligence for the Air Force before retirement as a colonel.

Engeman, Len. The 9th Armored Division tank battalion commander who directed the capture of the vital bridge at Remagen remained in the Army until retirement as a colonel. He lives in California.

Erwin, Henry. The Air Corps crewman badly burned by

an incendiary and who received a Medal of Honor is deceased.

Eubank, Eugene. The commander of the B-17 19th Bomb Group in the Philippines on 7 December 1941, he earned Army wings almost thirty years earlier. He recalled that when Boeing produced the first Flying Fortress he and his associates immediately recognized it was far superior to any competitor's wares. However, while the prototype was being tested in 1935 at Wright Field, Ohio, the plane crashed. "We damned near sat down and cried when the first one was wrecked. In those days the manufacturer had to submit an article [a plane] that was tested, evaluated, and the board decided which one was going to win. If it hadn't been for that accident, Boeing would have won the competition and we would have had the B-17 two or three years ahead of what we did." He retired as a major general.

Evans, Bing. An original Ranger who was Darby's sergeant major, he received a commission before being captured at Cisterna. He noted that his experiences as a POW so scarred him that throughout his life he was subject to "black rages." He worked in private industry and now lives in Huntington, Indiana.

Gage, Tom. The Air Corps clerk captured on Bataan acts as a clearinghouse for information about prisoners of war from that period and lives in Tulsa, Oklahoma.

Gangel, Dick. The P-38 pilot came home from the Fifteenth Air Force in Italy to teach other flyers. After his honorable discharge he became an art director, first in advertising and then for *Sports Illustrated*. He lives in Weston, Connecticut, where he creates sculptures.

Gilliam, Tom. As an officer with the 2d Division, he recovered from wounds after a three-month hospital stay in time to participate in the final drives against the Germans.

After the enemy repulsed the unit in a brutal confrontation in the vicinity of Eisenschmitt, Gilliam noted to his superior that for the third time he had wound up the senior company commander in the battalion. He added that the only other officer of that responsibility who was left from their arrival in France on 9 July was home on a forty-five-days leave. Told he was regarded as the best in the division, Gilliam said he replied, " 'Colonel, I am going to be a dead company commander if this keeps up.' We retook the town the next day, but we lost 117 men up there that night. Less than three weeks later I was on orders to return home for a forty-five-day leave. But that three weeks included the second crossing of the Moselle, the closing of the Trier pocket, the crossing of the Rhine at Oppenheim, the capture of Frankfurt am Main, and the memorial service for President Roosevelt aboard ship." He lives in Lakeport, California.

Goode, John. The 36th Division officer shattered by the Rapido River experience is deceased.

Hartman, Tom. The Navy pilot recalled that while a student at Princeton, in his enthusiastic rush to enlist after the college requirements were lowered, his physical exam revealed possible problems with one eye. He was instructed to return for a second test. "A Navy corpsman was to be the examiner. His first question was, 'Are you another college boy?' I thought that I should drop through the floor. Princeton was like the kiss of death in that milieu. But I admitted my status. He said, 'Princeton! That's great.' He told me he had worked as an usher at the Chicago Opera House and the only company passing through that invited the ushers to their cast parties was the Triangle Club [the university's drama group]! He was so excited that he never gave my eye a look and signed my clearance." Hartman returned to his alma mater to complete his education and then taught at Rutgers. He lives in Princeton, New Jersey.

Hayes, Tommy. The Army fighter pilot who fought in both the Pacific and Europe retired as a colonel and lives in Pennsylvania.

Herder, Harry. The 2d Ranger Battalion replacement participated in the liberation of the Buchenwald concentration camp. "We were the last replacements taken into the battalion. Barely in my memory is the first job [that] rumor said we were scheduled to do. They were going to put us, a company at a time, in Piper Cubs and fly us over the Rhine. That was washed out when the Remagen Bridge stood. I remember a ballistic company commander. Being nearsighted made me less than perfect and unfit to be a Ranger. The way that man was mad at me was something else. With him, I did not belong. In 1947 I was accepted in jump school and allowed to be a member of the 82d Airborne for three years and they knew I wore glasses the whole time. Even jumped with them taped on once they found out. The helmet jammed them into my nose on 'opening shock.' They remained in my shirt pocket all the rest of the jumps."

Herder on his third military hitch joined the Navy and served as a corpsman for the Marines in Korea. He lives in Hayward, Wisconsin.

Hill, David (Tex). The former Navy flyer who enlisted in the American Volunteer Group under Gen. Clare Chennault retired as a colonel and is a resident of San Antonio.

Hite, Robert L. The last-minute addition to the Doolittle Raiders, who endured years of captivity, remained in the service after his liberation and worked as an air attaché in North Africa. He retired as a lieutenant colonel.

Hofrichter, Joe. The rifleman from the 24th Division entered a family construction business and makes his home in Port Charlotte, Florida.

Hostetter, Philip. The battalion surgeon with the 24th Division, after mustering out, opened a practice in family medicine and lives in Manhattan, Kansas.

Howze, Hamilton. The 1930 West Point alumnus who spent World War II with armored forces in North Africa and Italy switched to airborne in the 1950s to command the 82d Airborne Division and the Eighteenth Airborne Corps. He retired as a full general in 1965 and died in 1998.

Jackson, Schuyler. The 101st Airborne paratrooper worked in construction until his death in 1995.

Johnson, Fred. The former National Guardsman called up in 1940 and who fought with the 32d Division in the Pacific said, "I approved of what we did in the war then and still do. There was a sense of duty; you were scared, heck yes. But you just did what you thought you had to do. There was pride in not letting the others down. To bug out would make you ashamed. The worst food was in Buna, bully beef, and small rations, two spoons a day. I came home with malaria, having had three separate attacks." After his discharge he became a Superior, Wisconsin, policeman and then was elected sheriff ten times before retirement. He lives in Arizona.

Johnson, Leon. He was in the class of 1926 at the USMA. He led the 44th Bomb Group on the Ploesti raid, where he earned a Medal of Honor, and then commanded a bomber wing with the Eighth Air Force in England. He retired in 1961 as a general and died in 1998.

Johnson, Robert. The ground crew sergeant who volunteered for the 4th Armored Division was convicted of a 1971 murder and is serving a life term in North Carolina.

Johnson, Robert. The fighter pilot with the second highest number of planes shot down in Europe worked in the aircraft industry after the war. He died in 1998.

Jones, David M. The Doolittle Raider who parachuted into China then returned to duty was subsequently shot down in a B-26 during a raid on Bizerte. He became a prisoner of war in Germany. Following liberation he held positions in the Pentagon, with NASA, and other research projects. He retired as a major general.

Jones, Harry. The Navy pilot who helped sink the *Yamato* remarked, "I think it was a good idea to drop the atomic bomb because I think the invasion would have killed millions of Japanese. War is hell; stay the hell out of it. We had no business in Vietnam; in my opinion we should stay the hell out of Bosnia. They should have some sort of international police there." He became an FBI agent and now lives in Carlisle, Pennsylvania.

Jones, Homer. After the war ended, the paratroop platoon leader left the service but was recalled for the war in Korea. He remained on active duty until retirement and then taught Spanish in public schools. He lives in Florida.

Kelly, Walter. The Eighth Air Force pilot who flew the first B-17 raid on occupied Europe later flew missions against the Japanese in the Pacific. He continued his career in the Air Force after the end of hostilities and retired as a colonel. He worked in private industry before retiring to a home in Alexandria, Virginia.

Kidwell, Vance. The draftee from Illinois who became a replacement in a supply section of the 2d Armored Division while the outfit was in North Africa was with the outfit when it reached France on D plus 1. He lives in Donnellson, Illinois.

Kitzmann, Erich. The *Suwannee* crewman blown overboard after a Kamikaze explosion worked in aircraft maintenance until he retired to Sedona, Arizona.

Kunz, William J. The former 3d Infantry Division field artillery hand who campaigned through North Africa, Sicily, Italy, Anzio, southern France, and Germany lives in Illinois.

Loiacano, Leonard. An artilleryman, he said, "When the gun was fired it made so much noise that you had to keep your mouth open and if your hands were free you put them in your ears. We would be wet to the skin, cold and in total darkness. Most of the time we got six hours of sleep every other night. One time we went sixty hours without sleep. We were never relieved and always firing for somebody. We dug gun pits and cut down trees [to brace the artillery and cover foxholes] from Normandy to Czechoslovakia." The 105mm howitzer crewman with the 5th Infantry Division had amassed enough points to warrant discharge shortly after V-E Day. "When we were home, the two 'A' bombs were dropped and the war was over. Many years later the bleeding hearts would say what a terrible thing it was to drop the bomb. For all of those people I wish them ten months of combat and then let us hear what they have to say." He makes his home in Yeadon, Pennsylvania.

Lomell, Len (Bud). The Ranger sergeant involved in the destruction of enemy big guns atop Pointe du Hoc on D day received a battlefield commission before being wounded a second time. He studied law under the GI Bill and practiced in New Jersey where he makes his home.

Long, Stanley. The first P-38 pilot to shoot down a Japanese plane in the Aleutians, he remained in the Air Force, retiring as a colonel.

Low, Martin. The fighter pilot, who was at Hickam Field on 7 December 1941 and over the Normandy beaches on 6 June 1944, came home after seventy-five missions in Europe. "I had seen enough of the Army in peacetime to know that it was not for me. I applied to the airlines but they did not think fighter pilots had the right stuff. Because of my experience of war I took up the cause of the United Nations, which I believe is a much more viable method of settling differences." As a civilian he produced commercials for TV and lives in a suburb of New York City.

Lynd, J. Q. The 90th Division platoon leader recovered from his wounds and became a research scientist and teacher at Oklahoma State University in Stillwater, Oklahoma.

Mabry, George L. Jr. The 4th Division officer finally received a regular army commission in 1944 and by the time the war ended he was the second most decorated soldier of the conflict. He subsequently graduated from the Command and General Staff College, the National War College, and held a variety of command, training, and staff positions. He led a 100-man team of officers and civilians to evaluate operations in Vietnam and later served as chief of staff and assistant deputy commanding general for the U.S. Army Forces in Vietnam. In 1975 he retired as a major general and lived in Columbia, South Carolina, until his death in 1990.

McCubbin, James. The fighter pilot now lives in Garberville, California.

Meltessen, Clarence. The 4th Ranger Battalion lieutenant captured at Cisterna survived more than a year in the stalags. He remained on active duty after the war, retiring as a colonel. He has compiled an exhaustive record of what happened to his fellow Rangers and their experiences in the prisoner-of-war camps. He lives in California.

Merrill, Alan. The 2d Battalion Ranger wounded and temporarily captured near Anzio recovered in a Naples hospital. During his recuperation he met a captain who offered to wangle a transfer to the Air Corps, enabling Merrill to serve out his time as a limited-duty, noncombat soldier. Assigned to the 379th Bomb Group, a B-25 outfit, he learned aircraft recognition while assisting in tow-target practice. He even went along on missions that dumped aluminum foil to foul up enemy radar. But when a batch of replacement gunners failed to arrive, Merrill was pressed into service as a tail gunner beginning in October 1944. He flew twenty-four missions, occupying various positions manning a .50-caliber machine gun. Flak ripped into his airplanes on several occasions, killing other members of the crew, and he survived a crash landing in the sea near Corsica. Blackouts, bleeding from his left ear and nose on his last missions grounded him after his twenty-fourth. He waited several months before orders finally sent him home via Casablanca, where he said he visited bordellos supervised by the U.S. Army with military police on duty.

"I went away a frightened boy. I returned a frightened man. The actual battle of enduring a war in the various types of combat that I participated in was not as riveting an experience as the battles my mind fought daily in the ensuing peaceful years. When the actual fighting was done I had to conquer my own personal, mental war of nerves. I found out much later that I had no control over what happened to the unprepared, mindless, loose ends of my young manhood and the residue of the code of killing or being killed. I don't believe I ever really adjusted to this code of the military survivor. Everything I was taught to do to survive was diametrically opposed to a way of life I had been raised to believe in for eighteen years.

"How does one go about 'unlearning' to kill another human being? This unlearning process comes ever so slowly or it never comes at all. It is your own individual struggle.

No one can do it for you. If this cannot be done, then peace of mind eludes you all your days. In my half century, since World War II and with my battles over, I truly believe that war is like a malignant tumor on the face of mankind." He now lives in Florida.

Mott, Hugh. The platoon leader who helped preserve the Remagen Bridge over the Rhine went into politics and in 1949 was elected to the Tennessee State Legislature while remaining active in the National Guard. He retired from the Guard as a major general in 1972.

Mueller, Arndt. The 6th Infantry Division battalion commander attended the Command and General Staff College and eventually joined its faculty. He headed the ROTC program at the University of Miami, earned a law degree, and joined the Florida bar.

Newman, Stan. The P-51 pilot assigned to the Fifteenth Air Force in Italy redeployed to the States after V-E Day in preparation for the finale against Japan. "I changed my mind about a regular air force career, took a reserve commission, and made it back to start my interrupted college at the University of Illinois. I was one of the first vets back and was like a fish out of water. I really missed the Air Corps life, good pay, great airplanes, and wonderful friends. But I eventually adapted." As a reserve officer, however, he was recalled during the Korean War and flew 100 missions in that conflict. During the war in Vietnam he flew cargo missions to Southeast Asia. He retired in 1983 as a major general and lives in Oklahoma.

Northrup, Jay. The replacement officer with the Rangers had been reassigned, but a bout of malaria contracted in Sicily sent him back to the States. After he left the service he entered the field of banking before retirement to Florida.

Odell, Bill. The Eighth Air Force pilot involved in the organization's first raid moved first to North Africa and then the Pacific. After he retired as a colonel he embarked on a career as a writer publishing many novels in the mystery, adventure, and Western genres. He lives in Colorado Springs.

Olson, John E. After liberation from his Philippine prison camp, the 1939 USMA graduate remained in uniform until retirement as a colonel in 1967. He has done extensive research and writing on the Bataan fighting, the Death March, and Philippine guerrilla movements. He lives in Houston, Texas.

Paris, Dee. The 9th Armored Division tank commander retained a reserve commission after the war and made barbershop quartet music his avocation while living in Maryland.

Poston, Tom. The troop carrier pilot chose the life of an actor after being mustered out. He appeared on Broadway, and in numerous roles on radio and then television. He lives in California.

Raaen, John C. Jr. One of the few West Pointers (class of 1943) to volunteer for the Rangers, his jeep accident in France ended World War II for him. In 1951 he earned a master's degree from Johns Hopkins and then held command posts with various units before retirement as a major general. He lives in Florida.

Raila, Frank. The 106th Division soldier taken prisoner in the Ardennes became a radiologist in Mississippi. The emotional outbursts, triggered by his memories of the stalag that disturbed him in the years immediately after the war, subsided.

Rants, Hanford. The wireman with the 24th Infantry Division, which fought in the Pacific theater, used the GI Bill to complete his education at Washington State University, then taught in high school before becoming a principal. He lives in Downey, California.

Robison, Noel (Eugene). As a replacement, he joined the 90th Division in November 1944, where he served as a runner until his frozen feet disabled him during the Battle of the Bulge. He lives in Claremont, California.

Rosson, William. The officer with the 3d Infantry Division, as an honor student in the ROTC program at the University of Oregon in 1940, had obtained a regular army commission. His senior captain instructed a first sergeant, "I want you to make an officer of Lieutenant Rosson." Rosson says, "The training was rather rudimentary and simply wouldn't be accepted today. It was a peacetime oriented affair with more emphasis upon spit and polish, cleanliness of barracks and whatnot rather than combat readiness. I never attended the basic course of the infantry school. I went into the war and learned on the job."

When he visited the Dachau concentration camp after its liberation, he recalled, "I was shaken—so much so that when I left I was literally unable to speak as I drove back to the division. I had never seen such depravity and inhuman treatment." Following his service in Italy and France, Rosson qualified for airborne, was involved in the Vietnam conflict before his retirement in 1975 as a general, and resides in Florida.

Ruhlen, George. The commander of the 3d Field Artillery attached to the 9th Armored Division, a 1932 graduate of the USMA, retired on a disability in 1970 as a major general. He lives in San Antonio.

Salomon, Sid. The Ranger captain who captured Pointe et Raz de la Percée at Omaha Beach entered the paper products field after the war. He makes his home in Pennsylvania.

Salter, Cary. The P-47 and P-51 fighter pilot in the Ninth

Air Force said, "We were shooting down planes but we knew we were killing people, too. I don't know any of our guys who lost sleep over it. We were there to fight a war and the more we killed, the quicker it would be over and the less likely we would be killed." He became a pharmacist, then presided over a wholesale drug firm. Active in the P-40 Warhawk Pilots Association, he resides in Jackson, Mississippi.

Schueler, Jon. The B-17 navigator, invalided home for physical and emotional disabilities, became a well-known painter. His autobiography, *The Sound of Sleat*, was published posthumously in 1999.

Schwarz, Otto. A prisoner of war after the sinking of the USS *Houston*, he endured years of hard labor, beatings, and lack of food in a series of camps. "We were under strict orders that, whenever a Japanese of any rank approached us, the first person seeing him had to shout in good Japanese and call the group to attention. You then all had to properly bow to the person. You had to bow from the hips down with the face tilting up and facing the person. If you deviated from this at all, you very quickly got bashed."

Schwarz recalled that the British captives treated the problem of sanitation far more casually than the Americans and as a consequence suffered a much greater incidence of dysentery. However, they insisted upon maintaining a military mode. "These guys acted as if they were on regimental maneuvers. The British held regular drills—complete uniforms, full field packs—and they would march up and down the hills, and the officers with their little 'dog-chasers,' the little sticks they carried, would be marching alongside of them." The Americans in shorts and ragged garments refused to salute and an intense dislike grew between the two allies.

Shipped to Burma, Schwarz became part of the gangs constructing a railroad much like that described in the film *The Bridge on the River Kwai*. Along with the prisoners, the Japanese conscripted thousands of local people who, said Schwarz, "died like flies. Entire villages, the entire male populations of villages were just wiped out."

Toward the end of the war, while housed in Saigon, Schwarz and three companions escaped and sought refuge in the French quarter of the city, only to be caught up in the Vietnamese effort to oust the French. Jailed by the rebels along with the French, Schwarz convinced his captors that he was an American and was allowed to return to the Japanese prison camp. A U.S. Army officer parachuted in to the camp and officially freed all of the POWs.

"My service in the Navy and World War II were years of great pride and dedication to America. I have been in the presence of men who have cried openly when hearing our National Anthem, which was picked up by a Japanese radio in Saigon. These were the kinds of men I was privileged to serve with. Despite our disadvantage of being ill prepared, outnumbered, and outgunned at the beginning of World War II, and the horrendous ordeal of three and one-half years as Japanese POWs, we never wavered in our loyalty and faith in our country."

In 1948, Schwarz entered the U.S. Postal Service and on retirement in 1980 held a senior management position. He lives in Union, New Jersey.

Shapiro, Alan. After leaving the service, the 87th Division rifleman taught school and now lives in Ridgefield, Connecticut.

Sims, Ed. The paratrooper officer with the 504th Regiment went on inactive reserve after being demobilized, but said, "I returned to active duty because good employment was hard to find and I was more oriented toward military life." He retired as a colonel in 1968, then earned a college degree and held jobs with a title company and, later, as a county probation officer. He lives in New Jersey.

Smith, Robert. The Air Force B-26 pilot in the South Pacific became intelligence director of the Strategic Air Command during the 1950s, where he pioneered in the use of computers for dealing with intelligence. He retired as a lieutenant general.

South, Frank. "The death of FDR [12 April 1945] came as a shock. There was not a dry eye that could be found. I recall leaning against a tree and bawling like an infant." After V-E Day, South's unit became part of Patton's Third Army. For a review before himself and some Soviet officers, Patton ordered clean, pressed uniforms and polished boots, which South considered reasonable. Further instruction to coat helmets with shellac and all arms and vehicles oiled on the surfaces to provide a shine struck the Ranger as foolish because of the prevalence of road dust. "Most of us had long regarded Patton as a bloody popinjay whose exhibitionist streak was witnessed by his dress and pearl-handled revolvers." The medic with the 2d Ranger Battalion used his benefits to study biophysics and physiology. He lives in Maryland.

Southworth, Billy. The B-17 pilot completed his tour in the United Kingdom but was killed on a training flight in 1945.

Stroop, Paul D. A USNA 1926 alumnus, he retired as a vice admiral and died in 1995.

Strange, Glen. The 27th Armored Infantry officer required two years of medical treatment for his wounds before he recovered enough to work in manufacturing. He later became a postmaster in Oklahoma.

Swanson, Wallace. The 101st Airborne company commander worked in the petroleum industry and lives in Alabama.

Taylor, Harold. The 3d Division GI joined the Fort Wayne police department, put in twenty years, and then operated a part-time cabinet-making shop.

Thach, John (Jimmy). The naval aviator says, "Everybody's scared, but it isn't a thing you can let prey on your mind very long because there's always something to do. And you can function just as well, maybe a little better, if you're scared." He retired as a full admiral and died in 1981.

Turner, William (Pappy). The army pilot said, "I did not shoot at anyone in a parachute although I had several chances. I figured he had his problems. Also on the ground he could be captured, some information gained. On one occasion, one of the pilots asked me for permission to strafe the Jap in the parachute. I told him to let his conscience be his guide. He broke off, made a pass at the man, but did not shoot." After the war he worked briefly in private industry before signing on with the New York State Department of Public Works and switched to the Department of Transportation. He now lives in Florida.

Ullom, Madeline. The former army nurse, taken prisoner in the Philippines, now lives in Tucson.

Ulsaker, Carl. The USMA 1942 graduate finished the war with the 95th Division. He collected a master's degree and then taught English at West Point. He retired as a colonel in 1969 and resides in Virginia.

Uzemack, Ed. The 28th Division POW returned to a career as a newspaperman and then entered public relations in Chicago.

Vaccaro, Tony. Born in the United States to Italian émigrés, the 83d Division intelligence specialist had lived in

Italy for much of his childhood and early adolescence where he developed an abiding hatred of the fascist philosophy. After V-E Day he signed on as a photographer for the military newspaper *Stars and Stripes*, and then as a civilian remained in Europe several more years building a reputation for his photographs. Back in the States he worked on staff for *Look* and the short-lived but influential *Flair* before a long successful career as a freelancer. He lives in New York City.

Vogel, Walter. The 1937 enlistee in the Navy started his career in the Asiatic Fleet and served on the ill-fated *Houston* in the first months after the war began. Having survived the sinking of the destroyer *Blue* and other adventures, he was promoted to the rank of chief petty officer and assigned to the destroyer *Hyman* engaged in picket duty off Okinawa. The kamikaze hit on the *Hyman* brought a third Purple Heart to Vogel, but the full extent of his wounds only surfaced several months after V-J Day when he collapsed with ruptured lungs, apparently due to the explosion off Okinawa. He recovered after four months of hospitalization and served on a number of ships including support for the war in Korea. He taught at the USNA as well as other institutions and became a commissioned officer. He weathered an attack of blindness before retirement in 1970. He lives in Tennessee.

Walker, Anthony. The Yale graduate and Marine officer remained in the Corps. "I suppose I decided to stay on because I liked the life, was reasonably successful in the war and had nothing else to do, not being qualified or interested in other professions or business." His three sons all became leathernecks. He makes his home in Rhode Island.

Warneke, Bud. The paratrooper with the 508th Parachute Regimental Combat Team won a battlefield commission and remained in the service until 1964 when he retired and began a TV rental service. He lives in North Carolina.

Warriner, Vic. The glider pilot involved in the D day invasion, and the Market Garden and Varsity operations, completed his education at the University of Michigan and became a real estate developer in Texas. He lives in Fort Worth.

Widoff, Gerald. The interpreter with Merrill's Marauders began a career as a violinist with prominent orchestras before starting a chain of music record stores. His home is in New York City.

Yarborough, William. The USMA Class of 1936 paratrooper officer, following World War II, held top staff positions at home and abroad until his retirement in 1971 as a lieutenant general. He lives in North Carolina.

Bibliography

Adair, Charles. Oral History. Annapolis, Maryland: United States Naval Institute.

Alexander, Irvin. *Memoirs of Internment in the Philippines, 1942–45*. West Point: U.S. Military Academy.

Alison, John R. Oral Histories. Maxwell Field, Alabama: United States Air Force Historical Center, 1943, 1944, 1960, 1977, 1979.

Allen, Brooke E. Oral History. Maxwell Field, Alabama: United States Air Force Historical Center, 1965.

Altieri, James. *The Spearheaders*. Indianapolis: Bobbs-Merrill Company, Inc., 1960.

Ambrose, Stephen E. *Citizen Soldiers*. New York: Simon & Schuster, 1997.

Andrusko, Edward. Unpublished Stories. Denver, Colo.

Archer, Clark, ed. *Paratroopers' Odyssey*. Hudson, Florida: 517th Parachute Regimental Combat Team Association, 1985.

Ashworth, Frederick. Oral History. Annapolis, Maryland: United States Naval Institute.

Austin, Gordon H. Oral History. Maxwell Field, Alabama: United States Air Force Historical Center, 1982.

Benitez, R. C. *Battle Stations Submerged.* Annapolis, Maryland: *Proceedings*, January 1948.

Bidwell, Sheffield. *The Chindit War.* New York: Macmillan Publishing Co., Inc., 1979.

Blair, Clay. *Ridgway's Paratroopers.* Garden City, New York: Dial Press, 1985.

Bluemel, Clifford. Private Papers. West Point: U.S. Military Academy Library.

Blumenson, Martin. *Mark Clark.* New York: Congdon & Weed, 1984.

Bolt, Jones E. Oral History. Maxwell Field, Alabama: United States Air Force Historical Center, 1984.

Bower, William. Oral History. Maxwell Field, Alabama: United States Air Force Historical Center, 1971.

Bradley, Omar. *A Soldier's Story.* New York: Henry Holt and Company, Inc., 1951.

Breuer, William. *Geronimo!* New York: St. Martin's Press, 1989.

Budge, Joseph. Unpublished Memoir. Moraga, California.

Buffington, Herman. Unpublished Memoir. Jefferson, Georgia.

Bunker, Paul D. *The Bunker Diary.* West Point: U.S. Military Academy Library.

Burchinal, David A. Oral History. Maxwell Field, Alabama: United States Air Force Historical Center, 1975.

Byers, Dick. Unpublished Memoir. Mentor-on-the-Lake, Ohio.

Carlton, Paul K. Oral History. Maxwell Field, Alabama: United States Air Force Historical Center, 1979.

Carmichael, Richard. Oral Histories. Maxwell Field, Alabama: United States Air Force Historical Center, 1942, 1980.

Caron, George R. Oral History. Maxwell Field, Alabama: United States Air Force Historical Center, 1975.

Carpenter, John W. Oral History. Maxwell Field, Alabama: United States Air Force Historical Center, 1970.

Cass, Bevan, ed. *History of the 6th Marine Division.* Washington, D.C.: Infantry Journal, Inc., 1948.

Chandler, P. R. Oral History. Maxwell Field, Alabama: United States Air Force Historical Center, 1943.

Chernitsky, Dorothy. *Voices from the Foxholes.* Uniontown, Pennsylvania: Dorothy Chernitsky, 1991.

Cochran, Philip. Oral Histories. Maxwell Field, Alabama: United States Air Force Historical Center, 1943, 1975.

Cole, Hugh M. *The Ardennes: The Battle of the Bulge.* Washington, D.C.: Center of Military History, U.S. Army, 1965.

Cox, Luther C. *Always Fighting the Enemy.* Baltimore: Gateway, 1990.

Craig, Robert. Unpublished Memoir. Winter Haven, Florida.

Craven, Wesley Frank, and James Lea Cate. *The Army Air Force in World War II.* Vol. 1: vi. Chicago: U.S. Air Force History Office, University of Chicago Press, 1948.

Crosby, Harry H. *A Wing and a Prayer.* New York: Harper, 1993.

Cutter, Slade. Oral History. Annapolis, Maryland: United States Naval Institute.

Dacus, W. E., and E. Kitzmann. *As We Lived It—USS Suwannee (CVE-27).* USS Suwannee and its Air Groups, 27, 60, & 40. Reunion Association, 1992.

DeHaven, Robert M. Oral History. Maxwell Field, Alabama: United States Air Force Historical Center, 1977.

Dennison, Robert Lee. Oral History. Annapolis, Maryland: United States Naval Institute.

D'Este, Carlo. *Patton: A Genius for War.* New York: Harper-Collins, 1995.

Duckworth, George H. Unpublished memoir. Farmington, New Mexico.

Dunn, William. Oral History. Maxwell Field, Alabama: United States Air Force Historical Center, 1973.

Edlin, Robert. Unpublished Manuscript. Corpus Christi, Texas.

Edmonds, Walter D. *They Fought with What They Had.* Washington, D.C.: Center for Air Force History, 1951.

Eisenhower, David. *Eisenhower at War 1943–45.* New York: Random House, 1986.

Eisenhower, Dwight D. *Crusade in Europe.* Garden City, New York: Doubleday & Company, Inc., 1948.

Eisenhower, John. *The Bitter Woods: The Battle of the Bulge.* New York: G.P. Putnam's Sons, 1969.

Ellington, Paul. Oral History. American Air Power Heritage Museum, Midland, Texas, 1991.

Ellis, John. *Cassino: The Hollow Victory.* New York: Mc-Graw-Hill Book Company, 1984.

Ellis, Richard. Oral History. Maxwell Field, Alabama: United States Air Force Historical Center, 1987.

Emmens, Robert G. Oral History. Maxwell Field, Alabama: United States Air Force Historical Center, 1982.

Eubank, Eugene. Oral Histories. Maxwell Field, Alabama: United States Air Force Historical Center, 1942, 1982.

Fitzgerald, Ed. *A Penny an Inch.* New York: Atheneum, 1985.

Frank, Richard B. *Guadalcanal.* New York: Random House, 1990.

Freeman, Roger A., with Alan Crouchman and Vic Maslen.

The Mighty Eighth War Diary. London: Motorbooks International, 1990.

Gavin, James M. *On to Berlin.* New York: Viking Press, 1978.

Gelb, Norman. *Desperate Venture: The Story of Operation Torch.* New York: William Morrow and Company, 1992.

Gerevas, Larry. Unpublished Memoir. Napa, California.

Golubock, Ralph. *Hello, Pathway: A Bomber Pilot's Memories of Love and War.* Unpublished Manuscript. St. Louis.

Goodson, James. Oral History. American Air Power Heritage Museum, Midland, Texas, 1991.

Grashio, Samuel C., and Bernard Norling. *Return to Freedom.* Spokane, Washington: University Press, 1982

Hagerman, Bart., ed. *U.S. Airborne: 50th Anniversary.* Paducah, Kentucky: Turner Publishing Company, 1990.

Hall, Leonard G. *Brother of the Fox: Company F, 172d Infantry.* Orange, Texas, 1985.

Hallden, Charles. Unpublished Memoir. Madeira Beach, Florida.

Hamilton, Tom. Unpublished Memoir. Santa Barbara, California.

Hammel, Eric. *Guadalcanal: Starvation Island.* New York, Crown, 1987.

———*Munda Trail.* New York: Orion Books, 1989.

Hannon, Philip. Unpublished Memoir. Ellicott City, Maryland.

Hanson, Robert. *Memoirs.* Unpublished manuscript.

Harmon, Ernest. Oral History. Carlisle, Pennsylvania: United States Army History Institute.

Harrington, Jasper. Oral History. Maxwell Field, Alabama: United States Air Force Historical Center, 1981.

Hastings, Max. *Overlord: D-Day and the Battle for Normandy.* New York: Simon & Schuster, 1984.

Hawkins, Ian L. *B-17s Over Berlin*. Washington, D.C.: Brassey's, 1990.

Hechler, Ken. *The Bridge at Remagen*. Missoula, Montana: Pictorial Histories Publishing Company, 1993.

Heinl, Robert Debs Jr. *Soldiers of the Sea*. Annapolis: Naval Institute Press, 1962.

Herder, Harry J. Unpublished Memoir. Hayward, Wisconsin.

Hill, David (Tex). Oral History. Maxwell Field, Alabama: United States Air Force Historical Center, 1977.

Holloway, Bruce K. Oral History. Maxwell Field, Alabama: United States Air Force Historical Center, 1977.

Holloway, James L. III. *Historical Perspective: The Battle of Surigao Strait*. Naval Engineer's Journal, September 1994.

Hostetter, Philip H. *Doctor and Soldier in the South Pacific*. Unpublished Manuscript. Manhattan, Kansas.

Howard, Thomas. *All to This End: The Road to and through the Philippines*. Unpublished Manuscript. St. Charles, Missouri.

Howze, Hamilton. Oral History. Carlisle, Pennsylvania: United States Army Military History Institute.

Hoyt, Edwin P. *Submarines at War*. Briarcliff Manor, New York: Stein and Day, 1983.

Hudson, Ed. *The History of the USS Cabot (CVL-28)*. Hickory, North Carolina, 1988.

Jackson, Robert. *War Stories*. Unpublished Memoir. Anacortes, Washington.

Johnson, Robert S. Oral History. American Air Power Heritage Museum, Midland, Texas, 1977.

Kunz, William J. Unpublished Memoir. Rockford, Illinois, 1996.

LaMagna, Sam. *Silent Victory: Fox Company, 169th Regi-*

mental Combat Team, 43d Infantry Division. Unpublished Manuscript. Ocala, Florida.

Leckie, Robert. *Strong Men Armed.* New York: Random House, 1962.

Lee, Ulysses. *The Employment of Negro Troops.* Washington, D.C.: Center of Military History, 1994.

Leinbaugh, Harold P., and John D. Campbell. *The Men of Company K: The Autobiography of a World War II Rifle Company.* New York: William Morrow and Company, 1985.

Lynd, J. Q. *Château de Fontenay: Episode tragique de la libération 1944.* Unpublished Memoir. Stillwater, Oklahoma.

———*Legacy of Valor* [Video Script]. South Hill, Virginia: 90th Division Association.

MacArthur, Douglas. *Reminiscences.* New York: McGraw-Hill Book Company, 1964.

MacDonald, Charles. *A Time for Trumpets.* New York: William Morrow and Company, 1985.

———*Company Commander.* New York: Bantam, 1987.

———*The Mighty Endeavor: American Armed Forces in the European Theater in World War II.* New York: Oxford University Press, 1969.

McClintock, D. H. Narrative. Washington, D.C.: U.S. Naval Historical Center, 1945.

McClure, John. Oral History. American Air Power Heritage Museum, Midland, Texas, 1991.

McCubbin, James. Unpublished Memoirs. Garberville, California.

McManus, John. *The Deadly Brotherhood.* Novato, California: Presidio Press, 1998.

Mack, William. Oral History. Annapolis, Maryland: United States Naval Institute.

Manchester, William. *American Caesar.* Boston: Little, Brown & Company, 1978.

Martin, Harry. Unpublished Memoir. Mt. Arlington, New Jersey

Merillat, Herbert C. *Guadalcanal Remembered.* New York: Dodd, Mead & Company, 1982.

Milkovics, Lewis. *The Devils Have Landed.* Longwood, Florida: Creative Printing and Publishing, 1993.

Miller, Thomas G. Jr. *The Cactus Air Force.* New York: Harper & Row, 1969.

Mills, James. Unpublished Memoir. Vandalia, Ohio.

Moore, Ellis O. *Notes on Leaving Okinawa.* Pelham, New York: Privately Published, 1988.

Morison, Samuel Eliot. *The Battle of the Atlantic.* Boston: Little, Brown & Company, 1984.

————*Coral Sea, Midway and Submarine Actions.* Boston: Little, Brown & Company, 1984.

————*The Struggle for Guadalcanal.* Boston: Little, Brown & Company, 1949.

————*The Rising Sun in the Pacific.* Boston: Little, Brown & Company, 1961.

Morton, Louis. *The Fall of the Philippines, U.S. Army in World War II.* Washington, D.C.: Center of Military History, U.S. Army, 1953.

Muehrcke, Robert, ed. *Orchids in the Mud.* Chicago: Privately Published, 1985.

Mueller, Arndt. *Hill 400: The Destiny and the Agony.* Monograph.

Murphy, Robert. *Diplomat among Warriors.* Garden City, New York: Doubleday & Company, Inc. 1964.

Murray, S. S. Oral History. Annapolis, Maryland: United States Naval Institute.

Old, Archie Jr. Oral History. Maxwell Field, Alabama: Historical Research Center, Air University, 1982.

Olson, John E., assisted by Frank O. Anders. *Anywhere, Anytime: The History of the 57th Infantry (PS)*. Houston: John Olson, 1991.

————*O'Donnell: The Andersonville of the Pacific*. Houston: John Olson, 1985.

Patton, George. *War As I Knew It*. Boston: Houghton Mifflin, 1947.

Philos, C. D., and Ernie Hayhow. *1987 History of the 83d Infantry Division*. Hillsdale, Michigan: Ferguson Communications, 1986.

Potter, E. B. *Bull Halsey*. Annapolis, Maryland: United States Naval Institute, 1985.

Potts, Ramsay. Oral History. United States Air Force Historical Center, Maxwell Field, Alabama, 1960.

Prange, Gordon W. *Dec. 7 1941*. New York: McGraw-Hill Book Company, 1988.

Pyle, Ernie. *At Dawn We Slept*. New York: McGraw-Hill Book Company, 1981.

————*Here Is Your War*. New York: Henry Holt and Company, 1943.

————*Brave Men*. New York: Henry Holt and Company, 1944.

————*Last Chapter*. New York: Henry Holt and Company, 1946.

Rants, Hanford. *My Memories of World War II*. Unpublished Manuscript. Downey, California.

Rodman, Gage. Unpublished Memoir. Hurricane, Utah.

Rooney, Andy. *My War*. New York: Random House, 1996.

Rosson, William. Oral History. Carlisle, Pennsylvania: United States Army Military History Institute.

Ryan, Cornelius. *A Bridge Too Far*. New York: Simon & Schuster, 1974.

Salomon, Sidney. *2d Ranger Infantry Battalion*. Doylestown, Pennsylvania: Birchwood Books, 1991.

Samson, Jack. *Chennault*. New York: Doubleday & Company, Inc., 1987.

Schueler, Jon. *The Sound of Sleat*. Unpublished Manuscript.

Schultz, Duane. *The Maverick War*. New York: St. Martin's Press, 1987.

————*The Doolittle Raid*. New York: St. Martin's Press, 1988.

Schwarz, Otto. Unpublished Memoir.

Seibert, Donald A. Unpublished Memoir. Fort Belvoir, Virginia.

Shapiro, Alan. Unpublished Memoir. Ridgefield, Connecticut.

Sherrod, Robert. *Tarawa: The Story of a Battle*. New York: Duell, Sloan and Pearce, 1944.

Sledge, E. B. *With the Old Breed*. Novato, California: Presidio Press, 1981.

Smith, John F. *Hellcats Over the Philippine Deep*. Manhattan, Kansas: Sunflower Press, 1995.

Smith, Robert. Oral History. Maxwell Field, Alabama: United States Air Force Historical Center, 1983.

Spector, Ronald. *Eagle Against the Sun: The American War with Japan*. New York: Free Press, 1985.

Stroop, Paul. Oral History. Annapolis, Maryland: United States Naval Institute.

Svihra, Albert. Transcripts of letters to his family and Diary. West Point: U.S. Military Academy Library.

Teeples, Robert. *Jackson County Veterans,* Vol. II. Black River Falls, Wisconsin, 1986.

Thach, John (Jimmy). Oral History. Annapolis, Maryland: United States Naval Institute.

Tregaskis, Richard. *Guadalcanal Diary.* New York: Random House, 1943.

Ullom, Madeline. Memoir. Washington, D.C.: U.S. Army Center for Military History.

Van der Vat, Dan. *The Pacific Campaign.* New York: Simon & Schuster, 1991.

Walker, Anthony, ed., *Memorial to the Men of C/P Company, 4th Marine Raider Battalion.* Middletown, Rhode Island, 1994.

Ward, Norvell. Oral History. Annapolis, Maryland: United States Naval Institute.

White, W. L. *They Knew They Were Expendable.* New York: Harcourt Brace and Company, 1942.

Adair, Charles, 72, 142
Adair, Marion, 509
African Americans, 17
Agee, Walter, 447–49
Air war: Aleutians, 482–83;
  bombing, Europe, 1942, 430–49,
  455–81; Britain's and American
  airpower, 320–22, 329; Butt
  Committee, 325–26; casualties,
  planes lost, 326–27, 336; combat
  importance, 319–20; daytime
  precision vs. nightnight area
  bombing, 324–27, 338–40; debut
  of U.S. heavy bombers, 338–40;
  discord with British, 322, 324,
  327; first assault on Germany,
  476–77; first B-17 shot down,
  346; first units against Axis,
  Europe, 328–36; flak, 332;
  Independence Day raid, 330–36;
  Le May's theories, 462–65, 477;

N. Africa, 452–54; opening
  offensives, Europe, Eighth Air
  Force, 337–50; superiority of
  Germany and Japan, 320; Norden
  bombsight, 320, 327, 46; strategic
  bombing campaign, 324. See also
  Flying Tigers; Royal Airforce
  (RAF); U.S. Army Air Corps;
  U.S. Navy Air Corps
Aleutians, 303, 305–6, 317, 482–86
Alexander, Harold, 503
Alexander, Irvin, 77, 94, 196–98,
  213, 222–23, 224–26
Algeria, 390–421
Alicki, John, 1–2
Alison, John, 110–12, 509
Allen, Brooke, 5, 7, 24–25, 509
Allen, Terry de la Mesa, 402,
  408–10, 414, 501, 502, 509
Allied High Command: Meaulte,
  bombing, 344–46; meeting,

Allied High Command (*cont'd*)
Casablanca, 1943, 487–88;
Operation Husky, 503, 505;
Operation Jubilee, 386–87;
Operation Torch, 387, 390–421,
487–508; Rouen, Allied
bombings of, 338–40, 466–68

Altieri, James, 383, 413, 509

American-British-Dutch-Australian
Command, 158

American Caesar (Manchester),
46–47

Anderson, Jonathan, 411, 499

Andrusko, Ed, 354–55, 510

Armstrong, Frank, 339, 477

Arnim, Jurgen von, 490

Arnold, Henry "Hap," 82, 95, 103,
117, 245, 321, 324, 327, 329,
340, 351

Ashe, Walter, 510

Ashworth, Frederick, 510

Austin, Gordon, 6, 21–22, 27,
510–11

Austin, Paul, 511

Australia: 7th Div., 427–29;
Adelaide, 427; Brisbane, 300;
Canberra, 358; Darwin, 159,
162; *Perth*, 164; Philippine
evacuations, 206–7, 208; supplies
and, 167; threat of invasion, 350;
U.S. planes and pilots in, 161–62,
168

Axis powers. *See* Germany; Italy;
Japan

Backus, Paul, 4, 12–17, 38

Bali, 167

Barron, Frank, Jr., 511

Basset, Ed, 311

Bataan, 48, 53, 54, 74, 85; Death
March, 227–42; final assault by
Japan, 216–21; MacArthur
leaves, 209–11, 213–14; medical
care and casualties, 215–16, 217,
219, 224; morale, 207–8, 203–4,
207; Navy personnel, 194–95;
"Pockets," 203, 204; retreat to,
140–57, 159; siege, 178–79,
189–205, 212–16; supply
shortage, 153–54, 179, 190,
204–5, 215, 229; surrender,
221–26, 228; taking to the hills,
224–26; Washington writes off,
205–6

Batson, Shorty, 83

Battle of the Atlantic, 282–86

Battle of Britain, 102, 104, 105, 343

Battle of the Coral Sea, 294–303

Battle of the Java Sea, 162–66

Battle of Makassar Strait, 158–59,
160

Battle of Midway, 303–18, 328–29

Baum, Abe, 511

Beadle, Frank R., 339

Bean, Joe, 132

Beattie, T. T., 17

Beckwith, James, 348

Behlmer, Bill, 414, 490–91, 500,
511

Bell, Don, 94

Bellinger, Patrick N. L., 33

Bennion, Mervyn, 17

Berges, Col., 450–51

Bernheim, Eli, 511

Bianchi, Willibald C., 204

Biddle, Melvin, 511

Bither, Waldo, 252

Bluemel, Clifford, 52, 60–63,
76–77, 138–41, 153, 178–81,

201–2, 214–15, 219–20, 226, 232–35, 511

Bolt, Jones E., 511–12

Borneo, 73, 95

Bouck, Lyle, 512

Bower, William, 248, 249, 512

Boyington, Greg, 119–20, 243–44

Boyle, Bill, 512

Bradley, Omar, 495, 500, 502, 507

Bradshaw, Frederick W., 389

Brami, Russel, 377

Brandt, Waldo, 460

Bratton, Rufus S., 40

Bremen, 325, 476–77

Brereton, Lewis, 71–72, 74–75, 77–80, 86, 95, 137

Brett, Jimmy, 294, 295

Bridget, Francis J., 194–95

Britain: American airpower in, 320–36, 454–81; Army, 1st, 505; Army, 6th Armored Div., 496; Army, 8th, 387, 390, 420, 486, 505; Army, 61st Highland Div., 104; Battle of the Atlantic, 282–86; Battle of Britain, 102, 104, 105, 343; Battle of the Java Sea, 163–64; B-17s rejected, 111, 323; Commandos, 379, 386–87; Crete, 378; Dunkirk, 50, 328, 379; El Alamein, 420–21; Expeditionary Force, 103, 104; Navy, 282–86, 394, 410, N. Africa, 328, 329, 387, 390–421, 450–52, 496–97, 503, 505; P-40s rejected, 110–11; siege of London, 50; sinking of *Prince of Wales* and *Repulse*, 27, 158, 285; Tobruk, 391; U.S. Lend-Lease Act, 110–11, 283, 323. *See also*

Churchill, Winston; Royal Air Force

Brokaw, Frank, 128

Brown, Cecil, 347

Buckley, Pete, 512

Bulkeley, John D., 74, 97–99, 192, 210, 512

Bunker, Paul, 42, 185–86, 188, 198–99, 205, 210, 213–14, 262, 266

Burchinal, David, 512–13

Burma, 115–16, 117, 121–22, 123, 123–24, 242; Burma Road, 116, 387–88; Flying Tigers, 115–23, 162, 242; Merrill's Marauders, 388

Carlson, Evans F., 381

Carlton, Paul, 513

Carmichael, Richard, 7–9, 513–14

Caron, George, 513

Carpenter, John W., 90–93, 133, 137, 146–48, 159–61, 514

Carter, Norval, 514

Casey, Hugh J., 52

Celebes Island, 162

Champlin, Malcolm, 203–4

Chapman, Mary, 148

Cheek, Tom, 312

Chennault, Claire, 112–24, 242–43; Flying Tigers and, 115–24, 242–33; innovations in aerial warfare, 112, 115, 118

Chiang Kai-shek, 30, 113, 114, 253, 260, 387; Madame, 113

Childers, Don, 177

China: Air Force, 113; bomber pilots crash, 252–53; -Burma campaign, 387–88; -Burma-India Theater, 124; Chennault in,

China (cont'd)
112–24; international Squad,
113–14; Japanese in Manchuria,
28; Japanese reprisals, 261; P-40s
sent to, 115–16, 117–18, 121. See
also Flying Tigers
China Sea, 85, 86
Chism, John, 514
Christmas, Bert, 116–17, 122
Churchill, Winston, 123, 207, 244,
328, 329, 350, 379, 390–91,
395–96, 419–20, 446, 487
Clagett, Henry, 65
Clark, Albert, 341
Clark, Bob, 126
Clark, Mark Wayne, 395–99, 418
Clarke, George, 127–28, 173, 175,
178
Crete, 378
Clement, William T., 72, 74
Cochran, Philip, 452–54, 488–89,
514
Cole, Joe, 87
Coleman, L. A., 75
Coley, Clarence W., 491
Cologne, 325
Compton, John, 175–76
Compton, Kenneth, 432
Conver, Milt, 455–74, 477–81,
514–15
Cookson, George, 475
Cooper, Wibb, 272
Corregidor, 48, 85, 138, 145, 150,
159, 160, 181–88, 205, 208–11,
219, 227–28, 262–70; food and
supplies, 205, 228, 263; guns of,
199, 218; surrender, 262–74
Cox, Luther, 431–34, 452; Shoot
Luke and, 432–34
Cox, Nick, 434, 436

Creel, Buckner, 515
Creswell, L. B., 363
Crimmins, Fred T., Jr., 86–87
Cutter, Slade, 25–26, 515

D day, 1944, 393
Dakar, 394
Dammer, Herman, 412, 413
Darby, William, 382, 412–14, 515
Darlan, Jean Francois, 400, 412,
418–19, 420, 450, 451
Davenport, John, 16–17
Davidson, Howard, 27
Davison, Michael, 515
Davison, Miss, 272–73
Dawson, Frank "Buck," 515
de Gaulle, Charles, 394, 400, 419,
451
DeHaven, Robert, 515
DeLoach, James, 515
Dennison, Robert Lee, 58, 144–46,
186
DeShazer, Jacob, 258
D'Este, Carlo, 501
Devereaux, James P., 124
Dewey, Lawrence, 505
Dibb, Ram, 311–12
Dillon, John H., 41
Dixon, Bob, 298
Donaldson, Paddy, 107
Doolittle, James, 244–45, 321, 439
Douglas, Charles O., 349
Douhet, Giulio, 324
Drain, Paul, 345
Draper, Marshal, 330–32, 334–36
Duckworth, George, 515–16
Dunbar, William, 345, 346
Duncan, Paul, 194
Dunfee, Bill, 516
Dunn, Bill, 103–10, 327, 516

Dyess, Ed, 57, 75, 84, 88, 126, 200–201, 230

Eagle Squadrons, 102–10, 349–50, 429
Eagle Squadrons, The (Haugland), 108
Eaker, Ira, 321–22, 324, 327, 328, 329, 330–31, 337, 339, 340, 430
Earle, Mrs. John B., 11
East Indies, 54, 158–59, 160–68, 532
Eberhardt, Aubrey, 376
Edison, Dwight, 266
Edlin, Bob, 516
Edson, Merritt, 354–55, 365, 380, 386
Eisenhower, Dwight D., 329, 330–31, 336, 386, 391–92, 308; European invasion and, 392–93; MacArthur and, 47–48, 391, 420; Torch and N. Africa, 394, 399, 403–4, 419–20, 451–52, 487–88, 495–96
El Alamein, 420–21
Eller, Ernest, 516
Elliott, George E., 35
Ellis, Richard, 516
Emmens, Robert, 245–48, 249, 250, 253–57, 260, 516
Erwin, Henry, 516–17
Eubank, Eugene, 79, 90, 517
Evans, Warren "Bing," 382, 386, 387, 413, 517

Fall of the Philippines, The (U.S. Army), 193
Farrow, Bill, 257–60
Ferrall, Pete, 96–97
Fife, James, 73

Finn, John, 21
Fitch, Alva, 93, 127, 129, 140–41, 188–92, 217, 223–24, 231–32, 235–40
Fitch, Aubrey W., 301–2
Fleming, Bill, 458–74, 477–81
Fletcher, Jack, 305, 353, 359
Flying Tigers (AVG), 115–24, 162, 242–44
Formosa, 44, 57, 65, 78–79
Forrest, Nathan Bedford, 176, 251
Forte, Floyd, 52
Fowler, Halstead, 189–90, 191–92
France: defeat, 282, 373, 394; Dieppe, 340–43, 386–87; Free French, 394, 451; La Pallice, 459, 461; Lille, 430–39, 472; Lorient, 460, 472–74; Maquis, guerrilla fighters, 345–46; Meaulte, 344–46; Navy, 394; Rouen, 338–40, 466–68; Saint-Nazaire, 459–61, 468–69, 478–79; Torch and N. Africa, 399–40, 451; Vichy govt, 393–94, 419, 420
Fredendall, Lloyd, 487–88, 495, 497, 499
Fry, Philip, 56, 127–29, 141, 170–77
Funk, Arnold, 226

Gage, Thomas, Jr., 66–67, 83, 130–31, 133, 168–69, 193–94, 229, 275–76, 517
Gallery, Dan, 285
Gangel, Dick, 517
Gavin, James M., 371, 374
Gay, George H., 308–10, 314
Gayer, Noel, 291
George, Harold, 57, 65, 66, 200

Germany: advances in Europe, 1939–40, 50, 104; *Afrika Korps* and N. Africa, 328, 329, 387, 390, 420–21, 490–508; airborne troops, 373, 377–78; attacks on convoys, 282–86; bombing, Coventry and London, 326; bombing, Poland, 326' bombing raids by Allies, 325; declares war on U.S., 102, 282; El Alamein, 420–21; first Allied air assault on, 476–77; JU-88s, 112; *Luftwaffe*, 284–86, 322, 325; ME109s, 105, 108, 431, 460; ME210s, 440–41; Messerschmitts and Focke-Wulfs, 327, 338, 342–43, 466, 468; Stuka bombers, 104; surrender of N. Africa, 507–8; *Tirpitz* (battleship), 285–86; Tripartite Pact, 30; U-boats, 282, 284, 437, 440–44

Gerth, Herman, 171, 175, 176

Ghormley, Robert, 353, 365, 422

Gibraltar, 393, 395–96

Gilliam, Tom, 517–18

Giraud, Henri, 399–400, 403–4, 418, 419

Glidermen, 377–79

Goering, Hermann, 325, 430

Goettge, Frank, 360–61

Goode, John, 518

Goodson, James, 102–3, 327

Granberry, Hal, 199

Grashio, Sam, 56–57, 75, 84–86, 87–89, 126–27, 200–201, 212, 214, 230–31, 277–78

Green, Arthur, 175–76

Green, Ross, 251

Grier, Frank, 410

Griffith, John, 347–49

Griffith, Samuel, 354

Guadalcanal, 353–68, 422–27; Operation Watchtower, 353–54; sea battles, 357–59, 367–68; the Slot, 357–59, 423–26

Guam, 44, 53, 124

Haas, Capt., 171–74, 176

Halsey, William "Bull," 248, 422–23, 426

Hamblin, Archelaus, 395

Hansell, Haywood, 467–68, 477

Hapgood, Howard, 406

Hardy, mess Sgt., 230

Harmon, Ernest, 410–11, 412, 495–99, 503–8

Harrington, Jasper, 117

Harrington, Mary Rose, 74, 148, 168

Harris, Arthur, 327, 339, 447

Hart, Thomas, 31, 53, 54, 58, 70, 72, 74, 95, 100–101, 141–42, 145, 156, 163

Hartle, Russell, P., 382

Hartman, Tom, 518–19

Haugland, Vern, 108

Hayes, Tommy, 161–62, 167–68, 519

Hechler, Ted, Jr., 3, 18–20, 38

Hedman, Robert "Duke," 121–22

Hein, Douglas, 14

Henderson, Harry H., 13

Herder, Harry, 519

Hightower, Louis, 491–95, 496, 498

Hilger, Jack, 245–46

Hill, David Lee "Tex," 116–17, 122–23, 243, 519

Hill, Frank, 341–43

Hill, Whit, 444–45

Hirohito, 39, 264

Hite, Robert L., 257–60, 519
Hitler, Adolph, 420–21. *See also* Germany
HMS *Exeter*, 163
HMS *King George V*, 285
Hoffman, Norm, 14
Hofrichter, Joe, 519–20
Holmberg, Paul, 315
Holmes, Julian, 395
Homma, Masaharu, 137, 143, 151–52, 169, 170, 192, 204, 214, 216, 223, 268–69, 270, 271
Hopkins, Harry, 39
Hostetter, Philip, 520
Howard, Jim, 122–23
Howze, Hamilton, 401–2, 500, 504, 520
Huff, Sidney, 207
Hull, Cordell, 37
Hunter, Charles, 388
Hunter, Sam, 97, 223, 224
Huntington, Bob, 309
Husky (Operation), 503, 505

Ichiki, Kiyano, 361, 363
Ind, Allison, 81
Ingraham, Robert, 343
Intelligence and decryption, U.S., 31–32, 39, 40, 303–4
Irwin, John, 61, 76, 219
Irwin, Stafford LeRoy, 497
Italy: Allied invasion, 350; bombing of Ethiopia, 326; Corsica and S. France, 420; Greece, invasion, 378; Sicily, Allied invasion of (Operation Husky), 503; Tripartite Pact, 30

Jackson, Schulyer, 520
Janic, Ed, 434

Japan: air superiority, 131, 162; *Akagi* (carrier), 314–15; Aleutians, 305–6, 317, 482–86; attack on Pearl Harbor, 1–27, 41–42, 43, 70; attack on Malaya, Thailand, Singapore, Shanghai, 72; attitude toward prisoners, 228–29; banzai charge, Aleutians, 484–85; barbarity, 361; Bataan, 189–226; Battle of Coral Sea, 294–303; Battle of Java Sea, 162–66; Battle of Makassar Strait, 158–59, 160; Battle of Midway, 303–18; battleships built by, 28; Betty bombers, 162, 293; bombing by American B-29s, 326–27; *Bushido*, 228; in China, Manchuria, 28; Corregidor, bombardment and occupation, 262–71; declaration of war, 41–42; East Indies campaign, 158; Emily bomber, 290, 291; French Indochina, invasion, 29, 37, 51; Guadalcanal, 353–68, 423–27; Guam invasion, 125; *Hiryu* (carrier), 315–16; improvising avoided by, 151–52; *Jintsu* (cruiser), 364; *Kaga* (carrier), 314; *Kinryu Maru* (transport), 364; Navy, 315–16, 423–27; in New Guinea, 294–95, 350–51, 361, 427–29; night charge tactic, 355; offensive into China-Burma-India, 123–24; Philippines, 70, 83–101, 129–55, 168–81; POWs held by, 228–41, 272–81; *Shoho* (carrier), 297; *Shokaku* (carrier), 298, 363–64; sinking of U.S. Navy *Panay*, 29; *Soryu* (carrier), 309–10, 315;

Japan (cont'd)
  stereotyping, 157; strategy, post-Philippine, 295–96; Tokyo, Doolittle's bombing, 244–61; Tripartite Pact, 30; U.S. diplomacy, 29–30, 37, 39; *Tyujo* (carrier), 363–64; Wake Island, 125–26; Zeros, 81, 88, 118–19, 162, 288, 305, 312–13; *Zuikaku* (carrier), 298, 363–64
Java, 158, 160, 161, 167
Jennings, Jack, 83, 194
Jewell, Norman, 396
Johnson, Fred, 427–29, 520
Johnson, Harold K., 76, 175, 177–81, 239
Johnson, Leon, 520
Johnson, Robert, 520–21
Jones, David M., 252–53, 416, 447–49
Jones, Harry, 521
Jones, Homer, 521
Julian, Harry, 185
June 6, 1944: The Voices of D-Day (Astor), 514
Junkin, Samuel, 344

Kasserine Pass, 490–91, 497–99
Kegelman, Charles, 329–31, 417–18
Kelly, Colin P., 52, 131–33
Kelly, John, 192
Kelly, Walter, 338–40, 349–50, 430, 431, 439–40, 452, 521
Kenworthy, J. W., 14
Keough, Shorty, 105
Kesselring, Alfred, 421
Kidd, Isaac, 12
Kidwell, Vance, 521

Kimmel, Husband E., 9, 11–12, 31–32, 33, 36, 37–38, 41
King, Edward P., 222–23, 225
King, Ernest J., 244, 340, 351–53
Kinkaid, Thomas, 484
Kitzmann, Erich, 521–22
Knox, Frank, 41
Kolendorfski, Mike, 105
Komarek, W. J. "Red," 436–39
Krueger, Walter, 388–89
Kunz, Bill, 505–6, 522
Kurusu, Saburo, 37
Kusiamata, Lt. Col., 232–33

LaBan, Theodore H., 255
La Chaussee, Charles, 376
Landon, Truman H., 7, 9
Le May, Curtis, 461–65, 477
Leahy, William, 340
Leary, Fairfax, 38
Lee, William, 374n.
Leigh-Mallory, Trafford, 103
Lemnitzer, Lyman, 395
Levin, Meyer, 132
Libya (Tobruk), 391
Liebling, A. J., 409
Lille, bombing of, 430–39
Lilly, Edmund "Ted," 56, 232
Lim, Vincente, 52, 180
Lipsky, Clarence, 346
Lockard, Joseph L., 35
Loiacano, Leonard, 522
Lomell, Len "Bud," 522
Long, Stanley, 482, 483, 522
Loustalot, Edward, 387
Low, Martin, 1, 6, 25, 522–23
Lown, Frank, 433
Lucas, John, 502
Lynd, J. Q., 523

Mabry, George L, Jr., 523
MacArthur, Arthur, 45
MacArthur, Douglas: in Australia,
    220–21; background, 45–47;
    Bataan inspection, 178–79;
    character, 74, 178–79, 186–87,
    206–7, 352; Commander,
    USAFE, 31, 51–54, 58–59,
    60–61, 70, 351; Corregidor, 138,
    150, 184, 186–88; Corregidor
    surrender, 266–67, 271; declares
    Manila an open city, 143–45;
    departure from Philippines,
    208–11; "Dugout Doug," 207,
    214; as figurehead, 206; Filipino
    faith in, 207, 211–12; half-rations
    ordered, 179; "I shall return,"
    211–12; informed of Pearl
    Harbor attack, 74, 75; King,
    Ernest and, 351–52; lack of
    communication with Navy,
    144–45; lack of offensive after
    Pearl Harbor, 78–81; logistics
    ignored, 154; Medal of Honor,
    212; New Guinea, 427–29;
    Philippines, pre-war, 31, 45,
    47–54; Philippines surrender,
    206, 220–22; poor defense of
    Philippines, 136–39; Rainbow
    Five, 53, 58, 138, 150, 153; wife,
    Jean, 74, 207
MacArthur, Robert, 485
Mack, William, 55, 95–96
Magsaysay, Ramón, 139–40
Makin Island, 381
Mamedoff, Andrew, 105
Manchester, William, 46–47
Manion, Harry, 380–81
Marrett, Samuel, 130–31, 133
Marshall, George C., 32, 40, 41, 51,
    95, 143, 213, 221, 271, 324, 350,
    351–52, 372, 381, 391, 392, 403
Martelino, Pastor, 139
Martin, Frederick L., 33
Massey, Lance, 310–11, 314
Mast, Charles, 397, 400, 408, 412
Matson, Thomas, 345
McCubbin, James, 523
Medal of Honor, 21, 175, 204, 212
Meltessen, Clarence, 523
Merrill, Alan, 523–25
Merrill, Allen E., 383–85
Merrill, Frank, 388
Mers el-Kébir, 394
Miller, Dorie, 17–18
Mitchell, Billy, 320, 372
Mollison, James A., 10
Montgomery, Bernard, 420, 505
Moore, George F., 185
Morison, Samuel Eliot, ix
Morrell, John W., 194
Morton, Louis, 79
Mott, Hugh, 525
Mountbatten, Louis, 379, 381, 395
Mow, Peter (Mow Pan-Tzu), 113
Muehrcke, Robert, 426–27
Mueller, Arndt, 525
Murphy, John, 433
Murphy, Robert, 394–95, 397, 398,
    412, 419
Murray, Roy, 413
Murray, S. S., 72–73, 146
Mussolini, Benito, 378, 420

Nagano, Kameichiro, 223
Nakayama, Motto, 268
Nara, Akira, 170
Nesbit, Josephine "Josie," 149,
    280–81
Netherlands, 158, 331–36, 344

New Britain Island, Rabaul, 289, 294, 350, 356, 360

New Guinea, 294–96, 350–51, 361, 427–29

New Ireland, 350

Newkirk, Jack, 120, 122

Newman, Stan, 525

Nicholls, G. V., 400–401

Nimitz, Chester, 287, 352, 422

Nininger, Alexander, 52, 174–75

Nitto Maru, sinking of, 248–49

Nomura, Kichisaburo, 30, 37, 39, 40, 62

North Africa, 328, 329, 387, 420–21, 450–54, 487–508, *see also* Torch

Northrup, Jay, 525

Odell, Bill, 330, 332–34, 346–49, 452, 525–26

O'Hare, Butch, 289, 291, 292, 293

Olds, Robert S., 463

Olsen, Arvid "Oley," 120

Olson, John E., 152–53, 174–75, 177, 190, 214, 216–17, 238–39, 240–41, 276–77, 278, 526

Osmeña, Sergio, 206

OSS, 394

Pames, George, 336

Paratroopers, 370–77, 403; Torch and, 400, 405–8, 450–51, 488–89; training, 374–76, 374n., 377

Paris, Dee, 526

Parker, Edward, 73

Parker, George N., 169, 178–79, 180, 198, 220

Parks, Lewis, 26

Patton: A Genius for War (D'Este), 501

Patton, George S., 400–401, 404–5, 409, 411; character, 404, 411, 500–502; Husky, 503, 505; II Corps, N. Africa, 499–505

Paxton, George, 243

Pearl Harbor, 1–27, 41–42, 43; *Arizona*, 11–12, 13–14, 19, 27; *California*, 17; casualties, 10, 12, 13, 16, 17, 20, 21, 24; *Curtiss*, 19; damage, 24–25, 26–27; *Enterprise*, 7, 38; Ewa Field, 22; failed warnings, 31–32, 34–36, 40–41, 43–44; Ford Island, 3, 7, 19, 26–27; Fort Shafter, 10–11, 35; Haleiwa Field, 6, 9, 22, 25, 32–33; Hickam Field, 5, 7, 8, 19, 24, 26, 32; Japanese sub, 11, 12, 36; Japanese targets, 23, 24; Kaneohe, 2, 20–21; lack of preparation, 37–38, 40–41, 43; *Lexington*, 38; Marine barracks, 4–5; *Maryland*, 14, 15, 17; Medal of Honor, 21; Navy Cross, 17; Navy Patrol Wing 2, 2, 3, 12; *Nevada*, 26–27; *Oklahoma*, 4, 12–13, 14–17, 27; PBYs (surveillance), 12–13, 20, 21, 34; *Phoenix*, 3, 18, 19–20, 38; planes lost, 21; *Pompano*, 25–26; sabotage, 32, 36, 43; *St. Louis*, 2–3, 22–24; survivors in sea, 15–17; *Utah*, 27; *Vestal*, 12; *Ward*, 11, 12, 36; *W. Virginia*, 17; Wheeler Field, 1, 6–8, 24, 32. *See also* Kimmel, Husband; Short, Walter

Peltier, Bill, 345–46

Pershing, John "Black Jack," 372

Petain, Marshall, 419
Philippines, 44–69; air defenses, 65, 83–86, 87, 96, 141; airfields, 65–66, 68, 83; Army Air Corps 19th Bomb Grp, 79, 86; Army Air Corps 20th Pursuit Sqd, 86; Army Air Corps 21st Pursuit Sqd, 56–58, 87–88, 126–27; Army Air Corps 27th Bomb Grp, 71; Army Air Corps 34th Pursuit Sqd, 66–68, 83, 134, 193–94, 195, 230; Army Div., 52, 58–59, 61, 63, 77, 127–29, 140–41, 170–71, 180, 196, 198–99, 201–3, 204–5, 226; Asiatic Fleet, 95; B-10s, 68, 69; B-17s, 67, 68–69, 81, 83, 89–93, 94, 131–32, 133, 137; B-18s, 68; Baguio, 94; casualties, 89, 94, 97, 99–100, 126–27, 168; Clark Field, 65, 83–84, 85, 86, 87–88, 89, 93, 94, 126–27, 132; Coast Artillery, 59th, 185; Coast Artillery, 200th, 87; defense of, 66–67, 69–70, 126–37, 168–81; equipment, training, troop build-up, 59–62, 64–67, 87; fifth columnists, 136; first USMA grad to die, 133; "I shall return," 211–12; Iba Field, 65, 83, 85, 139; Japanese assault, Dec. 8, 83–101; Japanese invasion, 168–81; Japanese landing at Aparri, Vigan, Legaspi, 129–30, 136, 137; *John D. Ford*, 95–96; Lingayen "victory," 135, 137; losses, Dec. 8, 84, 89–90, 94, 95–99, 126–27, 136–37, 152–53; Luzon, 53, 54, 63, 81, 129–30; MacArthur and, 31, 41, 45–46, 47–54, 58–59, 70, 78–81; Manila,

as open city, 138, 144–45, 146, 148, 169; Manila Bay, 53, 264–65; Marine Rgmt, 4th, 62, 183–84; Motor Torpedo Boat Sqd 3, 64–65, 74, 97–99; news of Pearl Harbor, 71–77; Nichols Field, 65–66, 75, 79, 84–85, 87, 126; Nielson Field, 65, 85; P-13a, 79; P-26s, 69; P-35s, 66, 67, 130–31; P-40s, 56, 66, 67, 75, 80–81, 83, 84–86, 88–89, 96, 126, 130–31,133, 200, 242, 452; *Pillsbury* and *Perry*, 96; portents of war, 55–57; retreat, 139–55, 168–69; Scouts, 53, 60, 63–64, 76, 93, 127, 140, 143, 170–77, 180–81, 198–99, 201, 204, 225–26, 227, 239; *Seadragon* and *Sealion*, 96–97, 205; Sternberg Hospital, 56, 78, 99–100, 135, 149; Stotsenburg, 127, 152–53; submarine Divs, 72–73, 141–42; tanks, 64, 152, 169; USAFFE, 51–64; U.S. history with, 44; War Plan Orange, 48, 58, 129, 143–44, 150, 153, 154, 182, 205–6. *See also* Bataan; Corregidor; Quezon, Manuel
Phillips, Walter, 10
Pierce, Clinton, 224–25
Pinney, Charles, 482–83
Polla, Hector, 52
Portal, Charles, 446
Poston, Tom, 526
Potts, Ramsay, 434–36, 440–42
Price, Arthur, Jr., 2, 12, 20–21
Pride, Lewis Bailey, Jr., 12, 13
Priestly, William J., 233–34
Prisoners of war: Bataan, 223; Bataan Death March, 227–42;

Prisoners of war (*cont'd*)
Bilibid Prison, 280–81; bombers, Tokyo raid, 259–61; Clark, first pilot POW, Eighth Air Force, 341; Corregidor, 272–74, 278–79; Draper, first U.S. Air Corps POW in Europe, 336; in Europe, 336, 341, 343, 346, 387, 448–49, 512; Filipinos, 278, 281; Geneva Convention and Japanese, 223, 276; German, N. Africa, 508; O'Donnell camp, 240, 242, 275–78; Santo Tomas Camp, 281; women, 272–73, 280–81

Purnell, William R., 71

Pyle, Ernie, 409

Quezon, Manuel Luis, 44, 46, 47, 50, 137–38, 143, 184, 206–7

Raaen, John C., Jr., 526

Raff, Edson, 405, 406–7, 451, 489

Raila, Frank, 526

Ramsey, Logan, 3

Randall, Joseph H., 387

Rants, Hanford, 526–27

Rector, Ed, 116–17

Regan, John, 430–31, 474–77

Reminiscences (MacArthur), 47, 50, 51, 79, 136, 178, 188, 208–10

Reynolds, Royal, 153

Robins, Donald, 132

Robison, Noel (Eugene), 527

Rochefort, Joseph, 304

Rockwell, Francis, 74, 145

Rohow, Fred M., 16

Rommel, Erwin, 329, 421, 487, 489, 497, 500, 508

Rommel, Herb, 4

Romulo, Carlos P., 211

Rood, George A., 22–23

Rooks, Capt., 162

Roosevelt, Franklin, 29–30, 37, 39–40, 42, 47, 103, 244, 266, 267, 331, 390–91, 395

Roosevelt, James, 381

Roosevelt, Theodore, Jr., 402, 501

Rosson, William, 402–3, 415, 527

Royal Air Force (RAF): Blenheim and Stirling bombers, 108, 325; Brewster Buffalo fighters, 121; Eagle Sqds, 102–10, 327, 429; Hurricane, 104–5; mixed squadrons, 102, 327; Lancasters, 325; nighttime blitz bombing vs. daytime, 323, 324–27; Operation Millennium, 325; radar-based bombing systems, 326; Sperry bombsight, 323; Spitfire, 105, 107–8, 325, 331, 341, 429; U-boat attacks and, 282; Vickers Wellingtons, 323

Ruhlen, George, ix, x, 527

Ruhr valley, 325

Russia (Soviet Union), 111–12, 255–57, 284–86, 328

Ryder, Charles Doc, 418

Salomon, Sid, 527

Salter, Cary, 527–28

Sandell, Robert, 120

Sayre, Francis, 54, 184, 186–87

Scheuler, Jon, 455–74, 477–81, 528

Schneider, Max, 413

Schofield, William C., 406

Scholes, Robert, 199

Schwarz, Otto, 156–59, 162, 164–67; as POW, 167, 528–29

Segundo, Fidel V., 52

Selleck, Clyde, 195–96, 198
Seton, Adolph, 2–3, 22–24
Shapiro, Alan, 529
Sharp, William F., 209, 267, 271
Shaw, Samuel R., 4–5
Sheedy, Dan, 312
Sherrod, Robert, 364, 380
Short, Walter C., 9–11, 32, 33–35, 36, 38, 41
Shulz, Lester, 39
Sims, Ed, 529–30
Smith, Cornelius C., Jr., 5
Smith, D. K., 342, 343
Smith, Ed, 483–84
Smith, Robert, 530
Smith, Walter Bedell, 419
Solomon Islands, 295–96, 353, 355, 365, 386. *See also* Guadalcanal
Soong, T. V., 114–15
South, Frank, 530
Southworth, Billy, Jr., 455–74, 530
Spaatz, Carl, 321, 323–24, 327, 329, 330–31, 337
Spain: Guenica, 326
Spruance, Ray, 287, 305, 308
Stark, Harold, 39–40, 41, 283, 353
Stevens, Luther, 223, 224, 233–34
Stilwell, Joseph, 242, 388, 390
Stimson, Henry L., 392
Strange, Glen, 530
Stroop, Paul, 297–303, 530
Sullivan brothers, 424–25
Sutherland, Richard, 73–74, 78–79, 80, 138, 154, 178, 208, 211
Svihra, Albert, 52, 262–64, 269–70, 273–74, 279–80
Swanson, Wallace, 531

Tash, Earl, 91
Taylor, Harold J., 414, 531

Taylor, Kenneth, 22
Taylor, William, 103
Tessier, Henri, 397
Thach, John "Jimmy," 118, 287–93, 304–5, 310–14, 531
Tibbets, Paul W., 339
Timor, 162
Tobin, Gene "Red," 105
Togo, Shigenori, 39, 40
Tokyo, bombing of, 244–61
Topping, Bill, 442–44
Torch, 390–421, 429; air war, 452–54, 495; casualties and losses, 500, 508; clandestine meeting, Algeria, 395–99; foot soldiers, 489–90, 504–5; German surrender, 507–8; Kasserine Pass, 490–91, 497–99; opening phase, 410–18; Patton, 499–505; POWs, 508 Tafaraoui and La Senia airfields, 405–7; tank war, 491–508; Thelepte, 453–54, 490, 495; Tunisia, 450–52, 487–508; Twelfth Air Force in, 439–40; weakness of U.S. troops, 451. *See also* Darlan, Jean Francois; Giraud, Henri
Townsend, Glen, 58–59, 135, 204–5
Travinek, Charles, 344–46
Tregaskis, Richard, 354–55, 256–57, 362–63, 365–67, 368
Trenary, Mel, 370–71
Truscott, Lucian K., 381–82, 386
Tsuneyoshi, Yoshio, 276–78
Turner, Richmond, 352, 365
Turner, William "Pappy," 531
Tunisia, 450–52, 487–508
Twaddell, Jim, 9
Tyler, Kermit, 35–36

Ullom, Madeline, 55–56, 78, 99–100, 135, 148–59, 188, 215–16, 217, 218, 266, 272–73, 531

Ulsaker, Carl, 531

United States: Bolero, Sledgehammer, Round-up invasion plan, 350, 392; "bomb plot message," 32; China and, 114–15; convoy protection, N. Atlantic, 282–86; first casualties, Europe, 387; Germany declares war, 102; negotiations with Japan, 29–30, 37, 39–40, 62; Rainbow Five, 53, 58, 129, 153; readiness for war, 31, 39; Torch, 390–421; war declared with Japan, 41–42; War Plan Orange (WPO), 48, 58, 129, 143–44, 150, 153, 154, 182, 205–6; warnings of Japanese attack, 31–32, 39–41; "winds" dispatches, 39. See also Air war, American, concepts; Allied High Command; Intelligence and encryption; specific military branches

U.S. Army: 1st Armored Div., 382, 401, 451, 491–95, 498–99, 504–5, 506; 1st Div., 408, 410; 1st Infantry Div., 387, 402, 414, 490–91, 496, 502; 1st Ranger Battalion, 382–87, 400, 412; 2d Armored Div., 400, 410–11, 495, 503; 3d Infantry Div., 400, 402–3, 414–16, 505–6; 6th Army, 388; 7th Infantry Div., 483–86; 9th Infantry Div., 400; 32d Infantry Div., 427–29; 34th Infantry Div., 382, 418; 82d Airborne Div., 371; 503d Parachute Regiment, 405; 504th Parachute Regiment, 400; 509th Parachute Regiment, 450; 517 Parachute Regimental Combat Team, 370, 376, 377; 5307 Composite Unit, 388; airborne, 370–79, 403, 450; Alamo Scouts, 288–89; Americal Div., 423–27; M3 Honey tank, 491; M4 Sherman tank, 491–92; Marauders, 388; Rangers, 381–87. See also Philippines

U.S. Army Air Corps: 1st Fighter Grp, 328–36, 429, 454; 8th Pursuit Sqd, 1; 15th Bomb Grp, 329–36, 337, 452; 17th Bomb Grp, 245; 19th Bomb Grp, 79, 86; 20th Pursuit Sqd, 86; 21st Pursuit Sqd, 56–57, 58, 87–88; 27th Bomb Grp, 71; 31st Fighter Grp, 328–36, 340–41, 346, 429, 454; 33d Fighter Grp, 452–54; 34th Pursuit Sqd, 66–68, 83; 35th Fighter Grp, 161–62; 44th Bomb Grp, 452, 454, 476; 47th Pursuit Sqd, 6, 21; 53rd Antiaircraft Brigade, 1–2, 6; 78th Pursuit Sqd, 35; 82d Fighter Grp, 454; 91st Bomb Grp, 476; 92nd Bomb Grp, 349, 454; 93d Bomb Grp, 431–34, 437, 454, 476; 97th Bomb Grp, 328, 337–40, 344–46, 349–50, 439–40, 452, 454; 301st Bomb Grp, 349, 454; 303d, 454–81; 305th, 461–63, 476–77; 306th Bomb Grp, 430, 455, 476; A-20s (Bostons), 33, 329–36, 417–18; aerial warfare, 118; antisub patrols, 437, 440–44; B-

10s, 68, 69; B-17s, B-17Es, B-
17Fs, B-17Gs, (Flying
Fortresses), 7, 8–9, 24–25, 31,
67, 68–69, 81, 83, 89–93, 94,
111, 160–61, 304, 306, 307, 322,
327–28, 337–38, 349, 430, 431,
458–76; B-18s, 68; B-24s, 322,
323, 327–28, 349, 430–35,
440–44, 476; B-25s, 244–46,
247, 257, 482; B-26s (Marauder),
416–17; B-29s, 326–27; C-47s,
405–7; Eighth Air Force (Mighty
Eighth), 318, 321, 331, 337–50,
429–49, 454–81; *Enola Gay*, 339,
513; maintenance, modification,
repair, 444–46; Midway, 318; N.
Atlantic passage to England, 429;
obsolete pre-war force, 33, 34,
68; P-13s, 79; P-26s, 69; P-35s,
66, 67; P-38s (Lightnings), 328,
417, 429–30, 483; P-39s
(Airacobras), 328, 340–41; P-40s,
P-40E Warhawks, 56, 66, 67, 75,
80–81, 83, 84–86, 88–89, 96,
110–11, 117–18, 121, 161–62,
200, 341, 490; P-47s, 322; P-51s,
322; in Philippines, *see*
Philippines; Tokyo, Doolittle's
bombers, 244–61; Twelfth Air
Force, 439; weaknesses of, 322

U.S. Army Force in the Far East
(USAFFE), 51–54, 59–63,
78–81, 145. *See also* Philippines

U.S. Marines: 1st Div., 354–55; 2d
Raider Battalion, 381; 4th Raider
Battalion, 380; 7th Regiment,
365; Boyington and, 244;
Brewster Buffalo, 306; fighters
and dive bombers, 304, 306–7;
Guadalcanal, 353–68; at Pearl

Harbor, 4–5; Philippines, 62,
183–84; Raider Battalions,
379–81; Wake Island, 125–26;
Wildcat, 306, 356

U.S. Navy, 38, 43, 156–57, 244,
247–50, 253–54, 284–87,
351–52, 359, 423–26; Asiatic
Fleet, 31, 53, 54–55, 64–65,
95–98, 141–42; Pacific Fleet,
287, 350–68. *See also* U.S. ships;
U.S. subs; *specific battles*

U.S. Navy Air Corps: battles,
Pacific, 287–318, 350–368;
Devastators, 294, 308, 309–10,
314; Marauder, 307; SBD
Dauntless dive bombers, 314;
TBF Avenger, 307; Thachweave
tactic, 118, 288, 305; Wildcat,
288, 316; *See also battles*

U.S. Ships (*USS*): *Arizona*, 11–12,
13–14, 19, 27; *Astoria*, 358–59;
Atlanta, 424; *Blue*, 359–60, 532;
California, 17; *Chicago*, 358,
359; *Christopher Newport*, 284;
Curtiss, 19; *Enterprise*, 7, 38,
248, 249, 304–5, 308–10, 314,
316, 356, 425; *Gold Star*, 159 ;
Hammann, 317; *Helena*, 424;
Henley, 360; *Hornet*, 247–51,
253, 257–58, 304, 305, 316, 367;
Houston, 54, 156–59, 162–66,
359, 532; *Jarvis*, 359; *John D.
Ford*, 95–96; *Juneau*, 425;
Kearny, 283; *Lark*, 156;
Lexington, 38, 289–302, 314;
Long Island, 361; *Marblehead*,
73, 158; *Maryland*, 14, 15, 17;
Mindanao, 265; *Minneapolis*,
302; *Nashville*, 249; *Neosho*, 296;
Nevada, 26–27; *North Carolina*,

U.S. Ships (cont'd)
367; Oklahoma, 4, 12–13, 14–17,
27; Pensacola, 143; Perry, 96;
Phoenix, 3, 18, 19–20, 38;
Pigeon, 265; Pillsbury, 96;
Portland, 424; President
Coolidge, 57, 66; PT-34, 192–93,
210; PT-41, 210–11; Quincy,
358–59; Ranger, 416; Reuben
James, 283; St. Louis, 2–3,
22–24; San Francisco, 424; San
Juan, 355; Saratoga, 287,
288–89, 313, 356; Sims, 296; S.
Dakota, 425–26; Suwannee, 416,
521; Tanager, 264; Utah, 27;
Vestal, 12; Vincennes, 358–59;
Ward, 11, 12, 36; Washington,
285, 425–26; Wasp, 367–68; W.
Virginia, 17; Yorktown, 294–300,
304–5, 310, 313, 315–17
U.S. submarines: Canopus (tender),
145, 194, 218–19; Pompano,
25–26; Salmon, 141; Saury, 141;
Seadragon, 73, 96–97, 205;
Sealion, 96–97; Sea Wolf,
160–61; Shark, 145; Stingray,
141; Swordfish, 206–7
Uzemack, Ed, 531

Vaccaro, Tony, 531–32
Van Valkenburg, Franklyn, 12
Vance, Lee, 232
Vandegrift, Alexander A., 353, 356,
361, 365, 366, 422, 424
Vaughn, Jimmy, 237
Vincent, Casey, 120

Voge, Dick, 96–97
Vogel, Walter, 159, 359–60, 532

Wainwright, Jonathan, 52, 129–30,
137, 150–52, 169, 178, 179–80,
190, 191, 203–4, 209, 213, 215,
222, 227, 265–66, 267–72
Wake Island, 44, 53, 125–26
Waldron, John C., 308–9
Walker, Anthony, 532
Ward, Norvell, 73, 96
Ward, Orlando, 498, 499, 503
Warneke, Bud, 532–33
Warriner, Vic, 533
Waters, John, 451, 491
Welch, George S., 21–22
Widoff, Gerald, 533
Williams, Gus, 87, 88
Willoughby, Charles, 144, 197–98
Wingate, Orde Charles, 388
Women; ix; nurses, ix, 55–56, 74,
148–50, 169, 188, 215–17, 218,
266; POWs, 272–73, 280–81
Wright, Jerauld, 395, 396, 399

Yamamoto, Isoroku, 303–4, 425
Yarborough, William, 373, 377,
403, 405–7, 450, 533
York, Ed "Ski" (Edward
Cichowski), 246, 247, 251, 260
Young, Cassin B., 12

Zemke, Hubert "Hub," 110
Zenie, George, 402
Zobel, Don, 361

AMERICA'S FIRST ROAD WARRIORS

They were a bunch of tough-as-nails drivers who ran the enormous crucial operation known as the "Red Ball Express." Almost all African-Americans, these truckers rushed the fuel and supplies the rapidly advancing American armies desperately needed after D-Day to crush the German Panzers. Now for the first time, and filled with thrilling firsthand accounts, here is the full story of this legendary unit: the attacks they faced from the Germans, the battles they fought with racist G.I.s, the heroism and respect they earned the hard way. Here are the men who helped shorten the war with the great effort that made the final victory possible. As Dwight D. Eisenhower declared, "Without it [Red Ball] the advance across France could not have been made."

THE ROAD TO VICTORY:
The Untold Story of World War II's Red Ball Express
(0-446-66768-4)

by David P. Colley

"A CLASSIC AMERICAN TALE OF PERSEVERANCE, APTITUDE, AND ADAPTATION."
—*Bloomsbury Review*

AVAILABLE AT BOOKSTORES EVERYWHERE FROM WARNER BOOKS